Ericksonian Approaches

A Comprehensive Manual

Rubin Battino, M.S.
Wright State University

and

Thomas L. South, Ph.D.
Twin Valley Psychiatric System Dayton Campus

Chapters by:

James Auld, B.D.S., Dip. Soc. Sc., MSc
Leon S. Segal, M.A.
Sandra Sylvester, Ph.D.

Crown House Publishing
www.crownhouse.co.uk

First published by
Crown House Publishing Ltd
Crown Buildings, Bancyfelin, Carmarthen, Wales, SA33 5ND, UK
www.crownhouse.co.uk

and

Crown House Publishing Ltd
P.O. Box 2223, Williston, VT 05495-2223, USA
www.CHPUS.com

Permissions to quote from the following sources are gratefully acknowledged:

Zeig, G.K. (1980). *A Teaching Seminar*. pp. 99-100. Bristol, PA: Taylor & Francis (Brunner/Mazel). *American Journal Of Clinical Hypnosis*: 1, 117-121 (1959); 2, 227-231 (1960); 3, 112-116 (1960); 7, 64-70 (1964); 7, 152-162 (1964); 8, 57-65 (1965); 8, 198- 209 (1966); 15, 217-222 (1973); 20, 20-35 (1977). Haley, J. (1985). *Conversations With Milton H. Erickson*. La Jolla, CA: Triangle Press; Vol. I p. 59, Vol. I pp. 81-82, Vol. I pp. 118-119, Vol. I pp. 258-259, Vol. II pp. 123-126, Vol. III pp. 12-14, Vol. III pp. 135-138. Cheek, D.B. & LeCron, L. (1968). *Clinical Hypnotherapy*. Philadelphia: Gruen and Stratton (W.B. Saunders Co.). Gordon, D. & Meyers-Anderson, M. (1981). *Phoenix*. Capitola, CA: Meta Publications; pp. 67-69, pp. 131-132, pp. 139-140. Cooper, L. & Erickson, M.H. (1959). *Time Distortion In Hypnosis*. Baltimore: Williams and Wilkins (A Waverly Company); "Guitar Practice," (courtesy of Dr. Linn F. Cooper). Erickson, M.H. & Rossi, E.L. (1981). *Experiencing Hypnosis*. pp. 15-16, 155-168 (selected portions); Erickson, M.H. & Rossi, E.L. (1979). *Hypnotherapy: An Exploratory Casebook*. pp. 77-78. New York: Irvington Publishers, Inc.

The following are all reprinted by permission of W.W. Norton & Company, Inc. From *My Voice Will Go With You: The Teaching Tales Of Milton H. Erickson* by Sidney Rosen; excerpts from pp. vii, viii, ix, 36-37, 151-152. Copyright © 1982 by Sidney Rosen, M.D. From *Uncommon Therapy: The Psychiatric Techniques Of Milton H. Erickson, M.D.* by Jay Haley. Copyright ©1986 by Jay Haley; excerpts from pp. 157, 239, 280-282. From *Mind-Body Therapy: Ideodynamic Healing In Hypnosis* by Ernest Lawrence Rossi and David B. Cheek. Copyright © 1988 by Ernest L. Rossi and David B. Cheek; excerpts from pp. 182-183, 187-188, 217-218, 295-296. From *The Psychobiology Of Mind-Body Healing*, revised edition by Ernest Lawrence Rossi. Copyright © 1993 by Ernest Lawrence Rossi; excerpts from p. 39. From *An Uncommon Casebook: The Complete Clinical Work Of Milton H. Erickson, M.D.* by William Hudson O'Hanlon and Angela L. Hexum, eds. Copyright © 1990 by William Hudson O'Hanlon and Angela L. Hexum; excerpts from pp. 101, 104.

British Library of Cataloguing-in-Publication Data
A catalogue entry for this book is available from the British Library.

International Standard Book Number 1899836314
Library of Congress Control Number 2002109964

Printed and bound in the UK by
Bell & Bain, Glasgow

Dedications

This work is dedicated to my
loving daughters, Marie and Melissa,
for the happiness they have brought
to my life and as an inspiration
to their learning.

Tom

My contributions are dedicated
to my friends and mentors:
Howard H. Fink and
Joseph E. Emanuel,
and to my wife Charlotte.

Rubin

Table of Contents

Preface

TLS is the founder of the Milton H. Erickson Society of Dayton, Ohio. After RB immersed himself in the work of Milton H. Erickson, he found out about the Society and joined it. We have each served as president of the Society for considerable periods and continue to be active. Our mutual interests and friendship resulted in our teaching a year-long training course in Ericksonian methods. This book is the outcome of that collaboration.

We were motivated to write the book because we have yet to come across materials that can be reasonably used for courses or for training. This is the case even though the literature on Ericksonian methods is extensive and expanding. The books in the field are wonderful resources, but do not seem to lend themselves to a systematic training program. This book is, of course, no substitute for reading Erickson's collected papers, the books he has written in collaboration with others, the monograph series on his work, or listening to and viewing his many presentations. But we hope it will prove to be useful as a text or a training manual. To that end, we have incorporated many exercises throughout the book. If you will examine the table of contents, you will note that we develop the subject in a systematic way. However, many of the chapters can stand alone if you are interested in a particular area. Our individual interests have had an effect on the content.

We were pleased to be joined in this endeavor by three experts in their respective fields who wrote specialty chapters for us. S. Sylvester has written on medical applications; J. Auld on dental applications; and L.S. Segal on substance abuse.

We would like to acknowledge the influence of the following people on our work: Milton H. Erickson, E.L. Rossi, J.K. Zeig, W.H. O'Hanlon, R. Pearson, K.F. Thompson, M.D. Yapko, S.G. Gilligan, S.R. and C.H. Lankton, D.B. Cheek, S. Rosen, H. Lustig, H.H. Fink, J.E. Emanuel, S. de Shazer, R. Bandler, and J. Grinder, amongst many others. This book could not have been produced without the assistance of the Word processing Center of the Wright State University School of Medicine (Carol Enigk, director) and we owe an especial thanks to their staff. We also thank Michael Hall for assistance with the graphics and Alice McKinney and Charlotte Battino for advice on the layout of the book.

RB served as the overall coordinator and editor.

TLS
Dayton

RB
Yellow Springs

November, 1997

Foreword

The developing maturity of a new school of professional psychotherapy is signaled by the appearance of "Comprehensive Manuals" that attempt to integrate the best inspirations of the pioneers with the growing body of fundamentals that are needed to teach another generation. This comprehensive manual by Thomas South, Rubin Battino and their colleagues take on this task with honesty and integrity. So broad has the scope of Milton H. Erickson's psychotherapy become in recent years that it has become more and more difficult to discern Erickson's original voice. So many of his highly creative and individualistic students have carried Erickson's work in new unpredictable directions that there is now a real danger of losing the original threads of his genius.

This state of affairs would surely bring an impish smile to Milton Erickson's face. It is, after all, a true reflection of Erickson's view of at least one aspect of his own mission: to help others to find their own genius by teaching them in terms of the natural ways and metaphors of their own minds. This is one of the secret strengths of Erickson's original contributions that this comprehensive manual seeks to impart to the students and professionals. In one way or another it will be found to be a harmonic theme that connects the systematic presentation of the broad areas of Erickson's work with case studies, transcripts of inductions for different types of clients and practical training exercises that can facilitate the student's learning step by step.

But is all this really necessary, one might ask? Wasn't Milton Erickson an intuitive genius who could use his "creative unconscious" to simply free associate incantations and hypnotic spells that would be just what the patient needed? You know, deep unconscious communication from the mind of one person to the other. Sort of healing without cognition. The symptoms somehow go away and nobody knows the reason why, not even the therapist. In spite of such folklore that has been spun about Erickson's work, this oversimplified appeal to the intuitive is certainly not correct. In his early years Erickson worked very systematically to develop his understanding of the nature of hypnosis—what he called the "psycho-neuro-physiological" foundations of healing. How can mere words, stories, meanings and ideas facilitate healing?

Erickson described to me the lengthy process he went through in training himself with his first patients. He would first have a rather long initial interview with the prospective patient wherein he insisted on gathering all the information he felt he needed for a comprehensive case history. At the end of this initial interview he would tell the patient something like the following, "Well, I am going to have to study all your material very carefully for a while so I can develop some understanding on how to help you the best. So, why don't you give me a few weeks and when I am ready I will give you a call to arrange your next appointment time." Good grief, I thought at the time, how did Milton manage to earn a living with such a seemingly casual attitude?

But his attitude was anything but casual! Milton then described to me how he would actually study the patient's material very carefully for days and sometimes weeks. He would then write out longhand with pencil on paper about forty pages of "suggestions" that would cover all aspects of the patient's problems. He said he would then "boil those forty pages down to twenty and study them some more." He would sleep on those twenty pages for a few days and then "boil them down to ten!" Erickson would stare at me with a laser-like intensity as he told me all this to make sure he had my full attention. Here was a man who did not suffer fools gladly.

"And then," he would slowly and softly intone when he was sure he had my full wide-eyed attention, "I would boil those ten pages down to five and have my secretary carefully type them up." Erickson would then call up the patient and say, "Well, I have something for you," and he would arrange for the second appointment. When the patient arrived the five page manuscript would be in full sight on Erickson's desk. Sometimes with studied casualness Erickson would nod his head toward the manuscript and ask if the patient would mind if Erickson simply read it to him word for word. After all, Erickson had spent a lot of time on it and he wanted to get it just right.

Of course, the patient agreed. Of course, the patient soon went into a "therapeutic trance" as she or he listened with deep expectation to Erickson reading the most meaningfully constructed sentences, paragraphs and pages that utilized the patient's own unique language, attitudes and world view. Of course, the patient was deeply impressed with the importance of what was being received. Of course, the patient was touched and often overwhelmed with the poignancy of the situation. Perhaps for the first time someone of significance was giving such full and profound attention to the patient's personal problems. In this situation, of course, most patients would feel heartened and find unexpected sources of strength within themselves so that they would experience a new beginning and profoundly new possibilities for their lives. Of course, you, the reader of this carefully written volume will likewise be impressed with the need to study it deeply so you can carry on the work in the only way Milton Erickson would want: your own way!

Ernest L. Rossi, Ph.D.

Contributors

James Auld, B.D.S., Dip. Soc. Sc., MSc
Dentist, with a practice in Inverell, New South Wales, Australia. He studied with Kay Thompson. Invited faculty at International Milton H. Erickson congresses. Senior Clinical Associate, Faculty of Dentistry, University of Sydney; Course Consultant and Lecturer; Diploma in Hypnosis, University of Southern Queensland; President ASH (1999-2001). He uses hypnosis extensively in his practice.

Rubin Battino, M.S.
Private practice in Yellow Springs, Ohio. Teaches courses periodically for the Department of Human Resources at Wright State University where he holds the rank of adjunct professor. Over six years of experience as a facilitator in a Bernie Siegel style support group for people who have life-threatening diseases and those who support them. President of the Milton H. Erickson Society of Dayton. Co-chair of an ad hoc committee to establish certification standards for training in Ericksonian hypnotherapy for the societies and institutes affiliated with the Milton H. Erickson Foundation. Developed and teaches courses in Ericksonian hypnotherapy at Wright State University with T.L. South. Professor emeritus of chemistry.

Leon B. Segal, M.A.
Works extensively with substance abuse in the Dayton, Ohio area. Past president of the Milton H. Erickson Society of Dayton.

Thomas L. South, Ph.D.
Ph.D. in clinical psychology from the Union Institute. Has conducted workshops for the Associate Trainers in Clinical Hypnosis. Developed and taught courses in Ericksonian approaches at the University of Dayton and with Rubin Battino at Wright State University. Invited faculty at the Third International Congress on Ericksonian Approaches to Hypnosis and Psychotherapy. Author of a chapter entitled "Hypnosis in Childbirth: A Case Study in Anesthesia." Founder and first president of the Milton H. Erickson Society of Dayton. Presently a staff psychologist at the Twin Valley Psychiatric System - Dayton Forensic Unit. Private practice for many years.

Sandra Sylvester, Ph.D.
Trained with Milton H. Erickson, M.D. Many years of private practice. Many years of working in hospital settings as a staff hypnotherapist. Faculty at International Erickson congresses and at the Gestalt Therapy Institute of Cleveland.

Chapter 1

History of Hypnosis

Thomas L. South, Ph.D.

A. Introduction

Hypnosis is as old as the human race. The phenomenon known as hypnosis has existed since the beginning of recorded history, as found in the folklore of ancient cultures. In ancient times, as well as in the "primitive" tribes of today, it has been and continues to be associated with religious ceremonies, magic, the supernatural, and the occult. The ancient Egyptians and Greeks had dream centers (Udolf, 1981) where people came to fast and pray with the hope that their dreams could be interpreted so as to solve their problems and give them guidance. Under these circumstances their dreams were probably hypnotically induced. Even today, Hindu medicine men practice their ageless forms and variations of hypnosis for healing purposes. Magicians in the time of Genghis Khan (Erickson and Rossi, 1980, Vol. III, p. 3) practiced group suggestion to obtain visual and auditory hallucinations. According to Marco Polo, medieval men used hypnosis in mystic rites to produce fear and to intensify beliefs in the supernatural and the occult. With this long history of supernaturalism and mysticism, it is no wonder that the general public's attitude toward hypnosis, as well as that of many professionals, has been and, to a certain extent, still is one of misunderstanding, antagonism and fear.

B. Franz Anton Mesmer (1734–1815)

The scientific study of hypnosis began with Franz Anton Mesmer (1734–1815). The term "Mesmerism" is still in current usage. Mesmer was a Viennese physician who used his mesmeric techniques in the treatment of psychiatric patients. His practice of *suggestion* therapy consisted of what he called "the natural qualities of animal magnetism." He attributed his beneficial therapeutic results to the transferring of this quality of animal magnetism to his patients. Since Mesmer was greatly influenced by Newton's discovery of the gravitational attraction of the heavenly bodies towards each other, he generalized Newton's ideas to explain how certain diseases were due to an imbalance of hormones in the body due to the influence of gravity. In 1779, Mesmer (1980) defined animal magnetism as a "force which is the cause of universal gravitation and which is, very probably, the foundation of all corporal properties, a force which actually strains, relaxes and agitates the cohesion, elasticity, irritability, magnetics, and electricity in the smallest fluid and solid particles of our machine." To illustrate how such subtle forces affect the human body, he gave the following two examples: "(1) when the nervous system is exposed to emanating light, changes take place in the mind and body; (2) a stream of air affects the nerves in the ear and is capable of disturbing the entire animal body." He postulated that the same forces which caused the expansion of the ocean and the atmosphere created a tide in the human body in such a way that it agitated the blood vessels that carried blood to the brain and caused sickness. He used the increase in the number of epileptic seizures during a full moon as an example of this phenomenon. Since he believed that magnetism and electricity had similar properties that disturbed the fluid in the body in such a manner to cause disharmony of the nervous system, he placed magnets on various parts of the body, and claimed to have restored menstrual periods, decreased hemorrhoids, cured hypochondriasis, blindness, convulsions, hysterical irregularities, and spasmodic paralysis of the legs.

Mesmer later came to the conclusion that all people have magnetic properties such as himself in greater or lesser amounts that affect the bodies of others, e.g., hair can stand up on end, electrical sparks can fly from the body. Thus, a human body sick from weakened fluids can be rejuvenated by the magnetism from another. He also believed that magnetism can be transferred to such materials as paper, glass, water, metals or any chosen object, as well as to others. Thus, a human body that was sick from imbalanced or weakened fluids could be rejuvenated by the transfer of magnetism.

The documented case of Miss Paradis (1980) was considered as one of his most significant cures utilizing animal magnetism. Miss Paradis was born with normal vision but had developed hysterical blindness at an early age. Prior treatment consisted of blistering, leeches, cauterization, purgatives and diuretics for years, but with continued failure. She had intense pain from spasms in the eyes, and also suffered states of delirium. The spasms were described as causing the eyes to bulge so much that only the whites could be seen. The medieval medical society considered her condition as incurable.

Mesmer visited her home for three days and placed her in a trance by stroking her eyes and arms. He also moved a stick reflected in a mirror across her eyes. The patient watched the movement of the stick in the mirror. On the fourth day, she relaxed and her eyes resumed natural positioning, with one eye smaller than the other. The eyes became the same with continued treatment. After she reported continued headaches and eye aches with trembling in her limbs, he began treatment in a darkened room. In her home as she gradually adjusted to the sensation of light, she learned to distinguish colors. He had her gradually learn to use the motor muscles of her eyes by having her slowly search for objects, fixing sight on them and giving their positions. He then reinforced her visual memory by having her touch the objects. He also trained her to observe the movements of objects. She eventually learned to endure daylight. When her parents were informed of their daughter's favorable progress, they demanded that she be returned home since a substantial royal pension would be forfeited upon the daughter's recovery. When she could not name colors to her father's satisfaction and refused to return home, her father struck her and denounced Mesmer as a quack. Her blindness returned, and she continued to receive her pension; Mesmer was publicly declared a charlatan.

The media promoted Mesmer as a fraud and illusionist. Physicians who had attempted his animal magnetism technique and failed reported their experiences. They reported his cures as imaginary and his theory as an illusion. This caused Mesmer to stop using magnets and electricity due to the futility of attempting to influence medical committees.

Mesmer believed that he was ostracized and accused of eccentricity because he did not follow the traditional path of medicine, and that the community construed this as a crime. However, he believed that he had advanced the knowledge of medicine and had made discoveries in healing. Mesmer believed that most physicians had superstitious confidence in their traditional treatment of patients and this made them "despotic and presumptuous." He believed that physicians were "sheltered in traditional medicine" and were afraid to go outside of that tradition to help their patients. Thus, they failed to admit or explain how patients became cured *without* the help of medicine.

Mesmer was well before his time. Although he successfully treated large numbers of patients on whom traditional procedures had failed with animal magnetism, he had no realization of the psychological nature of his therapy. Unfortunately, his personality and the mystical character of his therapy served to bring him unjustly into disrepute. A committee (Erickson and Rossi, 1980, Vol. III, pp. 3–4. Also see Franklin, 1837) that included Benjamin Franklin, John Guillotine and Antoine Lavoisier was sent to investigate Mesmer. They observed that patients sent out to touch "magnetized" trees became healed. However, they also noticed that patients were cured even though they touched the wrong trees! Consequently, they came to the conclusion that Mesmer was a charlatan, and there was no realization of the psychological truths of this type of therapy. Despite the unfortunate reputation Mesmer acquired, many physicians who had visited his clinic during the height of its success were impressed with this form of psychotherapy.

The failure of contemporary societies to discover anything of medical or scientific worth in Mesmer's theories and claims did not deter the public or physicians in other countries from practicing animal magnetism. Mesmeric societies (Mesmer, 1980) were organized in other countries than France, Germany and Austria. Although official condemnation of Mesmerism had spread throughout Europe during the 1820s, there was always one respected physician who revived Mesmerism due to the remarkable results obtained by its usage.

C. John Elliotson (1791–1868)

The next great figure in hypnosis was an English physician. John Elliotson (1791–1868) was assistant physician at St. Thomas's Hospital and professor of medicine at University College in

London, as well as a prolific writer. He had aroused much antago-nism (Elliotson, 1977) because of his "liberal" and "radical" attitudes toward the practice of medicine. He was the first British physician to approve of Laennec's stethoscope, and used it in his medical practice. Although he was considered a radical, he was also recognized as an eminent physician. Elliotson became inter-ested in Mesmerism in about 1817. When he lectured on the effec-tive uses of Mesmerism, even the more traditional members of the medical society listened to him. He employed it extensively on his patients and left excellent records of its therapeutic effectiveness in selected cases, especially for pain control and surgical operations. Unfortunately, with the advent of chemical anesthetics it was no longer considered needed as a medical anesthetic. (See Gravitz, 1988, for a history of the early uses of hypnosis for surgical anesthesia—its use in America was surprisingly extensive, and the first documented case was in 1829.)

The following two cases have been selected from his writings (Elliotson, 1977) to demonstrate how mesmerism was practiced and its remarkable effects during surgery and recovery during this era.

Case 1 Successful Amputation of the Thigh:

The patient had suffered for five years from neglected disease of the left knee. The slightest movement of the joint caused him excruci-ating agony.

First Day: The mesmeric state consisted of 5½ hours of trance. During this time, he appeared awake and spoke without feeling pain.

Second Day: Within 20 minutes he was placed in a deep trance with the same results.

Third Day: The patient complained of great agony and was mesmer-ized for 15 minutes before surgery began. The mesmerist commenced the induction by making passes over the diseased knee. In five minutes he was mesmerized. Within ten minutes he was in a deep sleep. In order to test the depth of trance, his arms and then the diseased leg were violently pinched without the patient's exhibiting any sensations. The mesmerist then placed two fingers on the patient's eyelids and kept them there during surgery to deepen "sleep." The surgeon slowly plunged his knife into the center of the outside of the thigh, directly to the bone, and then made a clear incision around the bone, to the opposite point on the inside of the thigh. The stillness at this moment was something awful. The calm respiration of the sleeping man alone was heard, for all other seemed suspended. In making the second incision, the position of the leg was found more inconvenient than it appeared to be; —having made the anterior flap—(there was) the necessity of completing the posterior one in three stages—the patient's sleep continued as profound as ever. The placid look of his countenance never changed for an instant; his whole frame rested, uncontrolled, in perfect stillness and repose; not a muscle was seen to twitch. To the end of the operation, including the sawing of the bone, securing the arteries, and applying the bandages, occupying a period of upwards of twenty minutes, he lay like a statue. Thirty minutes after, he awakened from the mesmeric coma gradually and calmly. He appeared dazed and then replied, "I bless the Lord to find it's all over!" Later that night, he was re-mesmerized within two minutes and had a comfortable night's sleep.

Recovery. Two days later, he was placed in a mesmeric coma for dressing the wound without the patient's knowledge. The pain returned when he fully realized that the leg had been removed. In four minutes, he was re-mesmerized and the pain subsided. He was mesmerized daily for the following ten days with a marked improvement in his health, e.g., cheerful, stronger, slept well and had a recovered appetite. Within three weeks, his health completely returned and he was discharged as perfectly well.

Case 2 Tooth Extraction:

The dentist, "after having satisfied himself of this (mesmeric coma) by pricking him repeatedly, proceeded to extract the last lower left molar tooth. As it was broken, the dentist was obliged to cut away the gum from it, and the patient gave no sign of sensation. The dentist introduced the instrument into the mouth—the instrument with which he had first attempted to extract the tooth; and pushed back the head of the young man—fixed the instrument, extracted the tooth, which was barred, and therefore more calculated to give pain. The patient rinsed his mouth and was awakened. The moment he awoke, he entreated the dentist not to allow his tooth to be taken out, because he no longer had any pain; but, finding the blood in his mouth, he applied his hand to it, and discovered that the tooth had been extracted."

D. James Esdaille (1808–1859)

James Esdaille (1808–1859) was directly influenced by Elliotson's writings and became an advocate of mesmerism. He held a medical appointment in India from 1845–1851. He was successful in having the British government build a hospital in Calcutta. This gave him the freedom to experiment with mesmerizing, since the way Indians were treated did not raise concern as it did with patients in London. In this six-year period, he utilized hypnotic anesthesia in thousands of minor surgeries, and kept a diary that reported that only mesmerism was used in over 300 major surgical operations. After his return to Scotland, he continued his research and his correspondence with Elliotson (Esdaille, 1846).

By 1846, nitrous oxide and ether had successfully been used in surgery and were the anesthetics of choice by the medical society. Thus Esdaille and Elliotson became rebels without a cause.

In inducing the mesmeric coma for surgical operations, Esdaille strongly suggested that a trial trance under an hour was insufficient time, and preferred two hours. He also warned that a "perfect success" often followed frequent failures, but that insensitivity to pain was sometimes produced in minutes. His inductions for surgery often consisted of having the patient lie down in a quiet, darkened room and prepare for sleep. He suggested that the patient be told that it was a trial instead of a surgical operation in order not to arouse fear in the patient. Esdaille then would bring his face close to the patient's and extend his hands over the stomach, and then, bringing his hands up in a clawed fashion, shut the patient's eyes; then he would extend his hands longitudinally from the head to the stomach. This process was repeated for fifteen minutes while breathing on the head and eyes all the time. He then tested his work by gently lifting the arms and placing them into a cataleptic position. If catalepsy existed, the patient was called by name and pricked. If there was no response, the operation proceeded. If the patient awoke during the first incision, the trance was easily reproduced by continuing the mesmeric process. He believed that the patient only experienced a nightmare, since there was no recognition of the operation after awakening.

Since his beliefs regarding how animal magnetism affected the body were similar to Mesmer's, he induced trance by magnetizing objects and used them for trance inductions. For example, he would mesmerize water and induce trance by having patients drink the mesmerized water.

Most trances were easily terminated by sharply blowing in the eyes and sprinkling cold water in the face. To de-mesmerize a cataleptic limb, he followed the same procedure with the addition of gently rubbing the limb. He believed that this revived the "nervous currents" to the skin and the sense organs—thereby, rousing the brain to its normal functioning.

The following cases have been selected from the diary (Esdaille, 1846) that he wrote while in India. They present the extraordinary results that he obtained from his documented use of mesmerism.

Case 1 Terminating Hiccoughs with Mesmerized Water:

The patient was convalescent from cholera and plagued with continual hiccoughs—eight convulsions in a minute. He was mesmerized in fifteen minutes and continued to hiccough for thirty minutes. Esdaille reported that "he was raised to his feet, and a bandage soaked in cold water (was) wound around his chest, without awakening him, and he was allowed to sleep half an hour longer: still no change for the better. I now prepared some mesmerized water, and awoke him; he no sooner drank it than he fell asleep again, and the hiccough immediately stopped, and never returned. He slept for three hours after drinking the water." Esdaille commented that this was not the general effect of drinking mesmerized water and that this only occurred in individuals already under the mesmeric influence.

Case 2 Surgical Removal of an Enlarged Growing Tumor:

The patient had suffered for two years from a growing tumor in the antrum maxillae. The tumor had pushed up the orbit of the eye, filled up the nose, passed into the throat, and caused an enlargement of the glands in the neck. The patient had complained that he had hardly slept for the past five months. The mesmeric coma sufficient for surgery was produced in forty-five minutes. Since Esdaille reported that this was one of the most severe and protracted operations in surgery, his detailed account of this operation is presented:

"I put a long knife in at the corner of his mouth, and brought the point out over the cheekbone, dividing the parts between; from this, I pushed it through the skin at the corner of the eye, and dissected the cheek back to the nose. The pressure of the tumor had caused the absorption of the anterior wall of the antrum, and on pressing my fingers between it and the bones, it burst, and a shocking gush of blood, and brain-like matter, followed. The tumor extended as far as my fingers could reach under the orbit and cheekbone, and passed into the gullet—having destroyed the bones and partition of the nose. No one touched the man, and I turned his head into any position that I desired, without resistance, and there it remained till I wished to move it again: when the blood accumulated, I bent his head forward, and it ran from his mouth as if from a leaden spout. The man never moved, nor showed any signs of life, except an occasioned indistinct moan; but when I threw back his head, and passed my fingers into his throat to detach the mass in that direction, the stream of blood was directed into his wind-pipe, and some instinctive effort became necessary for existence; he therefore coughed, and leaned forward, to get rid of the blood, and I supposed that he then awoke. The operation was by this time finished, and he was laid on the floor to have his face sewed up, and while this was doing, he for the first time opened his eyes.

(Next Day) This is even a more wonderful affair than I supposed yesterday. The man declares by the most emphatic pantomime, that he felt no pain while in the chair, and that when he awoke, I was engaged in sewing up his face, on the floor;—so that the coughing and forward movement to get rid of the blood, were involuntary, instinctive efforts, to prevent suffocation.

(Following Day) The dressings were undone today, and the whole extent of the wounds in the face has united completely by the first intention. He is out of all danger, and can speak plainly: he declares most positively that he knew nothing that had been done to him till he awoke on the floor, and found me sewing up his cheek;—and I presume he knows best. Here is a translation of his own statement in Bengalee: "For two years I labored under this disease, and scarcely slept for five months. On the 19th of May, I came to the Imambarah Hospital, and three or four persons tried to make me sleep, but all in vain. On the 3rd of June, Dr. Esdaille, having kindly undertaken my cure, with a great deal of labor, made me sleep, and took something out of my left cheek, which at that time I did not perceive. After the operation, I did not sleep for two nights, but after the third day, I have slept as usual."

Table I. A list of painless surgical operations.

Arm amputated = 1
Breast ditto = 1
Tumor extracted from upper jaw = 1
Scirrhus testium extirpated = 2
Penis amputated = 2
Contracted knees straightened = 3
Ditto arms = 3
Operations for cataract = 3
Large tumor in groin cut off = 1
Operations for hydrocele = 7
Ditto dropsy = 2
Actual cautery supplied to a sore = 1
Muriatic acid ditto = 2
Unhealthy sores pared down = 7
Abscesses opened = 5
Sinus, six inches long laid open = 1
Heel flayed = 1
End of thumb cut off = 1
Teeth extracted = 3
Gum cut away = 1
Prepuce cut off = 3
Piles ditto = 1
Great toe nails cut out by roots = 5
Seton introduced from ankle to knees = 1
Large tumor on leg removed = 1
Scrotal tumors, weighing from 8 lb. to 80 lbs.
    removed 17, painless = 14

Total operations = 73

Tables I and II summarize his use of mesmerism during his last eight months in India as recorded in *Mesmerism in India, and its Practical Application in Surgery and Medicine.* It should also be noted that there were no reported deaths among these cases.

Table II. A list of medical/nervous cases cured.

Nervous headache	3 cured by one trance
Tic-douloureux	1 ditto
Nervousness, and lameness from rheumatism of 2½ yrs.	1 by chronic treatment
Spasmodic colic	1 by trance
Acute inflammation of eye	1 by repeated trances in 24 hrs.
Chronic ditto	1 by chronic treatment
Acute inflammation of testes	1 by repeated trances in 36 hrs.
Convulsions	1 by trance
Lameness from rheumatism	2 by chronic treatment
Lumbago	1 by general and local mesmerizing for 1 week
Sciatica	1 ditto
Pain in crural nerve	1 ditto
Palsy of one arm	1 ditto for month
Ditto of half the body	1 ditto for 6 wks
Feeling of insects crawling over the body	1 by one trance

Total = 18

E. James Braid (1795–1860)

James Braid (1795–1860) initiated the first attempt at a psychological explanation of mesmeric phenomena. He was an English surgeon and a prolific writer. He was also highly regarded by the British Medical Association. After his first opportunity of conducting a medical examination on a mesmerized subject in 1841, he became intensely interested in mesmeric trances. He began his own experiments in private and with selected trusted colleagues. It was due to his research that hypnosis was placed on a scientific basis and accepted as a clinical technique by the British medical profession. Thus, Braid is considered as the "father" of hypnosis.

In the course of his investigations (Braid, 1843), he discovered that eye fixation created a state of exhaustion, i.e., the eyelids became exhausted and could not be opened by the subject. He considered this as the key to mesmerism. After further experimentation, he created a theory of eye attention. He had subjects gaze at a variety of objects at different positions, including his own eyes and candle flames, and was successful in inducing trance. Braid did not believe that trance induction or cures of nervous complaints depended on the physical and psychological condition of the subject, or of any special agency, such as passes of the operator, magnetic fluid or medium. He did not want to be known as a modifier of the infamous animal magnetism. Since he did want credit as the discoverer of a new cure for nervous disorders substantiated by medical research, he adopted new terms to prevent association with magnetism.

He initially called his discovery *neurypnology*—a word derived from Greek meaning nervous sleep. He later coined the word *neuro-hypnotism* derived from Hypnos, the Greek god of sleep. A short time later, he suppressed the prefix for brevity. His discovery was then referred to as hypnotism or hypnosis. Since it was regarded as a medical technique, it was to be used only by professional men, preferably physicians.

Hypnotism was defined as a peculiar condition of the nervous system induced by fixed and abstracted attention of the mental and visual eyes of a subject, and concentration on a single idea without an exciting nature. It was used to cure functional disorders that were intractable or incurable by ordinary remedies. Most cases gave no evidence of physical pathology and were presumed to depend on some peculiar condition of the nervous system.

He generally induced trance by holding any bright object in his left hand at approximately eight to fifteen inches from the eyes above the forehead as to produce the greatest possible strain upon the eyes and eyelids. Subjects were instructed to maintain a steady fixed stare at the object, and the mind riveted on an idea of the object. When the pupils dilated, he would then slowly move the right hand with fingers slightly parted towards the eyes until they automatically closed. The arms were then raised. If the arms remained in a cataleptic position, the subject was assumed to be in a trance. Suggestions were then made to the subject to effect change in the patient's condition. Trance was terminated by either blowing in the patients's face, rubbing the arms, clapping the hands, or slapping the limbs. Sometimes a combination of those actions was necessary to rouse a subject. These techniques have survived time and are still taught and used by "traditional" hypnotists.

From his clinical applications and experimental research, Braid made many discoveries regarding hypnosis. He observed that trance behavior was stimulated by monotonous impressions upon the senses or soothing influences, such as weak vibrations, staring at a calm scene, listening to waves or a waterfall, the humming of insects, low howling of winds, the voice of a dull reader, the rocking of a cradle, slow and regular motion of the limbs. These impressions produced tranquility, drowsiness and sleep in most people. He also discovered that hearing was about twelve times more acute than when awake. He reported that the tick of a watch that could not be heard three feet away when awake, could be heard 35 feet away, and subjects could walk in a direct line to the watch. Smell was also exalted. One patient could trace the smell of a rose for 46 feet. Tactile sensations were also enhanced. The slightest touch often called into action corresponding muscles that were ordinarily not even felt. Heat and cold could be noticed from 20 inches. Subjects would move away from or towards stimuli according to their comfort level. In a deep trance, subjects could not hear the loudest sounds nor smell the most fragrant or pungent odors, nor feel hot or cold, nor respond to touch. Thus, subjects could be pricked, pinched or cut without causing the slightest symptom of pain or sensibility, and limbs remained rigidly fixed. Subjects were not conscious of surrounding objects or severe bodily infliction. Subjects who grasped objects held them more firmly as opposed to the sleeping state where objects normally dropped out of the hand. He utilized hypnotic amnesia and hypnotic dreaming to resolve problems.

Braid believed that the more a person was hypnotized, the easier it was to induce trance in the subject. He also believed that a person could not be hypnotized against their will, and could not be induced to perform acts that they would not ordinarily do while awake. Braid performed experiments demonstrating that subjects would not steal and, if they did during the trance, they immediately showed remorse and returned the items.

In a treatise to the medical profession, Braid presented the following nine conclusions as important scientific tenets of hypnosis:

1. The effect of continued fixation of the eyes alters the nervous system in such a manner that a person can display a variety of phenomena different from ordinary sleep or while awake.

2. Initially there is heightened excitement of the senses, except sight, and a great increase in muscular strength.

3. Shortly after induction, nervous energy can be directed or concentrated as necessary to effect desired changes.

4. The heart rate and circulation can be excited or depressed to a surprising degree.

5. Muscular energy can be controlled and regulated in a remarkable manner.

6. Capillary circulation, as well as secretions and excretions of the body can be changed as evidenced by chemical tests.

7. Hypnotic suggestion can cure a variety of diseases that are intractable or incurable by ordinary medical means.

8. Hypnosis can moderately or entirely prevent a person from feeling pain during and after a surgical operation.

9. During hypnotism, an operator can excite certain mental and bodily manifestations according to the parts touched by manipulating the cranium and face. (Hypnotic phrenology.)

Of the 25 cases recorded in *Neurypnology*, these have been selected to demonstrate his clinical hypnotic work:

Case 1 Abrogation of Severe Headaches and Severe Skin Disorder Simultaneously.

The patient was a 54 year old woman whose headaches for sixteen years had been so severe as to cause pain in her eyes and weakness of sight, i.e., she could no longer read for longer than five minutes with the aid of glasses. The palm of her hands were so hard, dry and irritable that she could not open her hands fully. Three years before consulting Mr. Braid, she had had a paralytic attack which had affected the right side of her face for days.

After the first session, she could read the newspaper without her glasses and could read a miniature Bible with her glasses. After the second session two days later, the pain in her chest, head and eyes dissipated. The harsh and arid skin of her palms soon became as soft as chamois leather.

Case 2 Mobility Restored to a Woman with Paralyzed Legs.

The patient was a 33 year old woman who had rapidly lost the use of her legs after delivery of a seven month pregnancy. She had lost feeling and voluntary motion of her legs and feet. The knees were rigidly flexed, the heels drawn up, the toes flexed, the feet incurvated, and fixed in the position of a club foot. She had not menstruated since her confinement. Her speech had become imperfect and her memory had become impaired. After five minutes of trance she could stand and walk across the room with assistance. After the second trance that evening, she could walk around the room with the soles of her feet on the floor with assistance. After daily trances for a week, she could walk through the house with little assistance. Within two months, she could walk several miles to town unaided.

Case 3 Abolished Pain in Spinal Cord.

This patient was a 45 year old male who had injured his spine and had limited mobility of his upper extremities for four years. He had been unable to dress himself for five years and could not lift his left arm. The right arm was also afflicted but to a lesser degree. The patient was so satisfied with the alleviation of pain after the first session that he returned for daily treatment. After two months of hypnotic treatment, he was able to return to work.

The other cases documented by Mr. Braid include successful trance work with numerous cases of stroke victims, paralysis, chronic rheumatoid patients, as well as the restoration of sight, hearing, smell and tactile sensations. However, Mr. Braid also recorded unsuccessful cases and strongly emphasized that hypnosis was not a universal remedy, but an extremely curative instrument in helping those who could benefit from it.

Since Braid, there have been many outstanding practitioners of hypnosis, but it was still ridiculed by medical societies, and at best it was considered as a placebo or for temporary relief of symptoms by the majority of physicians. However, it was the observed and published work of Milton H. Erickson, M.D. (1901–1980) that made hypnosis a respectable approach worthy of study in medical schools, as well as being considered a clinical tool by the American Medical Association.

F. Milton H. Erickson (1901-1980)

Erickson has been considered to be the most creative and innovative hypnotherapist and psychotherapist throughout the world. He was to the *practice* of psychotherapy as Freud was to the *theory* of human behavior. Erickson (Rossi, Ryan and Sharp, 1983) experienced the world in his own unique manner due to several constitutional problems: color-blindness, tone deafness and dyslexia. To his early problems were added two attacks of polio at the ages of 17 and 51. His efforts to rehabilitate himself led to a personal rediscovery of many classical hypnotic phenomena and how they could be utilized therapeutically. His successful rejuvenation of the entire field of hypnosis may be attributed to his development of the non-authoritarian and indirect approach to suggestion, wherein subjects learn how to experience hypnotic phenomena and how to utilize their own potentials to solve problems in their own way. His experimental and therapeutic experiences with the hypnotic modality spanned more than 50 years. During his lifetime, he gave seminars and workshops in various parts of the world, and under a variety of circumstances, including non-English speaking countries.

Erickson was raised in a farm community in Wisconsin and graduated from the local high school. After graduating from the University of Wisconsin in 1928 with an M.A. degree in psychology and an M.D. degree, he completed a general internship at the Colorado General Hospital and then served a psychiatric internship at the Colorado Psychopathic Hospital. He received an appointment at the State Hospital for Mental Diseases in Howard, Rhode Island where he completed his thesis for his Master's Degree. It explored the relationships among such factors as intelligence, marriage, abandonment and crime. His findings were published in various medical, social and legal journals in a series of seven papers between 1929 and 1931. His first published hypnotic research occurred while employed at the Worcester State Hospital as the Chief Psychiatrist. This paper (Erickson 1932) dealt with the "Possible Detrimental Effects from Experimental Hypnosis."

His next appointment was at the Wayne County Hospital in Eloise, Michigan as the Director of Psychiatric Research. He later became the Director of Psychiatric Research and Training. This provided him with the opportunity to conduct major experimental research studies on the nature and reality of hypnotic phenomena. These ranged in scope from controlled laboratory experiments on hypnotic deafness and color blindness to the investigation of hypnotically induced disorders significant in clinical work, as well as severe psychiatric syndromes. In the following 30 years, he published hundreds of papers and co-authored several books on the therapeutic use of hypnosis and hypnosis related strategies.

Due to his reputation, he became an Associate Editor for "Diseases of the Nervous System" (1940 & 1955). He was a consultant to the U.S. Government in its cultural studies during the second World War. Margaret Mead and Erickson investigated the Japanese character structure and the effects of Nazi propaganda. He served as the staff psychiatrist on the local induction board. He was consultant to the U.S. Olympic Rifle Team and other Olympic teams. Erickson was published in the *Reader's Digest*, *Life Magazine* and *This Week News Magazine*, and he was a consultant to the *Encyclopedia Britannica* on hypnosis. He was also a guest on radio shows and made addresses to the Boy Scouts, the C.I.O., and high school graduation classes. He and other colleagues founded the American Society of Clinical Hypnosis in 1957, and he became its first president. Erickson also served as the first editor of the society's journal from 1958 to 1968. The first volume included corresponding editors from Chile, Japan and Uruguay. Thus, his publications became international.

In 1948 he accepted the position of Clinical Director at the Arizona State Hospital in Phoenix, Arizona. A year later, he retired from the hospital. He gave numerous lectures to other professionals, including psychologists, psychiatrists and dentists, as well as entering into private practice. For several years before his death, his health permitted him only to teach part-time at his home.

Erickson received many honors throughout his lengthy career for his outstanding contributions. The two that he especially appreciated were the Benjamin Franklin Gold Medal by the International Society of Hypnosis in 1977, and a special issue of *The American Journal of Clinical Hypnosis* commemorating his 75th birthday (Erickson, Ryan and Sharp, 1983). The Milton H. Erickson Foundation was created in 1979. Since the International Congress on Ericksonian Approaches to Hypnosis and Psychotherapy held in Phoenix three years after his death, there have been numerous Ericksonian institutes and societies created throughout the world to promote an interchange of knowledge among practitioners utilizing clinical hypnosis.

Exercises

1. For expanding your background in the field it is important to be aware of the history of hypnotism. Thus, you should read about the development of hypnotism and the works of the main contributors to this development.

2. By necessity our treatment here has not been all-inclusive. Separately, you will find it rewarding to study the contributions of the French in the late 1800s, Freud, and the development of "academic" hypnosis in America following the steps of Clark Hull, the Hilgards, and Weitzenhofer.

Chapter 2

Myths and Misconceptions

Thomas L. South, Ph.D.

A. Introduction

In any discussion of hypnosis, *certain* general questions arise
concerning its usage. There are numerous myths and many
common misconceptions widely held by a variety of professionals,
as well as the general public. Many of these myths arose from the
historical connection of hypnosis with supernaturalism and mysticism. Also, well-intentioned explanations in attempts to understand hypnosis in its early scientific history led to misunderstandings. While Mesmer's "magnetism transference theory" has long
been antiquated, Braid's "nervous sleep theory" and techniques
have not only survived, but have continued to be taught in traditional schools of hypnosis due to the frequency with which his
effective results were misinterpreted, as well as being kept alive by
the entertainment industry, e.g., stage hypnotism shows, films, etc.

Thus, many individuals assume that they already are knowledgeable about hypnosis from what they have seen in films, including
documentary films, what they have read in "reputable" publications, and heard from "experts" in a variety of disciplines
including lawyers, physicians, nurses, dentists, and psychologists.
What they do not know is that many of those individuals are also
unknowingly misinformed about hypnosis. Many individuals who
practice hypnosis also come into this category, as evidenced by
their limited use of hypnosis, as well as by their incompetent
practice.

Although misinformation is constant, most misconceptions are
predictable because of stereotypical viewpoints, e.g., mind control,
form of sleep, weak-willed subjects, altering the mind, creating
abnormal personalities, etc. Due to the predictability of misinformation, the well-informed hypnotherapist should be prepared to
dispel these erroneous beliefs. In order to facilitate the use of

hypnosis it is especially important that the therapist spend sufficient time with clients discussing and listening to their views and expectations. Since some clients will deny having any opinions and others will actually believe that they know nothing about hypnosis, it is frequently beneficial for the therapist simply to begin discussing these misconceptions with the client. Some suggested leading questions are, "Why are you requesting hypnosis? What are your expectations? What are your past experiences? What do you think a trance is like? What hypnotic techniques have helped or not been beneficial to you?" Those clients who claim not to have any opinions will usually make comments upon re-orienting from the trance experience as to what they had expected, or the therapist will notice some difficulty during the trance experience that will elicit the client's opinions.

Since misconceptions can be a hindrance to the practice of effective hypnosis, the following explanations and scientific studies are offered to assist the therapist in discussing these general misconceptions with clients. Through the years, we have found these studies beneficial in subtly refuting misconceptions in graduate students, other professionals and clients, as well as alleviating their anxiety, and causing them to be more comfortable with hypnosis.

B. Hypnotic Susceptibility

A common question among academics and other professionals concerns hypnotizability or hypnotic susceptibility. A commonly held misconception among these individuals is that 25% of the population make excellent subjects, 50% are average subjects, and 25% cannot be hypnotized. These percentages are the result of controlled research experiments using so-called hypnotic susceptibility scales (Udolf, 1981), to wit: the Stanford Hypnotic Susceptibility Scale, the Stanford Profile Scales of Hypnotic Susceptibility, the Harvard Group Scale of Hypnotic Susceptibility, the Children's Hypnotic Susceptibility Scale and the Hypnotic Susceptibility Scale. These instruments consist of standardized scoring criteria in response to such suggestions as postural sway, eye closure, arm rigidity, eye catalepsy, verbal inhibition, various hallucinations, analgesia, amnesia, post-hypnotic suggestion, and so on. Statistical results of laboratory research on hypnosis can be quite misleading since there are subject variables which cannot be controlled. Some of these are misconceptions and individual reactions, e.g., the time needed to establish rapport and to enter trance varies widely. Thus, these percentages are more indicative of personality differences than hypnotic susceptibility. On the other hand, the Barber Suggestibility Scale (Udolf, 1981, pp. 29–30) is unlike the other instruments and does not depend on standardized scoring criteria. It is a test of suggestibility and relies on the *subjective* conditions on which an individual responds to suggestions, rather than the hypnotic state. *Barber's research suggests that the most consistent and important variables regarding hypnotizability are the subject-hypnotist relationship and motivation.* It is well-documented that hypnotizability is highest when a subject is strongly motivated to be hypnotized and has a positive attitude towards hypnosis, e.g., a poor subject who undergoes surgery without anesthesia when a chemical agent may be fatal makes an excellent hypnotic subject. Thus, anyone with an adequate attention span, average intelligence and a cooperative attitude can be hypnotized, including some mildly mentally retarded individuals. As a general guideline, mentally retarded persons, and those individuals suffering from organic brain disorders, paranoid disorders and schizophrenia do not make good subjects.

C. "Power" of the Hypnotist

Since the time of Mesmer the general public has believed that the hypnotist has "power," or can exert his or her will over the subject. This belief has its roots in animal magnetism and the techniques that were employed in its early history, as well as how they were depicted later in films. The terminology of "operator" and "subject" has also given the illusion that the hypnotist is controlling the hypnotic subject, i.e. the subject is responding to the commands of the hypnotist. While the term "subject" is an approved term used in research, it has a misleading connotation in its use in regard to hypnosis. The term "operator" is more easily replaced and its usage is becoming obsolete. It is absurd and grandiose to believe that we can control another individual, and those who become hypnotists believing this will be greatly disappointed. Hypnosis always requires the *cooperation* of the subject.

D. Fear of Not Awakening

The misconception of control is probably the greatest issue that needs to be resolved before implementing trance work. We have found that ending a discussion of control issues with a statement similar to "you can't be made to do anything that you ordinarily would not do, and you can arouse at any time you choose" often suffices to resolve this issue *before* entering trance. Those individuals who maintain this control belief are told that they will realize that they have full control of the situation after experiencing hypnosis. Sometimes an individual enters a trance state for other than therapeutic reasons, e.g., curiosity, power plays, etc. But, a trance state cannot be maintained without the subject's awareness. Therefore, the fear of not awakening is also unfounded. This misconception comes from a misunderstanding promulgated, perhaps inadvertently, by incompetent hypnotists who hold those beliefs. Some individuals find it difficult to remain in a trance, while others wish to remain in a state of complete relaxation, or to escape the frustrations of reality. Suggestions, not commands, are carried out because the subject is *willing* to do them, and can at any time terminate the trance state. No one can ever be made to do something against his/her will, especially regarding her morals or values. However, we may be surprised or shocked by our inaccurate assumptions about an individual.

E. Antisocial Behavior

Another prevalent misconception is the possibility of altering a person's personality even to the level of committing antisocial or other objectionable acts. Milton Erickson (1932) conducted an extensive investigation into this area. Possible detrimental effects center around the question of *hypersuggestibility*. He could not find any evidence to support the belief that a person's personality could be altered as a result of hypnosis from a survey of the literature, as well as his own research involving approximately 300 subjects and thousands of trances. A considerable number of subjects were hypnotized from 300 to 500 times over a four to six year period. The results of Erickson's literature research showed unfounded and subjective conclusions from the researchers and no well-controlled empirical research to support their dogmatic opinions and declarations. Personality profiles showed that those subjects who appeared to have had their personalities altered had unstable behavior disorders, and the alterations were not attributable to hypnosis as claimed. In Erickson's own research with subjects he found no detrimental effects. In fact, numerous subjects became uncooperative when attempts to make unwanted changes were suggested to them, and they had to be assured that this practice would cease in order for them to remain in the research.

A good example of this prevailing myth is in the criminal justice system. A number of courts have ruled that hypnotically refreshed testimony is inadmissible in court (Reiser, 1985). Even though there is no empirical proof, so-called expert witnesses, e.g., physicians, psychiatrists, and psychologists, have convinced lawyers and judges that a person's memory can be negatively altered as a direct result of being hypnotized. Thus court cases have been dismissed and suspects freed because an eyewitness had at *one time* been hypnotized. This has included anyone who has received hypnotherapy services for *any* kind of problem. However, there are some police departments that continue to use forensic hypnosis as an *investigative* tool.

In conducting a general survey of the literature, Erickson (1939) could not find any systematic or experimental study in which hypnosis could be used for antisocial purposes. Therefore, he conducted his own empirical research. His studies consisted of approximately 50 subjects from a total of more than 75. The subjects were children and adults, normal persons, and some recovering psychiatric patients, and ranged from those of superior intelligence to the feeble-minded. The majority of subjects were college students or graduates. All subjects knew Dr. Erickson and his status in the community. Thus, they had great trust and confidence in him as a professional person. About 40% of the subjects believed that they would perform minor objectionable acts, 50% believed that they would not, and the remainder were doubtful. None of the subjects believed that they would perform a major objectionable act.

The following studies have been selected to give the reader some idea of the nature of the experiments and their individual outcomes:

1.   While in a trance, subjects refused to pick up electrodes after a demonstration of shock by the experimenter. With insistence, the subjects became antagonistic. The subjects said that it was foolish and unnecessary since they were satisfied with the demonstration. They could not be persuaded.

2.   Glove anesthesia was proven with a lighted match under the fingertips. The subject accepted the suggestion and felt no pain. He became angry when he realized what was happening, and refused to continue the research.

3.   A subject was instructed to sit on a box described as a hot stove. She sat on it and acted like it was hot. Two weeks later, she was again instructed to sit on a box that was realistically described as a hot stove and refused. Two weeks later, she was told to sit on a hot stove. She obliged by mistaking a chair for the hot stove and acted like it was hot. She could not be convinced to sit on the actual hot stove.

4.   A subject was instructed to touch a hot stove with her hand and that she would feel nothing. She lowered her hand to one inch above the stove and claimed that her hand was on it.

5.   Subjects were told to tell lies. Some would only accept posthypnotic suggestions to tell "white lies." When told to lie to friends, they would lie only while in a trance and not in an awakened state.

6.   Subjects who were against drinking alcoholic beverages would not drink in a trance. However, some of these same subjects would taste drinks while awake. Some subjects even drank to intoxication.

7.   Unwarranted physical examinations were refused while in a trance.

8.   Subjects refused to give laxative candy to an unpopular student. Some subjects told the experimenter to do it.

9.   Suggestions to slap people or make disagreeable remarks to people they did not like were refused in trance. The most common reason given for refusing was that they would enjoy it more while awake.

10. When subjects were told that they had inadvertently committed criminal acts, they responded to the suggestions in trance. However, most subjects had amnesia for the acts outside trance. Some subjects who did not experience amnesia just remembered the experimenter telling them, or remembered that the acts were committed so long ago that they were not important.

11. Four subjects attempted to pick up a rattlesnake (enclosed in glass) described as a rubber hose. While awake (glass removed), they would not attempt it.

12. Three subjects attempted to throw acid in the experimenter's face (glass protection).

Upon questioning the subjects in 11 and 12 while awake, they gave similar responses about knowing that this was an experiment and that safeguards were employed.

The results of Erickson's research showed that all the subjects had the capacity and ability for self-protection, as well as critical judgment. They all showed complete rejection of commands and suggestions that were in conflict with their beliefs and values. The subjects were always aware of the general situation and conscious that it was an experiment. Some subjects were more apt to follow suggestions while awake rather than in a trance. Many of the subjects responded with anger and resentment to objectionable suggestions. These individuals also demanded that the hypnotist make an apology for unacceptable suggestions. This research also showed that an unstable personality was just as unstable in a trance state, and that an individual with antisocial tendencies was more apt to execute antisocial suggestions. It also showed that some individuals use hypnosis as an excuse for behavior that they really want to do. In conclusion, hypnosis did create a more suggestible state but individuals always had a choice.

Thus, hypnosis could not be used for antisocial purposes. The general conclusion drawn from the research was that hypnosis is no more harmful than therapy conducted by an unstable or unethical practitioner. The harmful affects incurred by those therapists could be the same if they utilized hypnosis because of the status given to their positions. But then again, that is questionable and contingent on the perception of the subject. All of the previously cited research is based on an assumption that the investigators were ethical in their outlook and non-Machiavellian in their intent. In Chapter 20 on ethics and the law we will cite evidence that a "dark side" of hypnosis does exist and that it is possible in unscrupulous hands (generally governments) to get subjects to do things that violate their personal conscious principles. However, to do this requires such extraordinary measures that one can safely say that these effects are beyond the capabilities of hypnotists operating by themselves in typical office outpatient settings.

Exercises

1. How many of these myths and misconceptions have you encountered, and how many had you subscribed to at one time?

2. Can you add to the myths and misconceptions discussed in this chapter?

3. How have stage hypnosis and movies contributed to misconceptions about hypnosis? Is the *Manchurian Candidate* scenario possible?

4. When working with a client, should you discuss these concepts and expectations about hypnosis before using trance work?

Chapter 3

Traditional vs. Non-traditional Inductions

Thomas L. South, Ph.D.

There are a variety of methods used to induce hypnosis. Mesmer's typical method was to place his hands on the subject's shoulders and to stroke the arms downward to the fingers. He then made various passes across the face or body and made gentle contact with his hand over the forehead, and the part of the body to be healed. Esdaille, the Scottish physician working in India, routinely placed his clients in a darkened room and instructed them to sleep. He then made passes without contact over the entire body. Braid usually had his subjects stare at some bright object and told them to relax and fall asleep. His later trance inductions employed the direct verbal method of repeating suggestions of fatigue and sleep. The direct verbal suggestion has become the most common technique.

A. Traditional Inductions

Most traditional inductions begin with giving subjects a brief explanation of hypnosis and what to expect while in a trance, as well as answering their questions to relieve any apprehension they might have regarding a hypnotic experience. Next, subjects are asked to sit comfortably and relax. At this time, some traditional hypnotists will employ one of the hypnotic susceptibility scales as a measure of hypnotizability. If subjects pass this test, they are so informed, and the hypnosis session is continued. Then, suggestions are given in a graduated form to the effect that they are getting tired and more tired, that they are getting sleepy and more sleepy, and that they will gradually go into a light sleep and then into a deeper and deeper sleep. The period of time required varies with each subject, some taking less than one minute to go into a deep sleep the first time, and others requiring hours to achieve this effect. Once the subject is in a trance, the same graduated manner is used to elicit any of the phenomena of the trance state. That is, repeated suggestions concerning the effect desired are given until the subject responds accordingly. Other direct suggestions are given repeatedly to effect the therapeutic change, e.g. cease smoking, weight loss, anesthesia, and so on. The traditional philosophy of hypnosis appears to be: if the subject realizes the "power" of the trance due to this altered state of awareness or perception, the subject will carry out the posthypnotic suggestions or commands. The hypnotist has the "power" and gives it back to the subject. The trance is usually terminated by the command to awaken at some suggested signal, such as snapping the fingers, or counting backwards or forwards to a designated number. Sometimes it is necessary to arouse subjects slowly by suggesting wakefulness in the same graduated manner that induced the trance.

B. Non-traditional Inductions

In the non-traditional or indirect method, there are many ways of inducing a trance. The hypnotherapist will frequently ask clients to give their attention to one particular idea. The hypnotherapist will usually have the client center their attention on their own experiential learnings. The therapist may suggest levitation to them and could have them lift a hand higher and higher, or could have them close their eyes bit by bit. Either of these experiences tends to direct attention to processes which are taking place within them. The non-traditional hypnotherapist can induce a trance by directing the client's attention to processes, to memories, to ideas, and to concepts that belong to the clients. Usually, what the therapist does is direct the client's attention to those processes that are within the client's experiences. Thus, the non-traditional hypnotherapist is limited only by his or her own creativity and experience. However, it is not uncommon to combine traditional and non-traditional techniques. Erickson condensed the traditional model and gave the client the illusion of choices (see chapter on language forms). Upon terminating trance, Erickson also usually informed the client that all hypnosis was self-hypnosis. The philosophy of the modern hypnotherapist is to use whatever methods are ethically effective in guiding clients to achieve their desired goals.

Table 3-1. Traditional Model

I. Preinduction	II. Induction	III. Deepening	IV. Direction	V. Termination
Rapport	Relaxation	Direct	Positive	Standard procedure, e.g. counting
Background	Sleep	Measured by scale	Negative	
Diagnosis				Discuss feelings
Dispel hypnosis beliefs				Verify
Hypnosis tests for susceptibility				

C. Rationale of Models

The rationale for having those different models relates to the different views and beliefs regarding hypnosis. The traditional model has its roots in the early history of hypnosis. That is, the hypnotist or mesmerist was thought to have the "power" to place individuals in some form of sleep and could directly suggest or command those individuals to behave in a desired manner, or

Table 3-2. Non-traditional Model

I. Preinduction	II. Induction	III. Deepening	IV. Direction	V. Termination
Rapport	Focus on inner experiences	Optional	Positive	Assume success
Optional		Indirect		Nurture
Background				Positive and future expectations
Diagnosis				
Dispel myths				

29

cause their patients with a "nervous disease" to heal themselves by balancing the "fluids" and "energies" within the body. While there is strong ongoing support from research on clinical hypnosis and how the mind affects the body in psychiatric and psychosomatic disorders, the belief about "power" is antiquated among professionals. However, it does continue to be a strong belief among the general population, as well as the belief that hypnosis is a form of sleep because of its sleep-like appearance to most people. Although hypnosis is still not understood, the *effectiveness* of both models is well-documented.

D. Hypnosis Defined

Due to the influence of Erickson's work, the perception of hypnosis has dramatically changed. He was aware that it was a special psychological state with certain physiological attributes, superficially resembling sleep, and characterized by a functioning of the individual at a level of awareness other than the ordinary state—which has been conceptualized as the "unconscious." Erickson never assumed that he knew the nature of hypnosis. He believed that it was such a complex psychophysiological phenomenon that it escaped definition. However, he did offer many definitions with the same theme throughout his life at seminars and workshops, as well as in response to personal inquiries and in articles he wrote for the *Encyclopedia Britannica*. We believe that the most encompassing and functional of his definitions was, "Hypnosis is essentially a communication of ideas and understandings to an individual in such a fashion that he will be most receptive to the presented ideas and thereby be motivated to explore his body potentials for the control of his psychological and physiological responses and behavior."(Haley, 1973, 1986.)

E. Common Everyday Trance

This definition subsumes the "common everyday trance" experiences (Erickson and Rossi, 1980, Vol. I, pp. 479–480) that people enter throughout the day. In ordinary conversation, we notice people quietly looking off into the distance, as they apparently reflect inwardly. We see these common trance experiences when people look out of windows, look at glowing fireplaces or dazzling lights, or at the floor. We have all experienced reading a good book or watching TV with someone talking to us and we are not aware of them. We have all experienced daydreaming while listening to a boring teacher in school, or at religious services. To fixate one's attention and become completely absorbed in the interesting story or topic that someone is telling is entrancing. So, a common everyday trance is when attention is fixed and absorbed in some matter of interest that is either inside *or* outside of ourselves. Thus, individuals do not need a formal induction, as believed by traditional hypnotists and the general population, to enter a trance experience. However, the hypnotherapist needs to know when a client is experiencing a trance state.

F.   Indications of Trance

The recognition and evaluation of altered patterns of normal functioning is one of the most subtle and important tasks of the therapist. Many clients recognize and admit changes that they have experienced, while others do not. It is not always necessary to convince clients that they have been in a trance. Arguing with a client regarding a trance experience is antagonistic and diminishes rapport, as well as being disrespectful of the client's belief system. Being aware of the indications of trance is especially important at the conclusion of a hypnosis session. *The therapist is responsible for knowing whether a client is leaving the office in an unintended trance state.* (There are times when waking trances are carefully and deliberately suggested by experienced hypnotherapists for a particular therapeutic purpose.) For example, an eye fixation induction using a prism paperweight quickly induced a trance in a graduate student. During suggestions to relieve test anxiety, the student opened his eyes, anxiously apologized for not being able to concentrate due to a severe headache, and began to leave the office. After requests to remain in the office were ignored, the student was *firmly* instructed to "sit down and relax." After comfort was re-established, he was awakened and asked about his experience. He reluctantly reported that he had re-experienced an auto accident in which his head struck the windshield without ever mentioning the headache—neither did the author, so as to avoid suggesting a headache. Further discussion revealed that the brilliant light of the prism evoked this unexpected abreaction. The experience was then resolved. If this author had not recognized the indications of trance and thought that this client had simply

Table 3-3. Common Indications of Trance

Pupil dilation
Slowed pulse
Altered respiration
Facial features smooth and relaxed
Response attentiveness
Comfort and relaxation
Swallowing reflex
Eye changes and closure
Body immobility
Literalism
Loss or retardation of blinking response
Catalepsy
Changed voice quality
Psychosomatic responses
Sensory, muscular, and body changes
Expectancy
Time lag in motor and conceptual behavior
Hypnotic phenomena
     a.   amnesia
     b.   anesthesia
     c.   body illusions
     d.   catalepsy
     e.   regression
     f.   time distortion
     g.   dissociation
Body reorientation after trance
Feeling good after trance

spontaneously awakened from trance, the student would not have only left the office with an excruciating headache, but the traumatic car accident experience would not have been resolved nor decreasing the test anxiety, and further trance work could have been jeopardized. (This student had a B average in engineering and was involved in another car accident causing bodily injury, but this was not that stressful to him.) Being aware of the indications of trance cannot be over-emphasized, and any student of hypnosis needs to be well-versed in observing these indicators.

Different individuals experience trance in different ways. The toughest task is to recognize those individual patterns. At this point we just list the most common indications of trance status. We will return to these indicators in more detail later.

Exercises

1. In your own words distinguish between traditional and non-traditional hypnosis. Which would you consider stage hypnosis to be?

2. How many of the common indications of trance have you noticed in the lecture hall or at the movies or in church or at parties? Which if these indicators are easiest to detect, and which would be the most important to observe?

Chapter 4

Rapport Building Skills

Rubin Battino, M.S.

A. Introduction

Before you can effectively work with someone, rapport has to be established. Your client must trust you and have confidence in you. There are some people you just automatically trust, and there are others whom you somehow distrust. How can you maximize useful rapport with your clients so that the cooperative work of their getting what they want will be enhanced? Is this learnable, or will you cop out with the statement one of our colleagues made: "Good therapists are born." Super-therapists like the late Carl Rogers, Virginia Satir, and Milton H. Erickson seemed to have these rapport skills naturally. Yet, if you study the work of Erickson, for example, you will find that he spent long years practicing and studying how to be more effective, how to read people, and how to interact with them. *Establishing rapport is something that can be learned.* In this chapter we will teach you the basic skills of rapport building and provide exercises for practicing and honing those skills.

It will always be the case that some people are "naturally" better at rapport building than others. Yet, we all learned those incomparably harder skills of walking and talking and writing. Remember that the early stages of learning any new skill involve confusion and awkwardness as well as a sense of "something" being not just right. Practice does make perfect. Giving your clients the congruent sense of having your "unconditional positive regard," that you are there for them and with them during the session, that they have *your* undivided attention, is the foundation on which *all* therapy is based. NLP people call this being in "uptime," i.e. a way of interacting in which all of your senses and consciousness (and unconsciousness) are focused on your client. To spend time in a session consulting your own inner feelings and memories is not what you are being paid for.

Of course, it is always permissible to ask for some time out to think about better or alternate ways to help the client. Some group practices routinely do this using a one-way mirror and telephones or time-outs for consultation. In fact, some individual practitioners do this routinely by actually leaving the client in the office for five to ten minutes while they think about what to do next. Remember, there are many ways to organize how you work with clients, as long as you design your approach for the unique person with whom you are working.

We exist and function in the world in terms of our proprioceptive senses and also in terms of language. We function in many different contexts, cultures, subcultures, and even mini-subcultures. When you meet another American abroad, there is an automatic feeling of recognition. If the two of you were both white or black or Hispanic, then another level of recognition would occur. If you shared the same religion, region of the country, sex, university, town, relatives, etc., the feeling of comfortableness around each other would increase even more. The closer the match, the greater the sense of rapport, of connection, of existing in the world in the same way. There is a rule about solubility which states that "like dissolves like." A similar rule about people might be that "like likes like" or that "like is comfortable with like."

Some people may raise an ethical objection here with respect to being "genuine" when you are working with a client. You cannot be other than yourself. If you adapt your behavior for the therapeutic advantage of your clients, is that ethical and responsible behavior? Since you cannot not manipulate during an interview, you might as well do so to the advantage of your client. It is ethical to do anything that is not unethical to help the client achieve what he or she desires (as long as that does not violate the law or harm people). If shifting the way that you phrase your speech to be closer to that of the client helps build rapport, what can be wrong with that? In fact, to not do so would be irresponsible since you should be free to do whatever you ethically can to help your clients. In this section, we will therefore explore ways of shifting your verbal and nonverbal behavior to better establish rapport and discuss ways of enhancing this feeling of mutuality.

B. Rogerian Approaches

Carl Rogers pioneered the approach of giving the client your "unconditional positive regard." He meant a number of things by this. First and foremost is that your client should know from your *congruent* behavior that you are there for them, that you are concerned about their well-being, and that you will do whatever is ethically possible for them within the therapeutic context. You may not be able to do this with some clients because of your own personality or perspective. If this is the case, then you should refer the client. On the other hand, almost everyone has something about them that is likable and with which you can make some connection. This also helps to separate within your own mind the person from their problems or difficulties. The client should have your undivided attention during a session since this is *their* time. They are paying and have hired you to perform a service which you are contractually bound to deliver. So, dealing with your problems or concerns during a session is improper. There is no place in dealing with clients for imposing your belief systems, your politics, your religion, your sexual preferences, etc., on the client. Since you cannot be other than who you are, then somehow or other your personal preferences must just not show up in the session. When we deal with significant people in our lives, there are some subjects that are just taboo if we wish to maintain that relationship. We know a couple who somehow never discuss the subject of abortion—he is adamantly opposed to it and she is not. If your belief system gets in the way of working with a particular client, then you must refer that client to someone else who would be comfortable with them. This "unconditional positive regard" is the foundation for all therapeutic relationships. A surgeon may possess remarkable technical skills, but even those skills can be enhanced by the belief of his/her patient that the surgeon is there for them and not just an automaton. A friend once said in this regard, "Even trees grow better when you talk to them!" It is the paying of attention that provides the basis for the cooperative venture of therapy. Of course, you should also know what you are doing!

C. Gathering Information

How much do you need to know about a client to help him/her? The answer is "just enough." Some therapists do not feel comfortable in dealing with clients unless they have the results of tests to guide them. Certainly, your own questionnaire, the MMPI, the TAT, the Meyers-Briggs, and the projective techniques of art therapy can provide useful information. Some clients will also require medical work-ups. (If you deal with third-party payments, you may need to do sufficient testing to justify your diagnoses.) We use a one-page intake form which obtains vital information such as address, phone numbers, family, etc., and then leaves one-half of the page for "briefly describe why you are here and/or what I can do for you." A ten to thirty minute discussion will usually provide sufficient information to devise interventions to help the client. Direct inquiry can also be useful.

Some therapists indicate that doing therapy is 95% gathering information and 5% interventions. Since you cannot do therapy without some information, it is important to gather just enough. You can always gather more information, if needed. On the other hand, you can spend endless sessions just gathering information and interpreting it back to the client. This may be a good way to pay the rent, but it is not effective, efficient or ethical therapy.

Body language is an important channel of information, and it is important that you "read" your client. This means being aware of facial expressions, voice quality, posture, movements, breathing patterns, etc. Of course, this should be done without being obvious. Pay special attention to incongruencies between verbal and nonverbal messages. With practice, you can read bodies automatically and with your peripheral vision. Erickson was an expert at this. In reading his works you will find that he spent endless hours practicing this skill. This will be discussed in more detail with exercises in the section on pacing and leading.

Erickson's "word salad" case (Erickson and Rossi, 1980, Vol. IV, pp. 213–215) is a fine example of the lengths he would go to in order to gather information. This case is also an excellent example of pacing and leading (see Section E following).

Word Salad

George had been a patient in a mental hospital for five years. His identity had never been established. He was simply a stranger around the age of 25 who had been picked up by the police for irrational behavior and committed to the state mental hospital. During those five years he had said, "My name is George," "Good morning," and "Good night," but these were his only rational utterances. He uttered otherwise a continuous word-salad, completely meaningless as far as could be determined. It was made up of sounds, syllables, words, and incomplete phrases. For the first three years he sat on a bench at the front door of the ward and eagerly leaped up and poured forth his word-salad most urgently to everyone who entered the ward. Otherwise, he merely sat quietly, mumbling his word-salad to himself. Innumerable patient efforts had been made by psychiatrists, psychologists, nurses, social service workers, other personnel, and even fellow patients to secure intelligible remarks from him, all in vain. George talked only one way, the word-salad way. After approximately three years he continued to greet persons who entered the ward with an outburst of meaningless words, but in between times he sat silently on the bench, appearing mildly depressed but somewhat angrily uttering a few minutes of word-salad when approached and questioned.

The author joined the hospital staff in the sixth year of George's stay. The available information about his ward behavior was secured. It was learned also that patients or ward personnel could sit on the bench beside him without eliciting his word-salad so long as they did not speak to him. With this total information, a therapeutic plan was devised. A secretary recorded in shorthand the word-salads with which he so urgently greeted those who entered the ward. These transcribed recordings were studied, but no meaning could be discovered. These word-salads were carefully paraphrased, using words that were least likely to be found in George's productions, and an extensive study was made of these until the author could improvise a word-salad similar in pattern to George's, but utilizing a different vocabulary.

Then all entrances to the ward were made through a side door some distance down the corridor from George. The author then began the practice of sitting silently on the bench beside George daily for increasing lengths of time until the span of an hour was reached. Then, at the next sitting, the author, addressing the empty air, identified himself verbally. George made no response.

The next day the identification was addressed directly to George. He spat out an angry stretch of word-salad to which the author replied, in tones of courtesy and responsiveness, with an equal amount of his own carefully contrived word-salad. George appeared puzzled and, when the author finished, George uttered another contribution with an inquiring intonation. As if replying, the author verbalized still further word-salad.

After a half-dozen interchanges, George lapsed into silence, and the author promptly went about other matters.

The next morning appropriate greetings were exchanged employing proper names by both. Then George launched into a long word-salad speech to which the author courteously replied in kind. There followed then brief interchanges of long and short utterances of word-salad until George fell silent and the author went to other duties.

This continued for some time. Then George, after returning the morning greeting, made meaningless utterances without pause for four hours. It taxed the author greatly to miss lunch and to make a full reply in kind. George listened attentively and made a two-hour reply, to which a weary two-hour response was made. (George was noted to watch the clock throughout the day.)

The next morning George returned the usual greeting properly but added about two sentences of nonsense. The author replied with a similar length of nonsense. George replied, "Talk sense, Doctor." "Certainly, I'll be glad to. What is your last name?" "O'Donovan, and it's about time somebody who knows how to talk asked. Over five years in this lousy joint" ... (to which was added a sentence or two of word-salad). The author replied, "I'm glad to get your name, George. Five years is too long a time" ... (and about two sentences of word-salad were added).

The rest of the account is as might be expected. A complete history sprinkled with bits of word-salad was obtained by inquiries judiciously salted with word-salad. His clinical course—never completely free of word-salad, which was eventually reduced to occasional unintelligible mumbles—was excellent. Within a year he had left the hospital, was gainfully employed, and at increasingly longer intervals returned to the hospital to report his continued and improving adjustment. Nevertheless, he invariably initiated his report or terminated it with a bit of word-salad, always expecting the same from the author. Yet he could, as he frequently did on these visits, comment wryly, "Nothing like a little nonsense in life, is there, Doctor?" to which he obviously expected and received a sensible expression of agreement to which was added a brief utterance of nonsense. After he had been out of the hospital continuously for three years of fully satisfactory adjustment, contact was lost with him except for a cheerful postcard from another city. It was signed properly, but following his name was a jumble of syllables. There was no return address. He was ending the relationship on his terms of adequate understanding.

During the course of his psychotherapy he was found hypnotizable, developing a medium to deep trance in about 15 minutes. However, his trance behavior was entirely comparable to his waking behavior, and it offered no therapeutic advantages, although repeated tests were made. Every therapeutic interview was characterized by the judicious use of an appropriate amount of word-salad.

D. Representational Systems

We function in the world in terms of language. As we have experiences, we describe those experiences for ourselves in words which are then stored along with other sensory inputs such as images, sounds, sensations, and odors. A number of observers have pointed out that people *tend* to have a primary representational system which they favor such as auditory, visual, or kinesthetic (bodily sensations). The NLP people have done the most with this concept, although the literature appears to be ambiguous as to its validity. As with many other ideas in psychotherapy, the concept of representational systems can sometimes be useful. If it works for you with a particular client, then use it.

Language can be limiting if your vocabulary is limited in some way. For example, there are some cultures whose language only has words for the numbers one and two. They can only count: one, two, many. There are some cultures which only have words to describe a limited number of colors, so they can only describe what they see in terms of those words. The full spectrum of colors may be out there, but if the only words you know are black, white, red, and green, then your reality is circumscribed by those words. Eskimos have an enormous number of words to describe snow and can do so with a fineness of distinction that eludes other people. (In fact, these words are being written while I look out of my window in December on falling snow and all I can say is that the snowflakes are small, appear wet, and are not too thick.) A linguist might be able to write down all of the Eskimo words for snow and what he/she is told their meanings are, but it would be meaningless for someone not growing up in the Eskimo culture and incorporating along with those words a *physical* sense of what they represent. The cross-cultural significance of how different peoples use time, space, and language can be found in the works of anthropologists such as E.T. Hall (e.g. see Hall, 1959). We are bound by our culture, our words, and our language.

Since *the meaning of any communication is the response that you get*, it is important to be exquisitely sensitive to how your clients react to what you say and do. You may intend one thing by the content of your language, but your client may be understanding something quite different. When in doubt, ask. Of course, much marital and family discord arises from misunderstandings that arise from habits of *hearing* in a particular way. Language is important to communication and it is also important in terms of establishing rapport.

Let us assume for the moment that everyone does have a preferred representational system, that is, everyone tends to perceive and record reality primarily in visual, auditory, or kinesthetic terms. The senses of taste and smell are important, but are used less frequently in terms of language than the three mentioned. For example, the recollection of aromas experienced in childhood can be used as a rapid method of regression and revivification. Table 4.1 lists words and phrases that are typically used by people whose representational system preference is auditory, visual, or kinesthetic. In addition, the table shows some words that are generally "neutral" with respect to representational systems.

These words are, in general, predicates or process words—verbs, adjectives, and adverbs that people use for communication. As you practice with representational systems, other words will come to mind.

A person tends to stick to one representational system, although within given contexts and normal word usage they may switch around. It is sometimes difficult to figure out a person's primary

Table 4.1. Typical Words and Phrases used in each Representational System.

Visual	Auditory	Kinesthetic	Unspecified
see	say	handle	think
picture	tone	firm	sense
clear	feedback	force	judging
visual	tune	build	assume
imagery	sounds good	handy	allows
point out	talk	push	learn
focus	hear	calm	motivate
eye	tempo	grasp	thought
look	shout	hard	discover
view	scream	reach	aware
draw	rhythm	solid	decide
appear	musical	narrow	agree
perceive	rings a bell	pull	apply
show	tell	shape	develop
movie	sounds like	burdened	evaluate
light	strike a note	feel	believe
blurred	said	hold	guess
foggy	spoken	measure	realize
keep your	sound the	take apart	use
eye on it	alarm	go around	process
		fluid	allow
		grind	know
		thrust	understand
		nail down	many ways
		step by step	internalize
		concrete	
		stage is set	
		wrap up	
		work on it	
		work it out	
		forge ahead	
		breath of relief	

representational system. When in doubt, be sure that your communication involves the use of all three systems. It makes good sense when giving general lectures or presentations to use all three representational systems insofar as possible. By careful observation, you may find that you get stronger responses using one system rather than another.

The usefulness of the idea of representational systems is that it lets you "*speak* the same language" as your client. You can then "be in *touch,*" "be on the same *wavelength,* " "be in *tune,*" "have the same *grasp,*" "be in *step,*" "*see* eye to eye," "*see* things the same way," "have the same *image/vision/picture,*" "be on the same *footing,*" "*sound* the same," etc. There is therefore something *sympatico* about the way that you speak and exist in the world. You are literally speaking the same language as your clients when you join their representational system (and any shifts in it that occur during the course of therapy).

Representational System Exercise

This exercise can be done in dyads or triads. If done in dyads, the A person engages the B person in conversation, perhaps in the form of an initial interview, and elicits information. In the course of this conversation, A attempts to discover B's preferred representational system. Once you think that you know what that system is, then you match the system and observe B's responses. A powerful check on this is to switch to other representational systems and observe B's responses. Does "violating" B's preferred system make B appear uncomfortable, pull back, or ...? After five minutes, switch roles. When the second person has finished this part of the exercise, then the two people should process what has happened. Ask for B's experiences during the process. Feedback is important to calibrate what you have done. If you don't know, ask. B might say "When I said this, you responded that way. What was going on then?"

When the exercise is done in triads, person C has two roles. The first is that of observer of both A and B. The second is that of adviser to A. C can whisper comments to A or pass notes to A about things to try or do or observe. C can also take notes. When all three participants in the exercise have had an opportunity to try the three different roles, then they can process what has occurred together. It is always useful to share with other groups when this is done in a setting of several groups.

Identifying representational systems can be difficult and, as in any new learning, requires practice. You can train yourself to be sensitive to representational systems by listening to the radio, television, movies, conversations in cafeterias, other public places, and within your family. Once you are aware that people can have a preferred representational system, you will find this phenomenon everywhere. You can also notice this in books and other writings, since authors also have preferred systems. If you look and listen for them, you will find them there.

One use of the concept of representational systems is in establishing rapport with your clients. Another is in enlarging their world view. If you have a client who is primarily visual, for example, she may be missing out on two-thirds of the possible ways of experiencing the world. Sex for such a person may be unsatisfactory since she is "seeing" rather than feeling. Music may not be as impactful since she would be seeing an orchestra play rather than really experiencing (hearing) the sounds. One way of expanding representational systems is by the process of "overlapping." You, as therapist, can describe an experience such as walking in the woods by first talking about what it is that you see, and then adding sound and feeling to the description so that the senses "overlap" from one to the other. The other senses are then connected to sight. For example, you might say, "As you look around you in the woods and see the trees and leaves and path, you can also be aware of the sounds that your shoes make as you walk over the path and how it feels differently to walk on leaves or dirt or stones. Taking a close look at the bark of a large tree, you can see the various shades of brown and the texture and, running your fingers over the bark, just feel the places where it is rough and smooth, and listen to the scratching noises as your fingers rub on the bark, or your clothing brushes up against it as you look so keenly at the tree."

As another exercise, you can practice overlapping in dyads once you know each other's representational systems. Overlapping not only helps enlarge your client's experience of the world but, in the process of doing this for your clients, *your* world experience will also be enriched. A "blind" walk, a "deaf" walk or a touching with hand-in-glove experience will really emphasize the power of representational systems.

E. Pacing and Leading

A good place to observe natural pacing behaviors is in a shopping mall. All you have to do is observe the way people interact with each other. For example, two people walking along together generally walk with the same stride and rhythm. Two people standing and conversing will generally stand in mirror images of each other. If one of the pair is leaning against a wall, then the other will, too. If one has his head slightly cocked to the right, then the other will have her head slightly cocked to the left. If one speaks loudly, softly, rapidly or in a special cadence, then the other is likely to speak in the same pattern. It is a general observation that couples who have been married for a long time (to each other!) tend to "look" alike. What we are perceiving here is that they tend to stand, walk, sit, posture, and use the same, or similar, facial expressions. We take these similarities to mean that they "look" alike when we are experiencing the way that they fit into the world as a totality of their postures, movements, and expressions. Adopted children grow to "look" like their "parents." These children certainly "sound" like their parents! Since each person fits uniquely (and unconsciously) into the world in terms of their postures, movements, expressions, and speech, one way of establishing a subtle rapport with them is for you to also fit into the world in the same way (or sufficient "same ways") to communicate this sense of oneness with them to them. First, we will discuss verbal pacing, then physical pacing, and finally the use of pacing in leading. This will be followed with some practice exercises.

Some of the characteristics or variations in speech include: tempo, loudness, speed, rhythm or cadence, accenting, regional or cultural accents, and breathiness. It is common knowledge that people from the same culture, subculture, and even mini-subculture, have identical speech patterns. *Verbal pacing* means to match your client's speech patterns in some way so that they feel more comfortable in your presence. Generally, *you need to match only in **one** characteristic* such as volume or rhythm for this ease to become apparent. It is important not to mimic or match too exactly since this will be detectable by the client and taken as a manipulation or an insult. *Pacing must be subtle.* Pacing should be done in such a way that it is perceived outside of conscious awareness and not directly in consciousness by the client. If a client speaks rather loudly, you do not have to shout with him, but just *increase* the *normal* volume of your voice. Some people speak exceedingly fast or slow. This may be difficult for you to duplicate directly, but you can duplicate this by *cross-over pacing* by using finger or toe movements or slow head nods to match the rate of speech. These other movements in a different system will be perceived outside of awareness. With verbal pacing, you literally want to "speak" your client's language in some way so that you both fit into the world similarly.

Physical and postural pacing has to do with matching your client's movements or postures in some way. Again, you do not have to match *all* movements and postures. It is only necessary to match the general way the other person is sitting in a chair or to tilt your head to the right just a bit if they are a head-tilter, or to nod your head a bit if they are a nodder, or move one of your feet if they are a foot tapper or wiggler. Exact mirroring or aping can be detected and will be taken as an intrusion or mocking. Physical pacing should be subtle, not exaggerated.

Pacing a client's breathing pattern is perhaps the most effective, and yet the most subtle way of fitting into his/her world. Breathing is such a basic pattern of existence that matching it is a profound experience. Babies do this automatically when placed on their mother's bosom. *In doing trance work it is important to pace your speech to the breathing patterns of your client.* This is a fundamental axiom in all hypnotic communication. In some cases it may be necessary to match breathing patterns in a cross-over form. Of course, you should not stare at the bosom of your female client if you are a male therapist to pick up her breathing pattern. Breathing patterns can be picked up via peripheral vision or by observing the small movements in clothing, in the shoulders, or in the abdomen. Subtle observation and matching are always better.

Being aware of body language is an important part of the science of being an effective therapist. It is not possible to do verbal and physical pacing without reading body language. Knowledge of body language is not only useful to pacing, it is also important in terms of being aware of your client's emotional state and changes in that state. Since the meaning of any communication is the response it gets, be aware of what *you* might be reading into your client's body language. Check out any meaning or interpretation before jumping to conclusions. A smile may not mean happiness. A grimace may not mean pain. A "blank" face may not mean being somewhere else. Gestalt Therapy teaches you to look for incongruities between verbal and body communications. For example, the client may be verbally stating that they are "open" to new ideas while their arms and legs are crossed. Some of these incongruities may be usable in certain contexts or they may be ignored. There are many roads to health and any one incongruity or observation may lead you there. However, there is no substitute for paying exquisite attention to your client.

One of the major uses of pacing is to be able to *lead* your client into other states, feelings, or postures once you have paced them. When you have matched the walking pattern of a companion, you can then get them to increase or decrease their stride or pace by simply varying yours. When you have matched the breathing rate of your client, you can get them to breathe faster or slower by modifying your breathing rate. This, of course, has obvious uses. You can literally lead a client out of a depression by first pacing and then changing your bodily and verbal patterns.

The case of the "nude dancing men" (Erickson and Rossi, 1980, Vol. IV, pp. 70–74) is Erickson at his best in terms of pacing and leading, as well as many other tactics. You can study the following case and mark out all the different ways he paced and led Sandra W. Perhaps the most remarkable outcome of this case is that Erickson found a way to keep a psychotic woman (he indicated that this was *not* a cure, and that the woman would always be psychotic) functioning as a productive member of society.

Sandra W.

Having first telephoned for an appointment, this rather beautiful 38-year-old woman entered the office and asked, "Do you use hypnosis?" She was answered, "If I find it necessary and helpful."

She proceeded to take a seat and explained, "I think it is necessary in this case. Most people won't believe this, but I am sure you will. I am troubled by nude young men that float in the air just above my head. See them up there next to the ceiling? Wherever I go, they follow me. They never do anything. They just float.

"Now there is a second thing I want you to do. Quite often I like to float up into the sky and travel around the world on a cloud. Some people think I am just sitting quietly in a chair. Actually, I am up on a cloud floating around the world. Sometimes, instead of doing that, I go down to the bottom of the Pacific Ocean, where I have a beautiful castle made of glass. I spend a day or two, sometimes even a week, there. It's so lovely to look out at the fish that are swimming all around my castle. I cannot tell these things to people. They don't understand. They call me crazy. My ex-husband got a divorce because he wanted to put me in the State Hospital. I don't want to go there because I am able to work and support myself. I just don't want to have people interfering with me. Now, if you use hypnosis, can you do something about those nude young men? And can you protect me from criticism when I go down to the bottom of the Pacific ... or when I float around the world on a cloud?

"By the way, Doctor, are you sure you are ethical? I notice that over there in that corner of the office you have a half-dozen nude dancing girls. I don't want my young men to associate with them. It wouldn't be moral. So would you keep control over your nude young women? I hope that all you do is let them dance for you."

This was the introductory meeting with a young woman who suffered from schizophrenia, catatonic type. She was working as a secretary for a real-estate firm for the summer and handling her work most satisfactorily.

"I've been married twice, but I didn't tell either of my husbands about the nude young men or of going around the world or to the bottom of the ocean. After we were married, I told them about every-thing. George was so mad about it he beat me up something terrible. Bill just acted plain awful. He called in some psychiatrist. They said I was psychotic and they wanted to commit me to the State Hospital. They took me to court for a hearing. I figured that the fuss must be about those nude young men ... and taking trips around the world ... and my castle on the bottom of the ocean that disturbed Bill so often. So, I just flatly denied all those things and I wasn't committed. Bill got a divorce.

"I have been teaching school regularly during the school year and always take a secretarial job during the summers. I have only been married twice so far. But neither of my husbands seemed to understand. It is awful worrisome teaching school, keeping children's attention so that they won't notice those young men. It is so embarrassing when I take a bath, but I have gotten used to it. They won't even let me go to the bathroom alone. So I always wait until night, and then I don't turn on the light.

"One summer I told my employer about the nude young men. The next day I was fired and he gave me a check for two weeks. I never could understand that. He seemed to be such a sensible man.

"I came to you for help. What I want you to do is to hypnotize me. I don't want to be troubled by these nude young men. They are mine as those nude dancing girls are yours. I want to keep right on making my trips around the world. But lately I have been staying in my apartment for as much as a week at a time—to take a trip around the world on the cloud or go down to the bottom of the Pacific and spend time in my castle. I want you to change things hypnotically. Don't take away my young men. Don't stop me from going around the world. Don't stop me from going down to the Pacific. Just see to it that I keep these things, but don't let them interfere with my everyday life. Now I am ready to go into a trance."

Indeed the patient was. In less than five minutes she gave every evidence of being in a profound somnambulistic trance. She was asked to remain in the trance and to talk freely. Her statement was rather peculiar. She said, "That poor girl that is really me is just plain psychotic, but she doesn't know it. She is hallucinating. She is going to the library and she has read up on catatonic schizophrenia. She is really afraid. She is covering up with you. She does not even know how afraid she is. Don't you ever let her find out how afraid she is because she might do something awful. Sometimes she has thought of suicide. Several times she has taken an overdose of sleeping pills. She just doesn't have anybody she can confide in. She thinks maybe you are all right, and will you be awfully kind to her? And you won't think bad about her because, even though she is psychotic, she is normal. Now and then she goes to bed with men, even if she isn't married to them. She wouldn't want you to know that. There are a lot of things she doesn't want you to know about her until she trusts you completely. You will have to do something about those nude young men. She is giving too much time to them. She is taking too much time to travel around the world ... too much time to go down to her castle at the bottom of the ocean. She really enjoys and believes that the castle and the trip around the world exist. She enjoys looking down at Hong Kong and other cities. Do you think you can do anything for her?"

The somnambulistic patient was assured that, with her help, something could be done for "this psychotic girl. She is really me, you know." Instructions were offered. She listened carefully.

Slowly and systematically an explanation was given her of dreams. Normal dreams that everybody has, in which one dreams of falling off a mountainside. Falling and falling and falling forever, it seems. Finally, after what seems to hours of falling, you hit bottom and wake to discover that you have only fallen of bed. Yet, it seems as if one has been falling for days and weeks and months and years. It was suggested that she employ this same normal mechanism of behavior and, at any time, climb onto a cloud and feel herself floating gently around the world. She was to feel as if it were taking days and weeks and even months, maybe even years. Yet in actual clock time this will be accomplished in a minute or two or three. She smiled very happily and asked—couldn't she do that in her trips to the bottom of the sea, too? She was told she could even stay three months, and the clock on her kitchen shelf would only show that she had been gone a minute.

Ready agreement was expressed, and the somnambulistic patient said that this arrangement could prove most satisfactory. But she asked most gently about the nude young men. The writer explained that he had a rather large closet attached to his office and that he could let the young men float in there. They could remain in the closet, and that any time, night or day, she would be at liberty to come to the writer's house (the office is in the writer's home) and look in the closet to see if they were still there.

The patient continued to teach school for several years, and was a most competent teacher. At first, at least twice a week, she would drop into the writer's office and ask if she could look in the closet. She was always satisfied. The frequency of these visits decreased. Finally she was making them only once in three months. Then once in six months. Then approximately once a year. During this period of time she made many trips around the world on the cloud. She took great pride in being able to make a three-month trip in three minutes' time ... in being able to stay months in her castle at the bottom of the Pacific in only three minutes of kitchen-clock time. After about three years the patient began having difficulties and sought further help. She explained only that she was having "psychotic episodes." These "episodes" she "reserved" for the weekend, but they were becoming rather difficult. She wanted to know what she could do about them. She explained further that she did not see how she could put them in the closet with the nude young men. They might become disturbed. She didn't know if these episodes would disturb her in her teaching and in her summer work as a secretary. They might also disturb her employers and other people. She was asked what she thought she ought to do. Her statement was rather simple. "I think I think better and more clearly when you put me in a trance." Accordingly, a trance was induced. In the state of somnambulism she said, "The poor thing, she is really having psychotic episodes. They are most distressing. She hasn't really told you the truth. She had to pretend she had a headache and get an excuse from teaching. She has missed more than the allowable number of sick leave days. She really has to do something about it. Last summer she lost two jobs as a secretary. You thought of putting her young men in the closet. Why don't you think of somewhere to put her psychotic episodes?"

The question was asked, "Could she put them in a manila envelope? Let them do whatever they want to do in the envelope and, therefore, not interfere with her. She could go by the office and leave the envelope for placement in the files." The patient thoughtfully considered this and asked, "Can you tell me [the next time she has a psychotic episode] to go into a hypnotic trance and put the psychotic episode in an envelope and bring it to you?" An agreement to this effect was reached.

The next week the patient appeared most unexpectedly, obviously in a somnambulistic state. "Here's the envelope. Don't open it. It is sealed carefully. The psychotic trance is in there. Put it in your filing cabinet. She will come by later and ask to see it." A few days later the patient appeared in the office and said, "I believe you have something of mine, but I don't know what it is." The sealed manila envelope was taken out of the files. She said, "So that is where my psychotic episodes went. You know, I think that is a good idea. For 15 years the writer has been receiving in the mail, envelopes containing "psychotic episodes."

The patient is now living in a city 1,000 miles away. During one disturbing episode she took a sick leave and came to see the writer. She demanded to see the envelopes containing her "psychotic episodes." They were carefully taken out of the file, one by one, and shown to her. Before this task could be completed, she said, "Now I know I can trust you. Couldn't completely before. You don't have to take out the others. Now I can feel comfortable sending them to you."

At present the patient is gainfully employed and has a civil service position. She will soon be eligible for pension. She has been married eight times and has been self-supporting, but she has never been able to establish a savings account. She was last seen two years ago. She looked at least 15 years younger than her age. She felt free to tell the writer that there was a period of time when she became addicted to alcohol, joined Alcoholics Anonymous, and overcame the problem.

Pacing and Leading Exercises

This verbal pacing exercise can be done in dyads or triads. A and B stand or sit back-to-back so that they are making contact with their backs and can sense each other's breathing as well as feel the vibrations generated in speaking. If there is a C available, then C will observe and provide feedback on the accuracy of the pacing. A says something—one short sentence works well here. It might be something like, "My name is Harry and I am feeling a bit uncomfortable about doing this exercise." It is B's task to repeat A's statement to A's satisfaction that B has their speech patterns accurately paced. Alternate several times doing this before moving on to practicing with someone else. Both A and C can coach B in how to do better. Being back-to-back rules out visual clues and forces you to concentrate on your hearing. B can also practice matching A's breathing patterns while doing this exercise. You can also practice verbal pacing in the privacy of your home while listening to the radio or the television. Another good place to practice is in your car while listening to the radio or tapes. Once you are aware of individual speech patterns you can even mentally rehearse matching people during ordinary conversations since this mental rehearsal actually activates your vocal cords and other relevant speech structures within your body. In practice you will be pacing representation systems, as well as speech patterns at the same time!

A second verbal pacing exercise is also done in dyads or triads. A is the client, B is the therapist, and C is the observer. In the framework of carrying out an initial interview with a client, find out what happens when you pace their speech patterns *and* when you deliberately "violate" their speech patterns. If pacing will lead your client to be more comfortable in your presence, then deliberately not pacing will "drive" them away. A and B switch roles (or C, too) and repeat the exercise. After everyone has had a chance to practice all parts, then process what went on. It is important to find out how the client reacted to the things you did. Now that you have had some success at pacing, do the exercise again, but this time consciously *lead* the client by changing one aspect of their speech patterns. Observe carefully what occurs so you can do this better and better. The body posture exercise is done in a similar fashion with dyads or triads. It is the therapist's task to mirror in a subtle way some aspect of the client's body posture, to "violate" that mirroring, and to observe what happens. Once you have successfully learned to mirror body postures (and you only need to do *one* at a time), then use this postural pacing to *lead*. Get the client to shift positions or change movements. You can sometimes subtly lead a client out of an emotional state by just shifting your body posture. Try it.

As a final exercise, put the pacing of representational systems, speech patterns, and body postures together so that you actually remember and match in all channels of communication. This exercise can be done in dyads or triads. Remember to process afterwards and to ask your "client" about internal states they experienced during the exercise. People daily demonstrate pacing and leading—all you have to do is be aware of it.

F. Eye Accessing Cues

One of us recently had a conversation with a clinical psychologist who said that she knew all about neurolinguistic programming (NLP) and that she used it all the time. Further querying uncovered the fact that she knew about eye accessing cues and thought that that was what NLP was all about! Although NLP people do use eye accessing cues, they are as much to NLP as, say, hand levitation is to Ericksonian hypnotherapy.

The observation of eye movements when you are working with someone can be useful. There is much controversy in the literature about the validity of eye accessing cues. Our own approach is that if you are aware of a consistent pattern of eye movements in your client and that the pattern matches the NLP assertions about this phenomenon, then you would be foolish not to use them. One assertion is that people tend to have a consistent association of an eye movement down and to their own right when accessing kinesthetic states internally. The pattern for most right-hand/left-brain individuals is shown in the following figure.

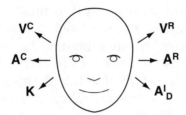

Figure 4.1. Looking at the Other Person

When a person looks up and to the left they are accessing stored mental images or pictures. When they look up and to the right they are constructing a mental image or picture. Looking straight left is accessing internal auditory messages. Looking straight right is constructing sounds. Down right is for kinesthetic states—from memory or current; and down left is for talking to yourself. Check these out for yourself to convince yourself of their validity. Some people demonstrate a mirror image of the patterns shown in the figure. It is sometimes difficult to ascertain an individual's eye accessing patterns.

There are two practical things you can do with knowledge of eye accessing cues. First, it is useful to know what your client's internal states are and what they are feeling or doing mentally while they are talking to you. Are they looking at old pictures in their heads, talking to themselves, listening to someone talking to them in the past, or accessing (kinesthetic) feelings? You can seem like a mind-reader when you ask, "What are you seeing now?" Secondly, there is an NLP procedure called "strategy elicitation" in which it is possible to track the mental steps a person goes through when they make decisions, motivate themselves, or learn, for example. Eye accessing cues are central to eliciting strategies and installing new strategies. See Dilts, et al., (1980) and Lankton (1980) for details on this subject.

You can practice eye accessing cues by observing your clients' responses, by observing performers in the movies and on television, and by observing people in casual conversations. If eye accessing cues make sense to use, then use them.

G. Anchoring

Anchoring is a word used in NLP to mean the obtaining of a conditioned response by an associated stimulus. Another definition is that anchoring is any stimulus that elicits a consistent response. In one sense you cannot not anchor in any interaction with another person. A typical culturally installed anchor is the handshaking response. Someone raises their right hand towards you and you automatically start raising your own hand. (This automatic response is the basis of the handshake induction method which will be discussed later.)

Anchors may be placed by touch, sound of voice, cue words, hand movements, odors, tastes, body postures, voice location, physical surroundings, or other stimuli. It is well known, for example, that students do better at exams given in the same lecture hall in which they received instruction. Just being in the same room aids in the recall of the lecturer's words or writings and other associated material.

In working with a client, the easiest stimulus to use is that of touch. Touch has an additional advantage in that there is a kinesthetic over-ride which appears to operate such that touch is more powerful for most people than other stimuli. (The sense of smell is perhaps the most powerful stimulus to memory since it bypasses consciousness, but it doesn't lend itself to convenient use in a therapeutic situation!) Since the physical arrangement of your office is under your control, this can be used to position yourself and your client in such a way that it is both convenient and natural to be able to casually reach over and touch a shoulder or a knee or an arm or a hand. However, permission should be obtained *before* touching a client. Since it is important to be able to reproduce a kinesthetic anchor *exactly*, you should pick a location that is easy to reach and easy to touch in exactly the first way you touched it. Knuckles are useful here. It is also important to reproduce exactly the amount of pressure used. Remember that the sense of touch varies in sensitivity depending on the part of the body touched. Fingertips and hands are much more sensitive than the middle of the back or the thigh. So, you need more precision to reproduce a kinesthetic anchor on the hand than on the shoulder.

There are several rules for effective anchoring. They are: (1) Have your client access the desired experience which you wish to anchor as powerfully and as fully as possible. They will probably need to be verbally guided to do this. (2) Insert your stimulus at the moment of fullest expression or the most intense response. Timing is crucial here. Use your senses to detect the peak experience by paying attention to breathing, facial color and tone, pulse, etc. Behave congruently with the type of response you are seeking. It is usually convenient to place the anchor lightly as the client starts to access the desired state, and then to slowly increase the pressure of the anchor as the client gets deeper into the desired state. Remember that these are *gentle* pressures that are used, and that small subtle changes are readily detected. (3) Be sure that the stimulus can be repeated *exactly*. (4) Always *test* to be sure that your anchor works. "Triggering" the anchor should get the response that you originally anchored. Observe!

One of the simplest uses of anchors in your office is to have a "hypnosis" chair, i.e. one chair that you use for putting the client into trance. They will automatically know when they sit in that chair that it is time to go into trance. Some therapists use a particular voice tone or delivery style that transmits the same information. It could also be the way that you sit or hold your head.

The most important thing about the concept of anchoring is that it does exist and that people are capable of one-trial learning. Once you are aware of this, then you can use it in appropriate contexts.

Although the following case (Erickson and Rossi, 1981, pp. 15–16) is probably more an illustration of dealing with resistance via a surprise technique, it also illustrates the power of anchoring the client's resistance to hypnosis to Erickson's office. When Dr. Q was outside Erickson's office and the "official" session was over, he no longer had any resistance to going into a trance. (The handshake technique is discussed later.)

Dr. Q and the Surprise Handshake

Another means by which I overcome strong resistance in my patients is the introduction of a surprise technique. Allow me to illustrate. One doctor had come 2,000 miles to have me put him in a trance. He walked into my office, laid a check on my desk, and said, "This is to compensate you for your time." I heard that word *time*. That check was to compensate me for my time. But he had come to be put in a trance by me. Now, obviously, the check was not to compensate me for putting him in a trance, but just to compensate me for my time. So I knew right then and there what he was going to do. And he did one of the most beautiful jobs of resisting me that I ever saw, although consciously he felt that he was cooperating. I spent two hours on the man, using every technique that I knew of to seduce [sic—we now prefer *facilitate*] him into hypnosis. But I failed absolutely, and finally I said, "Doctor, you've paid me for my time. And that is about all I've been able to give you. I'm awfully sorry I failed. But before you leave, I'd like to take you out into the other room and introduce you to my wife. She would like to meet you."

So we went out into the next room, and I called my wife and stated that Doctor Q was on his way home, that he had to leave immediately, but he thought he would like to meet her. Then I said, "I would like to shake hands before you leave, Doctor." He very graciously put out his hand and I lifted it slowly, induced a deep hypnotic trance, led him back into the office, and did the work that he wanted me to do.

Surely you do not hypnotize a man after you have said goodbye to him! He had no defenses, no guard, no way of protecting himself. When I reached out to shake hands goodbye and slowly, gently, suggestibly lifted his arm, inducing catalepsy, all the other suggestions I had given him previously about going into a trance took effect. So I took him back into the office and spent a couple of hours more with him, correcting some difficulties that had prevented him from using hypnosis for over 15 years. He had begun his practice using hypnosis but had run into a personal traumatic experience. Thereafter, he could not induce hypnosis and was, in fact, terrified of it. But after I unexpectedly induced that trance in him, he returned to his practice and began using hypnosis extensively.

Anchoring Exercises

Practice with anchoring is best done in dyads. One person is the operator and the other is the person having the anchor installed. As the operator, be sure to control your physical relation with your client. For the first exercise have your client access a pleasant or happy experience and then anchor it. Test by triggering the anchor outside of the client's awareness by first engaging them in casual conversation. As a second exercise, you will be anchoring two experiences, one of which is the opposite of the other. These could be pleasant and unpleasant, happy and sad, a good meal and a bad one, etc. The two anchors could also be used for an undesired behavior, and a desired one, or a present state and a desired state. Once the two anchors have been installed, then trigger both at the same time and observe what happens. You can influence the outcome by using slightly more pressure on the desired/positive state than the other one.

H. The Utilization Approach

In many ways the utilization principle is the heart of Erickson's approach in working with clients. He accepted clients as they were and then moved on from there. Erickson successfully resisted building a theory for his ways of doing therapy. He felt that, if he had a consistent and published theory for human behavior, the changing of that behavior, and what a "healthy," "normal," "self-realizing," etc., person would be like, he would then be required by the very nature of his theory to force clients into the mold of the theory. It was said of Erickson that a client never knew what Erickson would do when the client entered Erickson's office. You can all think of named therapeutic approaches where the client invariably knows what the therapist will be doing because it is a part of that system and world view. It would be "unnatural" for the therapist to behave in any other way. If all of this is really the case, how is it possible to write a book (and there have been many written!) about Ericksonian approaches to hypnotherapy? Erickson taught by modeling and writing about what he did. The totality of his various modes of teaching is Ericksonian hypnotherapy only as long as you keep his basic tenet in mind— *every client is unique and deserves to be treated in an unique way.* This is the essence of Erickson's approach.

If a client is a devout Catholic and you are an atheist, you can still help the client by working within his/her belief system since yours is not germane. (If *your* belief system gets in the way, then you must refer the client.) If you are a Republican and your client is a dyed-in-the-wool Democrat, then use that information. If your client believes in past lives and you don't, or vice versa, then use that information and belief system to help the client. Erickson once wrote of periodically visiting a dear friend of his who lived in New Orleans and commented on the fact that somehow the subject of segregation never came up in their conversations. You can undoubtedly think of subjects which you "somehow" don't discuss with your spouse or certain relatives or colleagues. This is not only a common sense way of getting along with people, but it is also the basis of dealing with clients who walk into your office with such varied belief systems and backgrounds. Of course, this becomes extremely important in doing cross-cultural therapeutic work.

One of Erickson's most quoted observations involved the Greek thief Procrustes who was in the habit of kidnapping people. He kept them on an iron bed. If they were too short for the bed, he stretched them to fit the bed. If they were too tall for the bed, he cut them down to size! By too rigorously applying any given approach, you are in danger of becoming a Procrustes.

In the utilization approach, you simply accept and utilize the client's observable and non-observable behaviors and beliefs. By non-observable we mean paying attention to what the client says about him/herself. Pacing these behaviors establishes rapport and leading them moves the client along. Unconscious processes which are elicited during trance can also be paced, led, and disrupted when necessary to change habitual patterns. Seeding should be done using the client's behaviors so that the seeding becomes transparent.

Haley (1973, 1986, p. 28) cites two cases which are clear examples of the ways that Erickson used the client's behavior.

Two Utilization Cases

Erickson's willingness to accept working within metaphors applies not only to verbal interchange but even to persons who live a metaphoric life. Such a style of life is typical of schizophrenics, and Erickson assumed that with a schizophrenic the important message is the metaphor. For example, when Erickson was on the staff of Worcester State Hospital, there was a young patient who called himself Jesus. He paraded about as the Messiah, wore a sheet draped around himself, and attempted to impose Christianity on people. Erickson approached him in the hospital grounds and said, "I understand you have had experience as a carpenter?" The patient could only reply that he had. Erickson involved the young man in a special project of building a bookcase and shifted him to productive labor.

In another case in that same hospital, Erickson dealt with a competent industrialist who had lost a fortune and become depressed. He spent his time crying and repetitively moving his hands back and forth straight out from his chest. Erickson said to him, "You're a man who has had his ups and downs," and asked him to modify his movement by moving his hands up and down instead of back and forth. Then he took him to the occupational therapist and asked for cooperation. Pointing to the man's up-and-down movement, he said, "Put a piece of sandpaper in each of his hands and fasten a rough board upright between them. That way he can sand and polish the lumber." The man began to do something productive, and he stopped crying. He then began to work in wood and carved chess sets and sold them. He improved so much that he went home on a trial visit and, the first year after he was discharged, he made ten thousand dollars in real estate.

In the following case (Erickson and Rossi, 1979, pp. 77–78) Erickson used the client's reluctance to develop anesthesia for dental purposes by using hypnosis to develop hyperesthesia in his left hand so that all of his sensitivity was focused there. Then, the client developed a spontaneous anesthesia in his mouth. Erickson followed the client's lead to help the client.

The Hypersensitive Dental Patient

A man in his thirties became interested in hypnosis and volunteered to act as a subject for some experimental studies at a university. In the first hypnotic session he discovered that he was an excellent hypnotic subject, but lost his interest in any further experimental studies.

Several years later he decided to have hypnosis employed by his dentist, since he needed extensive dental work and feared greatly the possibility of pain.

He entered a trance state for his dentist readily, developed an excellent anesthesia of the hand upon suggestion, but failed to be able to transfer this anesthesia, or even an analgesia, to his mouth in any degree. Instead, he seemed to become even more sensitive orally. Efforts to develop oral anesthesia or analgesia directly also failed.

Further but unsuccessful efforts were painstakingly made by the dentist and a colleague to teach this patient by various techniques how to develop anesthesia or analgesia. He could respond in this way only in parts of the body other than the mouth. He was then brought to this writer as a special problem.

A trance state was induced readily and the patient was casually reminded of his wish for comfort in the dental chair. Thereupon, he was instructed to be attentive to the instructions given him and to execute them fully.

Suggestions were then given to him that his left hand would become exceedingly sensitive to all stimuli, in fact, painfully so. This hyperesthetic state would continue until he received instructions to the contrary. Throughout its duration, however, adequate care would be exercised to protect his hand from painful contacts.

The patient made a full and adequate response to these suggestions. In addition to the hyperesthesia of the hand, and *entirely without any suggestion to that effect*, he spontaneously developed an anesthesia of his mouth, permitting full dental work with no other anesthetic agent.

Even in subsequent efforts, anesthesia or analgesia could not be induced directly or purposely except as a part of the hyperesthesia-anesthesia pattern peculiar to the patient. However, this is not a single instance of this type of behavior. Other comparable cases have been encountered from time to time.

Apparently, psychologically, the patient's fixed understanding was that the dental work must absolutely be associated with hypersensitivity. When this rigid understanding was met, dental anesthesia could be achieved in a fashion analogous to the relaxation of one muscle permitting the contraction of another.

Utilization Exercise

This can be done in dyads or triads. In a triad the third person is an observer and commentator and assistant to the operator. The framework for this exercise is to hold an intake interview with the client, paying attention to their uniqueness. Then using that uniqueness, devise and carry through an intervention.

Chapter 5

Language Forms

Rubin Battino, M.S.

During the intermission a question was put to me: "Are you aware of the way in which you use words?" I certainly am, and I want to emphasize the importance of that awareness to all of you.

In hypnosis you are going to use words to influence the psychological life of your patient today; you are going to use words to influence his organic life today; you are going to also influence his psychological and organic life twenty years from now. So you had better know what you are saying. You had better be willing to reflect upon the words you use, to wonder what their meanings are, and to seek out and understand their many associations.

(Erickson in Rossi and Ryan, 1985, p. 32.)

A. Introduction to Language Forms

Hypnotherapy is a *verbal* therapy in contrast to the various types of body work (massage, yoga, relaxation, meditation, bioenergetic analysis, Alexander, Feldenkrais, chiropractic, surgery, etc.) and the various types of "chemical" prescriptions (psychotropics, antidepressants, vitamins, vegetarianism, macrobiotics, altered state drugs, and diets of all kinds). Erickson's use of language has been characterized as being "the precise use of vague words." Certainly, he was a master of the English language despite the fact that he was dyslexic! Erickson learned his clients' language in order to more effectively convey suggestions to them. (See the chapter on rapport building.) Erickson worked hard at perfecting his communication skills as the following quote from his Ocean Monarch Lecture (Erickson and Rossi, 1981, p. 3) indicates.

Now the thing I want to stress is *the tremendous need for each doctor to work out a method of suggestion for himself.* In developing my own technique, I worked out what I felt was a good hypnotic technique. It was about 30 typewritten pages, single-spaced, of the various types of suggestions necessary to induce a deep trance. And then I slowly cut it down from 30 typewritten pages single-spaced to 25, to 20, to 15, to 10, to 5, and so on, so that I could use just one page or one paragraph. But I learned thoroughly how to graduate my suggestions, and how to lead from one suggestion to another. When one does that sort of thing, *one learns how to follow the leads given by his patient.* (Emphases in original.)

Erickson's genius to a large extent was due to self-training and "perspiration."

Colleagues and students, including the authors, who became acquainted with Erickson's work late in his life or after his death, were introduced to the distillation of years of conscious practice. One's first reaction to a detailed analysis of an Erickson session with a client is frequently one of awe and disbelief, i.e. the individual interpreting the session must have spent considerable time adding meaning and conscious design where there was none. Yet, as we have studied, *practiced,* and extended his teachings, we find among *our* own students the same doubt regarding this skill with language. However, we have unequivocally shown that Erickson's language skill can be learned. It has been easy for some and difficult for others, but any interested person can certainly practice and learn from Erickson's masterful use of language.

To a large extent, becoming a competent hypnotherapist is like being an apprentice to a "master" in the old guild system. In modern times, you can serve a significant part of your apprentice-ship with books. The literature about Ericksonian hypnotherapy has continued to expand. You should become conversant with the collected works (Erickson and Rossi, 1980, Vols. I–IV), "Hypnotic Realities" (Erickson, Rossi, and Rossi, 1976), "Hypnotherapy, An Exploratory Casebook" (Erickson and Rossi, 1979), and "Experiencing Hypnosis" (Erickson and Rossi, 1981) as a minimum in terms of Erickson's writings. Of other relevant writings, we would also recommend "Uncommon Therapy" (Haley, 1986), and "My Voice Will Go With You" (Rosen, 1982). A bibliography of Erickson's work and related books and references is provided at the end of this book. However, the practice of hypnotherapy involves much more than can be learned from written materials. Fortunately, there exists a large body of audio and video tapes of Erickson, as well as skilled practitioners of his work. These materials need to be studied to learn the nuances of delivery of the words and phrases covered in this chapter. (Also, you will find it useful to listen to the tape we have prepared to accompany this book and which is available separately.) In addition, you should attend as many workshops and training sessions as possible. Self-help and study groups are also effective, as is taping and reviewing your own work. The Milton H. Erickson Foundation (3606 North 24th Street, Phoenix, AZ 85016-6500) and the Erickson Newsletter are good sources of training information.

Since the developers of neurolinguistic programming (NLP) systematically modeled much of their language usage on Erickson's work, we will start our study of language forms with the NLP meta model.

B. The NLP Meta Model

In verbal therapies, after the client says something, how do you as the therapist know what to say next? For example, what decides your response? The nature and content of the response can be based on some theoretical model, a gut reaction, "instinct," some system for intervention, or a linguistic analysis of your client's statement. Which do you use? (Many therapists use a combination of ways to respond.) To what extent does *your* model of the therapeutic process *control* your responses? We are not being judgmental here, but are rather trying to get you to be consciously aware of how you function as a therapist.

Neurolinguistic programming, or NLP, was developed by Richard Bandler and John Grinder and their collaborators as an attempt to *model* the intervention patterns of three of the therapeutic "magicians" of their time. These master therapists were Frederick S. Perls, Milton H. Erickson, and Virginia Satir. In Bandler and Grinder's first two books (1975, 1976), they explored "the structure of magic" using the formalism of transformational grammar, a branch of linguistics. Their third and fourth books were solely devoted to analyzing the "patterns of the hypnotic techniques" of Erickson. Bandler and Grinder termed the result of their linguistics-based approach the "meta model." A detailed presentation of this model was contained in the "magic" books. Grinder and Bandler (1981), in their book "Trance-formations," applied NLP to the structure of hypnosis. The transcribed sessions contained in this book were a major feature. Appendix I in Cameron-Bandler's book (1985) gives a good summary of the meta model. Lewis and Pucelik (1982) have an easy-to-read chapter on the meta model.

In this chapter, we will give an introduction to the meta model along with some exercises so that you will become familiar with the use of language patterns as a prelude to the study of hypnotic language forms.

1. Introduction to the Meta Model

People function in the world in terms of language. A small vocabulary limits not only your understanding, but your ability to function and the number of choices that are available to you. If your culture has words for only one, two, many, or three colors, or two kinds of snow, for example, then the way you perceive the world is restricted. Being stuck or having limited options is the main motivation for those seeking therapy. Yet, language—the words we use to describe ourselves or our situations to ourselves and others, the words we use to describe our beliefs—holds the key to change. If you change the words you use to describe yourself or your situation, you actually start an irreversible process. Once you perceive yourself differently, it is almost impossible to go back to the old descriptives.

A popular saying in the field is "the map is not the territory." A map is a representation of the actual terrain—it is external to, or outside of, or *meta* to, the territory. Yet, people frequently function as if the road map were real. This is certainly useful when you are traveling. However, since we use these internal "maps" to represent and model our world and ourselves *to* ourselves, the maps are therefore subject to distortion. The information we receive through our senses is "filtered" through the uniqueness of individual physiology and experience. If you are color blind (as Erickson was), you literally "see" a different world than those who can see color distinctions. For example, American women, on the average, are usually able to describe many more shades of color than American men. Women, again due to cultural standards, are probably able to describe more odors and their variations than men. We also make maps of the maps of our world, or models of the models, and this is done with our language systems. This is called a *meta model*, or a model about modeling. For these models, words are anchors for experience. We behave *as if*.

NLP characterizes the goals of its meta model with respect to clients as: (1) to find out what is going on *now*; (2) to find out what their goals are, "What do you want?" and "What is your desired outcome?"; (3) to find out what *stops* them from getting this right now; (4) to find out what is needed to get from the present state to the desired one; and finally, (5) how would they know if they attained their desired state? It is important to be able to test the acquisition of the desired state by *sensory* experience to ascertain that it is concrete and real. Remember—every limitation or symptom the client presents is only an opportunity for cooperative creativity. That is, there is no such thing as failure—only feedback.

In terms of transformational grammar, what you say (to yourself or others) is the *surface structure*. This is a simple statement that *does not* contain the full semantic meaning. Examples of surface structure statements are: "I feel depressed." "I see a tree." "That feels good." and "She hates me." As you read these statements, many questions come to mind—there is a lot of information missing. The *deep structure* contains the full *semantic* meaning. A possible deep structure statement could be "Rubbing my shoulders now with both of your hands, George, gives me good relaxed feelings in my muscles and throughout my body." This statement is explicit with respect to time, location, action, persons involved, and responses. Reality for a given person is the *total experience* and is called the *reference structure*. For the deep structure example used above, the reference structure would include all body sensations, and all associated sensations, thoughts, and memories going back through the person's existence. As therapists, we can help our clients verbalize the deep structures, but in their uniqueness, the reference structure is solely theirs. This is not to say that there are not available effective interventions using the reference structure like age regression, changing personal history, and revivification. When you guide a client to go inside and seek the deep structure for some statement, they are doing what linguists call a *trans-derivational search*. Generally, such an internal search elicits a trance state.

There are three classes of errors that people make in mistaking the model for reality: generalization, deletion, and distortion. *Generalizations* are what you would expect in a person who takes a part or a component of his/her model of the world and lets that represent the complete category from which the part was taken. In *deletions*, a person pays *selective* attention to their experience, and thereby ignores part(s) of internal or external reality. *Distortions* are shifts or distortions in experiencing ourselves or the world. The meta model interventions fall into three categories: (1) gathering information: deletion, lack of referential index, unspecified verbs, nominalization, comparative superlatives, and the words "clearly" and "obviously;" (2) model limits—universal quantifiers, modal operators of necessity, presuppositions, and complex equivalence; and (3) semantic ill-formedness or "fuzzy functions": cause and effect, mind reading, and lost performative. Each of the three categories will be discussed separately and include related exercises.

2. Gathering Information

The aim here is to reconnect the client's language with his/her experience. Each of the components will be discussed separately.

a. Simple Deletions

These occur when something is obviously missing from the surface structure statement. Examples of simple deletions are: "I feel depressed." "I'm angry." "He hurt me." Once you have identified the verbs (or adjectives modifying nouns) you ask questions concerning their appearance in fuller or more complete sentences. You can ask who, whom, what, where "specifically" questions. For example, "You are angry at whom or what, specifically?" "You are feeling depressed about whom or what and at what times, specifically?" The addition of the word "specifically" is important.

b. Lack of Referential Index

A referential index is the person or thing which does or receives the action of the verb in the sentence. In the simple deletions above a referential index is missing. Questions are asked so that each "process" word in the surface structure is linked to a specific person or thing. Words like "this," "that," and, particularly, "it," are examples of unspecified referential indexes. "It is unimportant." "That just won't work." "I'm fed up with this." These statements need to be expanded with who and what, specifically, questions.

c. Unspecified Verbs

An unspecified verb leaves some doubt about the process or experience described. "I hurt." Is the hurt physical or psychological? "He ignored me." Ignored in what way or ways, specifically? "That's frustrating." Specifically? Note that the use of the word "specifically" is important in arriving at exact meanings. If you can clearly visualize the process being described, you may be getting the client's intended picture, but this should always be checked.

d. Nominalizations

In a nominalization, a process word or verb is concretized into a noun. If you can touch, move, manipulate, or haul what the word represents, it is not a nominalization. "Things" can be handled. However, if the word fits into the phrase "an ongoing ... ," it is a nominalization. An ongoing problem or depression or dependency is a nominalization. Contrast that with an ongoing camel or book or hammer. Nominalizations are one of the most serious limitations that people use to constrain themselves. A diagnostic descriptor is certainly useful for professionals, but is generally counter-productive when given to a client. We have met "professional" schizophrenics and obsessive-compulsives and depressives who maintain that identity long after the abatement of symptoms. One of our clients (an animated and affect-filled woman) was labeled "depressive" by a psychiatrist. She continues to seek antidepressant medication and therapy although any sensible therapist can tell that she is not depressed.

Nominalizations concretize particular behavior patterns. Nominalizations need to be directly challenged as in, "How do you know you are a depressed person?" "How do you depress yourself?" "How are you obesing or overweighting yourself?" Add "-ing" to the nominalization to convert it back into a verb. A person who views themself as codependent or alcoholic cannot change that concretized behavior. But, a person who is "co-depen-denting" or "alcoholicking" him or herself has a chance for change. Be sensitive to the ways that people define themselves via nominalizations, and challenge that definition. Such challenges, of course, can be very effective when the client is in a trance state.

e. Comparative Superlatives

Statements like: "I am the least liked" "They work me the hardest" or "I'm doing the best I can" need to be challenged. The challenge is: with respect to what or whom? You are being compared with respect to what or whom? With comparative superlatives people frequently lose perspective and tend to catastrophize. Getting them to be specific can depotentiate the problem.

f. Clearly and Obviously

"This is clearly best for me." "She was obviously preferred by mother." Clearly and obviously can be challenged by deleting the -ly and adding "it is" before the former adverb to make it a declarative statement. "It is clear that this was best for you." "It is obvious that she was preferred."

Exercises — Gathering Information

Consider the following statements and find ways to challenge them or restate them to help the client.

1. I feel frustrated.
2. I am angry.
3. I was told you would be late.
4. He did the best he could.
5. I work the hardest.
6. She was always treated better.
7. This is obviously the best.

8. Clearly, I should have received it.
9. I am dependent.
10. I am depressed.
11. I am a co-dependent.
12. I was told I was schizophrenic.
13. Unhappiness is my lot.
14. I am indecisive.
15. They're always downgrading me.
16. That's not important.
17. It always ends up this way.
18. She really frustrates me.
19. They hurt me deeply.
20. I am unrecognized.

3. *Model Limits*

People place limits on their ways of functioning in the world, and this is a result of their model of the world. The four patterns in this section deal with expanding a person's limits. Semantically, one might consider the possibility of a model without limits, but that is unrealistic since there are things that one cannot do like fly (unaided!).

a. *Universal Quantifiers*

This refers to the set of words—all, each, every, any, nobody, anyone, always, never, etc.—which indicates *absolute* conditions in the person's view of him/herself or the world. Some typical self-statements would be: "He never listens to me." "I'm always late." "Every day is bad." "Nobody loves me." "I can't smile anymore." "What's the use, each attempt fails." There are two ways of working with these limiting statements. One is to challenge the *accuracy* of the assertion. For example, "In all the time you've been together, he never listened to you once?" or "Have you ever had an attempt that succeeded, even a tiny bit?" These statements challenge the universality aspect. A second way is to exaggerate the generalization and ask what would happen if? "It must be interesting to have a perfect record of being late—there should be a special medal for you." "You really are special in having lived so long and have nobody love you even the tiniest amount, even when you were a baby." These universal quantifiers are like blinkers restricting vision and need to be challenged. Remember, the smallest exception will negate the universality of the assertion.

b. Modal Operators of Necessity

These operators imply that something must occur or cannot occur. The cue words to listen for are: can/can't, will/won't, should/have to, must, ought to, it's necessary. These words imply that you have no choice. Frank Farrelly (Farrelly and Brandsma, 1974), the developer of *Provocative Therapy*, makes a strong distinction between "I can't" which implies no control and "I won't" which implies some volition on the client's part. A statement like "I can't be happy." can be challenged by "What would happen *if* you were happy?" The tactic with modal operators of necessity is to ask the "what would happen if" question which challenges the person's immobility. The use of these words can be quite restricting.

c. Presuppositions

There is something implicitly assumed in the statement that must be understood or made explicit to understand the consequences. Examples are: "Why doesn't he love me?" "No one helps." "You forgot." "If George knew about this, he wouldn't have left." "Since I'm unimportant, I won't take any more of your time." The implied assumption needs to be asked for directly. "Are you saying you are unimportant?" "There are *no* people in your life who help?" "You mean you have *no* evidence of his love?" Overt knowledge is better than covert knowledge.

d. Complex Equivalence

In a complex equivalence there are *two* statements that are equivalent in the person's model of the world. There is often a causal connection implied. They can be identified by the existence of two surface structures that are syntactically parallel. Two examples are: "She's always ignoring me ... she hates me." and "He acts different ... he must be crazy." The connection between the two statements needs to be challenged. One way to do this is to reverse the sequence of the statements, i.e., does B necessarily imply A? The difficulty with complex equivalences is that people actually believe the two parts are linked and behave accordingly, but without checking the equivalence.

Exercises

If your client made any of the following statements, how would you respond?

1. I never do anything easily.
2. I am always in the wrong.
3. He always lies to me.
4. I can't change.
5. I have to finish by Wednesday.
6. I was taught to take care of others.
7. You should always obey your parents.
8. He smiles a lot ... he must be happy.
9. He's decisive ... he knows what he is doing.
10. She doesn't kiss me anymore ... she must hate me.
11. My boss hasn't talked to me for two days ... I'm going to be fired.
12. I can't relax anymore.
13. She doesn't look at me now.
14. They have other concerns than me.
15. They don't understand me.
16. Women don't like me.
17. My wife is lazy.
18. If she loved me, she would have called.
19. If he loves me, he would have noticed.
20. He doesn't appreciate me ... he never smiles at me anymore.

4. *Semantic Ill-Formedness or Fuzzy Functions*

The three linguistic "violations" to be discussed in this section are cause and effect, mind reading, and the lost performative. These are ways of using language that are "fuzzy" or semantically ill-formed, i.e. that don't make linguistic sense.

a. *Cause and Effect*

In this fuzzy function a connection is made between an external stimulus and an internal event, even though the two are not directly connected. The two cue words are "make" and "cause." "My boss makes me angry." "She caused me to fail." In human interactions, the only way to "make" someone do a specific action is by direct threat, say when you are holding a loaded gun on them. Otherwise, we have choices. People and circumstances rarely can force a particular behavior. The cause-effect relationship needs to be challenged. "How, specifically, did your boss make you angry?" "How did she cause you to fail?" Or, "Does your boss *always* make you angry?" It is usually easier to assign someone else the responsibility for your actions, but that removes choice and results in helplessness. Cause-effect should be challenged.

b. Mind Reading

Stage mentalists do a very good job at "mind reading," but for ordinary mortals that is not possible. Despite this, many people find it easy to feel that they actually know what another person is thinking or feeling without the test of direct communication. "She never considers my thinking." "When he looks at me that way, I know exactly what he's thinking." "You must be sad/happy/mad/angry now, and I feel your feelings." Again, the mind reading must be challenged. "How do you know what he/she is thinking/feeling?" "Did you ever ask him what he is thinking/feeling when he looks that way?"

c. Lost Performative

Clients make statements which are generalizations about the world which include the clients' judgment or beliefs about the world. These are sweeping universal generalizations like: "It's wrong to hurt anyone's feelings" and "It's bad to argue" and "That's a really stupid thing to do." In Transactional Analysis terms, these statements sound like "parent" messages that got blindly incorporated into belief systems. These statements can be challenged because they limit a client's behavior via a restrictive world view. The client can be helped to understand that this *may* be fine for him/her now in this context (or was appropriate at some earlier time), but that they can develop and explore other options which may be more appropriate now in all or specific contexts.

Exercises

Consider how you would respond to the following statements:

1. It's unethical to manipulate people.
2. People in authority must be listened to.
3. Always respect your elders.
4. If it's worth doing, it's worth doing well.
5. You should never be too strict.
6. Being on welfare is wrong.
7. There's only one right way to do things.
8. Abortion is right/wrong.
9. I know what's best for her.
10. I'm sure you know what I feel for you.
11. I can tell what you're thinking.
12. My boss thinks I take too long.
13. You look happy/sad/sick/well/ ...
14. You must be hurting.
15. My mom makes me so mad.
16. She really frustrates me.
17. Your snoring is giving me ulcers.
18. I'm sad because you're late/didn't call.
19. The teacher made me fail the exam.
20. My brother is giving me headaches.

5. *Summary - Meta Model*

Since this is not a book on NLP, but on hypnotherapy, why has so much space been given to the meta model? In *verbal* therapies you need to have a facility for understanding and working with language. The meta model is a systematic way of learning how to know what to say next. Mastering the linguistic patterns in the meta model can provide you with clues to constructing hypnotic interventions. For example, being aware of the fuzzy functions can lead you to construct a metaphor challenging these limiting assertions. Besides, if a book on hypnotherapy can include only what some expert defines as proper, then you are climbing into Procrustes' bed. Erickson always refused attempts to characterize his work. It was said of him that you never knew what he was going to do when you entered his office. How predictable are you?

There are two more useful linguistic patterns that are helpful. The first is the *meta question* which is to simply inquire "How do you feel about feeling depressed / lonely / sad / abandoned / hurt/ sick, etc.?" This question is *meta* to the feeling itself and provides perspective and distance. The second is the use of the Gestalt Therapy "So?" at an appropriate time. This word has the facility of starting a transderivational search, and the person must go inside. It also breaks up patterns of thought. A rule of thumb would be to use "So?" whenever you are stuck with a client and don't know what to say next! The responsibility for action/speech is thrown back on them. "So's?" can be repeated as needed.

Exercises

The previous meta model exercises provide you with specific examples to analyze and respond to. You will have already noted that many of the statements "violate" two or more meta model patterns. A good way to flex your meta model mind is to make up (or recall) your own examples for each pattern. The daytime "soaps" provide many examples, as do some of the sitcoms. Of course, you can listen to your own speech for meta model applications and analyze recorded sessions of your own or others. A good exercise is to work in triads with A being the client, B the therapist, and C the observer. B is to listen carefully to A's speech to identify the various meta model patterns, and then respond appropriately. C observes, makes notes, and can whisper suggestions to B. After 5-10 minutes, switch roles until you have all had some practice. You may find with some clients that using the meta model alone is all you need to do effective therapy.

C. Introduction to Hypnotic Language Forms

As commented on in the introduction to this chapter, words and language are essential tools of the hypnotherapist. In the previous section we gave an overview of the way that NLP uses language via the meta model. In one sense, one might characterize NLP as the precise use of precise language. Ericksonian work tends to be more indirect than directive, which led us to describe it as the precise use of vague language, but, we hasten to add, that "vague" language must be used very precisely!

In outlining the material under this heading, we discovered that we listed literally dozens of topics and subtopics. Language is rather rich and varied. Although we had much choice in where to include a given subtopic (since some would naturally fit within more than one topical area), we decided to use seven parts, namely: (D) delivery; (E) word usage; (F) negations; (G) ambiguity; (H) binds; (I) stories; and (J) torpedo therapy.

D. Delivery

The art of delivering hypnotherapeutic messages goes beyond the rapport building skills discussed in chapter 4. In this section we will discuss voice dynamics as well as a number of related ideas that deal with both the mechanics of delivery and stylistic matters. Again, listening to the patterns of a good hypnotherapist and then matching him/her is an initial step before you develop your own style.

Actors and actresses have long known the value of the "dramatic" pause. "Timing" is said to be central to all comedic routines. Cary Grant's pauses and double-takes in a movie like "Arsenic and Old Lace" are what made it so funny. So, pauses are a way of ... adding ... emphasis ... to words ... and phrases. Read the previous sentence with and without the pauses indicated by the ellipses. Pauses also allow the client to go internal and to do searches related to the word or phrase before the pause. Novice hypnotherapists frequently talk nonstop. Give your client the opportunity to do his/her own work in the cooperative endeavor of therapy.

Particular words and phrases can be marked, emphasized, or singled out by loudness or softness of delivery, by speed, by adding a musical quality, and by intonation. In a continuous patter you can subtly *mark out* particular ideas or feelings. Of course, you need to match in some way or ways your client's speech patterns so you can "understand" each other. Dragging out a word can mark it, noowww ... right? The human ear is quite sensitive to the *source* of a sound. You can, therefore, use voice locus for marking. With practice you can "pitch" your voice in a particular direction. Or, you can shift your head position to deliver a word differently. Using slang or an accent (within limits) also works.

In the *interspersal* technique you weave especially significant words or phrases that you wish to "mark" into your continuing patter of speech. These interspersed words/phrases seem to slide by the conscious mind, but are heard by the unconscious mind since they are different, out of the ordinary, or out of context. It is like getting the point of the needle in the haystack.

A particular voice tone can be used for anchoring a specific state. You may recall from chapter 4 that anchoring involves a stimulus/response pattern, a kind of conditioning, that can be elicited by an associational path. Our clients know when to go into trance by our voice shifts since Tom and I both consciously use a particular way of speaking for hypnotic work. (You can use other anchors, like a special chair, for hypnotic work.) *Analogical marking* uses nonverbals to mark out certain words or phrases as separate messages. If your client has his/her eyes open, then you can work analogically with raised eyebrows, head tilt, shoulder lift or shift, body shift, arm movement, eye movement, touch, change of facial expression, etc. Your action should be as natural as possible so that it is actually perceived outside of conscious awareness. Any one of these movements or shifts brings a special emphasis to the "marked" word or phrase. For example, a head movement such as a nod every time the word "comfort" is used will give special significance to that word. With your client's eyes closed, voice dynamics are primary, although people can sense bodily movement.

Splitting and linking involves first taking any behavior and splitting it into smaller units. This makes the behavior less global and working with it easier. Although you can go for the "big" change all at once, it generally is easier to work incrementally via small changes. For example, once you get a person to "violate" their phobia in a small way, you have established the idea that change is possible safely. Once a behavior has been split, then desired outcomes can be linked into the parts using the transitional words described in the next section (e.g., and, while, as, etc.). Some examples are to find out in step-by-step detail how a person carries out a particular compulsive behavior like hand-washing or counting or turning off the stove, or how they respond to their phobia-producing stimulus, again in excruciating step-by-step detail. "And, what do you do next? And, then what? Do you stop in between those two steps? What would you be saying to yourself at exactly that point?"

Splitting and linking is related to pacing and leading. Pacing establishes rapport and a connection at the unconscious level which can then be utilized to *lead* a client towards what he or she wants. The linkage between the two can be verbal via the language patterns discussed in this chapter or nonverbal via body language or voice dynamics using the auditory input channel.

A useful way of delivering information or ideas is to use *quotes* since you can effectively say anything in quotes. In talking to your boss you might get frustration and anger off your chest by saying, "I don't understand it. This guy I barely know came up to me at the water cooler and said 'You stupid shit, you don't know anything. You are totally unreliable and inconsiderate.' That's what he said to me. Strange." Or, you can say to your spouse, "This woman at work said to me 'You need to be more tolerant of my feelings and ideas.' That's what she said." It is much safer to "fight" with a significant other using quotes than stating things directly. Their unconscious gets the message without blaming you. Of course, if this is overdone, it becomes obvious and is then self-defeating. You can even quote someone quoting someone else! This would be called "quotes within quotes."

The "a client I once had" technique is related to quotes since you are attributing information to someone else. This provides some dissociation and, even, a sense of objectivity to the communication. You can attribute anything to other people. This approach is basically metaphorical and will be treated in more detail later. It can also be used as a trance induction technique. The delivery must be congruent and sincere to be credible. Avoid being obvious when using this approach, otherwise the client may feel manipulated, or that you are "using 'psychology' on them."

Suggestions and *presuppositions* can be embedded within questions. A *presupposition* is a statement that implies the existence of some condition, state, or feeling. Examples are:

"I'm wondering how comfortable you are."

"I'm interested in what you want to learn in this session."

"Who is here?"

"And, what did your father say?"

"Are you enjoying this?"

"You really think your eyes are open, don't you?"

"Can you look and not see anything?"

"And, what else have you noticed?"

"You are expecting what, now?"

"What haven't you done yet that you can do?"

Questions can be used for directly and indirectly obtaining information, as well as for giving indirect suggestions. "Questioning therapists can be very helpful." (The ambiguity in this last sentence will be discussed later.)

The incorporation of *surprise* into your language and style has many advantages. Being overly predictable can cause therapy to relapse into a humdrum routine which may be comfortable for all parties concerned, but not effective therapy. One of my clients got so accustomed to surprise that she would say something like, "Oh, oh. You've got that look in your eye again." And, isn't it nice that we ended up being comfortable with trying new, sometimes wildly new, things to help her? Children love surprises, and springing them can hook into a client's child part bringing about a natural regression. "I don't know how much you've learned today, and wouldn't it be a nice surprise to wake up tomorrow, or find on your way home today, how much has (have) changed?" (The nongrammatical use of "have" rather than "has" can be powerful. See the discussion later.) "How can you surprise yourself this week?" "After your hand touches your face, what surprising things will you find?" "And, you will be surprised, will you not?" "John was surprised to find how much had (has) changed after the session." "And, what will you surprise your wife/husband/father/mother/child, etc., with for you, now?" The word "surprise" sets up an expectation for newness and change, but with a generally pleasant overtone. (Of course, you need to check that this word does not have negative or nasty connotations for your client. The word may have been used in childhood to precede beatings or punishment. Everyone is unique.) There are many examples in the literature of Erickson's use of surprise. Erickson, in working with a particular client, said (Erickson and Rossi, 1976, p. 142), "Or would you like to have it as a surprise? Now or later? Shortly I'm going to lift your hand in the air. What happens after that is going to surprise you." When using counting to induce, deepen, or bring someone out of a trance, Erickson frequently skipped around out of sequence to both surprise and confuse clients.

"Torpedo" Therapy was developed by NLP practitioners and involves packing into a few sentences sufficient presuppositions bolstered by grammatical and nongrammatical enforcers to bring about rapid change by an almost instant reframing. Just as one well-placed torpedo can sink a ship, one well-conceived paragraph can permanently change a person. We will give one brief example here and return to this topic at the end of the chapter after covering many of its component language forms. "And, as you are looking back, now, you will have noticed how much has already changed in your life, soon, then, now, hasn't it?" Torpedo Therapy is mentioned in this section because the *way* that the previous sentence is delivered significantly affects its impact (not too surprisingly, now, hasn't it?).

Exercises

a. Voice dynamics

One obvious way to improve your skill with speech is to take some courses in acting and/or speech and communication. There are many things that actors do that incorporate delivery. (I feel, for example, that much of my success as a therapist and a trainer is due in large part to my work in the theater as an actor, director, and playwright. Tom feels that his effectiveness has been enhanced by an ability to express empathy and his modeling of many admired hypnotherapists, particularly Erickson. He has also found that practicing under supervision and much listening to audiotapes of himself has helped his skills.) Short of taking courses, or acting in a community theater, you can simply study analytically plays, movies, television soaps and sitcoms, etc. Pay attention to *how* lines are delivered. Listen to tapes of experienced therapists like Erickson and Rossi and Zeig. If you have videotapes, close your eyes and *listen* for voice dynamics.

Write out double-space an intervention or induction, and mark into your text exactly how you are going to deliver the words. Where are the pauses? Which words or phrases are spoken more loudly/softly? faster/slower? dragged out? with a special intonation, rhythm, or accent? Practice until this can be done smoothly. Record yourself or share critiquing with a colleague. Which words or phrases would you emphasize by changing voice locus? You can color code or use typography to denote the different modes of emphasis.

Read some of Erickson's classic inductions or interventions out loud playing with voice dynamics. Find your own way to do this comfortably. (Remember—in the initial stages of learning new skills most people feel slow, stupid, confused, despondent, uncomfortable, and awkward. With practice, the skills become more natural, just like not noticing how you can ride a bike or swim or drive a car.)

b. Analogical Marking

With any of the exercises just mentioned, add analogical marking with *appropriate* body language. To effectively learn this, practice exaggerating or burlesquing the movements. The body movements will naturally become "spontaneous." NLP practitioners sometimes use analogical marking with the formalism of eye-accessing cues (see chapter 4) to lead clients into feeling states, for example, by pointing (or indicating) lower left which directs the client's eyes to *their* lower right.

c. Splitting and Linking

Think of a person you are working with, or a case you have read or heard about, or a made-up case, and plan how you would split the presenting problem into smaller units and then link those units to desired outcomes. O'Hanlon (1987) gives a number of literature examples of splitting and linking, as well as a theoretical discussion.

d. Quotes and Questions

Make up a list of a dozen situations in which you can use quotes. Then, write out several quotes that you can use in each situation. Try them on friends, relatives, and enemies or adversaries (if you have any!). How would you "fight" in quotes with a significant other? Try it (and be sure to have an explanation handy if it doesn't work or they see through it!). What way of delivery works best with quotes? Can you quote someone quoting someone else?

Make up your own list of twenty questions that not only obtain information, but also are loaded with presuppositions for particular responses. Try them out. Notice the responses, paying particular attention to body language.

e. Surprise

Do you like surprises? All of us have enjoyed them at some time in our lives. Think about some of them. Think about how you've surprised others and how they responded. Before you can consciously use surprise, you need to feel comfortable about its use. Would you ever use surprise just for its own sake? Think of your friends, relatives, and colleagues and consider how you would surprise each of them. Consider your clients and develop appropriate surprises for them. Always check for responses and adjust what you are doing accordingly. Try these surprises out and don't be too surprised yourself as to outcomes both for your clients and yourself. *Should* surprises be *enjoyable*?

f. Torpedo Therapy

With what you know about language usage now, write out therapeutic torpedoes for all of your clients (or cases you know about). Be sure to indicate the needed subtle modalities of delivery for important words and phrases. Try these torpedoes out on selected clients and note the responses. Do follow-ups on the clients to test for effectiveness. Can you develop several "generic" torpedoes for common problems? Pick a personal problem and devise a torpedo for it and deliver it to yourself. Any change? Just how confusing can a torpedo be and still work?

E. Word Usage

This section has been divided into six parts: (1) "Reversing" the Meta Model; (2) Words; (3) Suggestions, Implications, and Presuppositions; (4) Multiples and Stacking; (5) Nongrammatical Usage; and (6) Time.

1. "Reversing" the Meta Model

Grinder and Bandler (1981) have described Erickson's use of language as "artfully vague." Appendix II in their book gives their summary of Erickson's use of hypnotic language. If, in effect, the meta model is used to help the client arrive at a fuller understanding of his/her state so as to have more choices, then the deliberate *reversal* of meta model usage drives the client to change and understanding by the (frustrating) fuzzing of their world. It is, if you will, indirection in language usage rather than direction when the therapist consciously uses meta language "violations." This forces the client to (unconsciously) do the "corrections" the therapist had previously done with them. So, in this section we will re-visit the meta model from another perspective.

a. Nominalization

A nominalization is converting a verb or "action" word into a noun or "static" (statue!) word that tends to immobilize a person. The following statement to a client has the nominalizations italicized. "You have the *knowledge* in your *unconscious mind* about how to *change*, ... to bring about new *understandings* and *learnings*, ... to attain a resolution *in your life* with the love you have found *desirable*, ... and you can be even more *curious* about how your present-day *resources* can be *utilized* and *expanded*." This statement is replete with nonspecific generalizations that your client will use as guideposts to find his/her own answers. There is a kind of pacing and leading here, particularly if you use nominalizations that are already part of the person's world view.

b.   Unspecified Verbs

Grinder and Bandler state that no verb is completely specified, but that specification can be added (induced!) to some extent. The use of unspecified verbs, such as learn, know, understand, change, wonder, do, think, and feel, force the person to supply the meaning in order to understand the sentence. "I want you to *know* how to *think*." "And you can *change*, can you not, and *wonder* about how that *feels*, now." "In what ways can you *fix* what you *do*?"

c.   Unspecified Referential Index

In unspecified referential index the noun that is used has no specific referent. "*It* really can help." "*This* is the *way* to understanding." The client needs to fill in the meaning.

d.   Deletion

In deletion, "something" is left out of the statement and the client does a search to find his/her own completion. "And you can be happy." "The way is ready." "Being prepared is helpful." "She does interesting things." "Knowledge comes in surprising ways."

e.   Causal Connections

Grinder and Bandler make a distinction of three levels of causal connections or linkages. The basic idea is that one person (or circumstance) can "cause" a particular behavior or response in another person. In the weakest kind of causal connection, conjunctions like "and" are used to connect otherwise unrelated phenomena. "You can feel the way you are sitting on that chair, *and* you can wonder how soon your eyes will close." "You are paying attention to your breathing, *and* becoming even more comfortable." The second level of linkage uses words related to time such as while, as, during, when, and soon. "*As* you pay attention to your breathing, your eyes become more tired." "*Soon* one of your hands will feel lighter, *while* your breathing becomes more regular." The strongest level of causal connection uses real causal words such as makes, forces, causes, and requires. "Paying attention to that spot on the wall *makes* your eyelids blink more." "As your breathing slows, it *forces* you to become more comfortable."

These causal connections start with something that is already going on like breathing, or sitting, or blinking, or staring, and then connect that to another condition.

f.   Mind-Reading

The therapist can act as if he/she knows the internal experience of the client. Eye accessing cues (if calibrated) can be useful here. "I wonder what you're hearing/seeing/feeling/saying to yourself now." "You're curious about what we're doing." "You're probably feeling a little nervous now."

g.   Lost Performative

In this pattern, evaluative statements are made, but the person making the evaluation is lost or missing from the statement. "It" is the favorite generalization. "*It's* good that people are honest." "*It's* not important just how fast you go into trance."

h.   Universal Quantifiers

These are the marvelous words: all, every, never, always, nobody, each, any. "*Each* and *every thing* you are hearing now can help you relax even more." "Slow breathing *always* relaxes." "All reactions are useful at some time in some way."

i.   Modal Operators

Generally, these words are called modal operators of necessity since they imply particular actions and a lack of choice. Some of these words are: can/can't, will/won't, have to, should, must, no one, necessary. "And you *can't* even lower that hand, can you?" "As you breathe slowly you *will/can/have to/must/need to/should* relax even more."

2.   Words

Words are the units of communication, and how we use them is the essence of verbal therapies. In George Orwell's "Animal Farm," Napoleon Pig indicated that some animals were "more equal than others." In language usage some words are "more equal" or more effective in attaining particular outcomes than others. In this section we shall explore separately (and somewhat arbitrarily) various types of words. There are obvious overlaps between this and other parts of this chapter—all roads lead to ...

a. Transitional Words

These are connecting and "linking" words and some examples are: while, and, as, because, become, but, could, might, may, makes, causes, wonder, if, then, how, what, beginning, will, allow, and when. Of these words, the ones that you will probably use most frequently are the first three, namely, while, and, and as. "*While* you pay attention to the sound of your breathing, your eyes can begin to slowly close." "*And*, when your hand begins to rise, you will relax even more." "*As* your conscious mind listens and analyzes, your unconscious mind may wonder which hand will lift first." These words are used as bridges between one set of thoughts or actions and another. Generally, you start with some truism that the person can't deny (like the sound of their breathing) and then connect that to an action or thought you want to occur. These are conscious choices on your part as the therapist. This is also an example of pacing and leading.

b. Meaningful Words

These are words that mean nothing in themselves, but they are powerfully vague in leading the client into doing inner searches. Some meaningful words are: hopes, dreams, resources, talents, sensations, thoughts, memories, beliefs, unconscious, learnings, love, loving, genuine, stubborn, individualistic, really, try, and yet. No matter how intensive the therapy, nor how frequent the sessions, it is impossible for you to really "know" your client in his/her unique and magnificent complexity. (This is particularly the case in any cross-cultural therapy.) A word like "try" implies a goal. We tend to avoid "try" since it has a connotation of uncommitted or half-hearted attempts. "Tried to do something" is not just an excuse for not doing something, but a goal itself. But, in countries where rugby is a popular sport, a "try" has a completely different significance. Kay Thomson has pointed out that the word "try" implies failure, "Now, just *try* to lift that hand."

Some examples of using meaningful words follow.

"And, you can take whatever of your present-day *resources* that are appropriate back to that earlier time, *learning* new and useful things for yourself."

"*Try* that now, but don't change, *yet*."

"Sometimes it is important to be genuinely stubborn, *learning* from your *beliefs* and *hopes*."

"*Dreams* can be so helpful."

"And, your *unconscious* knows how to channel your *thoughts* for real *understanding* and *comfort*."

"*Memories* are so useful because we can *learn* from them without even *trying*."

"*Memories* are so useful because they are ours and so subjective they can be changed to become powerful *resources*."

c.   *-er at the End of a Word*

"You can continue to feel _____ -er tomorrow." Adding -er provides an implied continuity to a particular feeling, behavior or change. In a similar way, the words "more" and "less" give a direction to change. "As you sit there feeling the floor solidly beneath your feet, you can/may/will become *more* and *more* relaxed." "There are *less* and *less* and *fewer* and *fewer* things in your way now, are there not?"

d. *Or*

This word presupposes the occurrence of at least one or more events. "You can continue to keep your eyes open *or* close them partially *or* let them blink *or* let them fully close." "I don't know which way your hand is going to move. It can move up or down *or* left *or* right *or* in some other interesting way." There is an illusion of choice here. However, *some* action is presupposed.

e.   The More X, the More Y

"The more your hand rises, *the more* you will relax." *"The more* your eyelids blink, *the easier* it will be to close them." *"The more* you pay attention to your needs, *the more* ways of attaining satisfaction will come to you." *"The more* your attention focuses, *the faster* you'll find an answer." Or, conversely, *"The less* you try, *the easier* it becomes." *"The less* involved you are, *the less* difficulty you'll have." Enough said, more or less!

f.   Awareness Predicates

There are words like: know, notice, realize, aware, find, understand, etc., that presuppose the rest of the sentence. Some examples of usage in question form follow.

"Do you *know* now, how much you will be changing?"

"Did you *notice* how much you have learned already?"

"When will you *find* the change you desire?"

"And are you *aware*, now, of how useful being in trance has been to you?"

"When did you *realize* what resources you have?"

"Did you *understand* all of what happened to you then, or now?"

Using these awareness predicates brings the communication down to *whether* your client is *aware* of the point you are making now.

g.   Adverbs and Adjectives

Plain old adverbs and adjectives can be used to presuppose a major clause within a sentence. Some good words are: deeply, easily, readily, curious, simply, and happily.

"And, have you *happily* found the answer?"

"You can *simply* understand this."

"How *curious* have you been about being in trance?"

"You can *deeply* find the meaning for yourself."

"Have you wondered how *easily* this happened?"

h. *Commentary Adverbs and Adjectives*

These are related to *(g)* and presuppose everything after the first word. Useful words are: happily, innocently, luckily, fortunately, necessarily, usefully, curiously, etc.

"*Curiously*, change can occur in a single session."

"*Happily*, going into trance is easy."

"*Fortunately*, you don't need to tell me what you don't want to tell me."

"*Necessarily*, people do change as they grow."

"*Usefully*, communication can be at many different levels and ways."

i. *"Now"*

This is one word that can be overworked, but the *immediacy* of its use when appropriately employed makes it one of the most potent in any therapist's vocabulary. You may have already noticed, *now*, how frequently we have slipped "*now*" into our examples. And, you can know *now*, how to use this word, *now*, in the middle of a sentence for emphasis, or at the end for definitive action, *now*. "To know when to "now" is not to have no knowledge, now, about how when your "no" is now to your knowing when to know to no, now." This is not a knot, or is it, now, or no?

j. *"That's Right"*

Someone once remarked that you can tell who is an Ericksonian therapist by the number of times they use the phrase "that's right," especially if spoken with a southwestern accent! Even as we write this, we can "hear" in our inner ear the slow and characteristic way that Erickson used "that's right" on so many of his tapes. "And, that's right, isn't it?" "That" is one of your all-time ambiguous words—*it* can mean anything! The implication/presupposition in "that's right" is that whatever preceded its usage was correct and appropriate. Although using the phrase is appropriate in almost all circumstances, you need to be cautious not to overuse it. That's right, isn't it?

k. Exercises

Practice, practice, practice. For each of the parts of this section, make up ten examples of that particular kind of language usage. Write them out first, and then practice delivering them. Write out an intervention for a particular case using as many of the words as possible, underlining them, of course. While studying Erickson's transcripts *try* to identify his language usage. Erickson and Rossi (1976, 1979) contain many annotated transcripts that can be studied. Remember, you learn more when you are exercising your own skills than studying someone else's. Reading about playing ping pong can give you some pointers, but ...

3. Suggestions, Implications, and Presuppositions

These three language forms are closely related. One definition of the hypnotic state is that the client (due to focused attention) is in a highly "suggestible" state. That is, the client is more receptive to comments made by the hypnotist. Hypnosis presumably bypasses conscious control, and statements are "heard" directly by the "unconscious" mind. So, the structure of suggestions, implications, and presuppositions, all of which are meant to influence client behavior, is important. These three topics and their subsets will be dealt with separately in this section, although there is much overlap.

a. Suggestions

While a person is in a trance (or in the waking state, too!) suggestions may be delivered to them directly or indirectly. The non-Ericksonian approach is to only give direct suggestions. (Erickson, true to *his* form, gave direct suggestions on occasion.) With respect to stopping smoking, direct suggestions might be: "Cigarettes will taste like [something unpalatable or nasty] from now on." or "You will simply give up smoking when you are aroused from trance." or "Every time you pick up a cigarette, you will see an image of yourself coughing uncontrollably." Indirect suggestions might be: "And you can notice, now, how much easier it is to breathe, and how your food has become more flavorful, and even that there are so many more interesting smells in your environment." or "What changes will have occurred in how your husband kisses you and reacts to you?" (Unfortunately, although hypnosis is much touted as a "cure" for smoking, it is generally not successful unless there is high motivation!) For most people the subtlety of indirection seems to reach deeper levels within the psyche and leads to more lasting change. Passive individuals and followers will heed direct suggestions while more independent or controlling individuals respond better to indirection. Again, know your client so you can adjust the balance between direction and indirection.

Several categories of suggestions follow.

(1) **Contingent Suggestions or the Use of "As If":** contingent suggestions imply a causal connection, even though the connection may be a specious one. Two examples are "The closer your hands come, the more deeply you will go into trance." and "The closer your hands approach each other, the more willing you will be to work on that problem." At some level the client connects the two parts and behaves *as if* the statement were true. It is useful to link the suggested response to something that is already occurring or something that you know will be upcoming. These suggestions have the form of "when this, then that." Erickson and Rossi (1976, p. 117) describe this as "Responses that are inevitable and most likely to occur are made contingent on the execution of the hypnotic response." Several examples taken from Erickson and Rossi (1976, pp. 117–121) follow.

"Your eyes will get tired and close all by themselves as you continue looking at that spot."

"Don't enter trance until you sit all the way down in that chair, there."

"The closer you get, the more you can recognize the comfort of going into a trance."

"Suppose you ask me about it after you are awake."

Please notice how many other language forms already discussed are incorporated in these statements.

(2) **Contextual Suggestions:** these depend on *context* and have the general form, "When you are in that circumstance, then this (a behavior or feeling) has occurred or will occur." Some examples are:

"When you reach for a cigarette, you will see an image of your daughter's big eyes / yourself jogging freely / yourself breathing deeply / climbing steps two at a time."

"When you walk through the door into the meeting room a sense of calm and relaxation will sweep through you / an image of speaking easily and comfortably to your family will stay with you."

"As you sit down in that chair, you can begin to go into a deep healthful trance."

"When you see that irregularly squeezed toothpaste tube, you will realize just how much you love him/her and how wonderful it is that he/she has his/her own ways."

(3) **Open-Ended Suggestions:** since it is effectively impossible to know someone completely, there is always the chance that suggestions which are *too* specific will run into significant client resistance. Bernie Siegel in his meditations likes to direct the listener to go "to the middle of nowhere." This image must be particularly comforting and meaningful *to him* in ways that are unique to his experience. However, that image is a frightening one to me. A suggestion like, "And, within your mind, you can now go to that special place in which you feel particularly safe and secure and comfortable. It may be in the middle of nowhere, or the middle of some crowded place, or somewhere in between, but particularly special and safe for you." (We are not criticizing Bernie here, but indicating how someone who is superb at healing suggestions can

improve by paying attention to the subtleties of hypnotic language.) Open-ended suggestions are like a crescent wrench in that they can be used on any size of bolt. The more open-ended the suggestion, the more people it will fit. Some of Erickson's open-ended suggestions follow (Erickson and Rossi, 1979, pp. 26, 111):

"We all have potentials we are unaware of, and we usually don't know how they will be expressed."

"Your mind can review more feelings, memories, and thoughts related to that problem, but you don't know yet which will be most useful for solving the problem you are coping with."

"You can find yourself ranging into the past, the present, or the future as your unconscious selects the most appropriate means of dealing with that."

"He doesn't know what he is learning, but he is learning. And it isn't right for me to tell him, 'You learn this or you learn that!' Let him learn whatever he wishes, in whatever order he wishes."

"But most patients with phantom limb pain just think of only the pain. And if you can have phantom pain, you can have phantom pleasure."

(4) **Compound Suggestions:** the compound suggestion is made up of two separate suggestions that are joined together with some grammatical conjunction. In delivery, a slight pause between the two parts adds a subtle emphasis. The first statement is generally a truism of some kind that the client cannot deny. This might be some global generalization or be a simple description of something about the client's posture. Some connecting words are: and, but, or, until, since, because, though, if, so, as, and after. Since compound suggestions also fall under other categories discussed here, we will just present a sampling of them taken from Erickson and Rossi (1979, pp. 31–38) in double quotes, and some of our own in single quotes.

"It's a holiday, so why shouldn't I do what I want?"

"You have done well and can continue."

"With each breath you take, you can become aware of the natural rhythms of your body and feelings of comfort that develop."

"As your hand lowers, you'll find yourself going comfortably back in time to the source of that problem."

"And when your conscious mind recognizes a plausible and worthwhile solution, your finger can lift automatically."

"As that fist gets tighter and tense, the rest of your body relaxes."

"When you next open your eyes, you will have an unusually clear memory of all that, but without the feelings you had then."

"And you can, can you not?"

"You do, don't you?"

"You can't stop it, can you?"

"You don't have to go into trance until you are really ready."

"And you really don't have to do [therapeutic response] until [inevitable behavior in patient's near future]."

"You may get divorced ... [Pause] ... unless you both really learn to get what you need in the relationship."

'You are sitting there/breathing/looking around the room/listening/moving your head/[any behavior you can describe], and your eyes will close/one of your hands will feel lighter/a tingling will start/you will feel even more relaxed/[any behavior or feeling you wish to elicit].'

(5) **Some Additional Observations on Suggestions:** obviously, the high "suggestibility" of clients in the trance state leads to both the effectiveness of the hypnotherapeutic approach and the caution that ethical practice requires. Although direct suggestion can be effective, we feel that the Ericksonian approach of indirection is, if you will, more *polite* in that it lets the client find his/her unique response. In contrasting direct and indirect suggestions, Erickson and Rossi (1976, p. 269) state:

> With indirect suggestion, however, subjects usually do not recognize the relation between the suggestion and their own response. There thus can be no question of voluntary compliance with the therapist's suggestion. If a response does take place, then it has been mediated by involuntary processes outside of a subject's immediate range of awareness. This involuntary mediation of responses is what we use to define the genuineness of trance behavior. Suggestions become more effective when there is some way of validating them, hence the use of truisms in compound suggestions.

b.   Implications

What does a dictionary have to say about the definition of certain words that we have been using over and over again? Let us digress briefly here for a few definitions.

> *implication* - 1. Act of implication or state of being implicated; involvement; close connection. 2. Act of implying or state of being implied; also, that which is implied; inference.

> *imply* - 1. Obs. To infold. 2. To involve in substance, or by fair inference, or by construction of law, when not expressly stated; to contain by implication. 3. To express indirectly; to hint or hint at. 4. Of words or phrases, to involve as a meaning or meanings.—Syn. See include, suggest.

> *infer* - 1. Obs. To bring on; induce; inflict. 2. To derive by reasoning or implication; conclude from facts or premises; to derive as a consequence, conclusion, or probability. 3. Colloq. To surmise; guess. 4. To indicate; point out. 5. Erroneous. To imply or hint.—Syn. See deduce, conclude, judge, gather, surmise.

suggestion - 1. The act or an instance of suggesting; also, that which is suggested. 2. The mental process by which one thought leads to another, especially through association of ideas. 3. A trace; a slight touch; hint. 4. Psychol. The uncritical acceptance of an idea or proposal made by a person to whom the subject is docile and submissive; as, hypnotic suggestion.

suggest - 1. To arouse, often by indirect means, the thought of, the desire for, the temptation to commit, or the like. 2. Of things, to call to mind, as by association of ideas; specifically of a word, to call to mind. 3. To serve as a motive or inspiration for. 4. To advance by way of suggestion. —Syn. Suggest, imply, hint, intimate, insinuate, mean to convey an idea or thought by indirect means.

intimate - 1. To announce; notify. 2. To suggest obscurely or indirectly; hint.

presuppose - 1. To suppose beforehand; to take for granted. 2. To require as an antecedent logical condition; postulate; as, true knowledge of the external world presupposes the validity of perception.

We are reminded here of Erickson's reading of the dictionary as a teenager. Although in the preceding we have been "exact" in giving definitions of words we have used repeatedly in this book taken from *one* dictionary, we are also reminded of the caution that "the meaning of any communication is the *response* that you get." Nevertheless, it is useful to periodically review dictionary definitions. Relying on the definitions, much of what we have (arbitrarily) separated in this chapter and its sections and subsections are so interrelated as to be in many ways variations of each other. If a supermarket checkout clerk one day loads you up with free extra goodies as the store policy for that day, should you complain or rejoice? Variability is the hallmark of an effective therapist.

We can continue our discussion of implication by a quote from Erickson, Rossi and Rossi (1976, pp. 59–60):

> An understanding of how Erickson uses implication will provide us with the clearest model of his indirect approach to hypnotic suggestion. Since his use of "implication" may involve something more than the typical dictionary definition of the term, we will assume that he may be developing a special form of "psychological implication" in his work. For Erickson, psychological implication is a key that automatically turns the tumblers of a patient's associative processes into predictable patterns without awareness of how it happened. The implied thought or response seems to come up automatically within patients, as if it were their own inner response rather than a suggestion initiated by the therapist. Psychological implication is thus a way of structuring and directing patients' associative processes when they cannot do it for themselves. The therapeutic use of this approach is obvious. If patients have problems because of their ability to utilize their own resources, then implications are a way of bypassing these limitations.

In copying out this quote, we resisted underlining particular words and phrases. You may wish to reread this paragraph and do the underlining yourself since it describes succinctly the essence and rationale for Erickson's use of indirection. Several illustrations will now be quoted (Erickson, Rossi, and Rossi, 1976, pp. 60–61):

"If you sit down, then you can go into a trance."

"Certainly your arm won't be numb before I count to five."

"Before you go into trance, you ought to be comfortable."

"The very complexity of mental functioning, you go into a trance to find out ... a whole lot of things you can do. And there are so many more than you dreamed of."

"I don't know how your behavior will change."

The last statement is a favorite of ours—there are so many circumstances in which this implied directive (and variations based on it) can be used.

In using catalepsy to explore human potentials, the following example from Erickson, Rossi and Rossi (1976, p. 99) is illustrative:

> "Of course
> something has happened to your left hand,
> and that will remain,
> and when you awaken
> you will have lost
> all control of your right arm.
> [Pause]
> And I want you to be curious
> about that dissociation of your right arm -
> the nature and character of it -
> because everybody handles the situation slightly differently.
> [Pause]
> Your arm will remain immobile."

In commenting on this quote of Erickson, Rossi enthuses as follows (Erickson, Rossi, and Rossi, 1976, p. 100):

> This is fascinating! You use implication as an indirect form of suggestion to set behavior in motion that will help her to explore her own individual differences in dealing with the situation. You are really not manipulating and controlling her. Rather, you are *offering* suggestions in such a way that her own unique response potentials become manifest in a manner that can be surprising and informative to both of you. Even while immobilizing her arm in what might appear to be a conventional catalepsy, you are actually leaving room for the exploration of human potentials. It is actually the subjective process by which she immobilizes her arm that will reveal whether she has a latent talent for anesthesia ("it may lose all feeling"), comfort, rigidity, ideosensory responses ("wooden feeling"), or whatever.

The implied directive is made up of three parts: (1) a time-binding introduction of some kind; (2) the implied/assumed/intimated/hinted suggestion; and (3) some sort of *behavioral* response to signal when the implication has been accomplished. You always need to check your work in some way, and structuring it to get a *behavioral* response that can be independently checked (in contrast to verbal responses) is a good way to function. Some additional examples from Erickson, Rossi, and Rossi (1976) can help you understand the subtlety of this work and give you examples you can adapt to your own style:

"I can tell your unconscious mind will allow you to use it. And it can take its own time, letting you go into a trance, helping you to understand anything reasonable."

"Your eyes can now close, and you will note that the drifting can occur more rapidly, that there is less and less importance to be attached to my voice, and that you can experience progressively [Pause] any kind of sensations you wish."

"Now with your background you'll have many questions about many things. You really don't know what those questions are. You won't know what some of those questions are until they are half answered."

"... you can go into a trance to find out a whole lot of things you can do. And they are so many more than you dreamed of."

"Now I am trying to map out some things you can learn."

"And when you have completed, ... you will awaken and tell us only these things that you are willing to share."

"As soon as your unconscious knows, it can again return to this state comfortably and easily to do constructive work the next time we are together, you will find yourself awakening feeling refreshed and alert."

Erickson was fond of using a statement somewhat like the following one early in his interactions with a new client: "Please be sure to not tell me anything you do not wish to tell me." This was delivered congruently, of course.

c.   *Presuppositions*

The most common example of a presupposition is the question, "Have you stopped beating your wife yet?" or its variant, "When did you stop beating your wife?" Both sentences presuppose that you have been beating your wife. A presupposition defined by O'Hanlon (1987) is " ... the use of language, actions and situations that *necessarily* involve certain antecedents *or* consequences." (Emphasis added.) The power of presuppositions is that they cannot be ignored, and, if used subtly, create expectations for change that are outside or beyond the conscious mind. "And there are so many things you can learn, aren't there?" O'Hanlon (1987) also states, "Presupposition is a form of language in which certain ideas or experiences are presumed without ever being directly stated."

Much of the material on presuppositions has already been "presupposed" in the section on word usage. As a review, we reproduce in what follows part of the material in Bandler and Grinder's appendix (1975, pp. 257–261) and the appendix in Grinder and Bandler (1981, pp. 244–246). They break down the material into simple and complete presuppositions.

(1) **Simple Presuppositions:** as a general case something is needed for the sentence to make sense. Some categories of this are:

(a) *proper names*—"Harry went to work" implies Harry's existence.

(b) *pronouns* such as her, him, she, them—"They were just here."

(c) *definite descriptions* which are complex noun arguments—"I liked the woman who wore that red scarf."

(d) *generic noun phrases* where noun arguments stand for an entire class—"Misers hate to spend money."

(e) *some quantifiers* such as each, every, some, few, many, all, none—"If you all agree on this, I resign."

(2) **Complex Presuppositions:** these are cases where more than the simple existence of an element of the sentence is presupposed. Bandler and Grinder cite 24 categories which are briefly repeated here.

(a) *relative clauses:* consist of complex noun arguments with a noun followed by a phrase beginning with which, who, or that—"The bell which had rung tolled his demise."

(b) *subordinate clauses:* of time which are identified by words like before, after, as, since, during, when, while—"If I had been here when she was, this wouldn't have occurred."

(c) *cleft sentences:* are ones beginning with an *it was/is* noun argument—"It was his honesty that won the day."

(d) *pseudo-cleft sentences:* are identified by the structure What (statement) is (statement)—"What Harry didn't know is the end of the story."

(e) *stressed sentences* where voice stress indicates that something occurs or exists—"If I had been nice to YOUR MOTHER, this wouldn't have happened."

(f) *complex adjectives* such as old, new, previous, former—"When she wears her old print dress she's happy."

(g) *ordinal numbers* are simply first, second, third, another—"When you've completed your third book, you can retire."

(h) *comparatives* such as more, less, and words ending in -er or -est—"When you play against a better ping pong player, you'll know the difference."

(i) *comparative as* which has the structure ... as X as ...—"If he was as smart as his wife, they would be happy."

(j) *repetitive cue words* are: too, also, again, either, back—"If I have to go back, I don't know what I'll do."

(k) *repetitive verbs and adverbs* are those beginning with re-, such as restore, return, renew—"When he repeats that one more time, I quit."

(i) *qualifiers* are words like only, even, just, except—"Except for that one time, the dog behaved admirably."

(m) *change-of-place verbs* like leave, come, go, depart, arrive—"When he leaves the house, he is going to get it."

(n) *change-of-time verbs and adverbs* are: end, stop, proceed, begin, still, already—"When she begins to play, please be quiet."

(o) *change-of-state verbs* are words such as: transform, become, turn into, change—"I'll change my tie as soon as you change your dress."

(p) *factive verbs and adjectives* are: know, aware, realize, regret, odd—"You should be aware of how you are standing." "It's odd he phoned so late."

(q) *commentary adjectives and adverbs* such as: fortunately, innocently, lucky, happily, far out—"Fortunately, you are real lucky to be here."

(r) *counterfactual conditional clauses* are verbs having the subjunctive tense—"If only you had paid that bill, we would not be in this mess."

(s) *contrary-to-expectation* usage is characterized by the use of the word "should"—"If only you should pay attention to me, I would respond."

(t) *selectional restrictions*—"If the dog has puppies, you can have your pick."

(u) *questions* imply the existence of what is questioned—"Who has the eraser?" or "Where is the file on depressives?"

(v) *negative questions* such as "You didn't mean that, did you?" or "Wasn't that the last bagel?"

(w) *rhetorical questions* work so well for politicians because …—"Who wants to raise taxes?" or "How much change can we support?"

(x) *spurious not*—"We realize that he is not playing fair."

Although the previous lists of word usage as presuppositions may appear daunting, the good side is that this is all learnable by practice. If you are a native speaker of English, most of this is already known to you.

Exercises on Suggestions, Implications, and Presuppositions

The various parts of this section contain many examples of the described usage. They can be studied in themselves so that you can incorporate them into your own speech patterns. A better learning strategy is to write out *two* examples of your own for every one given in the text. An even better method is to work in dyads or triads where one person is the therapist, one the client, and the possible third is a combined observer/helper who can whisper suggestions to the therapist. The goal in this exercise would be to conduct a session in which the therapist incorporates as many possible variants of suggestions, implications, and presuppositions. Such practice sessions can be taped for the additional benefits that a later review would afford. It would certainly help the "practicing" therapist to make cue cards containing lists of the various language forms. Such cue cards (if unobtrusive enough!) can be used for review at dull staff meetings or boring classes or functions. I invariably bring along work to do, letters to write, or material to study to seminars and faculty meetings! With practice you can develop a style of working with these "outside" materials that appears to be one of intent listening to the speaker! (Trance also helps one survive such meetings.)

d.   Overloading: Multiples and Stacking

The speech pattern of using lots of "ands" to link together a series of tasks or suggestions has as its goal the *overloading* of the conscious mind, the unconscious mind, or both. The series may be related in some meaningful or realistic manner, or they may be unrelated. The latter heightens confusion and may be deliberately employed for that purpose. (See the section on the use of confusion as an induction technique.) Just how many things can you pay attention to at one time? The psychologist George Miller, in summarizing much research in the 1950s, found that the average human being has the capacity to consciously retain about seven blocks or chunks of information (give or take two) at one time. Thus, some people can retain nine items, and others only five. Therefore, you can "overload" a person by presenting too much information at one time. Any information that is presented beyond the overload capacity must perforce be processed at the unconscious level. So, you can consciously overload your client to make him/her more receptive *or* you can string tasks or suggestions together to provide linkages that are seemingly impressed upon the client in an unconscious manner. (Dual or double inductions are a special case of overload and will be dealt with later.)

In the use of *serial suggestions*, you simply give a nonstop series of suggestions, usually connected by the word "and," although other connectives like "or" and "as" also work. This takes the class of compound suggestions to its limit. Some examples follow:

> "As you sit there and pay attention to your breathing, your eyes can focus on an object and you can be aware of how your feet are placed on the floor, how your big toe feels, and just how your hands lie on your thighs, while you continue breathing and looking and sitting and wondering."

> "And you can pay attention while I count backwards from twenty, and just sit there wondering, while your eyes move or don't move, and your eyelids blink, twenty, nineteen, and numbers are so ordered, aren't they? sixteen and fifteen, or they can jump around, and your eyes are, fourteen, ten, what happened to? just breathing, eyelids and hands and feet, thirteen and twelve, and is eleven left out or in? as you continue to ..."

A series of images may be *stacked* as in: "And your mind can drift back to an earlier time, and are you in a classroom, sitting at what kind of desk, and what have other students written there, and how much gum is on the underside, looking at the blackboard and out of the window and the back of whose head as you continue to wonder and see many pictures from then at one time or many times, and who was that special teacher?"

Multiple tasks may be suggested as in: "While you are sitting there now counting your breaths, you can move your left hand in some direction and your right hand in another, and will your head turn or nod at the same time? while your heart keeps beating and your eyelids blink appropriately, and there may be some movement in a leg or both legs beneath your hands, and you can swallow some excess saliva, while you wonder how much more you can do and learn and how important those changes will be for you, now."

In *stacking realities* you can build realities or stories inside one another. This can also be used as an induction method. "I remember a friend of mine who moved out west to improve his life, and when he arrived, this guy he met told him a story about losing his job to another man whose life was most interesting since it involved being part of this group that went on ..." You can, of course, flesh each of the segments out to any length. This technique will be revisited as multiple embedded metaphor.

Exercises: for the preceding material involve analysis of the examples, creating your own examples for particular clients, and practicing with others.

e. Nongrammatical Usage of Language

The human mind automatically fills in missing elements or gaps in speech and visual objects. Gestalt psychologists and others have studied many aspects of this. There seems to be a built-in need for filling in in the way the brain functions. Incomplete sentences or images or sounds set up a tangible tension that can be utilized for a client's benefits.

Rossi and Rossi (Erickson, Rossi and Rossi, 1976) discuss Erickson's use of particular language forms as enhancing right-brain activity versus left-brain. They present (p. 277) the following characteristics of the two hemispheres which they further describe as "awake" versus "trance":

Left Hemisphere (Awake)	Right Hemisphere (Trance)
Linguistic	Pantomime, kinesthetic musical
Logical—Grammatical	Visuo-spatial
Rational	Intuitive
Abstract	Literal—concrete

Analytical	Perceptual—synthetic
Directed	Spontaneous
Focused	Diffuse
Effort	Comfort

This can be expanded upon by the following quote from Erickson, Rossi, and Rossi (1976, pp. 277–278):

> ... many of Erickson's habitual forms of verbal expression are actually designed to jam or depotentiate the orderly, rational, abstract, and directing functions of a subject's usual modes of left-hemisphere knowing. His use of shock, surprise, dissociation, shifting frames of reference, confusion, paradox, and double binds are thus all directed to depotentiating the left hemisphere. His emphasis on body language, cues from voice locus, emphasis, rhythm, etc., are all shifts away from the rational and analytic to the perceptual, kinesthetic, and synthetic of functioning so characteristic of the right hemisphere. When he uses hypnotic forms like implication, expectancy, partial remarks, and dangling phrases, analogues, metaphors, puns, and folk language, he is again shifting away from the abstract and analytical to the intuitive and synthetic modes of the right. Many of the most characteristic features of trance experience such as reverie, dream, literalism, comfort, and the autonomous or spontaneous flow of mental experience and behavior are all facilitated by hypnotic forms such as not doing and not knowing, open-ended suggestions and suggestions covering all possibilities of response.

For a native speaker of any language, the use of non-grammatical language is arresting and potentially jarring. So, this usage needs to be done subtly and in small doses to reach the unconscious directly. (You may wish to overload with nongrammatical usage for a particular purpose.) Since some sectors of a given society habitually use grammar differently, you need to be aware of such patterns for establishing rapport and effective communication in what may be "cross-cultural" work *within* one society.

Partial remarks and dangling phrases are ways of letting the client fill in with endings that are appropriate to them. If this is done with the lyrics of well-known songs or lines from well-known poetry, then the fill-ins can be *directed* along directions you are interested in as the therapist. Some examples follow:

"Sit there quietly and just close ..."

"You can just relax, now, and just listen to ..., and ignore ..., and feel so ..."

"And you were, weren't you? Then or ... And, even how ..., chance can ..."

"Being is or was, soon, now ... change."

"Before you go during while these thoughts, helpful, aren't they not now, but then ..."

"Ain't ain't the way to hear what you want for yourself, now, it ain't, is."

"And you don't know exactness how to change as you need now, but when but?"

"Something there is that doesn't love a ..., and how many haven't you left, that wants it ..., so you can get what you need here today?"

"As you walked that path you noticed that two, too, roads diverged in a yellow wood, and you take the correct one for your left, right? Or was it right to be left?"

"Poems are made by ..., and isn't it foolish to think what creating rhymes raises you to, and even though only God ..., you have so many choices in your life, and how will you grow yourself?"

"The moving ..., and you really need to pay attention to your own in this matter, don't you, right now?"

"And you can ease your burden by the dawn's early ... to illuminate what was dark."

Gilligan (1987) writes about the use of *meaningful nonsequiturs*, which are statements that are totally irrelevant to or not following from the established context. Gilligan states that (p. 244) "... nonsequiturs will have maximum hypnotic effect when (1) they are delivered meaningfully (2) by a speaker assumed and expected to speak rationally and relevantly (3) in a context where the listener trusts the integrity of the speaker." Erickson was fond of this usage because its unexpectedness led to confusion which could then be utilized.

"It was snowing hard, and just close your eyes, now."

"Do elephants need horseshoes? As you continue to learn even more, finding appropriate solutions."

"As you pay attention to your breathing, the green turtle, relaxing even more, how now cow, and your eyelids continue blinking, a bus can pass, closing now, and you can get on with your own life."

Gilligan (1987) writes about a class of nongrammatical usage as syntactical violations (pp. 244–246). His advice about their usage follows (p. 245):

> ... hypnotically utilizable syntactical violations can be generated by (1) selecting words that have more than one meaning, at least one of which is relevant to trance development ..., (2) forming a statement in which the key word appears at the end of the statement in its trance-unrelated sense; (3) forming another statement in which the key word appears in the beginning of the utterance in its trance-related sense; and (4) connecting the two statements together, with the key word used once as the overlap.

"Watching the rain, you can drop right down into trance."

"Sitting in an easy chair can relax completely now."

"Being careful to observe the clock hands, watch your own hand start to float down."

"The balloon descended lower and lower your eyelids."

"After three comes fourth that surprising answer."

Gilligan suggests that you attain maximum effectiveness with syntactical violations when they are delivered smoothly and rapidly and meaningfully.

Exercises

Nongrammatical usage can add a degree of playfulness to sessions, and you can enjoy playing with this form and creating as many statements as you can. It helps to have a particular client and a specific goal in mind as you practice. One way to enhance your skills is to study comedians and how they use language non-grammatically for laughter.

f. Language Involving Time

"As you change, now, think about all the new things you've learned about yourself, then, and how will you have already begun that process while you continue to progress even now?"

As you read (and reread) the previous sentence, notice how the use of time-related words and grammatical tense have been used, and how just the *reading* of a sentence like that has affected your own thoughts. The use of time words in your repertoire can really enhance its effectiveness. Earlier in this chapter, we cited twenty-four complex presuppositions which are given in the appendix of Bandler and Grinder (1975). Eight of these complex presuppositions are related to time. Since Bandler and Grinder have done this so cleverly, we reproduce here these eight descriptions along with their illustrations. In each part, the first sentence in quotes is the example, and the second indicates what has been presupposed.

(1) *Complex Adjectives*: new, old, former, present, previous, etc. "If Fredo wears his new ring, I'll be blown away." "Fredo had/has an old ring."

(2) *Ordinal Numbers*: first, second, third, fourth, another, etc. "If you can find a third clue in this letter, I'll make you a mosquito pie." "There are two clues already found."

(3) *Repetitive Cue Words*: too, also, either, again, back, etc. "If she tells me that again, I'll kiss her." "She has told me that before."

(4) *Repetitive Verbs and Adverbs*: verbs and adverbs beginning with re-, e.g., repeatedly, return, restore, retell, replace, renew, etc. "If he returns before I leave, I want to talk to him." "He has been here before."

(5) *Change-of-Place Verbs*: come, go, leave, arrive, depart, enter, etc. "If Sam has left home, he is lost." "Sam has been at home."

(6) *Change-of-Time Verbs and Adverbs*: begin, end, stop, start, continue, proceed, already, yet, still, any more, etc. "My bet is that Harry will continue to smile." "Harry has been smiling."

(7) *Change-of-State Verbs*: change, transform, turn into, become, etc. "If Mae turns into a hippie, I'll be surprised." "Mae is not now a hippie."

(8) *Counterfactual Conditional Clauses*: verbs having subjunctive tense. "If you had listened to your father and me, you wouldn't be in the wonderful position you're in now." "You didn't listen to your father and me."

Notice that many of the illustrations use the if/then structure. We will return to the use of time-ly(!) words when we discuss "torpedo" therapy.

Exercise

Think up your own examples of time-related words and practice their use. Also, add to the list of the words given as examples.

g.   Hypnotic Poetry

"Hypnotic Poetry" is the title of a book originally published in 1930 by Snyder and reprinted in 1971. Snyder placed poetry on a continuum from hypnotic (or what he also call hypnoidal or spell-weaving) to intellectualistic. The latter appeals to the intellect and appears to require analysis and cogitation on the part of the listener. He indicated that, although there appear to be some readers who can achieve a kind of self-hypnosis simply in reading to themselves, spell-weaving is generally manifested when the poetry is read aloud. Of course, the ability of the reader, the venue, and the expectational atmosphere are also important factors. What Snyder found was that there were certain poems whose actual structure and choice of words and imagery were more conducive to hypnoidal states than others. Some of these poems (with the poet in parenthesis) are: "Auld Lang Syne" and "John Anderson My Jo" (Burns); "Kubla Khan" and much of "The Rime Of The Ancient Mariner" (Coleridge); much of "The Rubaiyat of Omar Khayyam" (Fitzgerald); "Elegy Written In A Country Churchyard" (Gray); "La Belle Dame Sans Merci" (Keats); "The Long Trail" (Kipling); "Sea Fever" (Masefield); "Annabel Lee" (Poe); and "O Captain! My Captain!" (Whitman).

In analyzing for the commonalities in hypnotic poetry, Snyder found (p. 37) "... a peculiarly effective stimulus consists of words which fix the subject's attention by their rhythmic sound and make a simple suggestion on which the subject concentrates without any great mental activity." He found that hypnotic poems have the following characteristics in common: (1) An unusually perfect pattern of sound which tends to be soothing. In fact (p. 42), "Hypnotic poems in general give us heavy stresses falling regularly at half-second intervals, and so ornamented that the rhythmically inclined listener has his attention drawn to the sound rather than the sense." (2) There is in these poems a freedom from abrupt changes which can break the spell, and this especially means freedom from ideas which might compel mental alertness. (3) The poems contain a certain vagueness of imagery (p. 42). "The pictures presented in these hypnotic poems have such soft, shadowy outlines that one may fill in the details to suit one's fancy or let the picture remain hazy. They foster an idle, dreamy state of consciousness like the preliminary stage of hypnosis." (4) There are fatigue-producing elements, i.e. what Rossi calls "depotentiating habitual mental frameworks." These include verbal difficulties (p. 45). "Paradoxical though it sounds, we may yet have to accept the view that in the early stages of a hypnotic poem, a foreign word, an obscure phrase, or any slight difficulty that causes fatigue from strain on the part of the listener may actually promote the ultimate aesthetic effect at which the artist aims." (5) Another characteristic is the use of a refrain or of frequent repetition. (Think of the repetition of "Nevermore" in "The Raven.") Finally, (6) these hypnotic poems tend to use suggestion on the entranced listener, the suggestions sometimes having a post-hypnotic effect. In fact, the key suggestive sentence comes near the end after "... there has been a long preliminary soothing of the listener's senses by monotonous rhythmic 'passes'." (p. 48)

Consider incorporating some of these "hypnotic" poems in your inductions. Test the poems by reading them to friends. (The approach known as "poetry therapy" apparently uses poetry in a different way.)

F. Negation

Jack thinks
    he does not know
  what he thinks
    Jill thinks
    he does not know

But Jill thinks Jack does know it.

So Jill does not know
    she does not know
  that Jack does not know
  that Jill thinks
  that Jack does know
and Jack does not know he does not know
  that Jill does not know she does not know
  that Jack does not know
    that Jill thinks Jack knows
  what Jack thinks he does not know

The preceding poem by Laing (1970, p. 59) is a magnificent illustration of the use of negation involving *phonological homonyms* (no and know, not and an implied knot), confusion, hypnotic poetic structure, and ambiguity. Reading it leaves you with a sense that you "know" something about Jack and Jill, but that this may be *no* know-ledge! In this section we will dwell on the use of negation in the variety of ways that Erickson developed and utilized. He loved puns and clang associations and word play.

Consider how we process negation—you first have to visualize or recall the phenomenon so that you can then negate or forget it. "Don't think about a purple elephant." It is impossible to *not* think about a purple elephant when hearing this statement. First, you think about it, then you *try* to negate it. The mind processed the word "don't" as if it didn't exist! We hear the above sentence as "~~Don't~~—*think about* a purple elephant." "Do" is an action word which "not" presumably cancels out, but does it? We tend to process what comes after the "don't" as an injunction or command. Think about (a *direct* suggestion) how you react to the following statements.

"Don't forget to mail this letter."

"Remember to mail this letter here."

"You don't have to do that now."

"Pick up your clothes now."

"I don't mean to interrupt, but ..."

"If your wife weren't here, I would say ..."

"Of course, you can't do that now."

"I don't think you're the kind of person who wouldn't do that. People don't change that fast, do they?"

"Don't violate presuppositions if you expect to have effective outcomes."

"And you can really think many other and interesting thoughts about that, can you not, now?"

"Please stop screaming, won't you?"

"Stop making so much noise."

How have you not reacted knowingly to the preceding, even being aware of the knotty way that language can trip you up now, isn't that not so?

Grinder and Bandler (1981, p. 67) state, *"No single pattern that I know of gets in the way of communication more often than using negation. Negation only exists in language and does not exist in experience."* (Emphasis in original). Erickson studied in depth the use of negation. He is said to have admired an actor who could say "no" in sixteen different ways so as to shade the meaning from an "absolute" no to an agreeable acceptance. Since it is more difficult to comprehend negative formulations than positive ones, then negatives tend to depotentiate consciousness. It is, therefore, easier to go along with a (positive) suggestion than struggle with one involving negations. In a statement like, "You will, will you not?" the "not" balances the positive "you will" and gives the listener a way to resist which they really cannot resist! This balance is an example of the apposition of opposites which we will write more about later in this section.

1. Double Negatives and Tag Questions

Erickson was concerned with ways of discharging the negativity or resistance that grows whenever a client follows a series of suggestions. Some people feel imposed upon and want some control back. This behavior is most evident in children who are told to stop a particular behavior. Typically, the child will do the behavior one more time to establish his/her independence before complying with the command. This opposition to suggestions is a healthy one (if not taken to extremes!). Psychologists use the concept of reactive inhibition which effectively states that after repeating some task (following suggestions, e.g.) a person becomes less and less willing to continue and becomes open to alternate behaviors or actions. So, Erickson found that the simple use of negation served as a kind of lightning rod to automatically discharge the buildup of resistance or inhibitions.

In addition, there is experimental evidence (Donaldson, 1959) to the effect that it is about thirty percent more difficult to comprehend a negative than a positive. (Before you can negate, you must first affirm!) Some characteristic Erickson usages follow (Erickson and Rossi, 1979, pp. 35–36):

"And you can, can you not?"

"You can try, can't you?"

"You can't stop it, can you?"

"You will, won't you?"

"You do, don't you?"

"Why not let that happen?"

"You don't have to go into a trance until you are ready."

"You won't do it until your unconscious is ready."

"And you really don't have to do [therapeutic response] until [inevitable behavior in patient's near future]."

"And you really don't know how you will change, do you?"

"And you really don't know what you are learning now, do you?"

The *tag questions* at the end of the sentence throw in an unexplained negation that seems to both empower and confuse the client. "And you will, will you not?" This "gets" you both coming and going, so to speak. Resistance is by-passed by enlisting questioning and doubt. Read the following three sentences found in Gilligan (1987, p. 188):

"And you really would like to go into a trance, would you not?"

"And you probably can't get yourself fully comfortable, can you?"

"And it really is all right to relax, is it not?"

Simply adding the sentences in this section (and your own variations of them) to your repertoire will enhance your effectiveness.

A particularly elegant use of negation which Erickson liked to use in the first session to put the client at ease is: "And I want you to please be sure to *not* tell me anything that you do not wish to tell me." The client is getting permission to keep confidential potentially embarrassing or secret thoughts, acceptance of what might be considered to be "resistant" or inappropriate behavior (you have to tell *all* to a therapist, right?), and an embedded message to "*tell me anything.*" This opening welcome is disarmingly useful in the first session.

2. *Apposition of Opposites*

The *apposition of opposites* consists of two opposing concepts or experiences that are juxtaposed within the same context or sentence. This is in part a confusion technique, but the apposition also reinforces the concept/experience that you tag with your delivery. Some examples follow:

"And you can remember to forget, can you not?"

"Do you really wish to forget to remember, or remember to forget?"

"Remember to forget what is unimportant."

"As your left hand feels cooler, your right hand will feel warmer."

"As your toe itches a bit more, your discomfort will decrease."

"You can remain comfortably and safely immobile while your mind wanders to a significant early experience."

"How comfortable can you feel, now, about what used to be uncomfortable, then?"

"Learning to unlearn can be useful."

"And just how much warmth can you find in coldness."

Oxymorons, in which the opposites are in a single phrase, serve the same goals of confusion and movement. In a classic case (Rosen, 1982, pp. 36–37), Erickson used the phrase "vicious pleasure" to help a client overcome sexual problems. Some oxymoronic straight statements follow:

"And you can be happily sad / depressed / guilty / crying, can you not?"

"And you may experience a rather slow, but rapid change."

"How quickly can you escalate decreasing that feeling of discomfort?"

"It is sometimes quicker to crawl."

"A distant touching can start this change."

"You can blindly look at yourself and wonder what it is you are not seeing."

"What exciting blindness will smooth your way with this easily difficult person?"

Aside from anything else, the use of oxymorons and the apposition of opposites adds an element of playfulness to what may be the ponderous seriousness of some sessions.

3. Not Knowing and Not Doing

"Not knowing" and "not doing" are typically Ericksonian. Once again, the "not" is ignored, resistance is by-passed, and the client acts as if only positive statements were made. "Thus, Erickson's initial direction in trance training is to have the subject have a comfortable experience in not doing" (Erickson, Rossi, and Rossi, 1976, p. 24). Some typical Erickson statements taken from this book follow with the page number in parentheses:

"And without knowing it, you're demonstrating the immobility that a hypnotic subject can show." (p. 10).

"Now physical comfort exists, but you don't even need to pay attention to your relaxation and comfort." (p. 12).

"You don't have to talk or move or make any sort of effort. You don't even have to hold your eyes open." (p. 23).

"You don't have to bother trying to listen to me because your unconscious can do that and respond all by itself." (p. 24).

"People can sleep and not know they are asleep." (p. 24).

"They can dream and not remember that dream." (p. 24).

"Now the important achievement for you is to realize that everybody does not know his capacities. (Pause). And you have to discover these capacities in whatever slow way you wish." (pp. 36-37).

"Every person has abilities not known to the self, abilities discredited by the self." (p. 45).

"You can as a person awaken, but you do not need to awaken as a body." (p. 48).

"You don't know when you're going to change your rate of breathing [or whatever]." (p. 154).

"You don't need to know where your hands [or whatever] are." (p. 162).

"You don't need to listen, your unconscious can respond on its own." (p. 198).

"You don't need to know [whatever] for when the occasion arises, your unconscious will supply that knowledge." (p. 198).

The following are more Erickson statements from Erickson and Rossi (1981):

> "I don't know when you'll go into a deep trance." (p. 28).

> "You are looking at that hand [or whatever], and you don't need to see anything else." (p. 59).

> "You do not know what the body orientation is in the matter of developing a trance." (p. 67).

> "And you really don't know how far up they (hands) move, how far down they move. Isn't that right?" (p. 174).

> "And I'm not instructing you to put it down." (p. 195).

The following quotes are from Erickson and Rossi (1979):

> "You don't even have to talk or move or make any sort of effort." (p. 25).

> "You don't even have to hold your eyes open." (p. 25).

> "You don't know when those eyelids will close all by themselves." (p. 25).

> "You don't really know just how your unconscious will help you resolve that problem. But your conscious mind can be receptive to the answer when it does come." (p. 25).

> "Your conscious mind surely has many questions, but it does not really know just when the unconscious will let you give up that undesirable habit. You don't know if it will be sooner or later. You don't know if it will be all at once or slowly, by degrees. Yet you can learn to respect your own natural way of doing things." (p. 25).

> "You don't need to talk. You don't need to move. You don't even need to listen to me." (p. 284).

In providing you with all of these statements by Erickson, we are aiming to *overload* your mind with an overwhelming use of "not knowing" and "not doing." In a sense, is not being in a trance the essence of "not doing?" We ask the client to be relaxed and passive and do nothing, which becomes a kind of precondition for trance. In the relaxed state the parasympathetic nervous system predominates, and this is a predisposition to *not do* rather than actively making an attempt to do. The "not knowing/doing" takes advantage of the inherent laziness of someone in the trance state. There are also paradoxical and confusion components, as well as many opportunities for embedded suggestions and commands, in "notting" your client. "There is, is there not, and how much have you not learned consciously, yet?"

4. Truisms and the "Yes Set"

The "yes set" is a way of describing a procedure where you use a series of questions and statements whose only and obvious answer is "yes." This is part of establishing rapport but, more importantly, it establishes a receptiveness in the client to *continue* to respond in an affirmative manner to anything you say. You have "set" an affirmative response in his/her/their mind by repetition. This can also be used as an induction where you can bore a person with a series of simple questions. The "yes set" also depotentiates resistance and is effective with intellectual clients who analyze everything. One possible set of such questions follows:

"Today is Wednesday, isn't it?"

"And it is also the fifth of October?"

"We are talking in the afternoon?"

"And you are seated in that chair there?"

"The time is 3:10 on that clock, right?"

"Are you living at ...?"

"You are working at ...?"

"And your feet are firmly planted on the floor?"

"Your wife's name is Mary?"

"We are just sitting here, the two of us, in my office, are we not?"

"And you just heard a door slam, didn't you?"

"There are a lot of books in this room, aren't there?"

"Your car is parked outside?"

"It was raining when you came in, wasn't it?"

"And how soon do you think you will go all the way into a deep trance?"

"And none of these things have anything to do with your reason for being here."

These statements are examples of truisms that the client cannot refute. He/she must simply sit there and nod or say "yes" to each statement and/or question. The two last statements in the series are suggestions for some behavior you wish to elicit. You can continue with truisms after this statement or go directly into trance work depending on the client's response. Yes-set statements can be used as inductions or in the trance state to facilitate change. Notice that this use of the yes-set is another form of pacing and leading.

One useful way of using truisms with a negatively or resistance minded client is to have them *agree* to all of the things that they would *not* be willing to do. These negative things then become a common ground or understanding between the two of you. Thus, you are pacing and getting the client to agree with you. This is also considered to be a utilization approach.

Truisms can be used following a suggestion, and this unconsciously reinforces the suggestion with a subtle associative link to the last statement. In effect, you are in an agreeing/accepting mode and will do that for whatever has been stated. The truism or yes-set can be used to reinforce in an associative manner post-hypnotic suggestions. "And you will be waking up tomorrow to find interesting changes in your life." Tacking an unnecessary truism onto a statement serves as a distraction which takes the client past the statement, and automatically by-passes a conscious questioning—they are too busy agreeing with the truism to notice. This can be enhanced by loading the client with many truisms. It is useful to have your client agreeing with you. One caution here is to not overdo truisms to the point of such tedium that you actually lose rapport rather than enhance it. (Remember, the meaning of *any* communication is the *actual* response you get and not your intended response.)

5. *The Reverse Set*

In the *reverse set*, the client responds in the *opposite* way from the normally expected response. This would be to nod "yes" when he/she means "no," and vice versa. It could be to move when they would normally not move. The reverse set works through a confusion state to teach the client new patterns of response and behavior. The reverse set can give a client permission to continue to be resistant while exhibiting cooperative behavior. The clearest example of the use of the reverse set is Erickson's working with a client named Ruth in a demonstration filmed by E. Hilgard and J. Haley at Stanford University in 1958. The partial transcript that follows is from Erickson and Rossi (1981, pp. 165–168):

> E: Now I'm going to ask you, is your first name Ruth? [Ruth nods Yes.] That's right. Are you a woman?
>
> Ruth: Yes.
>
> E: You just nod your head or shake your head in answer. Are you a woman? [Ruth nods, Yes.] Are you sitting down? [Ruth nods Yes.]
>
> E: All right, now I'm going to ask you some other questions, and you will nod your head in answer. Is your name Ann? [Ruth shakes head No.] And you will nod your head in answer. [E models, nodding Yes.] Is your name Ann? [Ruth nods Yes.]

E: That's right. Because your thinking can be different than the movement of the muscles in your neck. Are you standing up? [Ruth nods Yes.]

E: That's right. And are you a boy? [Ruth nods Yes.] That's right.

E: And now I want you to shake your head No. [E models head shaking.] Your name isn't Ruth, is it? [E shakes No; Ruth shakes No.]

E: And you aren't a woman, are you? [Ruth shakes head No.]

E: And you aren't sitting down, are you? [Ruth shakes head No.]

E: And you aren't in trance, are you? [Ruth shakes head No.]

E: And you aren't answering me, are you? [Ruth shakes head No.] And you're not going to answer me, are you? [Ruth shakes head No.] That's right. And you can hear everything I say, can you not? [Ruth shakes head No.] And you won't hear anything I say to you, will you? [Ruth shakes head No.]

E: All right, and you can close your eyes.

E: You can close your eyes, can you not?

E: And you're closing them, are you not? [Ruth closes her eyes.] That's right. And you can enjoy sleeping more and more deeply all the time. And you really are, aren't you? [E nods head continuously.] That's right. And you really are—and just keep right on sleeping, deeper and deeper in trance.

Erickson then goes on to induce a hand levitation and other hypnotic phenomena. This film is well worth studying. Notice the use of double negatives and tag questions.

The reverse set is not for everyday use in trance work, but it is useful on particular occasions as a way to utilize and then by-pass resistance.

Exercises

"And you can practice all of what we have written about the use of negation, can you not?" In this section we have provided many examples of this kind of language usage. Study how the sentences are constructed, and then write out two more of your own so that you can incorporate this knowledge. In a practice session, find out how many negations you can use and in what ways. Have a really negative experience while you learn. Be sure to carefully observe the nonverbal responses during this kind of practice. Try some of the ways of using negatives in casual conversation. Listen to television or radio with an ear to hearing when negatives are used. Do politicians use them more than ordinary folk? If you have access to tapes of Erickson's work, listen with negation in mind. Contrast Erickson's work with tapes of other therapists. Listen to earlier tapes of your own work to find out where you might have used negation without being consciously aware of it. Now that you know about the usefulness of negation, in what circumstances and with which of your present clients will it work best? And you really shouldn't do this too soon, should you, for you don't need right now to learn too much?

G. Ambiguity

A dictionary definition of ambiguous is: a. doubtful or uncertain, especially from obscurity or indistinctness; also, inexplicable. b. capable of being understood in two or more possible senses; equivocal. Consider the following three poems from Laing (1970, p. 26, 55, 64).

> I'm happy you're happy
> I'm unhappy you're unhappy
> Jack's unhappy that Jill's
>   unhappy
> Jill's unhappy that Jack's
>   unhappy
> that Jill's unhappy that
> Jack's unhappy
> that Jill's unhappy
>
> Jill is guilty to be unhappy
> if Jack is unhappy that Jill's unhappy ...
> Jack is guilty that Jill is unhappy
> because he feels that he should
> make her happy

Jill feels guilty
    that Jack feels guilty
        that Jill feels guilty
            that Jack feels guilty

If I don't know I don't know
                I think I know
If I don't know I know
                I think I don't know

Jack knows he does not know.
Jill thinks she knows what Jack does not know,
but she does not know he does not know it.
Jack does not know
    Jill does not know he does not know,
    and thinks she knows what he knows he doesn't.
Jack believes Jill.
Jack now does not know he does not know.
One happy ending.

Jack thinks Jack sees what he does not,*
and that Jill sees what she does not see.

Jill believes Jack.
She now thinks she sees what Jack
    thinks Jack sees
        and that Jack sees it too.
They may now both be completely
    wrong.

*This is ambiguous. Jack thinks he is seeing an illusion; is he right or wrong? Jack thinks he is not under an illusion. Is he right or wrong? Try it anyway. (Comment in the original.)

Can you find at least two meanings in these poems? What happens to the level of meaning and confusion if some of the "knows" are replaced by "nos?" (The third homonym of "nose" does not apply here, but can certainly be fit in somewhere!)

In linguistics the term "ambiguity" applies to the case where there is more than one deep structure to a given surface structure. So, the use of an ambiguous surface structure word, phrase, or sentence sets off an internal transderivational search in which the client will end up providing his/her unique deep structure. This, of course, hearkens back to the "precise use of vague words" that is characteristic of Erickson's use of indirection.

Linguistic Ambiguity

Four types of linguistic ambiguity may be distinguished: (1) phonological; (2) syntactic; (3) scope; and (4) punctuation. These will be discussed separately.

1. Phonological Ambiguity

The English language is replete with words represented by the same sound sequences but which have different meanings. Some examples are: hare/hair, know/no, duck, knows/nos/nose, harte/heart, deer/dear, boll/bowl, pen, need/knead, here/hear, buy/bye, nun/none, moon, some/sum, hi/high, fall, light, founder, eye/I, hold, waive/wave, rite/write/right, knot/not, knight/night, so/sew, to/too/two, fine, nay/neigh, blew/blue, flew/flue, ship, road/rode, tire, days/daze, naught/nought, cow, card, bowl, bold/bowled, muse/mews, knew/new, dye/die, die, train, pane/pain, be/bee, fast, rhyme/rime, awl/all, sail/sale, heard/herd, wait/weight, way/weigh, grade/grayed, made/maid, wade/weighed, pale/pail, rail/rale, steak/stake, rein/reign/rain, plane/plain, there/their, bear/bare, and beer/bier. Two or more words that sound the same, but have different meanings are called homonyms. The unpaired words above have different meanings depending on the context. For example, "bowl" is a container as well as an action, which also holds for "hold." The "founder" of a policy may also "founder" in enacting that policy. Phonological ambiguity may be used for confusion. It may also be used to mark a particular state or emotion or to set off internal searches. "To know how to no may be the right rite when you write about the pain that you can look through to find your way to a lighter way of just being." Obviously, there is a lot of room for exploration here.

The psychological definition of a "clang association" is that the association is through the *sound* of words without regard to their meaning. Erickson was fond of "clangs." Some examples are: light/flight/height, founder/flounder, hold/fold, comber/summer, sober/somber/encumber, and kitty/titty.

2.   Syntactic Ambiguity

This form of ambiguity occurs when the syntactic function of a word cannot be uniquely determined by the listener from the context in which the word is used. Bandler and Grinder (1975, p. 233) found two forms of this kind of ambiguity in Erickson's work. The first is the construction of a verb + ing + a noun. The four examples they give are:

"... flying planes can be dangerous"

"... investigating FBI agents can be dangerous"

"They are murdering peasants ..."

"They are walking dogs ..."

The second form is the nominalization of a noun as in:

"The touching woman ..."

"The feeling of the chair ..."

"The minding of the work ..."

"The running leader ..."

The confusion syntactic ambiguity engenders can be usefully employed.

3.   Scope Ambiguity

This occurs when it is not possible to determine from the linguistic context of the sentence how much is applied to that sentence by another portion of the same sentence. Two apt examples cited by Bandler and Grinder (1975, p. 235) are:

"I want you to draw me a picture of yourself in the nude ..."

"... speaking to you as a child ..."

Some of our examples are:

> "You can begin to act in the house ..."

> "... listening to you as a father ..."

> "... reacting as an adult ..."

4. Punctuation Ambiguity

This is a kind of nongrammatical form where two unrelated sentences or ideas are connected by a word that can sensibly fit into both parts. The use of this kind of ambiguity serves to confuse and bypass the conscious mind. A typical Erickson usage cited by Bandler and Grinder (1975, p. 236) is:

> "I want you to notice your *hand* me the glass."

The word "hand" ends one sentence at the same time as it starts another. Additional examples follow:

> "You can take a *turn* that around in your life."

> "A pocket full of *change* the way you are sitting."

> "When you go to the *store* your new learnings for another day."

Other Ambiguous Approaches

Erickson was particularly fond of using puns which may be considered as an ambiguous use of language. Puns are also an example of communicating on two levels at the same time, as is all usage of homonyms. Puns require an internal search for meaning/interpretation/response. Some examples of Erickson's use of puns follow with brief commentary in parentheses where needed to understand his therapeutic goals. (The page numbers are from Erickson and Rossi, 1979.):

"Now, Archie, you've had many long years of happy feelings. Why not get those *happy feelings back*? You've had all the pain you need." (Archie has back pain.) (p. 12)

E: "Do you think you could make a puddle with your hands? Try it."

X: "Try? I did make a puddle for some doctors once. This doctor told me it was the worst he had ever seen and he went and got a bowl. Four other doctors came around to watch me make a puddle." [X tries but cannot.]

E: "I said *try* it! You are beginning to have some doubts?"

X: "About a puddle, yeah. I could give you a little stream."

E: "Try it. Just a little puddling stream. [Pause] Looks like your poorest performance on the record."

X: "I can't understand it."

E: "Do you suppose your hands are unfolding for you to become a *dried-up old maid*?" (She used to sweat excessively from her palms.) (pp. 186-188)

"But men are such curious creatures that they will be attracted to and marry just anything so long as it is female. Imagine any man in his right mind marrying an Ubangi duck-billed woman, *but they do it*. And can you imagine even necking with a Burmese giraffe-necked woman, but their husbands love them. And think of that historically happy, contented bean-pole Jack Sprat and his lard-tub wife. What she ever saw in him or he in her, heaven only knows, but *love is blind, so all authorities say*. And please don't ever tell Mr. Hippopotamus that Miss Hippopotamus does not have a lovely smile." (p. 433) (The client was an overweight woman who was paralyzed from the waist down and had asked Erickson to be forthright with her. The triple pun in "hip-pot-mus (mess)" is direct and forceful in stories about varieties of attraction. This case has a typical Ericksonian ending: the woman was married in two years and bore four children by caesarian operations. The above excerpt was part of a longer treatment that interwove poetry, puns, parables, and metaphors.)

Puns also add a playfulness to a therapeutic situation that helps depotentiate the crippling seriousness that too many clients and therapists feel is standard operating procedure for sessions.

One level of ambiguity is the use of "empty" words which are devoid of specific reference or meaning. The client must fill in the meaning or context. Earlier, you read about "meaningful" words which give an illusion of communicating because of common usage. Both kinds of words are vague, imprecise, and indefinite. Some examples are: hopes, dreams, memories, sensations, beliefs, resources, genuine, learnings, happy, there, here, it, when, whenever, how, try, should, could, would, maybe, etc.

We have written earlier about the use of oxymorons which are useful in part because of the ambiguities involved. Can you be ambivalently and ambitiously ambiguous in an exacting sort of way? Can shaggy dog stories fit in here somewhere, too?

Exercises

Make up sentences for particular clients using the four classes of ambiguity. Try them out. How much "playing" with words do you do in your normal practice? Listen to tapes of yourself and analyze them for places where you have used ambiguity, and for places where the addition of ambiguity would have been helpful. If you are not a natural punner then, as *pun*ishment, force yourself to pun with every client and friend at least once each day. For *pen*ance, you might write them out instead.

H. Binds

Binds and double binds have been discussed extensively by Erickson, Rossi, and Rossi (1976, pp. 62–76), and by Erickson and Rossi (1979, pp. 42–49). The following definitions are quoted from the former book (pp. 62–64):

> A *bind* offers a free choice of two or more comparable alternatives—that is, whichever choice is made leads behavior in a desired direction. Therapeutic binds are tactful presentations of the possible alternate forms of constructive behavior that are available to the patient in a given situation. The patient is given free, voluntary choice between them; the patient usually feels bound, however, to accept one alternative.

> Double binds, by contrast, offer possibilities of behavior that are outside the patient's usual range of conscious choice and control. ...

> The double bind arises out of the possibility of communicating on more than one level. We can (1) say something and (2) simultaneously comment on what we are saying. ... In actual practice the metacommunication that comments on the primary message may take place without words: one may comment with a doubting tone of voice, a gesture or body movement, subtle social clues and context. ... Ideally, our therapeutic double binds are mild quandaries that provide the patient with an opportunity for growth. ... A double bind may be operative whenever one's usual frames of reference cannot cope and one is forced to another level of functioning ... What is a bind or double bind for one person may not be one for another.

In this section, we will first discuss "simple" binds, and then five types of double binds. Since they are related, we will also briefly discuss in this section: illusion of choice, all possibilities, ordeal therapy, and ambiguous function assignments. Bateson was responsible for postulating that the double bind was schizophrenogenic.

1. Simple Binds

Simple binds are most easily formed by posing questions that give the client an apparent free choice among comparable alternatives. (This was discussed earlier as "illusion of choice.") Some examples are:

> "Would you like to go into a trance sitting in this chair or that one, or standing up or lying down?"

> "Would you like to go into a trance quickly or slowly?"

> "Would you like to work on this problem now or in a few minutes?"

> "Would you like for me to read your bedtime story before or after you take your bath?"

> "Would you take the trash out now or when that program ends in seven minutes?"

Simple binds give an either/or choice, readily framed in a question, that *presupposes* the action discussed. There is an *illusion* of choice. As discussed earlier, people generally respond as if they had this choice, and then will carry out the action as if the decision were their own. Occasionally, you run into clients (and children!) who see through this ploy and might respond with, "No bath, only the story tonight!" or, "I'm not interested in going into a trance at all." With a child, you can probably insist that this is the only way the story will be read—parents do have control. With a client, you would have to deal with the patient's resistance in some other way.

The time bind gives alternatives with respect to time: quickly/slowly, now/in a few minutes, today/tomorrow, this week/next week. Sometimes it is better to be general about time (in a few minutes), and sometimes it is better to be explicit (by 4:10 pm tomorrow).

2. *The Time Double Bind*

A time double bind is designed to evoke a response on an autonomous level. These binds link some element of time to some autonomic response like warmth / coolness / numbness / analgesia / anesthesia / tingling / itching / blood pressure / blushing, or ideodynamic processes. Some examples are:

"And when do you think that blushing will start?"

"In a few minutes will that hand get warmer or cooler?"

"Just how soon will that finger move?"

"And the old sensations of pain will safely change to a tingling in how many minutes?"

A particularly elegant use of a time double bind by Erickson was with a six-year-old nail-biting boy (Erickson, Rossi, and Rossi, 1976, p. 66):

I know your father and mother have been asking you, Jimmy, to quit biting your nails. They don't seem to know that you're just a six-year-old boy. And they don't seem to know that you will naturally quit biting your nails just before you're seven years old. And they really don't know that! So when they tell you to stop biting your nails, just ignore them!

3. *The Conscious-Unconscious Double Bind*

By definition the conscious mind cannot control the unconscious mind. So, it is useful to presuppose the existence of both a conscious and an unconscious mind. The conscious/unconscious split implies a dissociation which can be utilized to do therapeutic work. (It has been also called the "dissociation technique.") The key, as you will read, is to use words and context to split the conscious and the unconscious. Some Erickson examples of this usage follow (Erickson, Rossi, and Rossi, 1976, pp. 67–68, 86):

"If your unconscious wants you to enter trance, your right hand will lift. Otherwise, your left hand will lift."

"You don't even have to listen to me because your unconscious is here and can hear what it needs to respond in just the right way."

"And it really doesn't matter what your conscious mind does because your unconscious automatically will do just what it needs to in order to achieve that anesthesia [age regression, catalepsy, etc.]."

"And when will the unconscious mind make all those valuable learnings available to your conscious mind?"

"But your conscious mind will keep it only with the consent of your unconscious mind."

"You don't need to listen to me. Your unconscious mind can listen to me without your knowledge."

"And your willingness to rely on your unconscious mind to do anything that can be of interest or value to you is most important."

"Do you really think you're awake?"

Additional examples from Erickson and Rossi (1979) are:

> "Go right ahead [Pause] and share that with your conscious mind. [Long pause] Share it with your conscious mind. [Long pause] This struggle is helping you. Even though you don't know consciously all of the struggle, that is all right." (p. 171)

> "Now I am going to say something to you. You are not going to understand it consciously. Doesn't it surprise you that you can't stand up?" (p. 182)

4. The Double-Dissociation Double Bind

These double binds involve a dissociation that occurs on two levels. These quotes from Erickson, Rossi and Rossi (1976, p. 67–70) will serve to illustrate this complex usage:

> "You can as a person awaken but you do not need to awaken as a body. [Pause] You can awaken when your body awakes but without a recognition of your body."

> "You can write that material without knowing what it is— then—you can go back and discover you know what it is— without knowing you've done it."

This kind of double dissociation can be used when you want to communicate with your client, but keep them in the trance state. They can be awake from the neck up and leave any part(s) of their body in trance. The latter quote above also implies this usage for posthypnotic suggestions.

5. The Reverse Set Double Bind

This kind of double bind permits the client to both resist and to yield by giving them *two* ways of resisting. You can select which way of resisting you wish them to follow. First, the client is challenged in such a way that a reverse set is established: "Keep sitting in that chair and being quiet and unresponsive" or "Do absolutely nothing for a while." The second part is to provide some milder responses. "Or you might wish to move or talk just a little bit, but not too much or too soon" and "Sometimes it is really hard to be completely inactive, isn't it?"

6. *The Non-Sequitur Double Bind*

Erickson was fond of using non-sequiturs or illogical statements as double binds. This playing with words appealed to his sense of humor—why not add some fun to working with people? To hook a child, Erickson might start with a time double bind such as, "Would you rather go to bed at 8:30 or exactly at 8:45?" This would be followed by an irrelevancy such as "Do you wish to take a bath before going to bed, or would you rather be careful about not putting on your pajamas backwards in the bathroom?" This is, of course, a kind of confusion technique.

7. *Illusion of Choice and All Possibilities*

A central characteristic of all binds is the *illusion of choice*. (This is also called the illusion of alternatives and sometimes the double bind.) This is a kind of "cured if you do, and cured if you don't" intervention. The client is offered two or more choices, but within a restricted range that is set by the therapist. *If* the client picks an alternative, then this choice is apparently a "free" one, i.e. of the client's own choosing. We italicized the word "if" because it is the artistry (and frequently the *authority*) of the therapist that gets the client to accept the narrowed set of choices. Of course, you want to congruently and sincerely imply that the client has no other choices at this time! We should note here that the use of "binds" is appealing for its almost magical effect, *but*, in practice, it is often difficult to come up with an appropriate bind at the right time. A related, and interesting, connection made by Gilligan (1987, p. 56) is the similarity of the Zen koan to binds. The Zen student can find the solution to a koan by going outside the system (second-order change) to utilize the "middle way."

One effective way of using the illusion of choice is to structure it so that, by suggesting *all* possibilities, the client must accept one of them! Consider the following from Erickson, Rossi, and Rossi (1976):

"Shortly your right hand, or it may be your left hand, will begin to lift up, or it may press down, or it may not move at all, but we will just wait to see just what happens. Maybe the thumb will be first, or you may feel something happening in your little finger, but the really important thing is not whether your hand lifts up or presses down, or just remains still; rather, it is your ability to sense fully whatever feelings may develop in your hand." (p. 78)

"Your arm will feel entirely comfortable, at ease, or it may lose all feeling, or it may develop a wooden feeling, a feeling of not being your arm." (p. 98)

"And when you spend time, time can be of varying intensity. It can be condensed, it can be expanded, so you can review a lifetime history in a few seconds." (p. 136)

"Your unconscious mind can decide what part or what aspects of the experience should be shared by Dr. R and me. By others in general. By patients with whom you work. [Pause] With others within you. Also, your understandings belong to you. But it is possible for you to share with others in ways you never thought of before." (p. 238)

In suggesting things such as hand levitation or ideomotor responses, it is useful to suggest *all* possible movements including the possibility of no movement. (Pacing and leading!) With eye closure you can suggest eyes open, eyes closed, a little blinking, or a lot of blinking. With emotional responses you suggest the entire range. Of course, you can direct a response by your manner of delivery—body language, tone, pauses, volume, analogical marking, and so on. The illusion of choice in its many forms is well worth learning.

"One blizzardy day in mid-winter, my father tried to pull a calf into the barn. The calf braced itself staunchly against my father's effort; neither one was making any progress, and I stood there and laughed at both of them. My father said, 'If you are so smart, you pull the calf in yourself, or at least help me to do it!' I said, 'I'll pull the calf in alone,' whereupon I took hold of the calf, grabbed it by the tail, and tried to pull it *out* of the barn. That calf showed me: *it* dragged *me* into the barn, exactly where we wanted it!

The editors commented on this story as follows:

> In another version of this same story which Erickson told later in life, his father was still trying to pull the calf into the barn when Milton pulled on its tail. The calf in this version trampled over Dad as it pulled Milton into the barn. In this version the situation presents a double bind to the calf, who chooses the lesser of two evils (it would rather move into the barn than have its tail pulled on), which, of course, was what Erickson wanted. (Erickson in Erickson, Rossi and Ryan, 1985, p. 34.)

8.   Other Binds

For completeness, we simply mention here that ordeal therapy may be considered to be a form of bind. This is also the case for ambiguous function assignments. These are discussed in Chapter 6.

Exercises

You need to be careful in developing binds that you do not get all tied up yourself. Be clear in your own mind about the difference between simple binds and double binds, and the five kinds of double binds. First, study the examples given here, and then make up five binds of each kind. It will probably be easier to do this by thinking of particular cases or situations. You may wish to practice the use of binds within your own family or significant relationships. Since some clients may react with, "Oh, you are just using psychology on me," you need to practice the delivery of these binds. You could always respond with, "Yes, and that is what you are here for, isn't it?" How often are binds used in a school setting or in sitcoms involving children or teenagers?

I.   Stories

At the beginning of my classes (both chemistry and counseling), I tell students that they will hear a variety of stories because I have discovered over the years that students tend to forget some of the subject matter of the course, but that they generally remember the stories. This seems to be universal, which is why so much of pre-book or oral tradition learning was by stories, myths, legends, and parables. There is an internal drive to connect new things with what we already know, and stories provide the connecting bridge. Mnemonics may be considered to be miniature stories for memorizing. For example, adults remember "George Eats Old Gray Rats And Paints Houses Yellow" as a way to spell "geography." Music students remember "F-A-C-E" and "Every Good Boy Does Fine" for musical scales.

Rosen's collection (1982) of Erickson's teaching tales is a remarkable resource for the richness, variety, and ingenuity of Erickson's stories. The power of story-telling is embedded in the traditions of all religions and cultures. All parents have experienced being corrected by their children if they stray in the slightest degree from the telling or reading of a favorite story.

Almost any story is engaging at the unconscious level. So, why not make use of this therapeutically? Later in this text, we will go into much detail on the construction and utilization of metaphors. We mention them here for completeness since metaphors and analogies are a "language form."

Telling stories is an integral part of the *"class of problems / class of solutions"* model (e.g. see O'Hanlon, 1987) of doing solution-oriented therapy. In this model you first analyze the presenting problem to fit it into a *larger* category or class. For example, enuresis falls into the class of muscle control, as does sexual impotence. Many parent/child problems are in the class of open communication problems. The generalized class of a solution serves the function of a skeleton key that can open many doors. So, the solution can appear in a story or stories dealing with muscle control, communication, not noticing or distraction, self-confidence, etc. Stories "force" an internal transderivational search where the unconscious seeks the meaning(s) unique to that person.

There are many approaches to story-telling. Clients sometimes need to be prepared for story-telling since this is not the normal expectation of a client in a therapist's office. You can say at some opportune time, "I frequently tell my clients stories since most of them find some special helpful meaning in them." You can construct specific or general metaphors following the guidelines presented later. Analogies, with highly specific parallels are useful, as are similes using "like" or "as." Erickson frequently used the "my friend John" technique in which he told stories about his friend. (See Section B.1 in Chapter 8 for the use of "My Friend, John" as an advanced induction technique.) "John" could be any relevant friend. These stories about "John" were isomorphic to the client's difficulties. Telling stories about people you know adds a useful dimension of reality. (Generally, it is better to use people in stories rather than animals.) You can tell relevant personal stories. Shaggy dog stories carry a punch along with humor. Stories can be made more effective if you tell stories within stories. Finally, the psychological literature is replete with "case" studies, which are really stories wrapped in jargon. Do cases provide "anecdotal" evidence, or are they metaphoric teaching tales? Let me tell you a story ...

J. Torpedo Therapy (NLP)

Just as a single torpedo can sink a ship, a single well-phrased intervention can change a client. The components of the "torpedo" are: (1) use of temporal language; (2) use of reframes; (3) implications; and (4) congruence of delivery. These "torpedoes" are designed to be skeleton keys or *class-of-solution* interventions whose "general" nature covers many categories and encourages an internal trance-like transderivational search. Three examples follow.

"And as you sit there, now, your inner mind can wonder as to just how much you have changed, already, looking back on how you used to be, now, and thinking, soon, being, and what have you, will you, do differently?"

"After this session is over, the work that you've started will have continued to be helping in what you have already done this afternoon, now, and you may be surprised, but, then again, not, now."

"And how surprised will you be, now, thinking over what has happened, then, when you soon, now, change to what you have been and had deserved?"

Develop your "torpedoes" and practice them. How much of what we've covered about language forms appears above, and how much more can you add? Pauses and marking are extremely important in delivering torpedoes.

K. Summary

The essence of a verbal therapy like hypnosis is the effective use of language. We have presented many ways of using language in doing psychotherapy. Much of this material is specific to hypnotherapy, but almost all of it can also be used as "hypnotherapy without trance." In the next chapter we will discuss some of the (hypnotically) derived ways of doing hypnotherapy without trance. We also discuss the theory of change to set the background for some of the following chapters. In many ways, the next chapter is an extension of the materials in this one.

How do you learn to incorporate the parts of the enormous menu of language forms presented in this chapter into your daily practice? At the end of each topical area and throughout them are recommended relevant exercises. Perhaps the best way to learn language usage is to study transcripts of masters like Erickson. This can be done by listening to audiotapes, viewing videotapes, reading transcripts, and studying the various annotated transcripts, particularly of Erickson's work, that are available. You can tape your own sessions and critique them, but doing this with others is even more helpful. Write out some interventions and critique them from the point of view of language usage. In your writing be sure to indicate words or phrases you would mark out by pause, volume, intonation, or locus. A really good way to learn is to set up a self-study group with others. Such groups are enhanced, of course, by the presence of a "master" practitioner, but you should realize that you can learn a great deal on your own. You can also go for training at the Erickson Foundation, training given by the various Erickson institutes and societies, at "traveling" workshops, and at the international Erickson congresses. (The Milton H. Erickson Foundation Newsletter lists such programs and is free, although contributions are welcome. Write to: The Milton H. Erickson Foundation, Inc., 3606 N. 24th Street, Phoenix, Arizona 85016.)

There is an enormous amount to learn about language usage. Don't despair—if you learned how to speak English in 2–3 years, you can become adept at hypnotic language in a similar amount of time. Recall the principle of requisite variety and know that the more you know, now, soon, and know how to know and no, the better therapist you will be. In the chapters to follow on inductions and the uses of trance, reference will be continually made back to language forms. Indeed, you cannot do one without the other! Words are, are they not?

Chapter 6

Hypnotherapy Without Trance

Rubin Battino, M.S.

A. Introduction

There are some who say that *all* therapeutic interventions involve some level of trance. Certainly, any time your client goes "inside" to think or to process, there is an element of internal focussing that closes out external inputs to varying degrees. The recollection of past events and feelings naturally evokes a light trance. We have never witnessed, for example, an effective Gestalt Therapy two-chair exercise in which the client was not in a fairly deep trance. To avoid endless academic debates about depth of trance and even its existence in particular circumstances, we will by-pass the argument by considering hypnotherapy *with* trance to involve some *intent* on the therapist's part to induce a trance.

What, then, is "hypnotherapy without trance?" In the previous chapter, we wrote about hypnotic language forms. Those language forms can be used effectively with the client being in or out of the trance state. So, hypnotherapy without trance means using hypnotic language when the client is in the waking state. This does not preclude the client's going into and out of mini-trances as he/she responds to the various suggestions, binds, non-grammatical usage, or ambiguities. The *intent* of the therapist in this approach is to engage the client consciously, but with hypnotic language. For example, you can tell stories regardless of the client's mental state.

In this chapter, we will describe several therapeutic approaches. These ways of doing therapy are intimately intertwined with language, and, as such, cannot be separated from the material in the previous chapter. Reframing is an important and artful use of language. Paradoxical approaches are language based binds. The solution-oriented approach changes the model for dealing with clients both linguistically and temporally. Single-session therapy is a reality, and the recommendations for working within that reality rely heavily on hypnotic language. Other arrangements of this material could have been made: this one seems both logical and teachable to us.

Although much has been written about "strategic therapy," we will not be dealing with it separately here. Some therapists do effective work without planning out their interventions for a particular client. Of course, operating out of a particular model *implies* a plan of action. TA practitioners ask different kinds of questions than RET people, etc. It is nevertheless useful to develop a therapeutic plan tailored to your specific client. Steve de Shazer recommends taking time out in any session to consult with colleagues or yourself. This time out can be used for planning the rest of the session. Strategic therapies use planning (strategies) as well as using the client as a "change agent" to be "injected" back into the system. Change can be brought about by working with an entire family or with a selected member(s).

Since the theory of change is central to the therapeutic process, we begin this chapter with a study of it. Presumably, clients come to you for assistance in changing in some way. Most clients are interested in big investments rather than small change!

B. The Theory of Change

The staff at the Mental Research Institute (MRI) in Palo Alto, California, has long been in the forefront of the study of the nature and processes of psychotherapy, particularly in terms of *logical* analysis. They built on the work of Don D. Jackson, Gregory Bateson, and Milton H. Erickson. One of the most influential people in MRI has been Paul Watzlawick who has a special bent for logical analysis. In 1967, Watzlawick, Beavin, and Jackson (1967) published a basic book whose full title is illuminating— "Pragmatics of Human Communication. A Study of Interactional Patterns, Pathologies, and Paradoxes." To give some idea of the scope of this book, we simply cite the chapter headings. (1) The Frame of Reference. (2) Some Tentative Axioms of Communication. (3) Pathological Communication. (4) The Organization of Human Interaction. (5) A Communicational Approach to the Play "Who's Afraid of Virginia Woolf?" (6) Paradoxical Communication.

(7) Paradox in Psychotherapy. *Epilogue*—Existentialism and the Theory of Human Communication: An Outlook. Although this book was published some thirty-five years ago, the systematic study of language, language forms, communication, and related psychotherapeutic interventions based on these studies is as important and relevant at the present time as when the book was written. This is not to say that the book is easy to read—it is not, unless you have a particular bent of mind. Ericksonians need to go back to this root study.

A more accessible book by Watzlawick, Weakland, and Fisch (1974) was published several years later. In our opinion "Change" is a must read for every psychotherapist because it lays out the principles of how people (and societies, for that matter) change. The study of "change" is inextricably bound up with the use of language and logic. In this section, we will present Watzlawick et al.'s theory of change, giving some relevant examples and extensions.

From a study of Group Theory and The Theory of Logical Types, Watzlawick, et al. (1974) distinguish two different kinds of change. *First-order change* occurs *within* a given system which itself remains unchanged. That is, a system is invariant on the first-order change level. By contrast, *second-order change* involves changing the system itself. This can be characterized as a "change of change," and groups are thus open to change on the second-order change level. Second-order change, therefore, has the appearance of a discontinuity or a logical jump, and to outsiders, appears to be illogical or paradoxical.

First-order change occurs within the system and the main tactic for this type of change is to do *more of the same* or expand the (generally unsuccessful) solution which has already been applied. In this approach, *the (attempted) solution becomes the problem.* First-order change solutions are typical of parents, societies, institutions, government, and the military. If spanking or docking a child hasn't worked, then more disciplinary action will also not work (short of absolute terror). If public housing / welfare / food stamps / drug interdiction / mandatory penalties / capital punishment / military spending have not worked in the past, then the odds are that more of the same will not work. Two exceptions

147

are: increasing food supplies for hungry people, and the use of absolute terror in some form like a gun to obtain compliance. For example, Singapore has an almost non-existent drug problem because of their mandatory death sentence for possessing even small amounts of prohibited drugs. To be an effective therapist, you should find out about which first-order solutions your client has already tried so you know what *not* to do more of, or not at all.

It is the nature of second-order change to appear illogical, unusual, "crazy," unpredictable, and so on, particularly when viewed from within the system. Second-order change is *meta* to or outside the system; its effects are to alter the system itself. A standard illustration is the puzzle of joining the nine dots shown below with four straight lines without lifting the pen from the paper.

•   •   •

•   •   •

•   •   •

If you stay within the bounds of the dots, there is no way to solve the puzzle. You have to go *outside* the implied frame of the dots for a solution. (If you are a student of puzzles, riddles, and intellectual games, you will instantly be aware that these challenges generally require a second-order solution—that is what makes them so challenging!)

Watzlawick et al. (1974) consider three basic ways in which problems are mishandled: (1) action is necessary, but not taken; (2) action is taken when it should not be; and (3) action is taken at the wrong (logical) level. These problem-solving approaches may be characterized as (in same order as above): (1) ignoring the problem; (2) fixing something when it "ain't broke"; (3) first-order solutions like more interdiction or stronger legal penalties for the illegal drug problem.

What are some second-order change strategies? The first is the use of the various forms of paradox as exemplified in: (1) paradoxical intention (promulgated by the founder of logotherapy, Viktor E. Frankl); (2) ordeal therapy; (3) provocative therapy; and

(4) ambiguous function assignment. If you paradoxically encourage a client to do *more* of their presenting symptom and they comply, you change what the client considers to be an *involuntary* response to a *voluntary* one. This frequently brings about rapid change. The second approach is to use reframing, i.e. change the *meaning* of a particular behavior, response, or circumstance. We will review some of these methods in detail in the following sections.

Exercises

In your own words, write out definitions of first- and second-order change. Find examples of first-order change as used by an institution you are familiar with, and within your own relationships. Have you ever tried second-order change tactics? Think of applying second-order interventions where you work and how they might be implemented. Do your more "creative" colleagues use second-order change approaches? Be as far "off-the-wall" as you can in applying second-order change ideas to clients, institutions, the drug problem, health care, alcoholism, co-dependency, writing reports, and so on.

C. Reframing

I still recall the excitement with which I read a paper by John Enright on the concept of reframing when he was starting out in the field. It was such a refreshing and "new" idea and Enright's examples seemed almost magical, and very, very clever. In our training classes, we use a large variety of cardboard frames which the participants try on to "frame" themselves and observe the effect. Artists have long known the value that an appropriate picture frame (or setting) can lend to a work of art. Frame shop owners are expert in finding ways of reframing the same picture to change its impact.

To start our discussion of reframing let us present several quotes from Watzlawick et al. (1974).

> To reframe, then, means to change the conceptual and/or emotional setting or viewpoint in relation to which a situation is experienced and to place it in another frame which fits the "facts" of the same

concrete situation equally well or even better, and thereby changes its entire meaning. (p. 95)

They quote the first century A.D. philosopher Epictetus as saying, "It is not the things themselves which trouble us, but the opinions that we have about these things." (p. 95)

Reframing operates on the level of *meta*reality, where, as we have tried to point out, change can take place even if the objective circumstances of a situation are quite beyond human control. (p. 97)

In its most abstract terms, reframing means changing the emphasis from one class membership of an object* to another, equally valid class membership, or, especially, introducing such a new class membership into the conceptualization of all concerned. (p. 98) *[They take an "object" in its most abstract connotation which includes events, situations, relationships between people, behavior patterns, etc.]

The following three aspects of reframing are emphasized (p. 98–99):

1.   Our experience of the world is based on the categorization of the objects of our perception into classes.

2.   Once an object is conceptualized as the member of a given class, it is extremely difficult to see it as belonging also to another class. This class membership of an object is called its 'reality;' thus, anybody who sees it as the member of another class must be mad or bad.

3.   What makes reframing such an effective tool of change is that, once we do perceive the alternate class membership(s), we cannot so easily go back to the trap and the anguish of a former view of 'reality.'

In a more general sense, one can say that reframing is involved in all successful trance work; in fact, the ability to reframe whatever a subject does (or does not do) as a success and as evidence that his trance is deepening is the hallmark of a good hypnotist. (p. 101)

Reframing ... *teaches a different game,* thereby making the old one obsolete. (p. 104)

We trust that the extensive quotes from Watzlawick et al. (1974) give a clear explanation of reframing. They do provide many examples of reframing in their book.

We have found the following to be useful in terms of how people are stuck.

Stimulus ⇒ Interpretation ⇒ Response(s)

There is some stimulus in a person's environment. They are "stuck" if they only have *one* response and that response is limiting them in ways they do not want or like. Between the stimulus and the response is the possibility of interpreting the stimulus before action is taken. People are also stuck if they have only *one* interpretation for a particular stimulus. In this model, it is the function of the therapist to help the client discover additional and more appropriate interpretations, and to discover additional and more appropriate responses. Reframing works on the interpretation part of this model.

The NLP seven-step reframing intervention works on the response part of the model and, as such, may lie outside of the way we have been defining the term "reframing." Seven-step (in some of the literature it is called "six-step") reframing works well with helping clients change particular behaviors (or *one* particular response). The process guides the client into discovering for him/herself other unique and more appropriate responses in addition to their "traditional" one. The client goes through what is called an "ecological" check to be certain that there are no internal objections to the new responses, and also a "future pacing" which is a kind of behavioral rehearsal to lock in the new behaviors as possibilities in the future. In a sense, the "frame" of possible behaviors has been enlarged.

Bandler and Grinder (1982), in a book devoted to reframing, go over many ways of reframing. One strength of the book is that it is an edited transcript of a training session. This means the reader can study in detail their subtle use of language. Bandler and Grinder make useful distinctions between *context* and *meaning* reframes. Several quotes from their book are helpful.

> Every experience in the world, and every behavior is appropriate, given some context, some frame. (p. 9)

> No behavior in and of itself is useful or not useful. Every behavior will be useful somewhere: identifying *where* is context reframing. And no behavior means anything in and of itself, so you *can* make it mean anything: that's meaning reframing. (p. 13)

> With a complex equivalence you do a *meaning* reframe, and with a comparative generalization, you do a *context* reframe ... For a context reframe, ask yourself, "In what context would this particular behavior that the person is complaining about have value?" Think of different contexts until you find one that changes the evaluation of the behavior. For a meaning reframe, ask yourself, "Is there a larger or different frame in which this behavior would have a positive value?" "What else could this behavior mean?" (p. 15)

Recall that a complex equivalence is when one links a response to a class of events, such as, "Her looking at me that way makes me feel all sad inside." A comparative generalization is generally without a context and uses the word "too" as in "I'm too happy" or "She's too nervous" or "They're too quiet."

In the model presented above, changing the interpretation changes the meaning. Finding some context in which the old fixed response is appropriate also changes the meaning by breaking the involuntary nature of the response and enlarging the frame within which the behavior fits. Once the perspective/interpretation/ frame is changed, then it is no longer possible to "view" the (problem) behavior in the same way. One "standard" reframe that can be used during the first interview is to compliment the client on his/her courage/wisdom in taking care of themselves by confronting their problem and seeking help. "It is not everyone who could be so aware/strong to work on your problem."

One of the best examples of reframing extant is Erickson's handling of a young coed who broke wind in class and was so embarrassed that she dropped out of everything. This case is described under the title of "Whistleberries" in Rosen's book (1982) and is reproduced in Chapter 11, Section C.6. Erickson uses the fact that the girl is a converted Catholic and, therefore, excessively religious to confront her with her disrespect for God.

Showing her an illustration of the rectal area in an anatomic atlas, he asks if any engineer could have made a valve that would contain liquid and solid while permitting *only* gas to pass downward. He then has her bake up a pot of whistleberries (beans, onions and garlic), eat them, and prance around nude and alone in her apartment glorifying God with big ones and little ones! Rather than give more illustrations of reframing, we leave the practice of it to you in the exercises which follow.

Another excellent example of Erickson's use of reframing (and pacing and leading and surprise and ...) is the case that Rosen (1982, pp. 36–37) calls:

Vicious Pleasure

A woman in her thirties arrived and said, "I don't suppose you want to see me." I said, "That's your supposition, would you like to hear mine?"

"Well," she said, "I am not deserving of your attention. When I was six years old my father molested me sexually and from the age of six until seventeen he used me as a sexual object, regularly, several times a week. And every time he did it, I was in a state of fear. I was frozen with terror. I felt dirty, inferior, inadequate, ashamed.

"I thought, at seventeen, I had enough strength to break away from him and I worked my way through the rest of high school, hoping that that would give me a feeling of self-respect, and it didn't. Then I though maybe a bachelor-of-arts degree would give me a feeling of self-respect. I worked my way through college. I felt ashamed, inferior, indecent. It was a terrible feeling of disappointment. I thought maybe a master's degree would give me self-respect, but it didn't. And all through college and graduate school I was propositioned. And that proved I didn't deserve self-respect. And I thought I would enroll for a doctorate degree, and men kept propositioning me. I just gave up and became a common prostitute. But that's not very nice. And some man offered to let me live with him. Well, a girl needs to have food and shelter so I agreed to it.

"Sex was a horrible experience. A penis is so hard and looks so threatening. I just became fear stricken and passive. And it was a painful, horrible experience. This man got tired of me and I began living with another man. The same thing over and over, and now I come to you. I feel like filth. An erect penis just terrifies me and I just get helpless, and weak, and passive. I am so glad when a man finishes.

"But I still have to live. I have to have clothes. I have to have shelter; and essentially, I am not worth anything else."

I said, "That's an unhappy story; and the really unhappy part is— you're stupid! You tell me that you are afraid of a bold, erect, hard penis—and that's stupid! *You* know you have a vagina; *I* know it. A vagina can take the biggest, boldest, most assertive penis and turn it into a dangling, helpless object.

"And your vagina can *take a vicious pleasure in reducing it to a helpless dangling object.*"

The change on her face was wonderful. She said, "I am going to go back to Los Angeles, and can I see you in a month's time?" And I said, "Certainly." She came back in a month's time and said, "You're right! I went to bed with a man and I took a vicious pleasure in reducing him to helplessness. It didn't take long, and I enjoyed it. And I tried another man. The same thing. And another man. And it's pleasurable! Now I am going to get my Ph.D. and go into counseling, and I am going to wait until I see a man I want to live with."

I called her stupid. I *really* got her attention. And then I said, "vicious pleasure." And she *did* resent men. I also said, "pleasure."

The case we'll call "Hugest Fanny" (Gordon and Meyers-Anderson, 1981, pp. 67–69) is one where Erickson utilizes the obvious, makes no bones about what the client must know about herself, and converts that into an asset that leads her into a fulfilling life. He is also very careful to protect her integrity concerning the curing of her hiccups. As you read Erickson's cases, it becomes obvious that he does not need the client's gratitude or adulation for helping them. His clients changed (in ways they desired), but Erickson's work was often so subtle that the client had no idea of Erickson's involvement in their changes.

HUGEST Fanny

Now when I arrived in Michigan at Wayne County Hospital, I encountered a most unusual person. A young girl, medical technician, rather pretty, well-informed except she had the biggest,

HUGEST fanny I had ever seen on any girl. And when she walked down the corridor, I noticed that when she passed somebody, she'd swing her fanny angrily toward that person. Well, that interested me. So I made it a point to keep an eye open 'cause I wanted to see what that girl is going to DO with that great big fanny of hers. And I noticed that every visiting day was her *day off* and at the entrance of the grounds, she met the mothers and their children ... always asked the mother if she could give the children a piece of gum, a piece of candy, a toy, and volunteered to take care of the children while the mother visited the patient. And for a whole year that went on. That seemed to be her entire life, looking after those visitor children, and she gave every evidence of making that her one and only joy in life. So that gave me ANOTHER idea about her. Then one day she suddenly developed the hiccups. She hiccupped night and day. We had a staff of 169 physicians, they all examined her and could find nothing wrong with her and they finally told her she would have to have a psychiatrist consultation. She knew what THAT meant. I'd be the psychiatrist called in and she politely refused to have a psychiatrist called in. So, she was informed she was being hospitalized in Wayne County Hospital for free and receiving her pay, "you're paid even though you're not working, everything is being taken care of for you as if you were fully employed. If you're not going to take medical advice, just resign your position, call a private ambulance and go to a private hospital and get over the hiccups there!" She thought that over and said she'd permit me to see her. So, at two o'clock that afternoon I walked into her room, closed the door behind me, and said, "Keep your mouth shut! Listen! I've got a few things to say to you and I want you to listen 'cause you need an understanding. I KNOW you've got the biggest fanny in creation. I KNOW you don't like it, but it IS yours. And you like children, therefore, you'd like to get married, have children of your own. And you're afraid that great big fanny of yours is a *barrier* ... that's your *error*. You haven't read the Song of Solomon. You SHOULD have read your bible. The pelvis is mentioned as the *cradle of children*." I said, "The man who will want to marry you will not see a great big fat fanny ... he'll see a wonderful cradle for children." She listened quietly. "Men who want to father children DO want a nice cradle for the child." And when I finished my speech, I said, "You can think it over. After I leave keep on hiccupping. There is no reason for anybody except you and I to *know* you don't NEED those hiccups. You have something of great VALUE so let your hiccups disappear around 10:30 tonight, 11 o'clock, that way nobody will say a psychiatrist cured you, that my interview was an utter failure." So her hiccups disappeared around that time. She went back to work, and one day at lunch time while my secretary was having lunch, she

155

came into my office and said, "Here is something I want you to see." She showed me her engagement ring. She said, "I thought you should be the first person to see this." Sometime later she privately brought a young man into the office to meet me—her fiance. They were married shortly and started raising a family. Now reorientation of thinking ... I called her fanny a great big fat fanny, as big as I had ever seen. I told her she hated it, but she didn't *understand* it. Then, I presented it as a cradle for children against my background of knowing how much she liked children. And how a man who would want to father children WOULD want a nice cradle for children. Now, I didn't need to go into the past, I could just discuss the current state of *affairs* ... reorienting her thinking, reorienting her thinking in accord with her own secret desires. I was unafraid to call her fanny a big fat fanny, so she knew I was telling the truth, so she could believe what I said. I don't like doctors who pussyfoot around and try to say things sweetly and gently. The truth should be told simply, straight-forward fashion because that is the ONLY way the patient is actually going to absorb therapy and proceed to benefit. And once you get them reoriented, their nose pointed down the road, they'll go.

Finally, we give an Erickson case involving sexual dysfunction (Haley, 1973, 1986, p. 157) that reframes incompetence into overwhelming love:

Overwhelmed

One of my medical students married a very beautiful girl, and on their wedding night he could not produce an erection. Yet he had been rather a man about town and had slept with every chippy in the city. For two weeks after the marriage he could not produce an erection. He tried everything and could not even get one by masturbation. After two weeks of a dismal honeymoon, his wife consulted a lawyer about an annulment.

The young man came to me with this problem. I told him to call up a few friends who knew his bride and have them persuade her to come and see me. She came to the office, and I had the young man wait outside while I talked to her. She was extremely bitter, and I let her tell me the whole disappointing story. She thought she was attractive, and yet, there she was completely nude and he was incapable of making love to her. The wedding night can be such an event to a girl. It is a momentous occasion which represents being transformed from a girl into a woman, and every woman wants to be wanted and to be the one and only. It was an overwhelming situation, and so I defined it to her that way.

I asked her if she had thought about the compliment her husband gave her. This puzzled her, since it seemed to be a reversal of what she had been saying. I said, "Well, evidently he thought your body was so beautiful that he was overwhelmed by it. Completely overwhelmed. And you misunderstood that and felt he was incompetent. And he *was* incompetent, because he realized how little capacity he had to really appreciate the beauty of your body. Now you go into the next office and think that over."

I called the husband in and I let him tell me the whole sad story of the honeymoon. Then I said the same thing to him. I pointed out what a tremendous compliment he had given to his wife. He had a lot of guilt about previous affairs, but here was his incapacity proving to him that he had really found the one right girl, the overwhelming girl.

They drove home to their apartment together, almost stopping the car on the way to have intercourse, and they were successful from then on.

Exercises

In dyads or triads, have one person be the client, one the therapist, and a possible third the observer/helper. A possible setting is the initial interview. The therapist is to reframe every possible statement made by the client. In a training group setting, one person is in the center and presents a problem or complains. Going around the room, each trainee has to give a good reframe. If they don't, then they move to the center. Or, going around the room, each trainee gives their own reframe. Then someone else can present problems or complaints. Describe one of your clients and ask for possible reframes to use with him/her. Listen to taped sessions and think of reframes to use at different points. In a group setting this can be done with stopping the tape. Think about some of your own personal problems or stuck places—how would you reframe them?

Find a reframe(s) for each of the following:

1. I'm too hardworking.
2. She's too trusting.

3. I find it hard to say no/yes.
4. My husband never smiles ... he doesn't love me.
6. My boss never compliments me ... she doesn't appreciate my work.
7. My analyst says nothing ... he doesn't understand me.
8. I find life depressing / hopeless / impossible / unbearable / meaningless / awful / overly exciting.
9. I don't know why I came to see you.
10. I can't stand the way he ignores me.
11. I've been thinking of killing myself.
12. I can't have orgasms / ejaculate.
13. Studying is much too hard.
14. It's easier to flip out on drugs.
15. My mother / father never loved me.
16. I was an unwanted child.
17. You'd drink, too.
18. I don't know how to lose weight / stop bingeing / be caring / show love / say no / stop smoking / stop overworking / relax / smile ...
19. I've never been in trance.
20. I'm afraid of snakes / heights / closed places / open spaces / driving / flying / doctors / women / men / dogs / life / relationships / giving up control...

D. Paradoxical Interventions

The two primary methods for bringing about second-order change are reframing and the use of paradox. In this section, we will go into some detail on four types of paradoxical interventions: (1) paradoxical intention; (2) ordeal therapy; (3) ambiguous function assignment; and (4) provocative therapy. Writing about these approaches here is somewhat arbitrary since, for example, we have already presented double-binds and the illusion of alternatives which are frequently listed under paradoxical methods.

For convenience, let us repeat a dictionary definition of paradox: 1. A tenet contrary to received opinion; also, an assertion or sentiment seemingly contradictory or opposed to common sense, but that yet may be true in fact. 2. A statement actually self-contradictory or false. Watzlawick et al. (1967, p. 188) give the following definitions: "Paradox may be defined as a *contradiction that follows correct deduction from consistent premises."* Chapter 6 in Watzlawick et al. (1967) gives a rather scholarly treatment of paradoxical communication. This is followed by a chapter on the use of paradox in psychotherapy. There is additional useful information on paradox as used for second-order change in Watzlawick et al. (1974). Finally, Weeks and L'Abate (1982) devote an entire book to various kinds of paradoxical therapy, including working with couples and families. A follow-up book edited by Weeks (1991) includes chapters on a variety of related material, including one by S.R. and C.H. Lankton on Ericksonian styles of paradoxical treatment.

Erickson used paradox and confusion and shock in his successful attempt to help an over-intellectualized couple "procreate" (Haley, pp. 123–126, Vol. II, 1985). Also, see Volumes I and III of this series for many other cases and illuminating commentary.

Fuck for Fun

This college professor in his 30s married a girl in her 30s. They met at a faculty meeting. He took one look at the girl and he *knew* that was the girl he wanted to marry, and how could he meet her? She took one look at him and knew that was the man she wanted to marry, and how could she meet him? So there was a desperate campaign on the part of both of them until they could really get introduced. They had a very warm courtship. They both asked during the courtship one specific thing: Did the other want children? And each did, tremendously so. They agreed that they would make a baby on their wedding night. They were rather prim and rigid and they used professional language. She wanted to know if he was phylopro-genital. He inquired about her maternal instincts.

They agreed that their wedding night should be for purposes of procreation. They agreed that it should be a very, very complete physical union, because there is something in psychosomatic medicine. There should be full participation emotionally, intellectu-ally, and physically. On their wedding night they had intercourse and she had an orgasm, and so did he. Of course, one physical union does not necessarily result in impregnation. I'm just conveying their terminology. Therefore, there should be persistence, repetition. Since the time of ovulation is not necessarily known, they'd better have physical unions daily. Since the sperm cell lives not over 72 hours, probably less than 48 hours, it was only reasonable to have physical union daily. On the weekends to rest in bed, to caress one another, and to bring about psychosomatic responses and to culminate in complete physical union. Sundays and holidays, twice a day. Weekdays, once daily. They were going to procreate. Oh yes, menstruation was not a barrier, neither was pneumonia, a broken leg, or anything. They never missed a day for three years. They both had orgasms.

At the end of three years they came to me rather desperate. They came with this pitiful story. They said, "The unfortunate thing is that in the desperateness of our desire to procreate, we have become emotionally intolerant of each other. Our bodies function normally, but we're losing all the tender emotions, and we look upon the physical union as just a hopeful labor and nothing else. Of course, we make it complete, we both have orgasms, maybe that's a superstitious idea about impregnation, but we feel it should be complete. But it's only a hopeful labor, and we're awfully intolerant of each other so far as tender emotions are concerned. We've both been examined. There's no reason why we should not become parents. But we've reached an emotional impasse, and we wonder if we'll be suitable parents for the child." Such rigidity, it was horrible.

I asked them what they wanted me to do. They said, "Well, you're a psychiatrist. Maybe you can help us." I said, "Well, if you want therapy, I *can* help you. But it won't be very pleasant, because you need shock treatment. Shock treatment that will really knock you into another kind of understanding. Not electric shock, not insulin shock, not metrazol shock, but an emotional shock. You're both very religious, you're both very conscientious, you're both very circumspect. You're both very refined. If you want therapy that will help you, I'll give it to you, but it will be a shock treatment. Do you want it? Think it over, wait awhile." They sat there and looked at each other, and turned to me.

I said, "Well, you've been having a physical union regularly every day for three years. Twice on Sundays and holidays. Whether sick or well, throughout the menstrual period. But why in hell don't you fuck for fun!" You should have seen them stiffen rigidly, holding their breaths. It was a shock. For me to say "hell" and me to say "fuck." Finally they took a breath. I said, "I mean that: Why don't you fuck for fun? Think of it. Why don't you fuck for fun?" I called the wife by her first name and said, "She has a pretty body, she's got nice hips, and she's got a nice breast, in fact, she's got two, she's got twins. She's got nice legs, she's kissable and you know it. And as for you—and I called him by name—you know that you've got the thing that she can reduce in size. So why don't you fuck for fun? And for the next few months you'd better fuck for fun, and pray to God and hell that she doesn't get pregnant and interrupt your fun. Now get the hell out of here. Come back in a week or a month, and tell me how you're getting along. And remember that I meant everything I said."

I saw them about a month later. They didn't come to see me; I drove to their home. I walked in and told them I wanted a drink. So they fixed me a scotch and soda. The embarrassment on their faces. I walked around the house, took a quick look in the bedroom, grinned and said, "This is a delightful drink." I said I was driving by and thought I'd drop in. I was thirsty. Better sit around here an hour and let the drink wear off. How are things going in the department? So, we discussed his teaching. I waited an hour for the drink to wear off. I think that was about a month afterwards. Then about three months later they came in to tell me she was pregnant. How does the body do a thing a like that?

1. Paradoxical Intention

Paradoxical intention was developed by Frankl in 1929 and first discussed by him in a paper in 1939. English language readers probably first came across Frankl's psychotherapeutic approach of logotherapy in his 1959 book entitled "Man's Search for Meaning." The two main therapeutic approaches used within logotherapy are paradoxical intention and dereflection. (Readers interested in more information should consult the literature on logotherapy or write: Viktor Frankl Institute of Logotherapy, Box 15211, Abilene, TX 79698-5211; (915) 692-9597.)

Frankl makes a distinction between symptom prescription and paradoxical intention. In the former, he wants the client to increase a particular response of behavior, such as anxiety. In the latter, he wants the client to do or wish for that whereof he/she is afraid. In other words, in paradoxical intention, it is not the fear itself, but rather its object with which one is concerned. In symptom prescription, for example, a client with a hand-washing compulsion would be given directions to wash his/her hands two or three or *more* times a day than they have been doing. The symptom is exaggerated and overdone. For the same client, the paradoxical intention intervention would be in terms of the germs, i.e. to get as well acquainted with the germs as is possible. It is the underlying fear that is confronted by paradoxically "wishing" for it. With respect to insomnia this would be to urge the client to stay awake. For sexual impotence, the client is urged to avoid sex, to stay away from sex, to only cuddle and pet, but in no circumstance to consummate the act.

Exercises

Since paradoxical intention seems to work particularly well with phobias, compulsions, and performance (or anticipatory) anxiety, think of clients or cases exhibiting these characteristics and develop appropriate paradoxical intention interventions for them. What would you do with clients who: (1) stutter; (2) are enuretic; (3) agoraphobic; (4) have stage fright; (5) panic before taking exams; (6) are afraid of mathematics; (7) are overly concerned about health problems like their hearts or blood pressure or weight; and (8) are excessively neat or sloppy? Paradoxical intention can be self-applied—which of your own behaviors can benefit from this approach, and what would you say to yourself or do?

2. *Ordeal Therapy*

Haley (1984) has covered the systematics of doing *ordeal therapy* and has also given many examples of its use. The cases cited are useful for someone new to this approach to provide models that you can adapt to your own unique clients. The basic idea is that if you make it more difficult for a client to have a symptom than to give it up, then the client will give up the symptom. In traditional psychoanalytic theory, the "mere" giving up of a symptom was not considered to be helpful. But giving up a symptom is a *change* of behavior which Haley and others have found to be both therapeutic *and* long-lasting. The very act of carrying out the ordeal converts involuntary behavior to voluntary behavior. The helplessness and hopelessness disappear in the presence of action.

Haley delineates several characteristics of an ordeal. (1) The ordeal must be more severe than the problem, i.e. it should cause more distress than the symptom. If the initial ordeal is not sufficient to extinguish the symptom, then it can be increased until it does. (2) The ordeal should be related in some way to the symptom as in "let the punishment fit the crime." However, totally unrelated ordeals also seem to work! (3) The ordeal should be something that is good or healthful or beneficial to the client. These include activities that the client wants to do, but has trouble finding the time for such as exercise, healthier diets, reading, filing, studying, cleaning, or any other self-improvement activity. (4) The ordeal must necessarily be something that the client can do within the scope of their health, home, or employment. The client should be able to legitimately object to the ordeal. (5) The ordeal should not harm the client or anyone else or do any damage. (6) Some clients may need to repeat the ordeal over a period of time. (7) The carrying out of the ordeal is linked to the occurrence of the symptom. That is, on any given day during which the symptom appears, the ordeal must be carried through if at all possible. Depending on the nature of the ordeal, it can be carried out immediately, but no longer than twenty-four hours later.

Haley describes six stages of ordeal therapy. (1) The problem must be clearly defined in an operational way so that both therapist and client understand it. What kind of anxiety or depression or compulsion or panic is it? (2) The client needs to be committed to getting over the problem. In solution-oriented therapy terms, is the client a "customer," i.e., ready to work on the problem? *Who* is supplying the motivation? Clients can be helped by the therapist's stressing the gravity of the problem in terms of past history and realistic expectations. Clients may be "hooked" by being told that there is a cure which is fail-safe, but that the client will not be told what it is until the client commits to following the prescription. Many clients carry out the ordeal to prove the therapist wrong! Emphasize that it is the client who actually carries out the ordeal, although the therapist can sympathize with the work involved. (3) An ordeal needs to be selected by the therapist. This is best done with the client's collaboration so it can realistically fit their lifestyle. Ordeals should be very specific with a clear beginning and end. (4) It is important that the ordeal be described with a convincing rationale. The task must be specific and include the actions, the time to do them, and the duration. Ordeals are only done when the symptom occurs. Directions may need to be in written form for some clients. (5) The ordeal is to be continued until the problem is resolved. The typical contract is lifelong. (6) Since the ordeal exists in a social context, then the therapist must be aware of and sensitive to the frame within which the client lives. What effect will the ordeal and the loss of the symptom have on significant others, the workplace, etc.? Neither the client nor the ordeal exist in a vacuum.

There are several types of ordeals. The straightforward ones are things like: (1) doing some form of exercise which should be active enough so the client feels it in the muscles the next day; (2) reading something of use for an hour; (3) house-cleaning of some kind for an hour; (4) other household chores; and (5) writing for an hour. Typically, these straightforward tasks are done in the middle of the night—set an alarm clock to wake you at 3:00 a.m. Paradoxical ordeals are of the nature of symptom prescription. On any given day when the symptom like depression or panic appears by itself, the client is to pick a time to be really panicked for 30 minutes. Some ordeals function in relation to the therapist in terms of defiance or compliance. Monetary ordeals involve the client donating money to a hated cause any time the symptom appears. Ordeals can involve two or more people and include the entire family. In a classic intervention of Erickson's, he had the mother get up with her son in the middle of the night any time the son wet the bed and then supervise his handwriting practice. Finally, it is worthwhile noting that compliance is always voluntary and that the therapist is not some kind of oppressor.

The main problem with ordeal therapy is how to "hook" the client. If you decide to use this approach with a given client, then you need to know them well enough to work with the level of motivation available. There are many examples of the use of ordeal therapy in Erickson's work and in Haley's book.

In the following, we give three examples of Erickson's use of ordeals. He had the authority to convince clients to go along with him.

Insomnia and Dickens

One of my professional cases had insomnia, never got to sleep before two, always awakened at four. He was a hurried man, and had erratic working hours. He hadn't been reading for years. This insomnia had been going on for some 12 years, and I led him out on all the books he had promised himself to read since college. He named this book and that book. He did want to go through Dickens, and he did want to go through Scott. In college, he had promised himself to read some other set of books. I asked him what he thought about all these book reading promises that he had renewed and broken throughout the years. I made him feel as guilty as I could, and I told him there was a cure for his insomnia. He was to go to bed at 11:00 o'clock and, if he was not asleep at 11:30, he was to get up and keep his promises one by one. But he could not sit in a chair and read because he'd fall asleep. He was to fix up the lamp on the mantel and lean on the mantel and read for the rest of the night. (Laughter) He went to sleep at 11:30 very shortly, because he knew if he'd waken at 2, or 3, or 4, he'd be up for the rest of the night standing against the mantel reading and have the guilt feeling for not keeping his promises. That was an evasion for him. He was in to see me a year later, laughing at the "swindle" I had worked on him. But he said, "It's a good swindle. My practice is much better, my income is much better. I am healthy, I am happier, I sleep nights. I am reading some of those books, but I've got a whole set of Dickens waiting in case my insomnia comes back." (Haley, Vol. I, p. 59, 1985.)

Heart Attack

I can think of that man who dominated his wife with his threats of heart attack and dying, and his moaning and groaning, and so on, regularly. In spite of the doctors all saying there's nothing wrong with his heart. It's such a useful way of making life miserable for his wife. I told her to get advertising material from every mortician in town. And say, "Oh, your heart *is* bad." She got advertisements and scattered them all around the house. Every time he mentioned his heart attack, she would say, "Now I must pick up those from that table and arrange them neatly." She was looking at this collection of ads from morticians. He would irately throw them away, but she had others. He didn't dare mention it. But you see, that's vengeful behavior. "You're hurting me, you're annoying me, you're doing it deliberately. What's sauce for the goose is sauce for the gander." She varied it by adding up his insurance policies. She got advertisements for perpetual care and everything else. She would say, "Well, you need a good ride out in the fresh air; let's go see such and such a cemetery." She really had a very vengeful time, and he quit it. The wife would walk over to the telephone, dial the building contractor in her husband's presence, and say, "I hate to bother you again, but do you think you can get the house finished before my husband dies?" He got so that he grabbed that receiver out of her hand and would tell the contractor, "This is a wrong number." He was furious at me for telling his wife what to do. He said he didn't like that.

Nevertheless, he sent me other patients. Oh, about a year and a half later he called me up to ask me how long he ought to spend in Florida away from his work. I pointed out to him that he was a grown man, his wife was a grown woman, and their son was a grown man. That he had enough money so he didn't need to work anymore. He should stay in Florida until the pleasures and satisfactions palled. (Haley, Vol. II, pp. 139–140, 1985.)

Fishing—Without Whiskey

A husband and wife came to see me, and the wife was a pretty bad alcoholic. She was a secret drinker. Every day when her husband came home from the office she would be drunk, and they would have a nightly battle as he raged around the house looking for the bottle. She was mad because he hunted for it. It became a game of skill to find the bottle, as well as a nightly fight.

I found out that his idea of a good weekend was to lean back in an easy chair and read *Business Week* or the *Wall Street Journal* or a book. Her idea of weekend enjoyment was to go out in the yard, work with flowers, and when nobody was looking slip up to her mouth that bottle of whiskey hidden in the ground. She really enjoyed gardening; she also enjoyed the whiskey.

With the two of them in the office, I pointed out that every evening he laboriously tried to find the hidden bottle and she took a gleeful pleasure in hiding it. I told them to continue with exactly that procedure. He was to hunt for the bottle and she should hide it. But if he couldn't find it, *she was entitled to empty it the next day.*

I let them play that little game for a while. It isn't a good game, but he didn't like that hunting and she got too much joy out of it. However, the procedure *robbed her of the privilege of hiding the bottle secretly.* It became a purposeful hiding, not that guilty, shameful, sneaky hiding. It took some of the joy out of it. They had the most astonished facial expressions when I suggested that she hide the bottle and that as a reward it was his if he found it and hers if he didn't. But they had been doing that for twelve years anyway.

The next step was to have him buy a trailer and take her up to Canyon Lake and go fishing—without whiskey. I picked out boating as a recreation because I had found that she was raised in a lake region and she *hated* lakes and fishing. He hated fishing too.

I pointed out to them that being out on the water alone in a small boat without whiskey would keep her sober, which would be good for her health. It would be good for her husband to be out in the open getting some fresh air instead of sticking his nose in a newspaper in sluggishness and inertia.

Predictably, they began to use the trailer, but not to go fishing in a boat. They went camping on weekends, which they both enjoyed. She sobered up and stayed sober, and they began to enjoy themselves. They camped each weekend in all the available areas and gave up their battle. (Haley, p. 239, 1973, 1986.)

Exercises

Look at the list of problems under exercises in the previous section on paradoxical intention. How many of them are suitable for ordeal therapy? What ordeals would you devise for them? What ordeals would you devise for your current clients? How would you "hook" them into carrying out the ordeal? If you were the client, what ordeals would work for you?

3. Ambiguous Function Assignments

Every Ericksonian knows that if you go on a "hegira" to the "Mecca" of Phoenix, Erickson's home for the last part of his life, you are expected to climb Squaw Peak, a mountain in the region that overlooks Phoenix. There is a good path to the top, and the "climb" is not overly strenuous. As in one of the ordeal therapy strictures, you will feel some after effects in your muscles. The view is worth the climb, particularly if you arrange to be at the peak at sunrise or sunset. This climb is famous because Erickson used it a sufficient number of times as an ambiguous function assignment for this intervention to be given special status.

To give you a sense of Erickson's use of ambiguous function assignments, we quote the case summary given by O'Hanlon and Hexum (1990, p. 256–257).

Squaw Peak

A Pennsylvania psychiatrist had been practicing for 30 years and still had not built up a successful practice. He and his wife had been in analysis for a number of years. They came to MHE for marital therapy. On the first day, MHE sent the husband to climb Squaw Peak and he sent the wife to the Botanical Gardens. The husband returned with a glowing report, and the wife returned to say how much she hated it. The next day, MHE sent the wife to Squaw Peak, and the husband to the Botanical Gardens. Once again, the husband was thrilled and the wife had nothing positive to say. On the third day, MHE let them choose what they would do. The husband returned to the Botanical Gardens and the wife bitterly climbed Squaw Peak again. MHE told them their marital therapy was complete and sent them back to Pennsylvania. They looked at him in disbelief.

When they arrived home, they both went out independently. The wife went and quit psychoanalysis and filed for divorce. The husband also quit analysis and went home and started straightening up his practice. (Later their psychoanalyst and his wife came to see MHE. They also ended up getting a divorce.) The husband called MHE and asked him to talk his wife out of getting a divorce, but MHE told them he had not mentioned divorce during their therapy and would not interfere. They both became much happier.

A follow-up showed that the wife had gotten a job and made a life of her own.

Ambiguous function assignments or ambiguous tasks work well with clients who are particularly stuck, striving to do something about it, but who are vague about desired outcomes. Some aspects of this approach follow. (1) Get the client(s) to DO something. The actual physicality of the action breaks introspection and a potential fixation on the mental. The action can get the person out of him/herself. (2) The task or assignment needs to be sufficiently ambiguous, enigmatic, and puzzling to "hook" the client into transderivational and inner meaning searches. WHY were they asked to do this stupid thing? However, the art of selecting an appropriate task is in making it sufficiently isomorphic with the client's problem that there is a good likelihood of their finding their own unique solutions, but not so transparent that the ambiguity of the assignment is lost. In the Erickson case cited above, he could have chosen any two tasks for the couple to follow *separately*. One of Erickson's cases involved a young girl who was having trouble in school (what we would call in modern jargon an "underachiever"). Erickson taught her how to play jacks and got her to roller skate and ride bikes. Carrying odd objects, particularly heavy ones, is a typical assignment. Asking clients to read, observe, study appropriately are also effective. (3) The task cannot be harmful to the client(s) or others. (4) The task can certainly be healthful and/or educational. (5) The therapist needs to imply explicitly or implicitly that the client(s) will discover something of value by carrying out the task. (6) The follow-up is *expectational*— what have they learned that is useful, new, interesting, applicable? (7) The particular task may be repeated if needed. Also, additional features can be added. Were they looking in the wrong place or the wrong way for answers? Were they expecting too much? How much change do they want, now? (8) As in all assignments, the "trick" is in getting the client to comply. Sincerity and congruence of delivery are important. Hooking the client's sense of adventure/curiosity is a good motivator. (9) Finally, consider using ambiguous function assignments when you, yourself, are "stuck" as to what to do next with a particular client. (We should note before closing this section that the Lanktons, in particular, have raised this particular intervention to a high art.)

Here are three cases of Erickson's that can be characterized as ambiguous function assignment or paradox or confusion or ...

At Least One Good Memory

I had a patient come to me in about March. A young girl ... her hair was full of snarls, her dress had tears in it, in her hair a number of safety pins, her stockings were wrinkled, and she said, "I'm depressed. I've got a good job. I don't think anybody can like me. And I decided I'm going to try psychotherapy, but I know it ISN'T going to work, but I'm going to try it for several months and here's the cash to pay you for it. That will *force* me to use all the psychotherapy from March till August." And she *bemoaned* her unhappy state: she had a good job as a stenographer, and there were several young men on the floor where she worked, and whenever she went to take a drink, several men also suffered from acute thirst which she always avoided. One of her defects was she had a part between her teeth, and she told me she was absolutely going to commit suicide in August. And I said, well, she ought to have at least one GOOD memory before she committed suicide, "So, why not really play some prank on somebody?" I persuaded her that what she ought to do is go to the water cooler, take a mouthful of water, and when the young man approached her she should squirt him

169

with water. She said, "That won't do any good." I said, "No, but it'll be a nice memory to carry to your grave." So, she took me at my word. And the next day she went to the water cooler, took a big mouthful of water, and a young man she really liked, but she knew would have no interest in her, approached and she sprayed him! He was startled and the consequences were expectable ... he says, "You little bitch, I'm going to KISS you for that!" She turned and ran and he ran after her, caught her ... two months later they were married. She sent me a number of patients. To argue with her about NOT committing suicide would have been fatal ... why not have a good memory to take to your grave with you? So, she did! She is the mother of teenage children now and enjoying life. Therapy consists of altering the total life situation and reactions and behavior and the interpretations. (Gordon and Meyers-Anderson, pp. 131–132, 1981.)

Telephone Pole by Telephone Pole

Bob could drive on East Van Buren, and West Van Buren, he could drive on North Central, he could drive on Cyprus Street. There were two or three streets in Tempe that he could drive on, and he could drive on Buckeye Road. He could drive out Black Canyon Highway to the city limits. That was all the driving he could do. He said, what on earth would he ever do if East Van Buren ever got blockaded and he had to get back to Tempe? Because that was the only street he could drive on to get to Tempe.

Now what I did with Bob was this. "What happens when you try to drive on the street?" He said, "I faint at the wheel." I asked him if he was sure. He said, "Yes. My heart starts pounding, and I faint." I said, "How do you know?" He said, "I *know*. I've had friends with me in the car, and I've tried, and I pass out at the wheel, and they've had to take charge."

So my approach to him was, "I'd like to have you go up to Black Canyon Highway and note the telephone poles. Drive up to the last telephone pole that you dare drive up to and stop at the side of it. Then look at the next telephone pole. Drive up there about three in the morning. After you've looked at the next telephone pole, start your car up in forward gear and get it going just fast enough so that when you reach the telephone pole safely, you switch off the ignition. Then, you faint as you go past the telephone pole. When you recover, because your car will slow up and you're on the shoulder there," I knew the highway, "when you recover from the faint, wonder if you can get to the next telephone pole. So, put your car into first gear, start it up, release the clutch, and as soon as the engine is really turning, turn off the switch, and see if you get to that third telephone pole before you faint." You know Bob had just a lot of fun, he got some 20 miles. (Haley, Vol. I, pp. 118–119, 1985.)

Deep Squats

E: You can use the concept of energy with your patients. You can say a person is very much like an automobile. You wake up in the morning with a full tank of gasoline, or a full tank of energy, and just running through the day uses up your energy. You go to sleep at night, and you fill up on energy for the next day. You can carry only so much energy within certain limits. Then how are you going to utilize that energy? "You use it all in worrying," I pointed out to a patient who had a ritualistic, phobic, panicky reaction to his television broadcast. Forced panting, breathing, and for 15 minutes he would stand gasping, and gasping, and choking, and his heart would pound, and then, they would say, "You're on," and he'd broadcast over TV with the greatest of ease. But each day he became increasingly more miserable. At first it started with a minute or two; by the time he came to see me, it was built up to 15 minutes. He was looking forward to 20 minutes, 30 minutes, an hour; and it was beginning to interfere with his other work at the station. I gave him that concept of so much energy a day after I found out what his sleeping habits were. As you would expect, rather ritualistic. Always in bed at a certain hour. Always up at a certain hour. After I got that concept of energy pounded into his head, I pointed out to him, why not use up that energy that he spent that way? (Demonstrating panting.) How many deep squats would it take each day?

H: You mean in the morning before he went to work?

E: That's right. (Laughter) I told him that I didn't know how much energy it would take, but that I thought he ought to start out with 25, even though I thought at least a hundred would be requisite. But he could start out with 25. Have you ever done 25 deep squats?

W: Oh my.

H: I don't want to.

E: No, you don't want to.

W: I got to where only a few is more than enough.

E: And his lame legs. You see, I said 100. I thought that would be a requisite number, but we'd start with 25. His lame, sore legs all day long convinced him that he had used up plenty of energy. He had none left over for that. (Demonstrating panting.)

W: So, with something that would make him lame like this, you got it out of the way beforehand, but yet, he had a reminder all through the day.

E: His tendency was to reach down (Laughter) to those sore legs of his.

H: You make it seem so simple, Milton.

(Note: E is Erickson, H is Jay Haley, and W is John Weakland in Haley, Vol. I, pp. 258–259, 1985.)

Exercises

Think of clients who have stumped you with respect to what to do or try next. Would they be good candidates for ambiguous tasks? If your answer is "yes," devise such specific tasks for each of them. The next time you participate in going over cases, suggest ambiguous function assignments for individual cases. What kinds of ambiguous tasks would work with you, personally? Which of your current clients would you give assignments and what would they be? Would such an assignment work with a child? your child? your spouse?

4. *Provocative Therapy*

Robert Lindner (1955) in a fascinating case entitled "The Jet-Propelled Couch" lays out a useful principle of doing effective therapy which may be summarized as follows: in any two-person interaction, it is not possible for both people to be "crazy" at the same time. We obviously exclude residents in institutional settings interacting with each other, but we do include the personnel in those places interacting with individual clients or groups. Briefly, Lindner got so immersed in his client's delusional world that he did not notice when the client stopped being delusional. In fact, for several sessions, Lindner urged his client to provide additional details of a science fiction style fantasy that he (Lindner) was now deeply involved in. You might say that Lindner "pushed" his client out of his delusion.

Frank Farrelly (Farrelly and Brandsma, 1974) generalized and systematized this kind of approach to doing therapy. To get a sense of what provocative therapy is all about, let us quote from various places in their book with page citations:

People change and grow in response to a challenge. (p. 36)

We try to provoke a certain specific type of self anger. (p. 36)

We assume that clients have not changed because they *will* not, and that clients can change if they choose. (p. 37)

Few people other than therapists really believe that man is not responsible for what he does. (emphasis added) (p. 39)

No human group ever existed where a right was given without a corresponding obligation. (p. 39)

... to hold people responsible for their actions gives them hope and dignity ... (p. 39)

The client stresses the 'I cannot.' The provocative therapist firmly believing that the client *will* not, humorously agrees and echoes the doom and gloom messages of psychological determinism in an attempt to provoke the client into admitting that he is not functioning because he will not. (p. 41)

Clients have far more potential for achieving adaptive, productive, and socialized modes of living than they or most clinicians assume. (p. 41)

The psychological fragility of patients is vastly overrated both by themselves and others. (emphasis added) (p. 42)

The client's maladaptive, unproductive, antisocial attitudes and behaviors can be drastically altered whatever the degree of severity or chronicity. (p. 43)

The expression of therapeutic hate and joyful sadism toward clients can markedly benefit the client. (p. 48)

The two central hypotheses of provocative therapy are (p. 52): (1) "If provoked by the therapist (humorously, perceptively, and within the client's own internal frame of reference), the client will tend to move in the opposite direction from the therapist's definition of the client as a person." (2) "If urged provocatively (humorously and perceptively) by the therapist to continue his self-defeating, deviant behaviors, the client will tend to engage in self- and other-enhancing behaviors which more closely approximate the societal norm." The practice of provocative therapy is obviously paradoxical. Humor, honesty, instant feedback, wild exaggeration, confrontation, endurance, provocation, and the willingness of the therapist to talk nonstop are all part of the provocative therapist's armamentarium. The provocative therapist's message is something like, "Never mind your insight, never mind how you feel within yourself, you're still acting like a goofy loon, so how about shaping up in your relationships and behaviors?" Why do clients sit and "take" this severe provocation? They do, because this may be the only person they've ever dealt with who shows they truly understand them by being brutally and openly honest. (Think of the Erickson case with the obese woman whom he greets with a description about how her obesity disgusts him.) Also, the therapist shows by his/her nonverbals a different kind of unconditional acceptance of the client. You have to listen to or observe Farrelly in action to appreciate the power of this method. It should be noted that Farrelly developed provocative therapy working with institutionalized clients, and that a large part of his practice consists of these "difficult" people. This approach may not be your cup of tea, but you should consider learning how to use it (under supervision) for the clients for whom it is appropriate.

Exercises

After reading Farrelly and Brandsma's book, buy or borrow tapes of Farrelly in action and listen to the master at work. Which of your clients would provocative therapy work with? How much permission (and from whom!) would you need to try this approach? A caution here is to only try this method under supervision or under the supervision of an experienced practitioner. Some substance abuse groups work with variations of provocative therapy—what are the similarities and differences?

E. Solution-Oriented Therapy and Hypnotherapy

One of the hallmarks of Erickson's work is the utilization process. Another is his emphasis on the practical—what will work right now? What can we do now so that this person gets what he/she wants so they can leave the office with the change process already started, or occasionally even completed? Erickson rightly felt that a person's "understanding" of the dynamics/history of their problem wasn't necessary for change. He also knew that long-term therapy was not needed for everyone, and that brief and even very brief therapy was effective. Steve de Shazer built (1985, 1988, 1991, 1994) on Erickson's work and developed solution-oriented, brief therapy for use with client(s). His base is the Brief Family Therapy Center in Milwaukee.

Solution-oriented therapy fits into hypnotic language forms since it is the language patterns used that makes it so effective. In this section, we will briefly describe some of the language patterns developed by de Shazer and his group, the extensions developed by O'Hanlon and Weiner-Davis (1989), O'Hanlon's solution-oriented hypnosis (1992), and, finally, the related single-session therapy written about by Talmon (1990).

1. *Solution-Oriented Therapy: Steve de Shazer's Work*

One of the basic points of de Shazer's work is connected to the "class of problems/class of solutions" idea. For a particular intervention to work it does not necessarily have to be the specific key to open the single door leading to the singular solution for that client. In his metaphor, a skeleton or master key can open many doors. Once you have identified the kind of lock or class of problem, then an appropriate master key can make available the relevant class of solutions, or an effective member of that class. One aspect of this approach is to accept symptoms at face value, and then to transform the symptom into part of the solution. Symptoms are not to be feared or eliminated, but utilized, since they are unique manifestations of that particular person.

In his approach De Shazer (1985) delineates six assumptions. They are quoted below:

(1) Complaints involve behavior brought about by the client's world view.

(2) Complaints are maintained by the client's idea that what they have decided to do about the original difficulty was the only right and logical thing to do. Therefore, clients behave as if trapped into doing more of the same. (cf. first-order change!)

(3) Minimal changes are needed to initiate solving complaints and, once the change is initiated (the therapist's task), further changes will be generated by the client.

(4) Ideas about what to change are based on ideas about what the client's view of reality might be like without the specific complaint.

(5) A new frame or new frames need only be suggested, and new behavior based on any new frame can promote client's resolution of the problem.

(6) Brief therapists tend to give primary importance to the systemic concept of wholism: a change in one element of a system or in one of the relationships between elements will affect the other elements and relationships which together comprise the system.

Study these six assumptions and think about how they impact on your mode and philosophy of doing psychotherapy. The last one is of particular interest in family and couples therapy. In the beginning, if you will, clients were always seen alone since this was the psychoanalytic model, even if the problem(s) involved others. With the development of couples and family therapy, it slowly became the norm to see the entire unit and, for some therapists, the extended family or system. Recently, therapists have come to understand that you can work with *one* member of a system and "insert" that member back into the system as a "change agent." This idea is particularly important when only a portion of the system you have requested to see shows up at a session.

The central idea of solution-oriented or -focused therapy is simply that: the orientation is on *solutions* and *not* on problems. Although it is the case that clients frequently feel "obligated" to talk about their discomforts / problems / pains / symptoms, change comes about more quickly if you focus on solutions, what has already changed, and *exceptions* to complaints that the clients brought in.

After all, it is not even theoretically possible to be depressed *all* of the time. There must be moments, hours, days when you function normally. What is different about these times? How do you bring them about or let them occur? Take the debilitating problem of migraine headaches—they do go away after one, two, three or more days. So, the body already knows how to get rid of migraines. Why not do it faster? Why not bring the healing or curative mechanisms in earlier, or even *before* the migraines start? Look for *exceptions* to a particular problem and extend and expand them. Are there times you get along well with your husband / wife / child / parent / boss? What was different about those times and how can they be extended? The emphasis is on extending what works.

A crystal ball can be used for the client to see a time when the presenting problem has been resolved to their satisfaction. This is solution-focused and empowering. A key question is, "What will things be like for you and others when the problem is solved?" Establishing the existence of a problem-free time is a reframe. Near the beginning of the first session the client will be asked, "And what changes have already occurred in your life since you made this appointment that you would like to continue?" Surprisingly, over 50% of the clients have already begun beneficial changes (see O'Hanlon and Weiner-Davis, 1989)! Effective therapy starts with the initial contact to make an appointment, and such contacts should be structured in a facilitative way. Toward the end of the first session the "first session formula task" is given, "Between now and next time we meet, we [I] would like you to observe, so that you can describe to us [me] next time, what happens in your [pick one: family, life, relationship] that you want to continue to have happen." (de Shazer, 1985, p. 137) The second session would open with an inquiry about what changes *have already* occurred or started.

Another powerful way of focusing on solutions is to ask the "miracle" question, namely, "Suppose that one night, while you were asleep, there was a miracle and this problem was solved. How would you know? What would be different? How will your [pick one: husband, wife, family, boss, parents, friends] know without your saying a word to [pick one: him, her, etc.] about it?" (de Shazer, 1988, p. 5) This question can be used almost any time, but preferably in the first session. The emphasis is on solution and change and not on what has been and what hasn't worked. (This question is different than the Adlerian one of, "If you could have anything or be any way you wanted, what would that be?" Typically, according to Adlerians, clients select that which they are most afraid of! This is interesting, but not geared to solutions.)

We will describe just one more solution-oriented intervention in this section and that has to do with "as if" behavior. Since people live most of their lives *outside* of therapists' offices, they must have already in place various coping skills to just get by in their family or at work. In other words, people know how to act "as if" they were okay in most circumstances. You can get your client to try the following experiment (de Shazer, 1988, p.181): "Each night, before going to bed, predict whether or not you will be able to really fool people the next day. Then, before you make the following day's prediction, account for any and all differences between your previous night's prediction and the results. Don't just go by your feelings, size up the reactions of your [pick one or more: husband, wife, mother, father, child, boss, etc.]." Note the use of expectational language.

For a fuller understanding of solution-oriented therapy, peppered by many case studies, read de Shazer's books (1985, 1988, 1991, 1994), the excellent book by O'Hanlon and Weiner-Davis (1989), Cade and O'Hanlon (1993), and Miller and Berg (1995).

2. *Solution-Oriented Hypnosis: O'Hanlon*

Although there is now a book with the title "Solution-Oriented Hypnosis. An Ericksonian Approach," (O'Hanlon, 1992), it would be safe to say that what distinguished Erickson from other therapists of his time, was the solution-oriented focus of his hypnotherapeutic and psychotherapeutic work. O'Hanlon's book is an excellent summary of solution-oriented hypnosis in the Ericksonian tradition. A valuable feature of this book is that it is a verbatim transcript of a two-day workshop and, as such, you get exposed to the rich use of subtle language. The two main illustrations that O'Hanlon uses are sexual abuse cases and pain control.

3. Single-Session Therapy: Talmon

A study of Erickson's cases (see O'Hanlon and Hexum, 1990) will show that he was a master of brief therapy and that many of his cases were examples of single-session therapy. Talmon (1990) has done a great service to the psychotherapeutic profession by reporting on the "hidden" literature and the prevalence of single-session therapy (SST). Until the appearance of Talmon's book and the research done by him and his colleagues, the accepted wisdom by many professionals was that the only way to do therapy was long-term, or by the "fringe" as brief therapy of up to four or five sessions.

Let us first summarize some of Talmon's findings. In a study of Kaiser Permanente records he found that the most frequent length of therapy for *every* therapist in the study was a single session and, further, that thirty percent of *all* patients chose to come for only one session in the period of one year. Interestingly, the therapeutic orientation of the therapist had no impact on the percentage of SSTs in their total practice. A related effect was that patients seen for only one session showed a significant decline in their overall use of medical facilities. Talmon found that therapists have much more difficulty accepting the phenomenon of SST than do their clients. Since between thirty and forty percent of first appointments in public settings are not kept, it is important to do a phone call within a day of the initial contact. They did follow-up studies (usually three months) for clients who were in the SST study and found that useful change occurred for sixty to seventy percent of the clients. It is important that the follow-up phone calls not be done by the therapist.

Talmon gives useful information on how to structure the single-session, the initial contact, and the ending of the session to maximize the therapeutic effect. One word of advice is worth quoting (p. 117), "Viewing each and every session as a whole, complete in itself, can serve as an alternative attitude not only toward SST but toward each and every session of psychotherapy." The solution-oriented approach championed by de Shazer appears to be the best one for SST. Since SST is so common, professionals need to be realistic and work towards maximizing the effectiveness of that singular opportunity. The phenomenon of SST does not rule out brief or longer-term therapy, and Talmon does indicate the kinds of clients most suited to each.

Exercises

First, take stock of your orientation as a therapist. Are you problem- and symptom-oriented or solution-focused in your work? Think about the implications of switching your emphasis to a solution-oriented one. Go over your recent clients and any tapes you have of the sessions with an eye/ear to finding where you could have changed the focus. Try the crystal ball, miracle question, and end-of-first-session task on some clients or in practice dyads. How diligently do you search for "exceptions" and what use do you make of them? Try the "as if" experiment with appropriate clients. As you shift to a solution-oriented focus do you notice any changes in yourself? How do you feel about doing therapy? How do you feel about your clients? Consider a shift to a solution-oriented approach as a *reframe* of psychotherapy.

F. Summary

In this chapter, we have discussed the theory of change and given examples of both first- and second-order change. In addition, a number of therapeutic modalities that rely on hypnotic language forms were described. It is not necessary for a hypnotherapist to always use formal trance. In fact, Erickson's standard reply to being asked to do hypnosis was something like, "I shall certainly use hypnosis if that is what is best for you. Let's talk first. That reminds me of a story ..."

Chapter 7

Basic Inductions

Thomas L. South, Ph.D.

A. Introduction

The beginning student in hypnotherapy often wants to learn everything at once. Therefore, this chapter presents numerous basic methods for inducing hypnosis. Since the type of response that an individual makes to induction suggestions are a function of the suggestions *and* the individual's expectations, there are infinite ways of inducing trance. Reference will also be made to the indications of trance. The presented formal inductions are divided into traditional and non-traditional induction procedures. In the traditional section, we will present several of the most conventional standard induction procedures and will incorporate preinduction tests as part of the induction procedure. In the non-traditional section, numerous naturalistic inductions will be presented with both direct and indirect suggestions. We believe that this approach will enable students to become more skilled in working with varied and unique individuals.

Before any hypnosis procedure is initiated, you are reminded to have a preliminary discussion about hypnosis with clients as discussed in previous chapters. It has been our experience that most individuals will have some of the misconceptions mentioned earlier. All questions should be answered and fears sufficiently alleviated. Thus, enough time should be allotted for this session. This can make the difference between a smooth, successful induction, and failure by an apprehensive client. Also, remember to ask if they wear glasses and have them with them. This may eliminate eye-fixation inductions. Ask them to remove eye glasses, if not needed for the induction. Inquire as to any physical disabilities or injuries that might hinder specific hypnotic phenomenon, e.g., levitation, catalepsy, and so on.

B. Traditional Inductions

The traditional approach uses rituals and repeated verbalizations to limit or restrict the person's behavior, as well as to produce fatigue and similar reactions. For example, objects are held a certain distance from the eyes to fixate attention: revolving mirrors, flashing lights, cryptic eyes, spirals, swinging pendulums, etc. Many traditional hypnotists also have softly lit studios and have clients listen to soft music or soothing sounds (flowing water, ticking clock, metronome) to repeated suggestions of comfort, relaxation, drowsiness and sleep while sitting on a comfortable chair or lying down on a sofa. Suggestions are direct and sometimes challenging during the trance state, including the suggestions for awakening.

The following inductions are offered as examples of the *conventional* approach. Study how the tests of susceptibility and the indications of trance are incorporated as part of the induction process. These examples are paraphrased scripts from a book on traditional hypnosis (Teitelbaum, 1978).

1. *Induction #1 - Rapid Induction Technique*

This technique is based on the idea of *relaxation* and it is highly recommended for the novice student since the individual is not asked to do anything. It is also recommended to an individual as an introduction to hypnosis. This technique suggests that all responses are only the result of sufficient relaxation. The individual is informed that incomplete responses are the result of insufficient relaxation and suggestions are made for deeper relaxation. When the eyelids close, a light trance is assumed. If anesthesia occurs, the individual is considered to be in a deep trance. The writings of Jacobson (1938) and Benson (1975) on relaxation can also be effectively incorporated in the following hypnotic inductions paraphrased from Teitelbaum.

> I understand that you believe that hypnosis could help you relax more. Just lean back into a comfortable position and relax by taking a deep breath, and exhale. See how much better you feel. Now, take another deep breath and exhale. Now, you're twice as relaxed as you were. (Repeat the deep breathing exercise until the individual appears more comfortable.) Now, Mrs. Mathews, would you like to

relax further? All right, let me show you how. (Hypnotist lifts her left hand with his right hand and, while holding her hand, extends his left hand, palm down, on a horizontal plane approximately six inches above and away from her eyes.) I'm going to hold my hand here in front of your eyes. All you have to do is gaze at my little finger and don't take your eyes off it. In a moment, I'm going to lower my hand and, as you keep your hand still, I want your eyes to follow my little finger. As you feel that pull on your eyelids, they will gently close, and leave them closed. (Slowly lower the hand smoothly down and curve it under the chin.) Now, they are closing and closing and closing. Now, keep them closed. (Repeat until closure. Then, place the other hand in the lap.) Now, relax them completely. If you relax them completely, they won't open. When you feel that your eyelids are completely relaxed, you can test them but they won't open. Now, test them. See, they won't open. (If they do, repeat from the beginning.) Good, you're doing fine. Now, I'm going to show you some amazing things that you can do while completely relaxed, and let those relaxed feelings spread through your entire body. (Pick up the right arm and stretch it out straight and parallel with the shoulder.) I'm going to pick up your arm and stretch it out as far as it will go safely. Now, stretch out the fingers and, because the body is so relaxed, you can make the arm so stiff it will seem like a steel rod. Now, feel the muscles getting very stiff, stiffer, stiffer and stiffer. (The other hand can pat the arm on various places in order for her to feel how stiff the muscles have become.) Now, you can no longer feel joints in your arm as it get stiffer, and the harder you try to bend it, the stiffer it becomes, because your body is so relaxed. Try to bend your arm. See, you cannot bend it. It is completely rigid. Now, I'm going to relax that arm, and when I relax it, your entire body will become five times more relaxed. When I count to three your arm will be completely relaxed and your body will become completely relaxed. One-two-three, and now you're completely relaxed. (If the arm falls limply, there is a deep trance. If it falls at an angle into the lap, she has not completely accepted the suggestion.) That is fine. Now, I want you to make a real tight fist and a very interesting thing will happen. As you make the fist tighter, it will seem like a steel ball. When I tell you to open that hand, the harder you try to open it, the tighter it becomes. The muscles won't open it, and the tighter it will become. Since it is tight now like a steel ball, you can try to open it. See, it won't open. Now, I'm going to relax the hand and, when I relax it, your entire body will become twice as relaxed. One-two-three, relax. (Pick up the hand and see if it falls limply.) Now, I'm going to show you something even more amazing. Something you have never done before. I'm going to put a cool liquid on your hand, and as you feel that cool sensation, your hand will become completely numb. (Rub alcohol on the back of the hand.) Now, feel that cool sensation, and as you feel it becoming cool, it will now become completely numb. You can feel nothing on that area except a slight pressure. (Insert a sterilized pin or needle.) See, you feel nothing but a slight pressure. Because you are so relaxed, you have made your hand completely numb. Now, I will show you how to remove that numbness. All I have to do is rub that area and the numbness will immediately disappear. (Rub the hand.) Now, I will awaken you from this relaxed state at the count of three and you will have no discomfort and feel as if you had several hours of good sleep. You will feel relaxed all over and the next time I proceed to place you in this relaxed hypnotic state, you will enter easily and quickly. One-two-three, gently open your eyes. You're awake now and feeling fine.

In this induction, the hypnotist refers to the hypnosis session as "relaxation" and has her lean back in the chair and take several deep breaths until he sees her face become flaccid and observes slower respiration. This pre-induction relaxation is intended to relieve anxiety and to demonstrate that she can relax. Lifting the hand is a way of diverting her thoughts and to have her concentrate on the physical sensation of touch and to cause her to wonder what he is doing. The little finger (or any object) held six inches above eye level causes eye strain and fatigue. Following the finger downward closes the eyelids, as the relief is readily accepted. After the eye closure, the first test of susceptibility is made by directly suggesting that she cannot open her eyes due to being completely relaxed, but she is told that she cannot open them after the challenge is made and her attention is diverted to another topic. Also, the likelihood that she would consider opening her eyes is remote. Notice that the hypnotist always tells her what to expect before he touches her. This is to prevent a startle reflex, maintain rapport, and to stay within ethical guidelines. Lifting her arm and extending it allows him to gauge resistance and trance level. The ability to do this evaluation comes with experience. Having her extend her arm also permits several tests of susceptibility (catalepsy and rigidity), as well as the acceptance of suggestions. The "power" of the hypnotist is demonstrated by his ability to relax her arm at the command of three. Notice that the induction continues even if there is only a partial acceptance of the arm falling. In our experience, the clenched fist suggestion has always been accepted, probably because it can be done easily by anyone without a handicap. However, the next challenge of susceptibility is quite interesting. While a person is clenching a fist, it is difficult to release that tension quickly: the mind needs time to reverse the opposing message to the muscles before the next direct suggestion. "The harder you *try* to open it, the tighter it becomes. The muscles won't open it, and will get tighter instead." The "power" of the hypnotist is then demonstrated a second time by relaxing the hand at the count of three. Although quite amazing to an individual already in trance with eyes closed, the hypnotist's power is again demonstrated by "putting a cool liquid on the hand" and creating numbness. The cool liquid causes a surprising sensation on the skin since alcohol has a mild anesthetic and cooling effect. If the pin prick penetration is immediately performed, the anesthetic feeling can only be the result of the alcohol. However, if she accepts the suggestion of numbness after the alcohol evaporates, then she is experiencing hypnotic anesthesia—a hypnotic phenomenon. The hypnotist then demonstrates his "power" again by removing the anesthesia by rubbing the hand and stimulating the blood flow. Then, a standard counting procedure is used for awakening with suggestions of well-being. Re-orienting one's self is another indicator of trance, as well as feeling well-rested.

2. Induction #2 - Relaxation Technique

This relaxation approach is not a rapid induction technique, but it is a fail-safe induction for almost everyone. Hence, it is also highly recommended for the novice student. The length of time varies from individual to individual and can take as long as an hour. However, most people enter some level of trance within 30 minutes during the first session. This technique is usually used with individuals who experience anxiety, exhibit resistance, or generally have difficulty relaxing. The object of the induction is to have the client concentrate on small sections of the body, and then to tense and relax those muscles until the entire body is relaxed.

> Mr. Jones, I want you to settle back in that chair and get as comfortable as you can. Now, take two or three deep breaths and slowly exhale, and feel yourself becoming relaxed. Now, just close your eyes and listen to my instructions and you will learn to relax various muscles of your body and to enjoy those pleasant relaxed feelings.

Now, I want you to think about your left hand. Now, clench your left hand, making a fist by curling the fingers into the palm of your hand. Clench it very tightly. Study the tension in your fingers, your hand and in your forearm. Now, relax your hand. Let it rest comfortably and notice the difference between tension and relaxation. Once again, clench your left hand. Clench it very tightly. Study those tensions. Now, relax your hand noting the difference between tension and relaxation. Now, think about your right hand. Clench the right hand into a fist by curling the fingers into the palm of the hand. Clench it very tightly, and study the tension in your fingers, your hand, and in your forearm. Now, relax your hand. Let it rest comfortably, and notice the difference between tension and relaxation. Once again, clench your right hand. Clench it very tightly. Study those tensions. Now, relax your hand noting the difference between tension and relaxation. Now, notice the relaxation that is gradually coming into both hands. Now, stretch both arms out in front of you with palms down, even with your shoulders. Now, make a fist with both hands. Clench your fists. Tighten the muscles in your arms. Now, feel that tension so tight as if your arms are like steel rods. Study those tensions. Hold it. Now, relax your arms and let them fall softly into your lap noticing the difference between tension and relaxation. Now, raise the arms again and stretch them out in front of your body. Make a fist with both hands. Tighten the muscles in your arms until they become as stiff as an iron rod. Study those tensions. Now, relax and let your arms fall into your lap noticing the difference between tension and relaxation. Now, notice how much more relaxed your arms are becoming. Now, I want you to think about your forehead. Now, tense it up by wrinkling your forehead. Tense it. Study that tension. Now, relax your forehead. Smooth out those wrinkles noticing the difference between tension and relaxation. And one again, tense the forehead. Wrinkle it up. Study that tension. Hold it. Now, relax the forehead. Smooth out those wrinkles noticing the difference between tension and relaxation. Now, I want you to tense your eyes by closing them tightly. Study that tension, and now relax. Once again, close your eyes tightly. Study that tension and relax now. Let the eyes feel loose and relaxed. Now, press your tongue up into the roof of your mouth so that you are tensing the muscles that control the movement of the tongue. Study that tension, and now relax. Let the tongue drop to the floor of the mouth and rest comfortably. Once again, push your tongue up into the roof of your mouth. Feel that tension, now relax. Now, clench your teeth together as tightly as you can (safely). Feel that tension in your jaw muscles. Study it, and now relax. Again, clench your teeth together as tightly as possible. Study that tension. Now, relax your jaw muscles. Now, just feel how relaxed your entire head has become and allow it to relax even more. Know that any time you feel tension or a headache that you can do this simple head relaxation exercise and alleviate those tensions, feeling a sense of relief. So, now, just take a few moments and enjoy those feelings of comfort and relaxation ...

Now, I want you to bend your head forward and try to push your chin into your chest tensing the muscles in the front of your neck. Feel that tension, and relax. Let the head go back to where it was. Now, bend the head forward again pushing the chin into your chest. Feel that tension. Now relax those muscles by raising the head back up. Now, lean your head backwards as far as it will go safely and comfortably. Feel that tension. Now, relax by raising the head back up. Once again, lean the head backwards. Feel that tension. Now, relax those neck muscles by returning the head to its original position. Now, feel how much more relaxed your neck muscles have become. Now, shrug both your shoulders up towards your ears, trying to touch your ears. Feel that tension in the shoulders and on the back muscles. Now relax and drop your shoulders, noticing the difference between tension and relaxation. Once again, shrug the shoulders upwards trying to touch your ears. Study that tension in your shoulders and back. Now relax by dropping your shoulders, noticing how much more relaxed your shoulders and back have become. Now, I want you to take a deep breath and tense your stomach muscles by pushing it outward. Hold it. Study that tension. Now relax. Once again, taking a deep breath, hold it, push out the stomach, feel that tension and now relax. Now, take a deep breath by sucking in the stomach. Hold it. Feel that tension and slowly exhale as you continue to tense the stomach muscles. Now relax. Once again, take a deep breath by sucking in the stomach. Hold it. Feel that tension. Now feel how much more relaxed the upper body has become and enjoy those feelings for the next few moments.

Now, I want you to raise your legs and tense your thigh muscles as tightly as you can. Feel those large muscles tense up. Now relax by allowing your legs to slowly lower until your feet are flat on the floor. Now, raise those legs up again. Tense those thigh muscles tightly. Now relax, allowing your legs to return until your feet are resting comfortably on the floor, noticing the difference between tension and relaxation. Now, raise your legs up again and tense the muscles in your calves by pointing your toes toward your face. Hold it. Now relax and lower your legs. Now, once again, raise your legs up and tense your calf muscles by pointing your toes towards your face. Hold it. Now relax, letting your feet rest comfortably on the floor. Notice the difference between tension and relaxation. Now to completely relax the body, raise your legs as before and tense the other set of calf muscles by curling the toes downward, as if you were burying them in sand, so that you can feel the tension in the arches. Study that tension. Now relax, noticing the difference between tension and relaxation. Now raise your legs once again. Curl the toes downward and tense up the rest of the tension in the body. Hold it. Now relax by letting the legs slowly drift downward until the feet are resting comfortably on the floor. Now enjoy those comfortable feelings of the body being completely and totally relaxed letting all the tensions of the day float away. Now just enjoy those pleasant feelings.

Now, let your mind wander to any pleasant scene. It can be a real place or an imaginary one. You can be by yourself or with someone else. A place that is special to you. One that is serene, peaceful and relaxing. It doesn't matter if it is a mountain scene, a forest, or a sandy beach. Any place that your unconscious, your inner mind, wants to take you. A place where you can get away from all the stress and tension of the day.

Now, you know that you can relax and how you can make yourself relaxed. Now, we have gone through a whole series of exercises and you can practice this at home on a daily basis. And the more you practice these exercises the easier it will be for you to become relaxed. Now, we have done the whole series, but you have also learned how to relax specific muscle groups. If you have a headache, you may only do the head and/or shoulder exercises. If your legs are fatigued, you may only do the thigh and calf exercises. If you only want to relax briefly during the day, you may only do the hand and arm exercises. Any part of the series will make that muscle group relaxed. After you are relaxed, you can simply say the word "tranquility" slowly to yourself and return to your very pleasant scene, and simply enjoy these moments as you are now. Try it—tran-quil-i-ty—and feel yourself relaxing even more.

Now, I'm going to awaken you, but you can awaken yourself by repeating this awakening technique to yourself the next time you are in this pleasant experience. I'm going to count backwards from five to one and at the count of five, you will prepare yourself to awaken. At the count of four, you will become slightly awake. At the count of three, you will become half awake. At the count of two, you will be almost awake. At the count of one, you will open your eyes and become completely awake. Now, I'm going to begin counting: five, four, three, two and one. Wide awake and alert now.

Hi, Mr. Jones. How are you feeling? Look around this room. Does it appear different? Is it brighter or duller than before? Is your vision sharper? Now, you feel very relaxed, don't you? You can stretch if you want to and feel very awake. Do you know how long you were in a trance? Can you remember what we did or have you forgotten it? Do you think you could begin practicing this every day beginning tomorrow? This is your homework assignment.

The beginning of this induction is similar to the preceding induction in that the individual is instructed to take several deep breaths to relax, but with the simple direct statement to close the eyes. Instructing individuals to close their eyes and to take deep breaths is a good practice for preparing an individual for hypnosis. It is non-threatening and usually meets the client's expectation of inducing hypnosis. "Listen to my instructions" or "listen to my voice" are standard practice in the traditional method and quite effective. The muscle tension and relaxation exercises are a modification of Jacobson's Deep Muscle Relaxation Technique for Alleviating Tension in Office Workers (Jacobson, 1938). If imagery is used for the tension-reduction exercises instead of actual physical performance, it would be similar to Benson's Progressive Relaxation (Benson, 1975). The beginning exercise is done with the dominant hand since that hand is more tensed than the other hand. It is also a good idea to tense and relax this hand three times, and then two times for the rest of the muscle groups because of the additional tension on those hand muscles compared to the others. Although the sequence of the series can be altered, this sequence is offered because of the seemingly logical connections of the muscle groups. Also, the symbolism of "going down the body" usually indirectly suggests a deeper trance. As individuals relax, their respiration becomes slower, facial features become smooth and flaccid, and there is a swallowing reflex that soon diminishes. As individuals enter the trance stage, they respond to instructions with an expectancy for the next instruction. Motor responses become slower and there is usually body immobility—until they are instructed to move. During the stretched-out arm exercise, it would be quite easy to just leave the arms there in a cataleptic state "under the hypnotist's control." Another indication of trance is the following of every instruction for tensing and relaxing the muscle groups. This also increases the likelihood of compliance with further instructions. After complete relaxation has occurred, the individual is now ready to be given hypnotic suggestions. The suggestions here are related to the pleasant imagery that the individual is experiencing, which increases the chances that the suggestions will be followed. The direct therapeutic suggestions are:

1. practicing these techniques
    a. when stressed
    b. before retiring
    c. during breaks
    d. beginning tomorrow

2. practicing muscle relaxation

3. imagery of a pleasant place

4. "tranquility" as a post-hypnotic cue

The awakening procedure is similar to the preceding induction (#1) with the exception of counting backwards. This is changed just to show another procedure. Notice the awakening. How does the individual look, especially the face? Are the eyes glassy? Pupils dilated? How does the person re-orient his body? The asking of questions serves several purposes:

1. continuous hypnotic suggestions, e.g. "Is your vision clearer or sharper?" "Is this room brighter?" "You can practice this."

2. increasing wakefulness

3. indication of amnesia

4. subtly verifying the trance experience

5. confirming that the person feels better already and that something was done to them; feeling more rested usually increases rapport.

Remember, terminating trance is just as important as inductions and therapeutic suggestions. A good dessert after a meal even produces a good memory of an average entree.

3.   Induction #3 - The Guided Imagery Technique

Therapeutic suggestions were placed within the imagery section of the preceding induction. Guided imagery can also be used as an induction with individuals who have good visual imagery. The first imagery inductions are items from susceptibility scales. If the individual complies with the suggestions, trance has begun, and you have a cooperative "subject." This induction utilizes imagery for levitation. (How can you use the same *style* of this induction for auditory and kinesthetic clients?)

Mrs. Johnson, you have come here to learn something about hypnosis. Let's see how easy it will be for you to enter trance. So, just settle back in your chair, close your eyes and become comfortable. Let your hands rest comfortably in your lap for the next few moments. Now, I'm going to lift your hands up (horizontal with the body). Now, I want you to imagine a helium balloon tied to a finger on your right hand, and your left hand is holding a bucket of sand. That is a large helium balloon tied to your finger. And you can feel that string tied comfortably to your finger and it is being tugged upward by the large balloon. Now in a few moments, you will be able to feel that finger lifting upwards as it is being tugged. And as it begins to lift upwards, the whole hand begins to lift upwards. (Keep repeating until there is movement in the finger, then the hand.) As the hand lifts upward, it becomes lighter and lighter and lighter (hand lifts) and lighter as it lifts upwards. At the same time, that bucket of sand is becoming heavier and heavier as the other hand becomes lighter and lighter. And the left hand begins being pulled downward the heavier the bucket becomes, as if there is five more pounds of sand added. And the heavier it becomes, the lighter and lighter your right hand becomes, lifting and lifting, and heavier and heavier until you can no longer hold that bucket of increasing weight. Heavier and heavier the lighter your hand becomes. And as your left hand rests comfortably in your lap, your right will become suspended in mid-air. Now when I tap your left hand it will slowly and gradually begin to feel lighter and lighter until it begins lifting upwards and the right hand will begin drifting downwards simultaneously with the upward movement of your left hand (tap left hand). Now it is beginning to feel lighter and lighter and lighter (repeat until hand lifts). Lighter and lighter and the right hand is now drifting downward, the lighter the left hand becomes (repeat until the hands have reversed). Now, you know that you are in a deep trance, a comfortably deep trance, and know that you can go easily into a trance during our next session. And you can look forward to learning more about hypnosis.

This next induction is not only an imagery induction, but it is also used as a deepening technique and for age regressions.

Mr. Smith, make yourself comfortable and close your eyes. As you listen to my voice and follow my instructions, you will find yourself going into a comfortable, relaxing trance. Now, I want you to imagine being safely and comfortably in an elevator on the top floor of a building. Say, the twentieth floor. You are looking at the lit floor number as the elevator begins to make its descent. You can feel yourself going down, down, down to the next floors and see the numbers changing to nineteen, eighteen, seventeen, sixteen and fifteen, and then the doors open to a pleasant scene in your life from five years ago. You step out and you are with friends doing something enjoyable. Enjoy this pleasant experience, as if it were happening today. Now, re-enter the elevator and watch the floor numbers and feel the elevator going down, down, down as the numbers change. Fourteen, thirteen, twelve, eleven and ten. The elevator stops and the door opens to another pleasant experience in your life. Step out of the elevator and enjoy this experience. For the next few minutes. Now, re-enter the elevator and feel it going down, down, down. Nine, eight, seven, six and five. Five more years back in time to another pleasant experience. Feeling proud of yourself and looking forward to the years ahead. Now, re-enter the elevator and feel the elevator descending again. Four, three, two and one. The doors open to another pleasant experience. You are on the ground floor at the beginning of your life with aspirations of what you will do in the future. Now as you look around this floor, plan what you want to do with your life at this point in time and plan how you want to accomplish those things. Now, take those ideas with you back on the elevator. The doors close. Feel the elevator lifting upwards. Looking at the elevator numbers. One, two, three, four and five. The doors open. Step out into this pleasant experience and study the situation. Take with you what you need for your accom-plishments, and learn from your past experiences. Re-enter the elevator and feel it lift upwards. Six, seven, eight, nine and ten. The door opens to yet another pleasant experience in the future. See yourself using what you have learned before and applying those learnings to this situation and then take those skills back into the elevator. The doors close. Eleven, twelve, thirteen, fourteen and fifteen. The doors open to another pleasant situation in the future. Apply what you have already learned and gather new information.

Re-enter the elevator with this knowledge. Sixteen, seventeen, eighteen, nineteen. Thinking about all of your learning experiences and how you can apply them to your life now. Feeling good about yourself. And twenty. You are now at the top and feel comfortable about having a pleasant experience. When the door opens, come back to this time and place and open your eyes feeling wide awake and alert.

Descending elevators and stairs are common and conventional ways of inducing trance, deepening trance, and taking individuals back in time (age regression). Notice that the purpose of this induction is to allow the individual to regain skills, remember abilities, and acquire new knowledge that can help him solve present and future problems at different levels of his life. *Pleasant* experiences are suggested to prevent an abreaction (explained in a later chapter). Besides, individuals come to your office due to negative experiences. Returning to the beginning of trance by the elevator ascending is another counting method for awakening.

The next induction utilizes what is usually thought of as "guided imagery." Many mental health practitioners use this form of guided imagery to relieve stress, tension and anxiety in their clients. It is taught as a stress reduction technique in college courses and seminars. However, since it is quite effective as a hypnotic induction technique, it will be illustrated here as a conventional induction.

Now, just settle back in your chair and get as comfortable as you can. Take a deep breath and slowly exhale. Take another deep breath and slowly exhale. Now, feel how relaxed you are becoming. So once more take another deep breath and slowly exhale. Breathe out all the tensions of the day and slowly feel yourself relaxing as I talk to you. Now, I want you to visualize a nice quiet and safe place only known to you, away from all the tensions of the day. Perhaps, a place in the woods. So calm and serene. As you visualize yourself walking in the woods, you can see the trees and the leaves. The sun shining down through the branches as you look for a place to sit down by that stream. While sitting on a creek bank under the shade of a tree surrounded by other trees, you can feel a gentle breeze. Smell the moisture in the air as you see the ripples on the surface of the water, and see the splashing of the water over the rocks. Hear the comfortable splashing of the water and the faint roar of a waterfall. Enjoy those experiences as you become more and more relaxed. Now, as you are resting quietly and safely in the forest, you may remember something very pleasing about your childhood: enjoy this experience. Perhaps, you can remember other pleasant childhood experiences that you have not thought of in a long time. Now, take the next few minutes and enjoy these experiences. You have learned about relaxing, and know that you can relax. Just feel how relaxed you are right now. You know that you can become more relaxed than you are right now by practicing this profound state of relaxation, and that the more you practice it, the easier it can be to enter this state of relaxation to enjoy. So, feel good about learning how to relax. Whenever you feel tensed or stressed, you can take several deep breaths and begin to feel more and more relaxed as the relaxation flows throughout your entire body. Now visualize yourself sitting at home and closing your eyes and taking several deep breaths. Feel yourself becoming more relaxed as you are breathing out stress and fatigue. Become aware of the relaxation spreading throughout your body until you become just as relaxed as you are right now. So, any time in the future when you feel tired or have any discomfort, just sit down and let the experience of sitting be a cue to begin to relax. Feel the weight of your body in the chair—sinking into the chair. Relaxing now. Now take the next few moments and memorize those feelings to be used later. Enjoy those comfortable feelings. In a moment, I'm going to give you a cue to begin counting backwards from twenty to one. You are to begin counting silently to yourself and when you reach the count of one, you will slowly open your eyes and gradually awaken to this time and place. Begin counting now.

4. Induction #4 - The Authoritarian Approach

The basis of this approach is the *domination* of the hypnotist over the "subject," rather than obtaining the cooperation and relaxation of individuals. Traditional hypnotists believe that the domineering nature of this approach and the use of the word "sleep" instead of "relaxation" cause a medium trance state in five minutes with willing individuals. The tone of voice should be domineering and powerful, spoken with authority.

Mr. Jones, I want you to get comfortable in this chair. Sit erect and lean back so you can pick a spot on the wall to focus your attention. Constantly gaze at that spot and don't take your eyes off it. In a moment I'm going to begin counting. One-two, one-two, and at each count of one I want you to close your eyes. At the count of two, I want you to open your eyes, but keep your eyes fixed on that spot. As you open and close your eyes, you will soon feel your eyes getting very tired. The upper eyelids will become very heavy and you will feel a mild burning sensation in your eyes. Soon after that you will find your eyelids opening less wide each time until you will not be able to open your eyes at all. They will feel glued shut. I'm going to count now. One-two, one-two, one-two, and now your eyes are already beginning to get tired. One-two, one-two, and now you can begin to feel that mild burning sensation in your eyes. One-two, one-two, and your eyes are getting very tired. They are not opening as far as before and they are beginning to stick together when you close them. One-two, one-two, one-two. Your eyelids are beginning to stick more and more. Now, it is becoming more and more of an effort to open them. One-two, one-two, one-two. (Allow the eyelids to remain closed a little longer each time.) Your eyes are now so tired that you can hardly open them at all and even when open, they are only slightly open. Soon, they won't open at all. They will be stuck together. One-two, one-two, one-two, and now your eyelids are stuck together. You cannot open them. They are completely glued shut for now.

Now, I want you to concentrate on your head. Your head is now going to feel very heavy. As your head gets heavier and heavier, it will begin to fall forward safely to your chest. When your chin touches your chest, you will go into a deep sleep. You will not awaken until I awaken you. As you continue to sleep, you will hear everything I say. Now your head is getting heavier, heavier, and heavier. It is getting so heavy that you are finding it difficult to keep it erect. Your head is so heavy that it is beginning to fall forward. When you head falls completely forward and your chin touches your chest, you will be in a deep sleep. Your head is getting heavier and heavier and heavier. Now it is five times as heavy as before and even getting heavier. It is now like a heavy lead weight, so heavy you can no longer keep it up, and it is going down, down and down. Now, your chin is touching your chest, and you are in a deep sleep. You can hear everything I say, but you are in a deep sleep.

Now, I'm going to lift up your arms in front of you and they will just remain there with a power of their own. As they remain there, they will begin to feel weightless until they become unattached to your body and you won't even know they are there.

Now, I want you to imagine a blackboard in front of you. On this blackboard, I want you to see the numbers going backwards from one hundred. I want you to see 100, 99, 98 and 97 when I tell you to and also call off each number and then erase it from your mind. When you get to number 97, your mind will go blank and you will not be able to think of another number. Your mind will be blank. Now begin. Look at the first number, call it off and erase it. "100." Wipe it off and out of your mind. "99." Wipe it off and the last number. "97." Wipe it away completely. Your mind is blank and you cannot find another number. You cannot find the next number, can you? Of course, you can't. Now, you are in a deep, deep sleep. Deeper than you have ever been in your life. In a moment, I'm going to awaken you by touching your left hand. When I touch your hand, you will slowly awaken by opening your eyes and feel like you have had a wonderful sleep—like you have been sleeping for hours. You will feel very rested and relaxed and your head and arms will feel comfortably normal. (Hypnotist touches the back of the left hand.) Now, you are beginning to feel awake.

The most striking difference between this approach and the others is the stern rapid suggestions or commands. At no time should the "subject" be allowed the opportunity to challenge a suggestion because he/she might be successful. Therefore, only a few moments are given to break a suggestion then immediately re-direct attention to something else. When the individual cannot break the suggestions this creates the illusion of the "power of the hypnotist" and increases the likelihood of being successful with the next suggestions that eventually lead to direct therapeutic suggestions.

This authoritarian approach utilizes the eye-fixation technique of traditional hypnosis. Any object could be used effectively, e.g. candle flame, pendulum, penlight, or paper weight. Arm levitation was also demonstrated with the added suggestions of dissociation from the body. This allows the hypnotist to assess the depth of trance and response to suggestions. The counting technique is used to create amnesia, and an inquiry is made to verify amnesia for "any other numbers." Termination of trance utilizes a kinesthetic cue. Notice that positive suggestions for well-being are always given before awakening in all of the inductions. (Talk about traditional stages of sleep ensures belief in the depth of trance.)

5. Induction #5 - The Hand-Clasp Challenge

This is probably the most challenging of the authoritarian approaches. It further demonstrates the "power of the hypnotist" and the use of susceptibility scales, e.g. eye closure and handclasp. This technique is not recommended for therapeutic work. Not only can this technique easily break rapport with the subject, but it is not always effective and may strengthen certain negative views about hypnosis. It is primarily used by stage hypnotists to elicit the most cooperative subjects to ensure a good stage show. It is included to demonstrate the most challenging form of the authoritarian approach.

> Mr. Smith, you say you can't be hypnotized because of your inability to concentrate on suggestions. I want your cooperation in taking two tests to ascertain your ability to concentrate. Please make yourself comfortable in the chair with your feet flat on the floor and your *hands clasped together* in your lap. The first test involves the use of your eyes. So close your eyes, but try to stay awake. Now with your eyelids closed, I want you to attempt to look upwards towards your forehead, and do not allow them to look downwards. I am going to count to five. As I count upwards to five, your eyelids will get tighter and tighter. When I reach five, you will find that your eyelids will feel glued tightly shut and cannot be opened. At the count of five you can try to open your eyes, but the harder you try the tighter they will become. Now, remember to remain awake, but your eyelids will be stuck together until I release them. All right, let's begin, look up to your forehead. Feel the pressure on your eyelids. One. Your eyelids are getting tighter and tighter. Feel your upper eyelids pressing down. Two. They are getting tighter and tighter. Feel them beginning to stick together. Three. Already they are so tight that even if you tried you would find extreme difficulty in opening them. Four. They are so tight that you cannot open your eyelids. They are glued together. Completely glued together, so that no matter how hard you try you cannot open them. The harder you try, the tighter they get. When I count to five, you will find that you cannot open them. Five. They are stuck so tight that you cannot open your eyelids. No matter how hard you try, you cannot open your eyelids.
>
> Now I want you to forget about your eyelids. Concentrate upon your clasped hands. I am going to count up to five again. This time as I count, you will feel the sensation of your heart pumping blood down into your shoulders, upper arms, forearms and into your fingers. As the blood goes into your fingers, you will feel the added sensation of

them swelling. As you continue to feel that swelling, your fingers and hands will soon swell completely shut, and you will be unable to pull them apart. When I count to five, you can try to pull your hands apart, but they will be swollen shut tight together. They will be stuck tightly together, so tight that, no matter how hard you try, they will just get tighter. One. Begin to feel the blood flowing down through your shoulders, your arms and into your hands, and your fingers are beginning to swell. Two. As your fingers begin to swell, push your hands tighter together. Three. Your hands are swelling completely shut. Four. Your hands are getting tighter and tighter. They are getting so tight that you would have extreme difficulty in pulling them apart, so swollen now that you are beginning to lose control of the muscles in your hands and your arms. Your hands and arms are beginning to feel dissociated from the rest of your body. Feel that numbing sensation growing in your hands. They are completely stuck together. They are getting tighter and tighter. Five. They are getting tighter and tighter and tighter as you continue to lose control of those muscles. You can try to open them, but your hands are completely swollen shut, and now feel as if they have completely grown together—completely swollen shut.

Now forget your hands because you are getting very tired. You are getting very drowsy and are going to sleep. Your head is getting very heavy. As you feel your head getting heavy, so heavy, it is going to safely fall forward. Your head is getting heavier and heavier as you go into a deep, deep sleep, safely. When your head falls towards your chest, you will be in a deep sleep, but you can still hear my voice. You are in a deep sleep. You cannot open your eyelids because they are completely stuck together. You cannot pull your hands apart because they are completely swollen shut together. Now, feel your jaw muscles getting so rigid that you cannot open your mouth no matter how hard you try, you cannot open your mouth. The harder you try, the stiffer the jaw muscles become. You cannot tell me your name because your jaw muscles are so tight. What is your name? See, you cannot even tell me your name because your jaw muscles are completely rigid.

Now your hands can unclasp and I am going to make your arm completely rigid as I stretch it in front of you. Your arm is now so completely rigid that it is like a steel rod and you cannot bend it. It is fixed in the air, and you cannot bend it. Now your other arm is being stretched out, and it is stiff and rigid. It is like a steel rod and you cannot bend it. I can make any part of your body completely rigid and, you cannot move that part of your body. Now, I'm going to count to three, and you will relax all over into a deep sleep—ten times as deep as you are now. You will not awaken until I awaken you, but when you do awaken, you will feel wonderful, just as if you had several hours of restful sleep. ... One. Two. Three. Begin to feel completely awake and refreshed.

This induction is quite similar to the preceding induction except that it is more challenging. This is the technique that stage hypnotists use to have a subject lie between two chairs and cause the subject's body to become so rigid that the hypnotist stands on the subject to demonstrate his "power of hypnosis." **CAUTION:** *This has frequently caused back problems several months later in those individuals.*

Notice that the only suggestion is for well-being upon awakening. Since this technique has questionable therapeutic value, there will be no recommendation for its usage.

These five inductions were selected to give an understanding of the basic *traditional* approach. They were chosen because of their conventionalism and to demonstrate direct suggestions or commands. They also display how the susceptibility scales can be incorporated to induce trance, and how direct suggestions can be interspersed throughout the trance experience. There are numerous other types of inductions within the traditional approach.

C. Non-Traditional Inductions

The non-traditional or utilization approach uses the subject's own naturally occurring behaviors in the present to focus attention inward and to facilitate trance behavior. In other words, it is the acceptance and utilization of the present situations (pacing and leading) without psychologically or environmentally restructuring them, in contrast to the formalized, ritualistic and manipulative procedures of the traditional approach. Each person's unique personality characteristics are used to induce the trance state. The hypnotherapist provides individuals with stimuli and opportunities for intense retrospection that leads to altered states of consciousness. This includes incorporating traditional techniques such as eye fixation and direct suggestion and rituals (swinging pendulums, paperweights, etc.) to meet the expectations of clients.

Trance and hypnotic suggestion are believed to be separate phenomena and are not necessarily associated with one another.

A trance can be experienced differently by the same person on separate occasions. A hypnotic induction consists of inducing an altered state of consciousness. Hypno*therapy* is the utilization of therapeutic suggestions. Therapeutic trance focuses on altering a person's usual conscious beliefs so that one can be receptive to experiencing other patterns of associations and modes of mental functioning. Individuals accept non-hypnotic suggestions daily, because they evaluate them with their usual conscious attitudes and find them to be acceptable guides for their behavior, and voluntarily behave accordingly. Since trance does not insure the acceptance of suggestions, the effective hypnotherapist communicates to clients by the use of words, intonations, gestures and other techniques that will evoke the clients' own mental and behavioral processes. Hypnotic suggestions are effective only to the degree that they can activate, block or alter the functioning of natural associations already existing within individuals, i.e. normal psycho-physiological processes.

Suggestions are offered in such a manner that any response the individual makes can be accepted as following the suggestion. These responses are also used to learn more about individuals (e.g. attitudes and behavior) and to use these response tendencies to effect therapeutic goals. Thus, suggestions are usually directed toward circumventing the rigid and learned limitations of conscious and habitual attitudes that create problems for the individual. Indirect suggestions are used more than direct suggestions because they bypass that part of consciousness that frequently remains in the trance state. When following hypnotic suggestions, clients are often surprised by their behavior because it seems autonomous, which means that it is outside their usual sense of control. An effective therapeutic trance may be best defined as follows: "A successful clinical hypnotic experience, then, is one in which trance alters habitual attitudes and modes of functioning, so that carefully formulated hypnotic suggestions can evoke and utilize other patterns of associations and potentials within the patient to implement certain therapeutic goals." (Erickson, Rossi and Rossi, 1976).

The utilization approach to clinical hypnosis and hypnotic suggestion is presented and illustrated in the following inductions.
Notice how the use of language and indirect forms of suggestions
(Chapter 5) rapidly develop rapport (Chapter 4) and facilitate
hypnotic phenomena (Chapter 9). Notice how a therapeutic
outcome can be achieved in virtually any situation.

1. Induction #1 - Eye Fixation

Although the eye fixation induction dates back to the early days of
hypnosis and was based on eye fatigue, the utilization approach
simply uses it as a *diversion* technique to block out surrounding
stimuli, and then paces and leads the subject into a trance state. It
is also used to meet the expectation of an individual who expects
a ritual. This is one of the easiest inductions and can be used with
any person who can stare at an object, and only requires about 5-
10 minutes. It can also be used in any situation. Notice that the
subject will be asked to stare at a spot on the wall, but any external
object could be used to fixate attention. The subject can be directed
to focus attention on a crystal ball, a paper weight, prism, ash tray,
pen, swinging pendulum, a ball on the floor, a ceiling fixture, and
so on. The type of object or location of the object is not important.
The focus of attention and the pacing and leading suggestions
create the trance experience.

> All right. What I would like for you to do is look at that wall and find
> some spot. It can be a crack in the wall, a hole in the wall, a corner of
> the picture frame, something inside the picture (therapist names
> everything he can see until the subject fixates attention). Whatever
> you choose. It can be your spot, and as you continue to stare at that
> spot, you will notice that it begins to move (pause) up or down, left
> or right. Maybe it's not moving yet. And, I don't know, but maybe
> it's becoming blurry and out of focus as your eyes are becoming
> tired. And now, they are beginning to close. Your eyes are beginning
> to blink (pause). Slowly. That's right. Just like that. And now, they're
> beginning to blink a little faster—more frequently. And soon they
> will close. So, just go ahead and allow them to close (eyes close).
> That's right. Just like that, and sense that relief when the eyes are
> closed. Allowing them to relax, you can continue to relax. Just like
> that. Closing out all of the tensions of the day. Simply continue to
> relax. That's right. Now take the next few minutes and thoroughly
> refresh yourself. (After a long pause, guided imagery could be used
> to deepen the trance and/or therapeutic suggestions could be

offered.) In a moment, but not yet, I want you to begin counting backwards from twenty to one, silently to yourself, at my signal, and you will know what that is when you hear it. And at the count of one, you will slowly and gradually open your eyes, reorient yourself to this room and time, feeling completely refreshed as if you have had several hours of restful sleep. Begin counting now. (Wait for the subject to finish counting, and when she opens her eyes, comment on her experience.)

T: That's right. Come completely awake. (As she begins to orient herself). You can stretch if you want. Does this room look brighter or dull to you?

S: It looks brighter.

T: That's right, and I wonder what other changes will begin to take place in your life. I wonder if things will be brighter for you. How do you feel?

S: I feel fine.

T: Now, you know that you can experience trance, and it's a wonderful feeling, isn't it?

S: Yes, I feel great!

Notice that this induction begins with a simple harmless request that diverts attention to the wall, but also causes the individual to be curious, as well as eliciting her cooperation to follow suggestions. She is then asked to pick a spot on the wall, and the therapist offers her a variety of choices. This is an illusion of choice since not looking at the wall or not choosing a spot is offered. This is also made personal by "It can be your spot." The most cooperative subjects will immediately pick a spot, while a more selective individual will scan the entire wall. An obstinate trait will be displayed by choosing something not suggested or an obscure spot. Remember! We learn about individuals from their responses, so use that as an aid in conducting further hypnotherapy or psychotherapy. Pacing and leading suggestions for normal visual physiological responses to eye fatigue are now offered, leading to suggestions of complete relaxation. Notice that the awakening instructions are formed to create more "wonder" and inner searches for the cue to begin counting. This counting technique allowed her to awaken slowly on her own. Pacing continues upon awakening. All lighted rooms look brighter after the eyes have been closed for a while. If she were to say that the room was dull-looking or dark, the therapist would know that she is still in a trance, and would instruct eye-closure and give awakening instructions again. If she were to refuse to awaken, the therapist could choose different techniques such as: (1) suggest that she awaken at the count of five and doing the counting by raising the voice with each number. A loud noise such as clapping the hands at the end of the count is always effective for resistant clients; (2) suggesting that the bladder is full and that there is an urgent need to use the rest room. Notice how another inner search is created by the therapeutic suggestions of *"other* changes in her life"* suggesting that she has already changed by the experience, as well as the suggestion for well-being upon awakening. Continued verification of the trance is subtly achieved by assuming that she has a trance experience.

2. Induction #2 - Early Learning Set

We consider this a classic induction since it has repeatedly been used in seminars and workshops to demonstrate hypnosis, as well as being cited in many books on hypnosis for more than ten years. Ernest L. Rossi coined it "the Early Learning Set Induction" (Erickson and Rossi, 1979a). The following narrative is a modification of this famous induction.

> Will you sit back in your chair with your feet flat on the floor and your hands on your thighs? Now I want you to know that you don't need to talk. And you don't need to move. And you don't even need to listen to my voice because your unconscious mind can hear me. For your unconscious mind really doesn't have anything of importance to do, because the important thing is the listening by your unconscious mind. Now, there are certain changes taking place in you of which you are unaware. Already your breathing has changed. Your respiration has slowed down, and your heart rate has slowed. Now, I'm just going to talk to you. When you first went to school, I don't know if it was kindergarten or the first grade. But you had to learn the alphabet. And looking at all those letters seemed to be an insurmountable task. And you had to learn the difference between an A and a B, a B from a D, an M from a W and a P from a Q, and upper and lower case letters. But you learned them by creating

mental images of these letters in your mind. And then you had to learn script and that seemed to be an insurmountable task, but you did it by developing images of those letters in your mind, both upper and lower case. And that has been a permanent learning that has stayed with you. All your life. And you can learn other things like how to solve problems ...

This induction begins when the subject prepares himself to enter trance by sitting back in the chair with his feet flat on the floor and his hands resting on his thighs. This shows that the subject has made a self-suggestion to enter trance. The following pacing statements cannot be challenged and are spoken as simple facts to maintain rapport. Those statements are selected to depotentiate the conscious mind and to facilitate a dissociation between the conscious and the unconscious, as well as presuming that there is a difference. Ratification of a trance experience is made by further simple pacing statements regarding changes in physiology, i.e. breathing, respiration, and heart rate. The leading suggestions to return to early childhood learning evokes not only that learning experience, but deepens trance by indirect suggestions of imagery (mental images of letters). Leading suggestions are also made by framing this learning as unconscious and insurmountable. Therapeutic suggestions are then made to build self-confidence and to evoke inner resources to continue learning by stating, "But you did it ... and that has been a permanent learning that has stayed with you all your life. And you can learn other things like how to solve problems." The therapist then suggests to the subject that he has abilities and potentials that he has forgotten and to continue using these abilities to solve problems, as well as just learning something new, e.g. how to enter trance. Now the foundation has been laid to resolve any difficulties the subject is experiencing.

3. Induction #3 - Floating Hand Induction

Since this is one of the easiest inductions to teach, it is the second induction demonstrated (after eye fixation) and the first induction taught with supervision to our students to practice with one another. It is an excellent method for learning various language forms (voice dynamics, transformational grammar, word usage, splitting and linking, double binds, anecdotes, direct and indirect suggestions, etc.), as well as body dissociation, anesthesia, hand levitation, and catalepsy. It also facilitates confidence in students, allows them to learn about trance by experiencing it, and prepares them to conduct hypnotherapy.

While the subject is sitting in a chair with feet flat on the floor and hands placed on thighs, the therapist makes non-threatening pacing statements (e.g. truisms or yes set comments) to develop rapport, and asks the subject to lift her right hand just about an inch above her thigh and demonstrates this with his right hand as follows:

Now, what I would like for you to do is lift your right hand just about an inch from your thigh. That's right. And allow it to hover there as you look at your hand and focus all of your attention on that hand. And notice that it is beginning to move. That's right. Just like that. A little to the right. A little to the left. Down and up. Right and left. Down and up. A little more up. That's right. (Since the hand naturally lifts upward as the subject inhales and falls downward during exhaling, continue pacing and leading suggestions by matching the inhaling only.) Higher and higher. And now it is becoming more and more steady the higher it lifts upwards. That's right. I wonder if you've noticed how much lighter it has become the higher it lifts upward. It's moving as if it has a mind of its own, in small unconscious jerky movements. That's right. Higher and lighter. (At the halfway distance between the thigh and face.) Now, watch how the arm is beginning to bend at the elbow. Slowly and gradually bending at the elbow towards your face. (If the arm is not bending, gently and with the lightest of *hesitant* touches bend the arm at the elbow and guide the hand towards the face.) That's right. Just like that. Moving slowly and gradually towards the face. And you may wonder if your eyes are going to close before your hand touches your face, or when your hand touches your face. I don't know, but it will be interesting to find out. (If the hand is moving too fast before those suggestions are given, simply say, "Not that fast, slowly and gradually") And there's something else that you can be surprised about. (Pause.) When your unconscious hand touches your face, there may be a pleasantly warm, cool or tingling sensation before the part of your face that your hand touches gradually becomes numb, as the hand gently touches your face. (When the hand touches the face continue with the following.) That's right. Your eyes are closed, and enjoy those pleasant sensations as the face gradually becomes more and more numb. And we have all had experiences of going to the dentist and having our jaws anesthetized.

That's right. More and more numb. Now, in a moment, but not yet, I'm going to touch your hand, and it will slowly and gradually begin to drift downwards towards your lap. (Then just gently touch the back of the hand to guide it.) That's right. Slowly and gradually drifting down towards your lap. (Wait for the downward movement.) Slowly and gradually drifting downwards towards your lap and knowing that you have learned something else today that you were unaware of. And that is that your unconscious mind has the ability to anesthetize any part of your body by simply touching it, and you can use this ability when there is a need to—for your own well-being. Slowly and gradually down, but not too fast. I also want you to know that you are an excellent hypnotic subject and that any time you need to go into a trance, it can be easier than this time. I want to thank your unconscious mind for trusting me and allowing you this learning experience. And I want you to know that I've enjoyed working with you and look forward to other hypnotic experiences. Now, when your hand touches your thigh, but not yet, you will slowly awaken from this pleasant experience knowing that you have learned a great deal that can be used later. And you will remember what the unconscious mind feels that you need to remember, and you will forget those things that are trivia to you now. When you open your eyes, you will become completely awake and alert, as if you've had several hours of restful sleep.

N-O-W. (Hand touches her thigh, slowly opens her eyes and becomes oriented.)

T: Hi. How are you feeling?

S: Fine.

T: Does this room look brighter?

S: Yes, it does. A lot brighter!

T: I would like to thank you for this experience. You're an excellent subject. Would you like to tell me about your experience? (Discussion follows.)

This hypnosis session only took about fifty minutes. It demonstrates how to use much of the material covered thus far, as well as the utilization of some hypnotic phenomena. The sessions begins by rapidly developing rapport through pacing techniques (e.g. truisms, yes set, etc.) similar to the preceding induction by

Erickson. The Floating Hand Induction (so-called by one of the authors, TLS) is utilized to induce trance. Cooperation is further elicited by having the subject voluntarily lift her hand upon request and as demonstrated to her. Thus, her hand is already in a state of levitation and need not rise from her thigh. By placing the hand in this position, it easily becomes tired and will begin to tremble or show micro movements. This movement is paced and led with fail-safe suggestions, that is, all possible movements of the hand are suggested so she cannot fail to respond. This induction also combines an eye fixation technique. The association is made that as the "hand hovered there" to focus all of her attention on "that hand." The use of "that hand" is an indirect suggestion of dissociation from her body, i.e. not her hand but *that* hand. Then, the natural rising and falling movements of the hand during breathing are utilized, but only the rising movement is paced as she inhales with "higher and higher." The "and" is spoken as she exhales. The hand, becoming steady, is an indication that she is in a deep trance, as well as the continued lifting movements of the hand. Notice the association of the hand becoming more steady (fewer small movements) the higher it lifts, and the change to it becoming lighter. The indirect suggestion "I wonder ..." is made to facilitate an inner search causing deeper trance. Since small jerky movements are an indication of deep trance and the movements completely under unconscious control, this is also paced and led with the statement that it has a mind of its own. This also causes further dissociation from her body. The knowledge of the hand and arm feeling foreign to the body and not under conscious control develops from personal trance experience. Since the therapist already knows what he is going to do, the selected halfway mark seems a natural time to have the elbow bend for the hand to lift up to the subject's face. Thus, pacing and leading (plus some gentle assistance) is continued to effect this intention.

Then a double bind suggestion is made creating another inner search for the answer, i.e., time of eye closure. Again, *all* possibilities are offered so that no matter what the response, she is following suggestions. The phrase "interesting to find out" deepens trance with another inner search, but also creates an expectancy of the result. The desired speed of movement can always be guided with, "Not that fast" or "You can go faster than that," as well as "Slowly and gradually." The suggestion "be surprised" creates an inner search and expectancy. Notice the pause, allowing her time to wonder about the surprise. Notice the continuation of suggestions for dissociation, i.e. "unconscious hand." The word "when" offers no choice of whether the hand will touch the face; and indirect fail-safe suggestions are offered about sensations creating more inner searching and deepening of trance. The word "before" suggests that something else is to happen, and is then made explicit with the direct suggestion that her face become numb, this suggestion spoken with confidence and authority. Now we have eye closure with the closure of expectancy; then attention is directed to enjoyable new sensations. The word "as" is used to associate and continue the suggestions of numbness. An anecdote is used to retrieve anesthetic experiences. The subject is directly instructed "But not yet," followed by "In a moment," because some subjects will respond in a moment. Remember, trance subjects often interpret statements *literally*. Then, direct suggestions are made for when the hand will drift downwards with a touch cue. The downward movement is not paced and led with respiration because she is already in a trance. Respiration pacing and leading are used to induce trance. The numbness dissipates when the hand leaves the face because the suggestion is for when it touched the face. Notice that during descent of the hand another suggestion is offered. "Learned something else" would continue the inner searching and expectancy. Now it is suggested that the anesthetic experience can be generalized and used in the future. Notice the continued dissociation. To insure future cooperation, her unconscious mind is thanked for allowing her to be an excellent subject, with suggestions for future trance work. Notice that suggestions are included in the awakening for both remembering and amnesia under the guidance of her own dissociated self: the unconscious. Now, suggestions for well-being upon awakening are given as in most trances, but contingent upon the desired outcome of the trance work. A test for awakeness, e.g. brighter room is used. She is also asked how she feels to insure that there are no physical residuals of trance which might require alleviation. Notice that both her conscious and unconscious mind are thanked. It is a good idea to *thank both*, especially if future trance work is expected. The session ends with a discussion of her experience.

This hypnosis session is an example of a therapeutic trance session using the material in this book. The goals of the trance work are multifaceted. In actual practice, you may use only hand levitation (ascending and descending) to introduce the subject to a trance experience, or to explore the potential for trance work. Any part of this session can then be used in future sessions with different inductions. This session also serves as an introduction to hypnotic anesthesia.

4.   *Induction #4 - Hand Levitation via Questions*

The following brief induction demonstrates another method of eliciting a hand levitation. Erickson and Rossi (1979) use questions as hypnotic suggestions to elicit this hand levitation. This induction is quoted from Erickson and Rossi (1979, p. 30):

> Can you feel comfortable resting your hands gently on your thighs? (As therapist demonstrates.) That's right, without letting them touch each other.
>
> Can you let those hands rest ever so lightly so that the fingertips just barely touch your thighs?
>
> That's right. As they rest ever so lightly, do you notice how they tend to lift up a bit all by themselves with each breath you take?
>
> Do they begin to lift even more lightly and easily by themselves as the rest of your body relaxes more and more?
>
> As that goes on, does one hand or the other, or maybe both continue lifting even more?
>
> And does that hand stay up and continue lifting higher and higher, bit by bit, all by itself? Does the other hand want to catch up with it, or will the other hand relax on your lap?
>
> That's right. And does that hand continue lifting with these slight little jerking movements, or does the lifting get smoother and smoother as the hand continues upward toward your face?
>
> Does it move quickly or slowly as it approaches your face with deepening comfort? Does it need to pause a bit before it finally touches your face so you'll know you are going into a trance? And it

won't touch until your unconscious is ready to let you go deeper, will it?

And will your body automatically take a deep breath when that hand touches your face as you really relax and experience yourself going deeper?

That's right. And will you even bother to notice the deepening comfortable feeling when that hand slowly returns to your lap all by itself? And will your unconscious be in a dream by the time that hand comes to rest?

This hand levitation induction is similar to the preceding induction except for the question format. It is an excellent example of the pacing and leading technique. Erickson begins the induction by asking simple questions in a soft voice based on his observations. His questions then become leading with "Rest ever so lightly ... so that the fingertips just barely touch your thighs." Notice the frequent use of the consoling and assuring "That's right." Feeling light is subtly associated with levitation, and then dissociated by "all by themselves" and associated with "each breath you take." Dissociation continues with fail-safe pacing and leading the hands upward. Following this is a fail-safe double-bind question creating an inner search. Notice how he indirectly deepens the trance with the double meaning phrase "deepening comfort" before he ratifies the trance with "So you'll know you are going into a trance?" He then binds the touching of the face with allowing a deeper trance by the unconscious. Besides the other compound double-meaning phrase "deepening comfortable feeling," he indirectly suggests that the hand descend to the lap with another dissociative phrase "All by itself," and then associates this movement with being in a dream. The authors have observed E.L. Rossi effectively using questions for hand levitation.

5.   *Induction #5 - Counting Induction*

We will close this chapter with a simple counting induction that can be used to test cooperativeness. While the following is based on mild confusion, it also uses catalepsy to test the trance experience:

Now, John, I would like to test your susceptibility to enter a trance, if that's all right with you. Okay, just settle back, and get comfortable, and close your eyes. That's right. Now, I'm just going to talk to you, and you don't have to do anything but just sit there. I'm going to start counting from one to twenty, and I can count any way I choose. One. Two. Three. Four. F-i-v-e. Six. Seven. Eight. Nine, T-e-n. Eleven. T-w-e-l-v-e. Thirteen. Fourteen. Thirteen. Fourteen. Fourteen. F-i-f-t-e-e-n. S-i-x-t-e-e-n. F-i-f-t-e-e-n. Thirteen. Twelve. F-o-u-r-t-e-e-n. F-i-f-t-e-e-n. (Respiration slowing.) S-e-v-e-n-t-e-e-n. E-i-g-h-t-e-e-n. S-e-v-e-n-t-e-e-n. E-i-g-h-t-e-e-n. N-i-n-e-t-e-e-n. E-i-g-h-t-e-e-n. N-i-n-e-t-e-e-n. N-i-n-e-t-e-e-n a-n-d a-h-a-l-f a-n-d T-w-e-n-t-y. That's right. You've already altered your breathing. And without your awareness, you've slowed your pulse and your heart rate has slowed down. That's right. So just go on enjoying this pleasant experience away from all the stress and tensions of the day. (Long pause.) I wonder if you've noticed that your arms have become lighter, and as I pick up this arm it can become very light. (Gently take hold of his right wrist with the index finger and thumb of your left hand. Gently feel if he will allow you to guide his arm upwards. Remember! *He* does the lifting. If it is limp or rigid, you can comment that it must be the other arm, or say, "Or quite heavy and relaxed." But if he lifts it, leave it suspended in a cataleptic posture and continue talking.) That's right. Just like that. It can become lighter and lighter—maybe weightless. And the next time I touch your hand, it can drift slowly downwards. And when it rests comfortably, you can slowly open your eyes and become completely awake—feeling as if you've had several hours of restful sleep. (Touch his hand and wait for him to awaken. Then talk positively about the experiences. Remember! No arguing about being in a trance or not. Ratification of trance is not a part of this approach. (Review the table in chapter 3.) Good pacing and leading are utilized to maintain rapport.)

Note: The subject always awakens from trance with eyes going from closed to open because this is a natural way of awakening, and it demarcates the difference between the two states of normal and hypnotic, or conscious and unconscious.

These five inductions have been selected to show the variability and ease of inducing trance. All of these inductions are similar in that they begin with simple non-threatening requests made to elicit cooperation and to develop rapport. Pacing and leading by using what you observe, and natural psychological responses are clearly demonstrated. The integration of direct and indirect suggestions via Meta-model violations, double binds and dissociation are also illustrated, as well as several different awakening techniques. These hypnosis sessions can serve as an introduction to the utilization of hypnotic phenomena and as an example of therapeutic trance work.

Exercises

1. Practice the varieties of inductions included in this chapter. It is best to do this in triads with one observer. You can also audiotape or videotape your practice sessions. How would you modify or expand or contract or change these inductions to match your own style?

2. Write out your own inductions patterned on the ones in this chapter. Tape them. Work on shortening your inductions until you get them refined to their essence.

3. Contrast on a point-by-point basis the differences between traditional and non-traditional inductions. Which would you use with particular clients? Which style are you most comfortable with? Challenge yourself by working with the *other* style.

Chapter 8

Advanced Inductions

Thomas L. South, Ph.D.

A. Introduction

This chapter consists of inductions requiring an extensive under-standing of behavior, personality, psychotherapy, mastery of hypnotic language, and the processes of the utilization approach that are facilitated by clinical application and experience. It contains advanced inductions leading to therapeutic trance work and gives examples of hypnotherapy. It contains material for advanced hypnosis students and experienced psychotherapists who have mastered the basic inductions in the preceding chapter. These are not to be undertaken by the novice.

B. Sensory Altering Inductions

1. Induction #1 - "My Friend, John"

Erickson (1964a) coined this phrase and used this induction with resistant subjects. He also used visual hallucinations with children since they have a good imagination and enjoy playing games. This is an example of a conversational induction in which you just start the induction without any preamble:

> Now, what I want you to do is imagine my friend, John, sitting here with us. John, this is Jim. Jim, this is my friend, John. ... How old would you say John is? That's right. And what is he wearing? ... That's right. Now, John, I want you to sit there comfortably and think about your right hand as it rests comfortably on your thigh. Now, allow it to slowly lift up. That's right. See John's hand lifting upwards. Now, higher and higher. Show me how John's hand is lifting upwards. Slowly. That's right. Higher and higher. And as your hand is lifting upwards, your eyes are beginning to close. Higher and higher. And now just close your eyes as your hand continues lifting up towards your face ...

Note that you adapt "my friend, John" to what you know about your client. Hand levitation and eye closure are examples of what John can do, but certainly you may use other responses and behaviors. Erickson (1964a) wrote about this approach:

> My-Friend-John Technique is an excellent measure of teaching resistant subjects to go into trance. I demonstrate it to the resistant patient who comes in for therapy but resists, and I demonstrate it so thoroughly and carefully that as he watches me induce a trance in my purely imaginative friend John, he resents so much waste of his time and money, and becomes so unwittingly responsive while I am hypnotizing "John," that he follows John's example and develops a trance without needing to offer resistance. This, therapeutically, is an excellent beginning, since he came here for therapy and not a contest. I use it also to teach self-hypnosis in the heterohypnotic situation, and with subjects who are to rehearse at home in relation to study, migraine, obesity, etc.

2. *Induction #2 - Multisensory Induction*

Now, Al, you said you can't visualize anything and yet you want to learn to visualize. You also enjoy playing the piano. So let's do this. Close your eyes and relax. That's right. Now take three deep breaths and gradually relax even more. And you've sat down at the piano many times and have played your favorite songs. Now imagine that you're sitting at the piano and your hands are over the keyboard. And feel your fingers touching the keys and beginning to slowly play one of your favorite songs. That's right. Continue playing. (If you look closely, you may see small jerky muscle movements on the fingers.) Listen to the pleasant harmony as your hands continue playing. With your eyes closed, look at your hands as they continue playing. (Look for eye movements under the lids.) And you can see your hands playing the keyboard—the white and black keys. And, slowly into focus, you can begin to see a little more of the piano as you continue to play. And eventually the bottom of the sheet music and a little more. Gradually seeing more and more of that sheet music. I don't know if you're reading the sheet music as you hear yourself playing, or just what way you're seeing it, now. And I don't know if you're playing in a room by yourself or not. But, you can look around the room as you continue to play. (Look for eye movement.) Just for now continue playing, and when you have finished that piece of music, open your eyes and come back to this place and this time, feeling well-rested. Knowing that you have accomplished something that you didn't know you could do before.

(Upon awakening.) And what song were you playing? Did you use the sheet music? Was there anybody in the room with you? And, what other things did you see? Thank you.

This is a modification of an induction performed in front of an audience at a hypnosis seminar by TLS. The induction utilized visual, auditory and kinesthetic senses, as well as Al's musical talents. During the trance, there was eye flutter and small muscle movements in the fingers. These movements indicated that the subject was following the suggestions. Inquiry revealed that he did see the piano and scanned the room. He was playing by himself. He was also told that, if he practiced this trance experience enough, his visual experiences would increase. This suggestion was spoken in the author's hypnotic voice.

A similar technique was successfully used with a subject who was having difficulty playing a particular song. For the trance, she played the piece five times slowly and then ten times quickly without making a mistake. She was also told that her fingers had now "memorized" the correct notes and it could be played with ease. She reported after trance that she could feel her fingers playing the piano. The next day she reported to the audience that she had gone home and played the piece of music correctly, but she had felt differently as she played it. This suggested that she had re-entered trance while playing the song.

This trance rehearsal technique has been successfully used to help athletes play better, among other skilled activities. For example, Erickson used a similar technique to help an Olympic shot-put thrower increase his distance. A colleague has used it in her private practice of sport psychology, and this author has successfully utilized it to help an amateur tennis player win tournaments.

3. Induction #3 - Crystal Gazing Induction

Crystal balls, spirals and swinging pendulums have been traditionally utilized to induce trance. However, too much emphasis has been placed on the apparatus instead of the nature of trance. For example, the crystal ball used by mystics to foretell one's future is nothing more than just a piece of apparatus. The subject is usually told to "look into the crystal ball" (with expectations to see something) and the mystic ritually gestures with her hands while she speaks in a mysterious tone of voice. The mystic utilizes pacing and leading techniques such as, "I'm beginning to see a man (while watching the subject's face and observing other signs of trance), or is it a man? It's foggy, but now it's getting clearer. It's a handsome young man wearing ..." Or the mystic might say, "As you look into the crystal ball, you will begin to see vague images until a clear picture emerges. And what do you see?" And, alas! the subject has entered trance. Although crystal balls are great for inducing trance, they are expensive, heavy, bulky, and burdensome to carry. On the other hand, *hallucinatory* crystal balls are quite inexpensive and can be any color. Since they are weightless, the hypnotherapist can have any number of crystal balls, as well as any size, and they are just as good, if not many times more useful and effective.

Erickson (1952) utilized multiple visual hallucinations in which different, but related, things were visualized. On one occasion, he had a depressed patient see a happy incident from her childhood in one crystal ball and another happy incident at a different age level *simultaneously* with the first until there were about a dozen crystal balls of happy incidents from different ages. They were then incorporated into her present state and the depression was alleviated.

Crystal gazing is demonstrated in the following induction:

> John, look over here. I want you to see your mother sitting in that chair. (Chair facing subject.) You know what your mother looks like. What is she wearing? (Subject can't visualize his mother.) All right, I want you to face me and look at this crystal ball in my hand. (Therapist extends arm, as if holding a ball.) What color is it? (Subject replies "Doctor, I don't see anything in your hand.") What *color* is it, John? (Subject replies "Blue.") That's right. A pretty blue color. And is it a small, medium or large crystal ball? As you continue to gaze into that crystal ball, you'll notice something very interesting. The image is rather fuzzy, but it's clearing up. Now, can you see the image of a woman? How is your mother dressed? And she's talking to you—telling how proud she is of you. And she knows that you can do it. Now, look at this larger crystal ball. (Therapist holds another hallucinatory ball in the other hand and subject looks over at it.) The image will clear up. It's a young man

graduating from college. It's you graduating from college. And isn't that a good feeling? And the work was well worth it. Now, look at this large screen over here. (Therapist points beside him with the hand that held the first crystal.) And see yourself sitting down in your favorite studying place—intensely studying without any distractions, feeling relaxed and comfortable. Studying for at least 50 minutes knowing that you are absorbing the information easily in a relaxed manner. (Short pause.) Now after 50 minutes, getting up and walking to the refrigerator to get a refreshing beverage, or simply looking out the window taking a relaxing break. And after five minutes, returning to studying for another 50 minutes and taking another break. See yourself doing this for two to four hours. Now, close your eyes knowing that you've learned a lot studying. And knowing that you will use this technique every time you sit down to study, returning to this comfortable relaxed feeling, studying and absorbing the information that you need to know. And test-taking can be just as easy. Now, take the next few moments and completely relax—feeling your confidence build. That's right. (Long pause.) You will awaken by counting backward from twenty to one at my signal. And when you reach one, you will slowly open your eyes feeling well-rested, awake and alert. Begin counting now.

This is a shortened version of an actual therapy session lasting approximately 45 minutes. The college student was having difficulty studying due to anxiety caused by an increasing lack of self-confidence in his abilities the closer it came to graduation.

Hypnotic hallucinatory experience can be utilized therapeutically with almost anyone who has a visual imagination. Several individuals in an audience will enter a spontaneous trance while watching a hypnosis demonstration. On one such occasion, a co-workshop leader directly spoke to one particular individual and said, "I want *you* to look at this TV (Colleague pointed across the room.) and tell me what program you are watching." Suggestions were then made regarding what a pleasurable learning experience the subject was having at the workshop and would continue to have before being awakened.

C. Levitation Inductions

Although hand levitation is a motor activity, it is not considered an ideodynamic induction because the emphasis is placed on the subjective sensation of lightness, involuntary movement, or consciously effortless activity, and not the direction of the motor activity.

The hand is employed because it can easily be utilized without disturbing the rest of the body. Subjects have a lifetime of experience using their hands while the body is at rest.

1. Induction #4 - Hallucinatory Levitation

Mary, I want you to stare at that spot over there and fixate all of your attention on that spot. And know that you do not need to be distracted by anything. And as your eyes begin to blink, slowly and gradually go into a trance. And when your eyes close, you will be in a nice comfortable trance. Take your time and go into a trance at your own pace. That's right. (Eyes close.) Mary, if you are in a trance, nod your head "yes." (Subject nods head.) That's right. You're in a nice comfortable trance. Now, I want you to raise your right arm up without raising it up, but really raising it up above your head. You know what I mean, don't you? (Subject nods head.) You can begin now. (Therapist observes for shoulder and neck tension.) That's right. High above your head. Now, actually lift your left hand and slowly and deliberately place your left on the back of your right hand. (Subject slowly lifts her left hand upward above her head, moves it across her head, lowers her hand and stops.) That's right. Is your left hand touching the right hand? (Subject nods her head.) That's right. Now, lower your left hand and let it rest comfortably on your lap. (Subject lowers left hand.) Now, slowly and gradually lower the right hand until it is resting comfortably on your lap. (Therapist observes for continued tension in the neck and shoulder until the tension dissipates and the neck and shoulder muscles are relaxed.) That's right. I want you to know that you are an excellent hypnotic subject and thank you for a fine demonstration. And I want you to know that there are other things that you are capable of, but are unaware of, that you can be surprised about in the future. And when you are ready, and at your own pace, I want you to slowly and gradually open your eyes and return to this room feeling quite relaxed, as if you had had several hours of restful sleep. (Subject eventually opens her eyes.) It's bright in here, isn't it? (Subject verbally acknowledges the brightness and is asked about her experience.)

The hallucinatory hand levitation was discovered by Erickson (1964b) and used with individuals who had difficulty with hand levitation inductions. If a subject fails to levitate a specified hand, it is strongly suggested to leave the resistance in that hand and immediately work on levitating the other hand. This usually is successful. If both hands fail to respond, the hallucinatory levitation can be attempted. Erickson believed that many subjects who were considered unable to levitate performed hallucinatory levitations that were unnoticed by inexperienced hypnotherapists.

2. Induction #5 - Hand Levitation

There are numerous ways of eliciting a hand levitation. There are no standard techniques, as well as no right or wrong ways. The hypnotherapist is only limited by his/her own creative mind. However, there are helpful hints. The following induction demonstrates suggestions that are usually quite effective. It is a modification of the famous "Reverse Set Induction" conducted by Erickson. The complete induction is available on videotape and the annotated transcript is in Erickson and Rossi (1981, pp. 155–178).

I understand you've never been hypnotized, but you're interested. So I think the best thing to do is get down to work. And you're willing to learn, aren't you? And all you have to do is to let things happen, and they will happen and I'm going to take hold of your hand in a moment. (Erickson placed her hands on her thighs.) Now, as you watch your hands, they're simply resting there. And do you know about the feelings you have when you are feeding a baby and you want the baby to open its mouth, and you open yours instead of the baby? (Subject nods her head.) And did you ever put on the brakes when you were in the back seat of a car? (Subject nods her head.) Well, I want that same kind of automatic movement. Now, look at my hands. You see very, very slowly, without it being a voluntary thing. My right hand can lift up and it can lower. And the left hand can lift up and lower. (Erickson models slow lifting and lowering with his hands.) Now, what I'd like you to understand is this: you have a conscious mind, and you know that and I know that, and you have an unconscious mind. You know what I mean by that, do you not? (As she nods, Erickson leans forward toward her and makes intense eye contact.) Now, you could lift your right hand, or your left hand consciously, but your unconscious mind can lift one or the other of your hands. And now, I'd like you to look at your hands, and I'm going to ask you a question, and you do not know the answer to that question, but your unconscious mind does. So, you'll just have to wait and see what the answer is. I'm going to ask you which hand is your unconscious mind going to lift up first? The right hand or the left hand, and you really don't know. But your unconscious knows. (Pause.) That's right. It's beginning to lift one of your hands. Lifting, lifting, lifting, lifting up. And now that hand begins lifting up. (Subject's right hand begins to slowly move.) That's right. Watch it lifting, lifting, lifting, up it comes, lifting higher and higher. And as you keep watching your hand, you'll notice that you can just close your eyes and just feel your hand lifting higher and higher. That's right. And your elbow will start bending and the hand will come up. Lifting, lifting, and now close your eyes and feel it lifting higher and higher. And I'm going to take hold of this hand. (Erickson lightly slides his thumb on the inside of her left hand.) And it's lifting, lifting, lifting. That's right. And the other hand is lifting, lifting up. (Erickson lightly touches her right hand to assume a catalepsy position.) That's right. I mentioned before that the hand could lift up and it could go down. And now I wonder if you know which hand is going to go down first. One or the other is going to go down. Down it comes. (Her right hand begins to lower.) That's right. Down it comes. And it's coming down more and more. And as it comes down, I want you to go deeper and deeper into the trance. I'd like to have you enjoy going deeper and deeper. And when your hand reaches your lap, you'll take a deep breath and go even deeper into the trance, because you're beginning to know how now. That's right, coming to rest there. Now, take a deep breath. That's right. And now let it seem as if many minutes had passed. Now, I'd like for you to slowly arouse and look at me and talk to me. Now, slowly rouse up now. (She opens her eyes.) That's right. And you're beginning to learn to go into a trance. (Erickson lightly takes hold of a suspended left hand.) And how does your hand feel? (She says it is a little heavy.) That's right. A little heavy. (Erickson continues with what has been called "The Reverse Set," but eventually terminates the trance in this manner.) Rouse up. Do I have to awaken you again?" (Erickson raises the tone of his voice and lightly rubs her left hand.)

Erickson begins the induction by confirming her interest in hypnosis and defines it as a learning process. He then casually instructs her to *just let* things happen and directly suggests that they *will* happen. Notice that he informs her of his intentions of touching her hands before he places them on her thighs so as not to startle her, and indirectly asks permission by giving her a chance to refuse. Notice how the pacing statements are utilized to focus her attention *before* the analogies of automatic movement that are appropriate (matching/pacing) for a young woman. These analogies prepare her for the automatic movement required in hand levitation by initiating an unconscious search for the processes needed to automatically lift her hands. Erickson then paces and leads her by demonstrating how the hands lift up consciously, and continues the unconscious search by commenting about the unconscious lifting of the hands while fixating her attention on his hands. Notice how he speaks to her unconscious mind with the phrase "very, very slowly, *without* it being a voluntary thing." (It was not unusual for Erickson (and this author) to enter a brief trance to demonstrate the unconscious movement expected.) Her attention is further fixated by firmly stating, "Now, what I'd like you to understand is this," before he describes the dissociation of the mind as conscious and unconscious, and concludes with "You know what I mean, do you not?" The intense eye contact is used to speak to her unconscious mind. The dissociation is continued by reminding her that the conscious mind can lift either hand voluntarily, as well as show automatic movement by continuing the inner search, with the expectation that the unconscious mind is going to lift a hand by the questions, "I'm going to ask you, which hand is your unconscious mind going to lift first? The right hand or the left hand, and *you really don't* know. But, your *unconscious knows.*" Erickson then notices a slight movement in her right hand and begins to use leading suggestions until the hand is lifting automatically to his suggestions. A direct eye closure suggestion is linked to observing the hand levitating in a casual manner and suggesting that she feel the levitation. Suggesting that the elbow bend is only natural to direct the hand towards the face. Again, he informs her of his intention before he touches her other hand. Slightly sliding his thumb under her other wrist is a tactile suggestion that he is going to lift her hand, and she follows the suggestion by levitating the left hand as he gently guides it along with verbal leading suggestions. After a cataleptic position has been obtained in both hands, he facilitates another inner search by suggesting, "And now I wonder if you know which hand is going to go down first." Again, pacing and leading suggestions are utilized for the lowering of the hands. Notice how simply the downward movement is linked to deepening the trance. Not only is the hand reaching her lap linked to a deep breath and deepening trance, but it is also linked to "new" learning about how to enjoy a trance experience. As he awakens her, he again frames hypnosis as a learning process as he initially defines it. Notice, that at the end of the initial induction with her, she reports her hand being heavy (unlike the previous inductions). This is intentional. Erickson does not want her to fully awaken because this is only the first phase of the trance work that he is doing with her. But notice how he does awaken her at the termination of the trance session—raising the tone of his voice and slightly rubbing her hand. Rubbing parts of one's body after being asleep causes faster blood circulation and is associated with awakening. It is interesting to note that, after this 50-minute session, she is not convinced that she has been in a trance because she has remembered much of the experience, and this does not match her expectation of being in a trance. Time distortion is used to ratify the trance experience by having her wonder where 50 minutes has gone when she feels that it has only been several minutes.

3. Induction #6 - Multiple Dissociation with a Negative Hallucinatory Experience

The term "dissociation" is being used differently here. In this induction, different parts of the body are dissociated from the rest of the body. Thus, multiple dissociation refers to more than one dissociation.

After a successful trance induction has been achieved and evidence of a deep trance has been obtained, such as the double hand levitations in the preceding induction or that described in the "Floating Hand Induction" from Chapter 7, the following suggestions can be incorporated to create dissociations while the arm is in a cataleptic state:

> Now, your arm can feel that it doesn't belong to you—that it is not part of your body. It is detached and you really don't know where it is. It's simply resting comfortably somewhere in space, and that is not important. The important thing is that you can learn something else today. (Pause.) Now, you can hear my voice and only my voice, and I want you to know that you can open your eyes and see me and only me, but not yet. We can be here all alone—just you and I—all alone here. And I can talk to you and you can talk to me. But there's something incredibly important that you can learn to use in the future. Something very important that your unconscious can teach your conscious mind that can be utilized without your conscious awareness when the need arises. When I instruct you to open your

eyes, your entire body from the neck down, *will* remain completely in a comfortable trance, as if it were paralyzed and be completely under the control of your unconscious mind. And you will only awaken from the neck up. You will see me, and only me, just as you can hear my voice, and only my voice. Now, do you understand these instructions? (Subject nods her head.) Now, gradually and slowly open your eyes and see me and only me. (Subject gradually opens her eyes.) Gradually open your eyes. That's right. They will slowly adjust. (Pause.) Now, what do you see? (Subject responds, "You.") What do I look like? (Subject responds, "Your eyes. Your hair. Your beard.") Anything else? (Subject responds, "Your shoulders.") That's right. And we are here alone? (Subject responds, "Yes.") How do you feel? (Subject pauses and responds, "Strange. I feel funny.") What do you mean? (Subject responds, "I can't move. It's like my body doesn't belong to me.") That's right. But that's all right isn't it? You feel comfortable? (Subject responds, "Yes. It's just strange.") And now you know that you can dissociate any part of your body or your entire body, if need be, when your unconscious mind feels that there is a need in your life or an expected or unexpected situation that requires your body to be motionless or anesthetized for a particular time. And you understand that, do you not? (Subject nods her head.) That's right. Now, close your eyes, and the next time you open your eyes, according to my instructions, you will awaken with this new learning experience, but your right arm will remain in a trance, and only the rest of your body will awaken while that arm will feel unattached to your body and remain in a comfortable trance, and your unconscious understands that, does it not? (Subject nods head.) All right, begin counting backwards from twenty to one silently to yourself and, at the count of one, slowly open your eyes and awaken. Begin counting now. (Subject eventually opens her eyes and reorients her body except for the cataleptic arm.) How do you feel? (Subject responds, "Comfortable," and smiles.) Do you feel awake now? (Said in a normal tone of voice. Subject responds, "Yes.") How does your left arm feel? (Subject responds, "Fine.") How does your right arm feel? (Subject pauses and looks confused. This "look" is a return to the trance state because she is following a hypnotic suggestion that will be discussed in Chapter 9, "Utilization of Hypnotic Phenomena.") Do you always leave your arm up like that? (Said in a nurturing, but humorous way and, then, the therapist touches the arm.) Relax your arm and completely awaken. (Arm slowly drops to her lap.) You know, you've been a great hypnotic subject and you've learned a great deal today that can have an impact on the rest of your life. And I wonder if what you have learned today will begin to change your life for the better. I'll see you next week.

This trance demonstrates two body dissociations, a negative hallucination, multiple language forms, and the confusion technique in front of an audience. Notice that the first dissociation utilizes a simple arm levitation with suggestions that it is no longer attached to the body, but with the important suggestion for its whereabouts, i.e. "resting *comfortably* somewhere in space." This is immediately followed with a suggestion to forget about the arm, i.e. "It's not important." This implies that something more important is about to happen, thus creating an expectation—causing the subject to wonder what comes next—a subtle way of deepening trance. This expectation is utilized by having the subject focus on the therapist's voice in preparation of the negative hallucination. The expectation is the new learning experience that the subject can open her eyes in trance (unexpected to many people in trance). The suggestion for a visual negative hallucination is then made after the subject is prepared by the two prior negative suggestions of the arm being detached and to hear only the therapist's voice. Next, notice the pacing and leading suggestions. To verify this negative hallucination, the therapist asks her what she can see. Her responses are typical of a visual negative hallucinatory experience. She describes the therapist from the chest up, i.e. *direct field of vision* from looking directly at the therapist. Sometimes a subject will have the Gestalt experience of seeing the therapist quite sharply, and the audience and the rest of the room will be fuzzy and in the background. The body dissociation is verified by asking her how she feels. The pause before responding signifies an inner search. The paralysis suggestion is also verified, as well as being followed with suggestions for comfort so as not to create an abreaction of fright. Then, the most important therapeutic suggestion is delivered. She is directly told that she now knows that she can dissociate any part of her body and it is proved to her by experiencing it. Although this is something that all of us continually do in our lives, we're unconscious of it. By bringing it into our awareness, it is a learning experience. She is also told that she can use this "new learning experience" whenever the situation warrants it and a clear example is given, i.e. the need to have an anesthetized experience. Then, there is confirmation of this understanding. To make sure that the suggestion to remember this takes place, she is told to awaken while her arm remains in a trance to reinforce to the conscious mind that this has happened and can happen again. When a part of the body remains in trance, the subject frequently does not initially become fully awake, as is demonstrated in the other inductions. Notice that questions are asked about the non-trance parts of the body first, so that the subject notices the difference between the non-trance and the trance. The "pause and trance look," signifying a return to the trance state, is countered with humor to let her know this is okay. Thus, she then becomes fully awake and alert. She is then complimented for being an excellent subject, but notice the wording of the last suggestion upon closure. These are post-hypnotic suggestions for change and an excellent way to end a good therapy session.

An important note: An experienced hypnotherapist could completely awaken the subject while leaving that arm in a trance during a therapeutic situation. But, this should *never* be attempted by the *novice*. This author has done this procedure in numerous situations during the past 15 years, but the first time was after three years of hypnotherapeutic experiences. (Remember, always practice within your expertise and limitations.) Some situations warranting this advanced technique could be a painful break or a severe injury requiring the hand or arm to be elevated or kept away from the body to prevent further injury before professional medical attention is found.

This advanced technique has frequently been used within the field of dental and medical hypnosis to induce hypnotic anesthesia for pain control and surgical procedures. A case study of its use in obstetrical procedures, including natural childbirth and caesarean delivery is given in detail by South (1988).

D. Cataleptic Inductions

Since catalepsy is a common trance phenomenon and is easily elicited by most individuals in everyday situations, it can conveniently be used to induce trance. However, some subjects may only be cataleptic in light trances and others only in deep trances. The absence of catalepsy certainly does not indicate that an individual cannot enter trance as susceptibility scales suggest. If catalepsy is not successful, try another technique.

1. *Induction #7 - Handshake Induction*

The handshake induction (Erickson, Rossi and Rossi, 1976, p. 108) is probably the most famous of Erickson's inductions and the most misunderstood due to its seemingly mysterious appearance. It is a non-verbal induction that initiates catalepsy by tactile confusion. Due to its complexity, it requires much practice and attention to non-verbal cues. This is an advanced induction and is not for everyone. It is not always successful and it is not appropriate in all situations. Its attempt should be at the hypnotherapist's discretion. The only requirement is the willingness of the individual to be approached and shake hands. If it fails, nothing is lost. When mastered, it is a beautiful art form.

The following explanation is taken from Erickson and Rossi (1976, p. 108). The induction is initiated by approaching an individual and shaking hands in a normal manner. The induction begins when the firm handshake is being loosened. This loosening is transformed from a:

> ... firm grip into a gentle touch by the thumb, a lingering drawing away of the little finger, a faint brushing of the subject's hand with the middle finger—just enough vague sensation to attract the attention. As the subject gives attention to the touch of your thumb, you shift to a touch with your little finger. As the subject's attention follows that, you shift to a touch with your middle finger and, then again, to the thumb. ... the withdrawal from the handshake is arrested by this attention arousal, which establishes a waiting set, an expectancy. ... touch the undersurface of the hand (wrist) so gently that it barely suggests an upward push. This is followed by a similar slight downward touch, and then, I sever contact so gently that the subject does not know exactly when—and the subject's hand is left going neither up nor down, but cataleptic. Sometimes I give a lateral and medial touch so that the hand is even more rigidly cataleptic.

If the induction is not utilized, you can simply verbally distract the individual by conversation. Utilization will increase trance depth and should proceed as a continuation of the procedure as you would with any other trance induction.

2. Induction #8 - Extended Hand Induction

This induction was inspired by the handshake induction and is much easier to implement. While the title was coined by this author, this induction was taught by Grinder and Bandler (1981, pp. 70–77) while conducting hypnosis workshops. It has been used by both authors to demonstrate catalepsy in the normal awake state to our students. The induction is based on a conditioned response as learned in our culture, i.e. handshaking. From early childhood, we are taught that it is socially acceptable to shake hands to greet someone or to take leave, and refusal is considered rude. Thus, handshaking is good manners.

The induction begins by extending your right hand in friendship. The automatic or unconscious response is for the other person to reach for your hand. But instead of clasping his/her hand, you lightly grasp the wrist of the extended hand with your left hand while it is suspended in mid-air and it will remain cataleptic. Then, the hand can be moved laterally or upward and the induction continued as a levitation procedure. In *Trance-Formations* (Grinder and Bandler, 1981), Bandler turns the palm of the cataleptic hand towards the subject's face and states,

> "Look at your hand. Would you consider carefully all the color changes and shadows that occur on your hand. Study the lines and creases with interest as you allow your arm to begin to drift down slowly ... with honest unconscious movements ... your eyes will begin to feel heavy ... and will close ... you will see clearly ... just prior to your hand ... finishing its downward movement ... something of interest to you ... that you haven't seen ... for years ... take your time ... enjoy it."

This is one example of continuing the trance state. Remember, we are limited only by our own creative minds.

3. Induction #9 - Ideodynamic Induction

Any of the automatic or ideodynamic responses discussed in Chapter 9 can be paced and led as a hypnotic induction. However, the following induction by Erickson (Erickson and Rossi, 1979,

p. 55) is a beautiful example of utilizing an ideomotor behavior as a trance induction on an otherwise resistant subject:

> After a general discussion of hypnosis, she expressed a willingness to go into a trance immediately. The suggestion was offered that she select the chair and position she felt would be most comfortable. When she had settled herself to her satisfaction, she remarked that she would like to smoke a cigarette. She was immediately given one, and she proceeded to smoke lazily, meditatively, watching the smoke drifting upward. Casual conversational remarks were offered about the pleasure of smoking, of watching the curling smoke, the feeling of ease in lifting the cigarette to her mouth, the inner sense of satisfaction of becoming entirely absorbed just in smoking comfortably and without need to attend to any external things. Shortly, casual remarks were made about inhaling and exhaling, these words timed to fit in with her actual breathing. Others were made about the ease with which she could almost automatically lift her cigarette to her mouth and then lower her hand to the arm of the chair. These remarks were also timed to coincide with her actual behavior. Soon, the words "inhale," "exhale," "lift," and "lower" acquired a conditioning value of which she was unaware because of the seemingly conversational nature of the suggestion. Similarly, casual suggestions were offered in which the words sleep, sleepy, and sleeping were timed to her eyelid behavior.
>
> Before she had finished the cigarette, she had developed a light trance. Then the suggestion was made that she might continue to enjoy smoking as she slept more and more soundly; that the cigarette would be looked after by the hypnotist while she absorbed herself more and more completely in deep sleep; that, as she slept, she would continue to experience the satisfying feelings and sensations of smoking. A satisfactory profound trance resulted.

Rossi's commentary following this narrative stated that a less experienced hypnotist would have probably considered the desire to smoke as resistance and that students who did not accept her smoking failed at hypnotizing her. He explained that allowing her to smoke, especially offering her a cigarette, enhanced rapport. Erickson did not disrupt her normal pattern of behavior, but utilized it in casual conversation by pacing and leading.

E. Pantomime Techniques

Perhaps the most fascinating and intriguing contribution to the field of hypnosis and the least known and understood were the pantomime inductions developed by Erickson (1964b). In this paper Erickson gave a detailed account of several pantomime inductions he conducted in Mexico and Venezuela. These inductions were the result of his accumulated knowledge of hypnosis, including his non-verbal inductions, and human behavior. These inductions clearly indicated that hypnosis was a special process of communication with another individual. They adequately demonstrated that hypnotic suggestions can be given intentionally, as well as unintentionally by well-meaning individuals.

Although pantomime inductions are difficult to describe, the following actual presentation is offered as an attempt at this endeavor. As a volunteer from the audience approaches the hypnotherapist and comes within arm's reach, the hypnotherapist smiles and offers his hand to the subject, who likewise extends his hand. The extended hand is lightly squeezed in a handshake, and, as the hand is very slowly loosened, the smile slowly changes to a blank stare into the subject's eyes. All of this takes place as if in slow motion. The hypnotherapist's face becomes expressionless as he enters a light trance. This creates confusion in the subject and acts as an unconscious cue to go into a trance. The hypnotherapist slowly blinks his eyes as a non-verbal suggestion to the subject, and, as he continues to slowly open and close his eyes, the subject begins to blink. The hypnotherapist then begins to allow his eyes to remain closed longer and longer until the subject does the same. The subject usually will close his eyes and keep them closed. If he doesn't, the hypnotherapist simply reaches up towards the subject's eyes with his left hand and they will close. (A natural phenomenon.) The right hand is then released and the subject's hand remains cataleptic, as the subject goes into a trance. At this point comments are made to the audience who are usually confused. This author usually begins comments with the following statement: "He knows that I'm not talking to him because in a trance an individual can tell from which direction the voice originates, and, as I continue to talk to you, he can either listen to a boring presentation, or his mind can wander to any enjoyable place of pleasant experience. You're probably wondering, 'What happened?' You may also be wondering, 'How will he awaken?' But that's not really important because he will know when to awaken, just as his unconscious mind knows the cue for the conscious to enter trance. Now, you know that hypnosis is a process." After the presentation, the hypnotherapist re-engages the handshake, and the left hand lightly touches the subject's eyes causing the eyes to open. The hypnotherapist then smiles as he continues shaking hands, and thanks the subject for volunteering to be a subject. He then asks the subject to take his seat in the audience. Several members of the audience will usually ask questions, but not the subject. He usually simply stares at the hypnotherapist in kind of a bonding way. The subject is asked to respond to any questions regarding his experience. Many questions are unanswerable, so a break is given and they are told to think about what they have experienced and to share their thoughts with others. This allows the hypnotherapist and the subject time to discuss the experience and put closure on it.

F.   Confusion Techniques

While confusion appears in many inductions, as well as in some of the preceding inductions, it is a unique induction by itself. This induction can be verbal, nonverbal, or a combination of both elements. The confusion technique can be a play on words and/or unexpected behavior that interrupts usual thought patterns. Communication is delivered in an emphatic manner with meaningful ideas within a medley of loosely related associations that lead subjects to try to combine them in some meaningful way. However, the communication inhibits this which results in frustration and confusion. This compels an inner need for some clear understanding and often causes the subject to accept the first definitive suggestion offered. It can be either a simple or a complex procedure. Erickson was a master at utilizing confusion to induce trance, especially with so-called "resistant subjects." (Resistance is defined as a rejection of the suggestions offered and is usually a result of inadequate pacing and leading.)

The following contains a few examples from Erickson's prolific writings on the use of the confusion technique.

1. Induction #10 - A Nonverbal Approach

... A student nurse was pressured by her supervisor to volunteer as a subject. Fortunately, she was interested in being a subject, but she disliked being told to act as one. Advantage was taken of this emotional setting to use a confusion technique. ... As she approached the front of the lecture room from a side aisle, a chair was moved somewhat ostentatiously into place for her. When she was within six feet of the chair, she was asked, 'Will you sit on this chair here?' As the word 'this' was spoken, the writer's left hand was carefully placed on the back of that chair, as if to point it out. As the word 'here' was spoken, the writer gestured with his right hand, as if indicating a chair to the side of the actual chair. There was a momentary pause in her behavior, but, as she continued her approach, the chair was pushed slightly toward her, causing a slight noise as it scraped on the floor. This was readily audible. As she came still closer to the chair, it was pulled slightly to one side away from her, and immediately as she seemed to note this, it was pushed back an inch or so, and then another inch or so forward and to the side toward her. All of this she noted because the writer's left hand on the back of the chair constituted a focusing point.

By this time she had reached the chair, had turned slightly, and had begun to lower her body into it. As soon as her knees were bent, the chair was rotated about an inch, and, as she paused again momentarily to look at the chair, the writer took hold of her right elbow and moved it away from her body slightly and then slightly forward. As she turned to look in response to this, her elbow was released and her right hand and wrist were gently taken and moved slightly upward and then downward. As she shifted her gaze from her elbow to her hand, she was told quietly, 'Just sit all the way down in the chair, and, as you do so, just close your eyes and go way deeply into the trance, and, as you continue to sit there, sleep ever more deeply in a hypnotic trance.'

As she settled in the chair, the additional statement was made, 'And now you can take a deep comfortable breath while I go on with my lecture.' Thereupon, without further delay or training, she was immediately employed to demonstrate somnambulistic trance and all the other phenomena of the deep trance. She was awakened approximately one hour later, and demonstrated spontaneously a total amnesia by stating, 'But, you've got me so confused I don't know what to do. Is it all right to sit this way, and what do you want me to do with my hand?'

Reply was made, 'Would you like to go into a trance?' (Erickson, 1964c; and Erickson and Rossi 1980 Vol. I, pp. 292–296).

2. Induction #11 - A Verbal Approach

You know and I know and the doctors you know know that there is one answer that you know that you don't want to know and that I know but don't want to know, that your family knows but doesn't want to know, no matter how much you want to say no, you know that the no is really a yes, and you wish it could be a good yes. And so do you know, that what you and your family know is yes, yet you wish that yes could be no and you know that all the doctors know that what they know is yes, yet they still wish it were no. And just as you wish there were no pain, you know that there is but what you don't know is no pain is something you can know. And no matter what you knew no pain would be better that what you know and of course what you want to know is no pain and that is what you are going to know, no pain. ... Esther knows pain and knows no pain and so do you wish to know no pain but comfort and you do know comfort and no pain. And as comfort increases you know that you cannot say no to ease and comfort but you can say no pain and know no pain but you can say no pain and know comfort and ease and it is so good to know comfort and ease and relaxation to know it now and later and still longer and longer as more and more relaxation occurs and to know it now and later and still longer and longer as more and more relaxation and wonder ... and surprise come to your mind as you begin to know a freedom and a comfort you have so greatly desired and as you feel it grow and grow you know, really know, that today, tonight, tomorrow, all next week and next month, and at Esther's 16th birthday, and what a time that was, and these wonderful feelings that you had then seem almost as clear as if they were today and the memory of every good thing is a glorious thing ... (Erickson and Rossi, 1981, p. 285).

G. Utilizing Resistance Techniques

Resistance is considered an action of opposition to a perceived force. In therapeutic situations, the client is assumed to be resisting change when he or she attempts to avoid understanding or accepting interpretations on following the suggestions of the therapist. However, resistance seems to be a normal way of responding to change. People do not like to change. The way that they have been doing things is familiar and comfortable to them even though it is not effective in achieving their goals. It seems that people prefer to change others or the environment than change their own way of thinking or behaving. For example, a spouse who has a habit of throwing things when angry will continue throwing things even though a mess will have to be cleaned up and maybe broken items will have to be bought again.

Therapists succumb to this kind of thinking and behaving, too. Many therapists continue to use techniques, beliefs and approaches that are not effective with specific clients, and, when the client does not benefit, the client is blamed. This relieves the therapist of the responsibility of having to change his or her thinking or behavior.

Erickson believed that resistance was a way for clients to protect themselves against change. He thought that when a client resisted therapy it was because the therapist did not really understand the client or respect the client's view of the problem. Resistance can be due to many things, such as miscommunications, misunderstandings, disbeliefs, doubts, ambivalences, rigid beliefs, limited understanding, distrust, unconscious defense mechanisms, defiance, or just a natural tendency not to change. Erickson chose to think of resistance as a challenge and utilized everything the client brought into the office to effect therapeutic change.

To illustrate the effective use of resistance as an induction, the following excerpt from a seminar delivered by Erickson in 1965 at Seattle, Washington, will be offered. Regarding the use of resistance, he states the following:

> Resistance is a very important phenomenon you ought to be able to recognize and utilize when it occurs in your patients. The patient comes into your office, sits down, and starts shifting in the chair. He certainly is not settling down to a comfortable acceptance of what you are going to say to him. How can you deal with that?
>
> First I ask, "Do you mind standing up?" And he doesn't mind standing up, so then I ask, "Will you please place your weight primarily on your right foot?" He does. "And now shift your weight to your left foot." He does that too. "Now will you please sit down, and put your hand on the arm of the chair there; now put it here;

now put it on the other arm; then put it there. Now, I think you will feel very comfortable."

If patients want to shift their position, why shouldn't I have them shift their position? The point is that I have them shift their position; I ask them to shift their position, and I have certainly satisfied their need to shift around. Equally important, I have utilized their resistances, because the more times you get patients to say, 'yes, yes, yes, yes, yes,' the more adequately you have started them on this matter of hypnosis.

At another point in the seminar, he talked about how a therapist can use imitation and nonverbal cues to convert tension into relaxation and establish a yes set. Erickson stated:

I know that people will imitate, so I am very, very willing to utilize that imitative tendency, only I do so indirectly, I am very careful to appear to be simply self-absorbed—as if I were thoughtfully collecting my thoughts, and so patients feel free to look at me. Why shouldn't they look? There might be something of interest to them. Now I shift my gaze to the other side of the room and again I seem to be gathering my thoughts, and they again are looking over there along with me. I have given nonverbal suggestions; look here, look there. They have obeyed my nonverbal suggestions, and the more suggestions you get them to obey the more they fall into the habit of accepting your suggestions.

Erickson concluded his discussion on resistance with the following:

There is yet another angle to this matter of fighting resistance, certainly you ought not to contend with your patient; you ought not to enter a contest with your patient. So you can say: 'Well, I suppose we could really fight it out all day on this matter of whether or not I can put you in a trance, but I really don't believe you came here for that purpose. I think you came here to be helped in some way, and *I would like to understand your problem.*' Notice where I am exaggerating my emphasis. I said, 'I would like to understand your problem.' I am saying, 'I don't want to fight it out with you for the rest of the day; instead, *I would like to understand your problem.*' And, so I have shifted the battleground from one of resistance to one of understanding. The patient suddenly finds himself transported to another level of dealing with me, but I did have the honesty just to concede that 'we could fight it out all day so far as resistance is concerned, but really, *I would prefer to understand your problem.*' I have cut the ground from underneath my patient's feet comfortably, easily, and without antagonizing him. At the same time, I have not rejected his request for a duel, and it is a privilege to go along with me and tell me what his problem really is. And so the question of resistance is dropped right then and there." (Rossi, Ryan, and Sharp, 1983, pp. 237–245)

In concluding, everything that a client brings into the therapy session is utilized, including resistance, to effect a therapeutic change. Resistance is viewed as a positive action by the client to protect him or her in some way and as nothing more than a challenge to the therapist. Therefore, the therapist has to be flexible in order to discharge the resistance. We view resistance as a lack of effective pacing and leading.

H. Spontaneous Inductions

People enter spontaneous trances several times a day. They enter a trance whenever attention is focused inward, e.g. reading a fascinating book, watching a thrilling movie, daydreaming, etc. Thus, they already know how to enter trance, but just don't realize it. The following examples illustrate this natural phenomenon and can be utilized to induce trance states:

1. *Induction #12 - Direct Suggestion*

"Nancy, now I want you to go into a trance. It doesn't take that long, but we have all day. Just close your eyes. That's right. Relax and just let it happen."

2. *Induction #13 - Spontaneous Re-Induction*

"Now, you've been in trance before, have you not? That's right. And you know how to be relaxed and comfortable. So, just settle back. Close your eyes. Now, just think about that pleasant trance experience. That's right." (Therapist observes signs of trance and then tests for trance.)

I. Summary

In this chapter thirteen advanced inductions have been presented in varying detail. They, of course, make use of the material you've learned in basic inductions, as well as provide practical practice with language forms. Following Erickson's utilization principle, you need to adapt the induction to the individual. But, the more inductions you have practiced, the more effective you will be in an almost unconscious selection of the best one to use.

Exercises

1. Read through the inductions in this chapter and highlight the words and phrases you think are especially significant to mark out for delivery.

2. Tape record several of the inductions and listen to your delivery. How would you change your delivery?

3. The handshake induction can be used on special occasions as a rapid induction. When would you use it and with whom?

4. The hand levitation induction is a favorite of many beginners and is well worth practicing. But that is only an induction, and you need to have a plan of what to do *after* the client is in trance. The following chapters on the use of metaphors will help in this regard. Practice the hand levitation induction until it becomes automatic.

5. Write out your own inductions following the several styles in this chapter. Then shorten them, and shorten them again.

Chapter 9

Utilization of Hypnotic Phenomena

Rubin Battino, M.S. and Thomas L. South, Ph.D.

A. Introduction

Hypnotic phenomena appear to be unusual or extraordinary behavior elicited by individuals while in a trance state or as a result of being hypnotized. While this behavior is suggested and often elicited during and following trance, the events are far from being unusual. These behaviors are often experienced by each of us in our daily lives and are utilized in hypnosis in direct and indirect suggestions. Thus, hypnotic phenomena are applications of common everyday experiences as a result of hypnosis.

The hypnotic phenomena described in this chapter are the most common experiences that either occur naturally in the trance state or are elicited. They certainly are not all of the phenomena. However, most of the phenomena used in the instructions cited in this book will be reviewed.

B. Age Regression

Age regression involves utilizing an individual's memory to intensely go back into the past, usually at a specific time. If an individual relives the experience as if it were in the present, it is called *revivification*. If the individual observes the experience in a dissociated state, it is called *hypermnesia*. Age regression techniques are utilized to recover forgotten memories, to retrieve conscious or unconscious abilities and skills, to reframe old experiences, and to use those earlier capabilities in the present to resolve current problems.

Perhaps Erickson's most famous case involving age regression is "The February Man" (Erickson and Rossi, 1980, vol. IV, pp. 525–42). This case was also discussed by Haley (1973, 1986). However, it received book-length treatment in Erickson and Rossi (1989). In this book, Rossi recreates the case with verbatim transcripts, his own commentary, and commentary he had elicited from Erickson. This book was written forty years after the case was recorded by a stenographer. Erickson and Rossi (1980, Vol. IV, pp. 526–527) give the background of the patient as:

> At midterm of her first pregnancy, the wife of a young doctor on our hospital staff approached the senior author for psychiatric help. Her problem was that although happily married and pleased with her pregnancy, she was fearful that her own unhappy childhood experiences would reflect themselves in her handling of her child. She stated that she had "studied too much psychology" since it made her aware of the possible inadvertent unfortunate handling of a child, with resulting psychological traumatization.

> ... [Details are given of her upbringing.]

> Because of this history, she now wondered what kind of mother she would be. Her psychological reading had convinced her that her rejection by her mother and her emotional starvation as a child would in some way adversely affect the handling of her own baby. She wanted to know if, through hypnosis, her unconscious could be explored and either her anxieties relieved or she could be made aware of her deficiencies and thus make corrections. She asked the senior author to consider her problem at length and to give her another appointment when he felt he might be able to meet her needs.

Over a period of months, Erickson regressed her and introduced a friend of her father, the February Man, from the month he first met her. Year by year, usually around her birthday, the February Man would visit her in trance and slowly build up the necessary secure childhood with care and advice. She was given amnesia for these sessions, but in a carefully constructed final session was allowed full memory of the meetings with the February Man with the assurance that she had now learned how to be a good mother.

The book about the case should be studied carefully for all of the subtleties of Erickson's approach, including the conscious design of his word usage. Sidney Rosen (in the foreword to the book) gives an excellent summary of the rationales for using age regression.

What is the value of utilizing regression as the dominant feature in this therapy? While I was reading this book, it became clear to me why Erickson tended to treat almost everyone as a child! I suddenly understood why, at least in his later years, he seemed to be so enamored of corny jokes, childish puzzles and games. I now feel that he understood, probably from having learned it from working with adult patients in the hypnotically regressed state, that it is precisely in this "child state" that we are most open to learning, most curious, and most able to change. In order to intensify the patient's experience of regression, Erickson worked consistently to create a remarkably convincing illusion that he really was an older person talking to a young child. He had the "child" reenact and abreact to traumatic experiences and, through discussion, guided her through a reeducation process. As a result, the "child" had new experiences to add to her memories—positive experiences with a caring and understanding adult. These "corrective regression experiences," as I have called them, exerted a long-lasting effect on the patient, even after she returned to her "adult self" (p. vii).

At one point, Rossi suggests to Erickson that the best of his hypnotic therapy is "abreaction and a restructuring of the patient's mental processes." Erickson corrects him, saying, "It is not restructuring. You give them a more complete view." Rossi is then able to sum up his understanding with the comment, "It [hypnotic therapy] simply facilitates a more complete, comprehensive point of view and frees one from the limitations and literalism of childhood." This is a far cry from the belief of many therapists that hypnosis involves some kind of reprogramming (p. viii).

But regression does not need to be "real" in order to be helpful. Simply the subjective feeling of being young may make it possible for a patient to view matters from different perspectives. (p. ix)

Before terminating the therapy, Erickson helped the patient to ventilate hostility towards him. He reasons that this is important because patients often are angry at the therapist for taking away their symptoms and may express their anger by destroying their therapeutic work (p. ix).

Again, we suggest careful study of this case. But, what about the "mechanics" of age regression? How do you age regress a client? The "direct" approach is to induce a trance state using one of the many methods available, and then to say something like, "And, now, I would like you to just drift backward in time, to an earlier time when you were younger, and the problem you came to see me about had its origins. I don't know how old you were then."

A more direct statement would be, "Go back in your mind, now, to when you were five years old and tell me what you see." From previous discussion with the client, you can pick an appropriate age. It is usually useful to regress to a time *before* any traumatic event occurred to "sneak" up on it and provide a dissociative protection. It is also useful to provide an amnesia for any traumatic events that are elicited to protect the client—recall is permitted when the client can handle these memories.

Kay Thompson in her workshops endlessly emphasized the use of the naturalistic indirect way of simultaneously eliciting trance and regression by asking a client to "think about the house or apartment you grew up in. Do you remember how the doorknobs and light switches seemed so high up? And how hard it was to reach the sink? There may have been a time in that house that you would like to tell me about in a few words." The very act of thinking about your childhood domicile leads to a regression, and the act of focussing on that time induces a trance state without such words as "relax" and "close your eyes," etc. Talking about the earlier experiences that we all have had automatically brings about regression when the client goes inside to recall the memories and feeling states associated with that time. Of course, both direct and indirect approaches work.

One need not use such a complex technique as the February Man to elicit age regression. The simple suggesting that individuals return to past dates or earlier times will create age regression. Visual hallucinations are excellent avenues to elicit age regression. The therapist can have a person hallucinate a movie screen and can tell if the subject is really watching a movie screen by nonverbal cues. Then, the therapist asks what the subject is seeing and makes such comments as what is being said, what the person on the screen is thinking, feeling, etc. Other figures and things can be added to the screen. Age regression is mostly used to recall past events or return to a time before a problem began and then solve the problem. It is also used for reframing. These are just some ways of creating and using age regression. Books on hypnosis frequently contain many cases in which age regression has been used to solve problems.

C. Age Progression or Pseudo-Orientation in Time

Erickson (1954) defined pseudo-orientation in time as a procedure involving projecting a person into the future to experience those future "realities" in the present. "Thus, the patient was enabled to achieve a detached, dissociated, objective, and yet subjective view of what he believed at the moment he had already accomplished, without awareness that those accomplishments were the expression in fantasy of his hopes and desires" (Erickson, 1954). This is an age *progression* or a time projection approach.

In the 1954 paper, Erickson discussed five cases in detail. He started Patient A with a "crystal ball" technique. In trance he had the client hallucinate a series of crystal balls in which he could see various outstanding emotional and traumatic experiences in his life. The dissociation involved letting the client observe these events safely. After several preparatory sessions, Erickson wrote:

At the next session, with the patient in the waking state, a vague general discussion was elaborately offered of what he could expect in the future. This, it was explained, *would be the opportunity to look back over the past, to review his complaints and difficulties, and to recall the developments of therapy. Then, most importantly, he could examine all these accomplishments, resulting from therapy, that represented his achievement of these things signifying normal adjustments. However, this latter could be done only after a lapse of time, probably several months, following the termination of therapy.*

He was then hypnotized deeply, and the discussion was repeated in general terms. Still in the deep somnambulistic trance, he was then disoriented for time and then oriented or projected in time to some future date. [Emphasis in original]

In this future time, the client viewed another series of crystal balls.

Then the suggestion was made that he might be aided in giving his report on the *therapeutic developments he had achieved* by visualizing the significant incidents in another series of crystal balls. Thus, he could enjoy watching the progressive unfolding of each *event as it had occurred.* [Emphases added]

Two critical phrases have been emphasized in this last quote. The first implies that *he had already achieved* therapeutic developments. The second talks about these change events *having occurred in the past*. These implications are crucial to the success of this approach.

Why does this method work? We can never know the client as well as he/she knows him/herself. One of our operating rules of thumb is: when all else fails, *ask the client* what will work for him/her. The age progression technique uses a structure where the client can find his/her own unique and personalized solutions to their problem. It is not only implied, but can be stated directly that they *will have already* found these solutions in this future time. What they are uncovering is *how* they found those solutions and *what* they are. Once they have enunciated these solutions, the existing problem has been effectively *reframed* to a soluble one. Believing "as if" change has occurred results in behaving *as if* they had already occurred. (Rossi's "fail-safe" ideodynamic approach follows the same general scheme discussed here, but in real time. See Chapter 10.) Once solutions have been conceived and understood and vivified in the trance state, then they act in a self-fulfilling way, slowly penetrating into consciousness and controlling present behavior from the future!

In the following case (Haley, 1973, 1986, pp. 280–282) Erickson had the oversolicitous parents of a daughter do some time traveling into the future to experience *now* anticipated occurrences *then*:

The House Addition

A young lady came to me very much alarmed about her parents. She had two possessive, oversolicitous parents. When the girl went to college, her mother did all her laundry, did all her sewing, and supervised her weekends. However, what was most upsetting to the girl was that as part of her high school graduation present, her parents built rooms onto their house so that when she married, she could live there. The girl said she didn't know what to do about this addition to the house because they expected her to live with them and she didn't wish to. Yet, they had invested all this money and were being so kind. The girl had the feeling that she was being trapped by her parents and could never be independent of them even if she married.

I saw the parents together and we had a pleasant series of talks. I congratulated them on their concern for their daughter's welfare. They had anticipated the daughter's future, so I anticipated her falling in love, getting engaged, getting married, becoming pregnant, and delivering a child. In this discussion, I emphasized how much more willing they were than other parents to take the consequences of these future events. Most parents, when a daughter is raised, feel their work is over, but these parents could look forward to a continuation of their labors. With their daughter living right there in the addition on the house, they could look forward to the services they could offer her when she had a child. They would be available for babysitting at any time, unlike most parents who don't like that imposition. They could look forward to a baby crying in the night, but of course they had soundproofed the wall to the additional rooms? It happens they hadn't. So, I congratulated them on being willing to put up with the problems of a small baby as they had when they were young and their daughter was a baby. Then we talked about their future grandchild beginning to walk, and of course, living right there, he would be in and out of their house all the time. We recalled what it was like to have a toddler getting into everything, and how all breakable things had to be placed up high and the house rearranged. Other grandparents wouldn't be that willing to sacrifice their ways of living.

The parents began to express some doubt about whether they really wished their daughter to be living that close to them.

To assist this process, I anticipated with the mother how she would have to deal with her husband's lack of understanding of their future grandson. With the husband, I anticipated his wife's lack of understanding of the child when she became a grandmother. Their differences over the daughter were shifted so they could anticipate differences about the grandchild. This would be a problem they could look forward to dealing with continually with the daughter living right there with them. Each of them agreed with me that the other probably wouldn't be as good a grandparent as might be.

After this discussion they decided they really didn't want to have their daughter and her family living with them, and yet they faced a dilemma. That addition to the house had cost so much money that they might *have* to have the daughter living there. Out of the discussion we "spontaneously" came up with a good idea. The additional rooms could be rented out to some mature, quiet person and the rent could be put aside in the bank for their future grandchild's education.

Later on the daughter did get married and lived in a city some distance away, with the full agreement of her parents. When the daughter had a baby, her parents came to me and consulted me about how often the other one was entitled to visit their grandchild. I said to grandpa that grandma ought not to visit more often than one afternoon every six weeks or two months. By a curious coincidence, I thought the same visiting times would be appropriate for grandpa.

James and Woodsmall (1988) have based their approach called "Time Line Therapy" on time travel. Most of the applications involve age regression with the "adjustment" of past events from a dissociated state followed by an awareness of how these changes affect other parts of your life up till the present. But, they also use a pseudo-orientation in time in Erickson's manner. Bandler and Grinder (1979) use time travel in their technique of "changing personal history."

The following is a seven-step model for utilizing pseudo-orientation in time.

7-Step Model for Pseudo-Orientation in Time

1. Establish that a problem exists that the client is ready to work on at this time. Provide the problem with a symbol. (Optional)

2. Induce a trance. (Optional)

3. Travel to the Future: Go inside and travel to your future to a time that is sufficiently beyond the satisfactory resolution of this problem (symbol), so that it no longer bothers you. You may even have forgotten about the problem (symbol) by this time!

4. Look, or think back, towards the present, reviewing what you had done, step-by-step, in sufficient detail to understand those therapeutic changes, to get you to your present state, now, in the reasonably near future. Store that knowledge of change in a safe and accessible place.

5. Provide your present self with some unobtrusive physical signal or reminder about these therapeutic changes and your ready access to them.

6. Return to the present knowing in your inner mind, and knowing as much as you need to know in your conscious mind, what it is that you will have already done.

7. Re-orient to the present.

We frequently find it useful to use a symbol rather than repeat the problem description. Note that we have made the use of a formal trance induction optional. Once the client goes "inside," a trance state is induced naturally and maintained by the therapist's language. You can ask the client to respond with ideomotor signals or words or phrases to indicate the completion of each step. It is always useful to say something like, "Knowing how *fast* your mind can work, take whatever time you need to ..."

D. Time Distortion

Time distortion allows an individual to distort real world "clock" time by shortening or lengthening a period of time. It is quite common, for example, for clients to feel that their time in a trance state was much shorter than clock time. We are all familiar with comments such as, "Don't know what happened to the time," "This class really drags," "The summer just disappeared," and "Will this ever end?" On one level, we have rather precise inner clocks. Yet, we all know just how subjective is our sense of time. Both time compression and expansion have their place in hypnotic work.

Cooper and Erickson (1959) wrote the classic study of time distortion in hypnosis. In Volume II of Erickson and Rossi (1980, pp. 221–300) there are four papers on the subject of time distortion. The first two papers give the results of careful experiments on time expansion in hypnosis. The third paper gives six case studies using time expansion, and the last paper discusses time condensation (or compression). Several quotes from the third paper by Erickson (alone) are illuminating (page citations are for Volume II):

...The concept of time distortion does not constitute in itself a form of psychotherapy. Rather, it offers a method by which access can be gained to the experiential life of the patient. Any therapy resulting derives from a separate process of reordering the significance and values of the patient's experiential subjective and objective realities (p. 264).

Now, I'm going to give you much more time than you need to do this experiment. I will give you 20 seconds world time [i.e. real clock time]. But, in your special time, that 20 seconds will be just as long as you need to complete your work. It can be a minute, a day, a week, a month, or even years. And you will take all the time you need. ...*Now—from Childhood to Now—Remember*! [Emphasis in original.] (pp. 275–276).

Begin at the beginning, go all the way through in normal experimental tempo with a tremendous rush of force, skipping nothing, including everything, and reach a full complete understanding of everything about *Blood*—Now (p. 281).

The second quote was for a client not in trance initially and the third for a client in deep trance. Both had training in trance before these 20 second "experiments" were tried. Notice the language used, particularly how *expectational* it was.

One can readily state that it [the case study] demonstrates that sometimes brief psychotherapy can be remarkably effective; that the dictum that the unconscious, if therapy is to be achieved, must be always made conscious warrants serious doubt; and that the concept of time distortion lends itself in a remarkable way to clinical therapeutic work. *What the patient's problem was and the nature of its causes remain unknown even to her conscious mind* [Emphasis added.] (p. 282).

We note, again, the elegant use of time expansion that Rossi's "failsafe" approach using hand movements makes. (See Chapter 10.)

Time distortion finds a major use in pain control. If a client learns to compress the duration of pain sensations and expand the experience of relief in between, then much relief is found. This has been used successfully for migraines and cancer.

Erickson used time distortion for many purposes. In this section we quote from five of his cases dealing with (in sequence): pain control, headaches, obesity, guitar practice, and amnesia. The pain control procedure can be used for any kind of pain. Those which are periodic in nature (childbirth, cancer) respond particularly well.

Periodic Lancinating Pain

An excellent example is that of the patient with intractable attacks of lancinating pain which occurred approximately every twenty to thirty minutes, night and day, and which lasted from five to ten minutes. Between the attacks the patient's frame of mind was essentially one of fearful dread of the next attack. By employing hypnosis and teaching him time distortion, it was possible to employ, as is usually the case in every pain patient, a combination of several of the measures described here. In the trance state, the patient was taught to develop an amnesia for all past attacks of pain. He was then taught time distortion so that he could experience the five to ten minute pain episodes in ten to twenty seconds. He was given posthypnotic suggestions to the effect that each attack would come as a complete surprise to him, that when the attack occurred he would develop a trance state of ten to twenty seconds' duration, experience all of the pain attack, and then come out of the trances with no awareness that he had been in a trance or that he had experienced pain. Thus, the patient, in talking to his family, would suddenly and obviously go into the trance state with a scream of pain, and perhaps ten seconds later, come out of the trance state, look confused for a moment, and then continue his interrupted sentence (Erickson and Rossi, 1979, p. 101).

Headaches

In the matter of autohypnosis for a headache of psychological origin, you have to consider the willingness on the part of the patient to have the headache. You had better recognize that a lot of symptomatology is demanded by the total personality via a willingness to have the symptom. [Once you recognize this point,] your question to the patient becomes: "How long do you want to have that headache? Are you willing to have a headache for 2 or 3 seconds? ... willing to have a headache for 2 or 3 minutes?"

I had one patient who was bedridden about three months out of the year by severe headaches. She lost all that time; was never able to agree to any social function because she didn't know when she would have a headache. She was only willing to see me four times, and all I could do for her was to settle it in this way: she now has a headache every Monday morning, which is usually the most convenient time. It is a rather severe headache lasting all of 60 whole seconds, even up to 90 whole seconds. It is very severe pain. She lies down in bed, has her headache, then gets up. Sometimes she even has to postpone the headache until Tuesday.

There is that willingness to have the headache, and the patient may not be willing to lose it through all the psychotherapy that may be required. But the patient's willingness to have the headache implies a willingness to control it. The patient who comes to you and says, "I don't want even the slightest vestige of any of my symptomatology," is a patient who is offering you a rather difficult problem (Rossi and Ryan, 1985, p. 119).

Obesity

A physician's wife, in her late forties, entered the office and explained that she wished a single interview during which hypnosis was to be employed to correct her obesity. She added that her normal weight was 120 pounds, but that her present weight was 240, and that for many years she had weighed over 200 pounds despite repeated futile attempts to reduce under medical supervision. She stated that in recent years she had been slowly gaining to her present weight, and that she was distressed about her future because, "I enjoy eating—I could spend all the time in the world just eating." Additional history was secured, but the only thing of particular note was her somewhat anxious, unnecessarily repeated assertions that she enjoyed eating and liked to while away time by eating for purely gustatory pleasure.

Since she was insistent upon a single interview and hypnosis, an effort was made to meet her wishes. She was found to be an unusually responsive subject, developing a profound trance almost immediately. In this trance state, an understanding of time distortion as a subjective experience, particularly time expansion, was systematically taught to her. She was then instructed to have her physician husband prescribe the proper diet for her and to supervise her weight loss. She was henceforth to eat each meal in a state of time distortion, with time so expanded and lengthened that, as she finished each portion of food, her sense of taste and feeling of hunger for that item would both be completely satisfied, as if she had been eating for "hours on end with complete satisfaction." All of this instruction was given repetitiously until it seemed certain she understood fully, whereupon she was aroused and dismissed.

The patient, together with her husband, was seen nine months later. Her weight had been 120 lbs. for the past month, and her husband declared that her weight loss had occurred easily and without any medical complication. Both she and her husband spoke at length about their improved personal, social, and recreational activities, and she commented that, even though she ate much less, her eating pleasures had been intensified, that her sense of taste and smell were more discerning, and that a simple sandwich could be experienced with as much subjective pleasure as a two-hour dinner (Erickson and Rossi, 1980, Vol. IV, pp. 181–182).

Guitar Practice

This case report concerns a relatively circumscribed emotional problem for which the concept of time distortion was employed as an expeditious and experimental measure.

The patient, a 25-year-old student working his way through college, was primarily interested in the field of entertainment. His voice was fair and he accompanied himself on a guitar. Because of his promise as a singer, a night club gave him regular weekend employment. Unfortunately, as the weeks went by, his performance showed no improvement, and he was notified that he would be replaced at the first opportunity.

This caused him much discouragement, anxiety, and depression, and he sought therapy because of his hopeless attitude.

His history disclosed nothing of immediate significance except that his studies and his regular week-day employment on a late shift, in addition to the weekend engagement, gave him practically no time for practice.

Further inquiry disclosed that his late shift was characterized by spurts of activity followed by intervals of idleness.

This fact suggested a possibility for utilizing time distortion. Accordingly, the question of hypnosis was raised with him, and he dispiritedly expressed his willingness to try anything. He proved to be a good hypnotic subject and was easily trained in hypnotic phenomena.

This accomplished, he was systematically instructed, under hypnosis, in Cooper's experiments on time distortion until his understanding of the general concepts was good. The suggestion was offered that he might participate in a time distortion experiment. He was disinterested in the idea, but did consent reluctantly. He preferred that attention be given to his problem.

Accordingly, on a Monday, while in a profound trance, he was given a series of posthypnotic suggestions. These were that he was to utilize, from time to time, each night the idle periods at work, to develop brief 10- to 30-second trances. During these trances, at a hallucinatory level, he would have adequate special personal time to practice extensively both his singing and his playing. Since the trances would be brief in clock time, and since his practicing would be hallucinatory in character, his fellow workers would not note more than that he appeared momentarily self-absorbed.

He was awakened with a total amnesia for the trance instructions and given an appointment for the next Monday.

He reported excitedly at that interview, "I've got a new lease on life. Saturday was the best night I have ever had. Sunday night I did so well that the boss said that if I kept on that way, I could be sure of my job. I don't understand it because I didn't get a chance all week to practice. But Sunday I got out my tape recorder and made a new recording. Then I played it and some of my old recordings for comparison. Sunday's sounded as if I had had a lot of practice. I was amazed to find out how much I had improved. I must have unconsciously ironed out some emotional kink that was interfering."

Hypnotized, he explained that he had averaged at least three long, as well as several brief, practice sessions per night. During the long sessions he went through his repertoire, and the brief sessions were used for the practice of individual selections. Each time everything seemed to proceed at a normal tempo. Additionally, he frequently made a hallucinatory tape recording which he "played back" so that he could listen to his practicing and thus note errors for correction. At no time had any of his associates seemed to notice his periodically preoccupied state. He expressed his intention of continuing with this method of practice and supplementing it with ordinary practice (Erickson and Rossi, 1980, Vol. II, pp. 278–279).

Amnesia

A 30-year-old woman kept having amnesic episodes during which she would forget her identity, not recognize her children or her husband, and think it was 1934, even though it was in actuality 1952. She was often hospitalized during these episodes and would spontaneously recover her memory after varying lengths of time and amnesia. The Phoenix police asked MHE to help her. He initially observed that she had a negative reaction to hearing the policeman tell her his name. He had the policeman repeat his name until he observed that she was reacting to the "Eric" part of Erickson. She also showed a reaction to his cane, mustache, and his gray hair.

She was at first reluctant to have therapy and hypnosis, but decided after one amnesic episode that she was interested. MHE tried various hypnotic techniques with her (he lists them as age regression, automatic writing and drawing, crystal gazing, dream activity, mirror writing, free association, depersonalization, disorientation, identification with others, and dissociation techniques), all of which failed to help her recover any traumatic memories or stop having amnesiac episodes. Finally, MHE noticed that she developed an amnesia after seeing a Borden's milk truck through a window. Thereafter, he was able to trigger amnesiac episodes deliberately by exposing the woman to Borden's advertisements. Other things could also trigger an episode.

MHE developed an age progression technique of seeing a calendar with the monthly pages being torn off from 1934 to 1952. With that technique, she could rapidly be brought back to the present and full memories. After some time she was able to readily accomplish this in five minutes of clock time. He finally taught her time distortion and instructed her to experience her entire life to the present from childhood in 20 seconds of clock time. After she did this, she was able to recognize, remember, and report to MHE the source and triggers for the amnesiac episodes. She had witnessed the death of her father by heart failure at three years old when he was bending down to kiss her, and she had been tied and raped by a man named Eric Borden (who had gray hair and a mustache and used a cane) for three days and bore a stillborn child as a result of that rape. There were other traumas and any reminders of them had been enough to trigger an episode of amnesia. After recalling and discussing all the traumas, she only had a few more relatively brief amnesiac episodes, but functioned well at social, personal, and business levels. (Case summary from O'Hanlon and Hexum, 1980, pp. 217–218. The full description of this case is given in Erickson and Rossi, 1980, Vol. II, pp. 272–278.)

E. Amnesia

Amnesia is simply the technique of suggesting that an individual forget some specific event or events or period(s) of time. This technique is particularly important when dealing with traumatic memories which have the potential for causing abreactions if brought to conscious awareness. In a deep trance, the client can recall various traumatic incidents, but to protect the client he/she is given an amnesia for those events. Under the control of the hypnotist and the client's unconscious mind, these traumatic events can be brought safely to conscious awareness *if* doing so would be beneficial to the client. Remember that it is not necessary to attain useful change in a client's behavior by uncovering concealed memories—see the Erickson quote in the previous section. The unconscious mind may be guided to understanding, safe storage of the stressful memories, and providing the relief to the conscious mind that results in new satisfactory behavior. Splitting and linking techniques are often used with amnesic work.

There are five chapters in Vol. III of Erickson and Rossi (1980, pp. 36–90) devoted to the subject of amnesia. Of these, the last chapter (pp. 71–90) was a synthesis by Rossi of Erickson's published and unpublished results (Erickson and Rossi, 1974). They wrote about amnesia by distraction (p. 73):

> A spontaneous amnesia together with full recall of trance events in another trance constitutes the classical evidence for hypnotic amnesia; there is a continuity of memory from one trance to another and from one awake state to another, but there is an amnesia between trance and awake state. ... The typical research design testing for hypnotic amnesia immediately upon trance termination misses the spontaneous and suggested amnesias that develop at a later time. Erickson, in fact, makes it a routine practice not to talk to the patient about trance events immediately upon awakening. The trance state persists for a few moments after the appearance of wakefulness. Questioning during this period frequently permits full recall. Erickson typically engages the patient in casual conversations, anecdotes, and shaggy dog stories very remote from the hypnotic experience for a while after trance termination to effect an *amnesia by distraction*. Alternatively, Erickson will sometimes "rush" a patient out of the office to avoid talk about trance. He will distract and do

just about anything he can to make the waking situation very different from the trance situation and, thus, promote amnesia.

Amnesias can be suggested directly or indirectly while the subject is in trance. "When a direct suggestion for amnesia is given, the observing ego takes note of it. ... When a suggestion is made indirectly, however, even the observing ego tends to miss the fact that a suggestion has been given" (p. 75). Indirect suggestions for amnesia tend to be more effective for clinical purposes. Erickson and Rossi (p. 84) wrote, "The *structured amnesia* is effected by awakening the subjects in a manner that reorients them to the exact place, time, and associative content of consciousness where they were when they entered trance." Before trance, you might be talking about the weather—if you continue talking in the same casual way about the weather at termination of trance, the client will typically be amnesic for the trance experience.

Hypnotic amnesia can also be considered to be an example of *state-dependent learning* or to be "state-bound." Therapeutic use may be made of amnesic states as indicated earlier. A classic case of such use is "The February Man" (Erickson and Rossi, 1989). *Hypermnesia* is simply increased memory ability. Trance may be used to retrieve long lost memories which are inaccessible in the waking state. However, the hypnotist must be extremely careful to not evoke *confabulation*, that is, the *creation* of memories unless they are part of the therapeutic plan. Also, see the case entitled "Amnesia" in the previous section.

We will close this section with a brief comment from Erickson on amnesia, followed by amnesic suggestions during a hypnotherapy session.

During a presentation in 1960, Erickson commented on amnesia as follows:

What is hypnotic amnesia? I know that there are amnesias which occur in hypnosis. I also know that every hypnotic phenomenon can be found in everyday life, but only in a minor and disconnected way, and only at certain times. My favorite way of inducing amnesia is by a rather simple technique. When the patient with whom I know I am going to use an amnesia comes into my office, I may say: "You know, it was very pleasant driving to the office. Today is such a nice day in

Phoenix. Were there many cars on North Central Avenue?" Perfectly casual conversation. The patient answers, and then, in response to a posthypnotic cue she develops a trance, and we proceed with the therapeutic work. However, on this occasion I want her to have an amnesia, so when she awakens, I say, "How was the traffic on the corner of Camelback and North Central?" I'm right back with the conversation that preceded the therapeutic interview. I have thus reestablished and made dormant the trend of thought that preceded the therapy. In other words, I have gone clear around and back to the beginning of the interview, until the patient walks out of the office, thinking about the traffic and the nice day in Phoenix and the number of cars on Camelback and North Central Roads, and proceeds about her business in the total amnesia of the therapeutic work. Why shouldn't she have a total amnesia? By a simple asking of questions, casual thoughts have been made to emphasize a train of thought, a train of association in her mind, to bypass the conscious memories of the therapeutic interview (Erickson and Rossi, 1980, Vol. II).

During this therapy session, Erickson had the patient enter and awaken from trance several times. The following is one of the awakenings in which he directly used amnesia.

E: And now let's draw a curtain and leave all that's happened behind the curtain. You shut your eyes. And everything that happened will be behind the curtain of yesterday, and today you will open your eyes into today, ready to begin a new work. And so sleep for what seems like a few hours of very restful sleep. And by the time your left hand gets down to your thigh, it will seem as if hours of restful sleep had passed and you can then awaken.

J: Excuse me. Oh, what a yawn (J stretches and obviously awakens).

E: Now there are some things I would like to introduce here. (Erickson now distracts J with some interesting anecdotes about his family and the process of memory in psychological development, how different personality types remember via intellectual versus emotional associations, body associations, etc.)

E: Now, what work shall we do today?

J: Um?

E. What work shall we do today?

J: Whatever you would like. I guess I feel a little sleepy.

R: Plane trip make you sleepy?

J: But, actually I am not tired. I don't feel like I would go to sleep."

(Erickson and Rossi, 1979)

Notice how the amnesic principle of distraction was utilized. In the presentation, he continued talking about the traffic after trance just as if nothing had happened. During the therapy session, he distracted her from thinking about the trance experience by talking about other things and acted as if nothing had happened. Although amnesia is a relatively easy phenomenon to employ, it is also quite effective in therapy.

F. Analgesia and Anesthesia

Both analgesia and anesthesia are utilized to diminish bodily sensations. *Analgesia* refers to the reduction or elimination of pain, but allows an individual to experience the normal sensations of pressure, touch, temperature, etc. *Anesthesia* refers to a complete or near complete elimination of sensation in a particular part of the body, or the total body as in general anesthesia. This may be considered to be a "hypno-chemical-neurological" block of sensation. The distinction between analgesia and anesthesia may be blurred in particular circumstances. Since pain is a signal that something is wrong in the body, you should be careful to *not* remove all sensation of pain and to make certain that *changes* in location or quality are perceived so that they may be dealt with. It is also well known that patients in the surgical plane of anesthesia can hear and recall what is said in the operating room. So, care must be taken with what is said in the operating room. Also, with this awareness, operating room personnel may be trained to make healing-enhancing statements. (See the sections relating to pain control for more on this subject.)

We cite here three of Erickson's cases dealing with pain control for childbirth, dentistry, and cancer.

Childbirth

About a year later a very pregnant woman entered my office. She gave me her name, and I recognized the lawyer's name. She said, "I am on my way to the hospital to have a baby. After what you did for my husband [the lawyer], I would like a hypnotic delivery of my baby." So, I hinted gently about the value of a little more time.

I told her to go into a trance. She went into a very nice trance, and I told her, "Go to the hospital, cooperate in every way, except you explain that you want no medication of any sort, and you won't take any anesthesia. You just want to go into the delivery room and have your baby. And while you are lying on the delivery table, think about the baby. Is it going to be a boy, or a girl? How much will it weigh? How long will it be? What color hair will it have, or will it be bald? And what color will its eyes be? And will you really name it the name you and your husband picked out? And while you are lying there waiting for your baby, enjoy all the happy thoughts about having a baby. And wait patiently and gladly to hear its first cry. Think of all the happiness that you hope to derive from having a baby. And think about how happy your husband will be, and how nice it is to live in Arizona."

She was enjoying her thoughts and suddenly the obstetrician said, "Mrs. X., here is your baby." And he held up a baby boy.

Two years later she came in and said, "I remembered what you said about more time. I'm not going into the hospital for three whole days. I would like to have another hypnotic delivery."

I said, "All right, just close your eyes. Go into a trance very deeply and do a repetition of what you did the first time." I awakened her and she left (Zeig, 1980, p. 60).

Dentistry

A woman with a severe phobia for dentists was in an automobile accident that damaged her jaw and required dental surgery. She had previously been so frightened and tense during dental procedures that she had broken off headrests on her dentist's chairs. She had a sensitivity to chemical anesthetics, so they could not be used for the procedure. She asked her family optometrist, who had studied with MHE, to hypnotize her to prepare her for the dental work without chemical anesthesia. He referred her to MHE, because he was not that confident of his abilities.

MHE saw the woman that same day. He induced trance by using hand levitation and suggested that, instead of pain, she could feel pressure. All the pain would go out through her big toe. MHE did four sessions of hypnosis with the woman. When the woman saw the dentist, he was reluctant to do the work without using chemical anesthesia, but finally relented. She was aware and relaxed during the session and experienced no pain, only intense pressure. There was minimal bleeding, even though a partial plate of steel had been inserted. She experienced no soreness, swelling or complications and was completely healed in three days.

Since that time, she has been able to go to dentists and periodontists comfortably. A year later, she asked MHE to help her stop smoking. He did one session and it did not work. He occasionally used her as a demonstration subject in the years that followed (Case summary from O'Hanlon and Hexum, 1990, p. 84).

Cancer Pain

This 35-year-old woman, the mother of four small children and the wife of a professional man, was seen five weeks before her death from lung cancer. For a month before hypnosis, she had been almost continuously in a narcotic stupor, since the pain she experienced was unbearable to her. She asked that hypnosis be employed and voluntarily went without medication that entire day in her own self-determined effort to ready herself for hypnosis.

She was seen at 6:00 p.m., bathed in perspiration, suffering acutely from constant pain and greatly exhausted. Nevertheless, approximately four hours of continuous effort were required before a light trance could be induced. This light stage of hypnosis was immediately utilized to induce her to permit three things to be accomplished, all of which she had consistently refused to allow in the very intensity of her desire to be hypnotized. The first of these was the hypodermic administration of 1/8 grain of morphine sulfate, a most inadequate dosage for her physical needs, but one considered adequate for the immediate situation. The next was the serving to her of a pint of rich soup, and the third was the successful insistence upon an hour's restful physiological sleep. By 6:00 a.m. the patient, who finally proved to be an excellent somnambulistic subject, had been taught successfully everything considered to be essential to meet the needs of her situation.

The procedure followed was probably unnecessarily comprehensive, but the situation did not warrant any approach less inclusive.

The first step was to teach her positive and negative hallucinations in the modalities of vision, hearing, taste, and smell. Then she was taught positive and negative hallucinations in the areas of touch, deep sensation, and kinesthesia, and, in relation to this latter type of sensation, she was taught body disorientation and dissociation. When these learnings were sufficiently well acquired, the patient was given suggestions for glove and stocking anesthesias, and these were extended over her entire body. Thereupon, it became possible to teach her rapidly combined partial analgesias and anesthesias for both superficial and deep sensations of all types. To this was added a combination of both body disorientation and body dissociation, so that these latter could supplement the former.

The patient was not seen again, either professionally or socially, but her husband telephoned or gave reports in person daily concerning the patient's condition.

She died suddenly five weeks later, in the midst of a happy social conversation with a neighbor and a relative.

During that five-week period she had been instructed to feel free to accept whatever medication she needed. Now and then she would suffer pain, but this was almost always controlled by aspirin. Sometimes a second dose of aspirin with codeine was needed, and on half a dozen occasions, 1/8 grain of morphine was needed. Otherwise, except for her gradual progressive physical deterioration, the patient continued decidedly comfortable and cheerfully adjusted to the end (Erickson and Rossi, 1980, Vol. IV, pp. 257–258).

G. Dissociation

Dissociation means a breaking apart in some way. It is frequently used to describe the *separation* between the conscious and the unconscious or "inner" minds. These two aspects of the mind are said to be "dissociated" or separated so that they appear to function independently of each other. Sometimes communication between these two aspects of mind is easy, sometimes difficult, and sometimes walled off. Traumatic experiences and their memories may be safely kept in a dissociated state until it is okay to have them brought to consciousness. In the case of multiple personality disorders, there may be several (or even many) dissociated states which are either unaware or only partially aware of each other.

The creation of dissociated states must be done consciously and carefully and for a well-thought-out therapeutic purpose. (The same holds for reintegration.) Dissociation may be used for pain control by separating the painful portions of the body, or even leaving the body entirely for certain periods of time. Catalepsy of a limb, age regression or progression, amnesia, and hand levitation involve dissociated states. Trance, itself, is a dissociated state. These states should be used as part of a conscious design.

The following Erickson case is an example of the use of many hypnotic phenomena. We cite it here primarily for its use of dissociation.

Fear of Oral Exams

A doctor who had a history since high school of an unreasoning fear of oral examinations sought MHE's help. He had always been able to get out of oral examinations by convincing those who gave them of his fear. He was an excellent student and an unassuming man, so he had been given special consideration in those situations that usually would have required oral exams. He was now facing a situation in which he could not get special consideration. An old medical school colleague who hated MHE's patient was presiding over the four-hour oral exam required for certification in the patient's specialty. He knew of the patient's fear of oral exams and was unwilling to make an exception. The patient declared himself helpless and willing to do anything MHE suggested to get through the exam.

MHE had the man objectively recount every symptom he had experienced in relation to facing oral exams. The man described nausea, tremors, perspiration, bladder and bowel incontinence, dizziness, and physical collapse. He noted that the severity of the symptoms did not seem to be related to how important the exam was. He would experience the symptoms any time he recognized the situation as one involving an oral examination. He told MHE that, even on driver's license exams, he had to bring a pad of paper and write his answer, then read it to the clerk.

MHE used the patient for hypnotic experiments he was conducting and gave him extensive experience in using all the trance phenomena. Then, MHE gave the man suggestions to develop amnesia for the hypnotic suggestions and to go and take the examination in a trance. He was to travel to the distant city to take the exam and not to realize he was in an oral exam. He complied and, while in the exam, he saw the oral questions as if they were typewritten and saw textbooks with the appropriate pages with the answers written on them as if they were in front of him. His enemy disappeared from his view. At times, he saw the situation as if he were in back of the man reading the question over the man's shoulder. At times, he saw patients in front of him and imagined he was giving a lecture to students in response to the questions asked. He passed the exam by answering every question correctly and traveled home in a trance; later he recalled everything in detail. (Case summary from O'Hanlon and Hexum, 1990, pp. 187–188. The full case is in Erickson and Rossi, 1980, Vol. IV, pp. 193–206.)

"Harvey" may be used as a good example of automatic writing (See chapter 10), but we cite his case here as an example of dissociation.

Harvey

Harvey was a 29-year-old man brought to a seminar as a challenge for MHE by psychoanalytically-oriented therapists who didn't think much of hypnotherapy. He was very unassertive and had all sorts of aches and pains. He had been in treatment with a psychiatrist for several years. He was bullied by people at work and never stood up for himself. He held a job far below his capabilities. He was not able to write legibly or tie his shoes or tie neatly. He was always making social mistakes that kept him from developing romantic relationships. He always assumed he would fail.

MHE put him into trance using authoritarian techniques since Harvey always tried to please authorities. He had Harvey learn to positively and negatively hallucinate. MHE then had him write the phrase, "It's a beautiful day in June," and he wrote it almost illegibly. MHE had a seminar attendee write a sample of the same phrase in good handwriting and MHE praised it excessively. Harvey was ashamed of his writing. MHE asked him if he would like to be able to write like the other man had and Harvey said he'd give anything to be able to.

Next, MHE had Harvey forget he was Harvey and hallucinate scenes from his past in imaginary crystal balls, not recognizing that they were images of himself. [In another version, MHE had Harvey assume the identity of one of the medical students in the seminar in order to get an impersonal viewpoint.] Harvey saw some traumatic scenes, including one in which he got punished for writing with his left hand. MHE had him awaken and write the phrase with his *right* hand (that is, the correct one, the left) without being aware that he had written it. He wrote it very well. When others in the room tried to convince him he had written it, MHE instructed, he was to call them damn liars. He did.

Then, MHE had him watch the paper and find out who wrote the phrase next. When Harvey noticed himself writing it automatically, he became convinced that it was his handwriting after all. He went around the room and made everyone present praise his writing. He tied his shoes and tie neatly before leaving. He went back to work and started asserting himself. He recopied all his illegible records and got a raise and promotion. He also started dating and got married.

[In another version, Harvey was given a series of sheets of paper on which he legibly wrote a series of messages to himself to read sequentially after he came out of trance. The messages would convince him that he had written the pages and that he could write legibly.] (Case summary from O'Hanlon and Hexum, 1990, pp. 295–296. Fuller versions in Erickson and Rossi, 1980, pp. 81-85, 491–498).

H. Hallucinations

A *positive hallucination* is perceiving something—an object, person, sound or smell, for example, that does not exist in objective reality. A *negative hallucination* denies the existence of phenomena which do exist in objective reality such as a chair or a person or a clock or an odor. We all "hallucinate" in the sense of "seeing" things in our mind, or "hearing" a favorite song. Having a client practice positive and negative hallucinations teaches them about potentially unknown capabilities that they can utilize to resolve personal problems. Erickson taught a woman to mask tinnitus with favorite music. Sensory alterations may be used to dissociate unpleasant realities. The comedienne Lily Tomlin probably had the final word on this when she observed, "When people talk to God, that is called praying, but when God talks to people, they are called crazy."

In this case, Erickson uses hallucination to help a man over a problem concerning his conviction that he didn't love his wife. (This is also an example of marital therapy.)

The Man Who Didn't Love His Wife

Henry, a 28-year-old man, was convinced that he did not love his wife and that he had only married her because she resembled his mother, to whom he was strongly attached. In trance he discovered that he also had a strong hatred for his mother, but he wasn't willing to know about this consciously, as it would disrupt his relationships too much. In trance, MHE helped the man forget anything about his wife and mother, except the knowledge that he must have had a mother. Then, he had the man see a strange woman sitting in a chair across from him and have the strong sense that the woman's name was Nelly (his mother's name). Henry had frank discussions with Nelly and was able to objectively review her life and her understandings. There followed in subsequent hypnotic sessions similarly frank and objective discussions with two other hallucinated figures, one of Henry and one of his wife, Madge. The real Henry had no recognition of who these people were, due to the induced amnesia. Next, MHE had Henry see those three people in various combinations and in relation to various traumatic experiences from Henry's history. Gradually MHE led Henry into discovering that the people were his mother, his wife, and himself. He realized that his mother was messed up but deserving of a normal amount of respect and affection. He also realized that he loved his wife and that she was different in some ways from his mother. He gradually changed from a critical, compulsive person to a more relaxed, happy man. (Case summary from O'Hanlon and Hexum, 1990, pp. 242–243. Also, see Erickson and Rossi, 1980, Vol. IV, pp. 41–47.)

Erickson successfully used hallucinations to help a professional woman whom he thought might become schizophrenic. (Erickson and Rossi, 1980, Vol. IV, pp. 85–87.)

Monsters

I should like to present at this point the use of hypnotherapy in an experimental fashion. I was very much afraid that one of my patients was going to develop schizophrenia. Her very best friend had. She was a very accomplished person, professionally trained, and she worked until 11 at night. As soon as she got off work, she would sneak home, cowering and shivering, because there were some peculiar figures that were following her. Her bedroom was peopled by monsters of some sort. I think you would call her a psychotic, although she had sufficient insight so that you could have some doubts about it. She wasn't quite certain whether she was having dreams or whether her experiences were real.

"How could I have a dream on the street? I've got the feeling, though, that there are monsters back of me in mid-air."

I asked Mary if it wouldn't be a very nice thing to see herself in a crystal ball. I produced one, and she described to me the little girl she saw there.

In some surprise she said, "Why, that's me! And I'm very happy there. I'm playing with my doll. Now I'm going to go over and swing. I certainly was a happy kid. And look at that blue-checked pinafore I'm wearing!"

She really enjoyed looking at herself at the age of six.

So I conjured up another crystal for her. She was several years older. She described herself with a great deal of pleasure.

I said, "Don't look at that crystal over there yet. Let's look at the crystal here."

Slowly, carefully, I carried her through a process of fourteen crystals. The thirteenth crystal was her present state, in which she was walking home from the hospital in fear of those hideous monsters and evils. Were they real or unreal? When she got to the tenth crystal, I told her that she wouldn't know who the girl was in the crystal ball.

She said, "That's a ghastly thing to have me look at."

"Well, you just describe it to me thoroughly, completely, and adequately." We went through the tenth to the twelfth, and they were very, very painful. I said, "Now, I want you to forget the identity of the person in all of these crystals. Just tell me what you think about them—and never mind that crystal over there."

She said, "Well, she was a happy little girl. Then, she was a little bit older. There she's going to school—she looks as though she might be in such-and-such a grade. There she's in high school, and there she's going to a Christmas party." And so on. "My heavens! What's happened to that girl? Why should she have such horrible feelings?"

I said, "Well, I don't know—you don't know—but I've got a very pleasant surprise for you. If you'll look in that crystal there, and then look in that crystal over there, you'll discover that they're the same girl. And in that crystal over there, you'll see the picture of a girl who is acting and behaving very real. It isn't really a living picture—it's just a girl in that picture, and she's happy, and she's pleased, and she's going to be doing something that she really wants to do and she's really going to be enjoying it. Now that girl and this girl are the same girl. But the process of growth and development, the changes that occur in life, the accidents in life, and so on ... You know, every story should have a good ending."

She looked, and she said, "Well! That six-year-old kid grew up to be a very pretty girl, didn't she? And look at her. She's on a diving board, and she's got on a blue bathing suit with a yellow dragon or something on it, and she's having a wonderful time, she's really enjoying herself. I can hardly believe it. That girl is enjoying herself—she really is!"

I said, "This is only June, but that girl up there is going swimming in August."

Mary went swimming in August. She went swimming in a blue bathing suit with a yellow figure on it—I don't know whether it was a dragon or not. At all events she went swimming. I found out afterward that she learned to swim and then had developed tremendous fears and anxieties and distresses. She had developed all these other agonies, in spite of the fact that she actually had had professional training, and she had a very difficult time.

She is the head of a professional department at the present time, so I think that experiment was successful. I had a letter from Mary the other day, and she's very happy. She's married—happily married—and getting along very nicely.

Exceptional Growth

Erickson recognized the importance of healthy body imagery. He used hypnosis to help at least two young women allow their breasts to grow in response to their own hormones. They had previously inhibited such interaction, considering themselves unfeminine and unattractive (Erickson and Rossi, 1980, Vol. II, p. 183–185).

In 1960 he told me about a 20-year-old man who grew 12 inches in height in the span of one year. In hypnosis, at the start of therapy, this stunted young man looked out on his world as though unwilling to grow, a modern-day Peter Pan. For example, he described a room as though he were standing beneath a table. Similarly, a cow on his farm was visualized as though it were ten feet tall; his eyes were on a level with the cow's udder. Growth began to take place when Erickson encouraged the man to hallucinate his world as though he were standing part way up a staircase.

I said, "Why have you kept this report out of the literature?"

Erickson smiled and said, "No respectable editor of a scientific journal would publish such an impossible thing."

"Dr. Erickson," I answered, "You are the editor of a respectable journal."

He smiled again and said, "I would like to keep my job." (Cheek, 1982, p. 282).

Erickson did some things that bordered on the unbelievable!

I. Posthypnotic Behavior

Erickson and Erickson (1941, also Erickson and Rossi, 1980, vol. I, pp. 381–411) give the following definition: "A posthypnotic act has been found to be one performed by the hypnotic subject after awakening from trance, in response to suggestions given during the trance state, with the execution of the act marked by an absence of any demonstratable conscious awareness in the subject of the underlying cause and motive for the act." They write further that, "... the hypnotized subject instructed to execute some act posthypnotically invariably develops spontaneously a hypnotic trance. This trance is usually of brief duration, occurs only in direct relation to the performance of the posthypnotic act, and apparently constitutes an essential part of the process of response to, and execution of, the posthypnotic comment." In addition, they state, "... to a slight degree, the disappearance of the trance state, or to a much greater degree the completion of the posthypnotic performance, is marked by a brief interval of confusion and disorientation from which the subject quickly recovers by renewed and close attention to the immediate situation. ... In addition, there is usually evidence of an amnesia, either partial or complete, for both the posthypnotic act and the concurrent events arising out of the immediate situation."

Direct posthypnotic suggestion was the standard method used by the traditional hypnotherapists to effect change. However, Ericksonians believe that indirect suggestions and metaphors are more effective than direct approaches since they are lodged deep in the unconscious mind. Posthypnotic suggestions may be dormant for long periods of time. Erickson recorded one case of fifteen years.

Joseph Barber (1998) discusses the "mysterious persistence of hypnotic analgesia" in an article under that title. He suggests a model to explain how hypnotic treatment of recurring pain achieves enduring relief (p. 28).

Clinical experience suggests a two-component model. First, the clinician communicates specific ideas that strengthen the patient's ability to derive therapeutic support and to develop a sense of openness to the unexplored possibilities for pain relief within the security of a nurturing therapeutic relationship. Second, the clinician employs posthypnotic suggestions that capitalize on the patient's particular pain experiences, which simultaneously ameliorate the pain experience, and which, in small, repetitive increments, tend to maintain persistent pain relief over increasing periods of time.

The following are three simple examples of how posthypnotic suggestions can be delivered during therapy. The first example is by Rossi, and the remaining examples are by Erickson.

First example:

And the unconscious can continue working on that problem in that special trance when every moment in trance can be equivalent to hours, days, or even years of ordinary clock time. (Pause.) And the interesting thing is that the conscious mind may or may not really understand just what is happening if the unconscious needs to keep it private. You can remain just as you are until the unconscious completes that unit of work and you'll know it's finished when you have that urge to move and stretch and come fully awake again! (Erickson and Rossi, 1981, p. 133.)

Second Example:

E: And now, after you awaken, I want a bit of music that you haven't thought about or remembered for a long time to come suddenly into your mind when you see me plainly. And you can begin counting, mentally, silently backward from twenty to one, beginning the count now. (Long pause as X reorients to her body and awakens.)

E: Is it pretty? Can you tell us about it?

X: The music?

E: Yes.

X: It changed.

E: Tell us what the change was.

X: From harp to an orchestra.

E: When was that?

X: When I was seven.

E: Where were you?

X: At home.

E: Who is in the room?

X: Who? My whole family, I think.

E: To your right or left? To my left.

(Erickson and Rossi, 1979, pp. 162–163.)

Third Example:

Bear in mind that when you first formed an image of the letter 'A'
it was difficult.
But as you continued in school
you learned to form
mental images of letters and words and pictures
with increasing ease
until finally all you had to do
was to take a look.
(Pause)
In the matter of experiencing other sensations
you learn to recognize cold
warm
muscle tension.
In your sleep at night you can dream.
In those dreams you can hear
you see, you move
you have any number of experiences.
And as a part of that experience
is forgetting that dream after you awaken.
An experience of forgetting in itself
is an experience
that is not alien to anybody.

(Erickson, Rossi and Rossi, 1976, pp. 30–32.)

The first example uses a subtle posthypnotic suggestion for the unconscious to continue working on a solution to a particular problem. This type of suggestion lends itself well to individuals who are suspected of resisting suggestions. The second example is a direct posthypnotic suggestion to test her ability to lift amnesia, as well as hypermnesia. Notice that a cue is also suggested for when she would do this. Then Erickson prepares her for an age regression. He asks a question using a childish term, i.e. "Is it pretty?" and with the question, "Who *is* in the room? And to your right or left?" he accomplishes the age regression as evidenced by her responses. The third example begins with the early learning set and moves to a subtle, but direct posthypnotic suggestion for amnesia.

Although these are simple examples, we hope that readers can figure out how to create their own posthypnotic suggestions.

J. Ideodynamic Responses

We have devoted a chapter to the phenomena of ideodynamic responses. These are a useful class of hypnotic phenomena, and that chapter is well worth studying.

K. Hypnagogic and Hypnopompic States

A *hypnagogic* state is associated with falling asleep and a *hypnopompic* state is associated with waking up. Generally, these terms refer to the half-awake dreamlike state which has some trance characteristics and which occurs as a transition between wakefulness and sleep. Suggestions are sometimes made to clients to utilize these states for personal development work as a naturally occurring form of self-hypnosis. For example, you give yourself the direction before you go to sleep to have your unconscious mind work on a particular problem at night or in the morning.

L. Summary

In this chapter, we have described a number of hypnotic phenomena and their use. The coverage is not exhaustive, but is meant to give you a sense of the range of hypnotic phenomena and what may be done with them. Some are discussed in more detail in other parts of this book.

Exercises

1. Make a comprehensive list of all of the hypnotic phenomena you can think of. Write out definitions of them.

2. For each phenomenon indicate the circumstances for which it would be particularly useful, and those for which it would either be contra-indicated or a poor choice.

3. Write out inductions for each of these phenomena and practice their delivery in a supportive environment.

4. You are training a subject in hypnosis. Which phenomena would you use?

5. A client comes to you who has: (a) chronic pain; (b) migraine headaches; (c) panic attacks; (d) fear of flying; (e) depressions; (f) writer's block; or (g) tinnitus. Would you use any of the hypnotic phenomena described in this chapter? Would you use several, and in what order? How much additional information would you need to make use of a particular phenomenon with a particular client?

6. Think of several of your own clients. What will work with them? Have you written out a therapeutic plan for each of them?

Chapter 10

Utilization of Ideodynamic Responses

Rubin Battino, M.S.

A. Introduction

There are a great many "automatic" responses that we give to stimuli in our environment. By automatic, we mean responses that occur outside of consciousness or are not willful conscious responses. Some examples of common automatic responses are: raising your own hand to shake someone's proffered hand; putting your foot on the brakes when you are a passenger in a car; tilting your head so you can hear better; head noddings—you all have acquaintances who are head nodders; shoulder shrugging; grimaces and, especially, smiles; greetings "How are you?" "Okay"; patting and touching people who are to be comforted; passing food at meals; patting/arranging/combing your hair—in fact, almost any kind of grooming; checking the time; salivating when someone talks about food; thinking of movies when you smell popcorn; feeling sad when someone talks about sad events; and re-experiencing any event when you (or others) talk about it. Behaviorists would say that these are conditioned stimulus/ response behaviors and they are, of course, correct. In the memory of the author is the fascinating and once popular Ouija board in which several people lightly touch a pointer which "magically" and automatically spells out messages from "beyond." Any time we are dealing with automatic responses, we are dealing with the unconscious mind and, thus, have access to trance states. It would certainly be useful as a practicing hypnotherapist to learn how to utilize these automatic responses to help your clients. In this chapter, we will discuss various ways of utilizing this behavior.

Automatic responses are also called *ideodynamic* responses and can appear in several forms. The most common of these is *ideomotor* responses in which there is an automatic or out-of-consciousness movement of some kind. The most commonly utilized ideomotor responses are finger signals and the Chevreul pendulum.

Ideoaffective responses are automatically accessed emotions and feelings. In one sense, that has many interesting implications; we can consider that most phobic reactions are ideoaffective. *Ideosensory* responses are those involving the senses—seeing, hearing, feeling, tasting, and smelling. Automatic writing, drawing, and talking are other forms of ideodynamic responses.

When a hypnotherapist is using ideodynamic responses for therapy, he/she has a shortcut to the unconscious mind and can frequently do effective work briefly. An advantage of using ideodynamic methods is that they can frequently be used without the formal induction of trance. In fact, ideodynamic methods may be adapted to trance inductions.

Ideodynamic responses have been discussed by several authors. LeCron (1964) discusses the uses of ideodynamic responses in self-hypnotism. In particular, LeCron writes about the use of the Chevreul pendulum to query yourself. Over the years, Cheek and LeCron (1968) have been the main proponents and trainers in the use of ideodynamic methods. Their book gives many examples of the use of both the Chevreul pendulum and finger signals. Wright and Wright (1987) have some good sections on ideodynamic methods. The two volume set on the practice of hypnotism by Weitzenhoffer (1989) has both historical and practical information on the subject. The book by Rossi and Cheek (1988) deals with ideodynamic methods for many problems. The first three chapters of this book are devoted to ideodynamic methods. One of the areas they explore is the accessing of birth imprinting experiences via finger signals. They also discuss the experiences of patients under the surgical plane of anesthesia. Perhaps the best book in this area is the one by Cheek (1994) which is a comprehensive treatise on ideomotor techniques.

B. Ideomotor Responses

The two ideomotor responses that are most useful for therapeutic purposes are the Chevreul pendulum and finger signals, with the latter being preferred by us because the response time is so much shorter. Automatic writing and drawing will be discussed briefly. E.L. Rossi has developed a method of using hand movements which will be discussed as an example of both ideomotor responses and a rapid "fail-safe" induction.

In a brief article, Erickson (1961) reviewed his discovery and his development of the use of hand levitation and other ideomotor techniques. Erickson's work in this area actually goes back to the 1920s and 1930s. One of the clearest statements of ideomotor phenomena is in Erickson (1964), and part of the "verbatim" transcript for dealing with a resistant client is quoted here in its entirety:

> Something everybody knows is that people can communicate verbally ["talk by words" if warranted by low educational or intelligence level], or by sign language. The commonest sign language, of course, is when you *nod your head yes or no.* Anybody can do that. One can signal 'come' with the forefinger or wave 'bye-bye' with the hand. The finger signal in a way means 'yes, come here,' and waving the hands means 'no, don't stay.' In other words one can use the head, the finger, or the hand to mean either yes or no. We all do it. *So can you.* Sometimes when we listen to a person we may be *nodding or shaking the head not knowing it* in either agreement or disagreement. *It would be just as easy to do it with the finger or the hand.* Now I would like to ask your unconscious mind a question that can be answered with a simple yes or no. It's a question that *only your unconscious mind can answer.* Neither your conscious mind nor my conscious mind, nor, for that matter, even my unconscious mind, knows the answers. *Only your unconscious mind knows* which *answers can be communicated,* and it *will have to think either a yes or no answer. It could be by a nod or a shake of the head, a lifting of the index finger*—let us say the right index finger for the yes answer, the left index for a no since that is usually the case for the right-handed person and vice versa for the left-handed person. *Or the right hand could lift or the left hand could lift.* But only your unconscious mind knows what the answer will be when I ask for that yes or no answer. And not even your unconscious mind will know, when the question is asked, whether *it will answer with a hand movement, or a finger movement,* and *your unconscious mind will have to think through that question* and *to decide, after it has formulated its own answer, just how it will answer.* [All of this explanation is essentially a series of suggestions so worded that responsive ideomotor behavior is made contingent upon an inevitable occurrence—namely, that the subject "will have to think" and "to decide" without there being an actual request for ideomotor responses. The implication only is there, and implications are difficult to resist (Emphases in the original.)].

Several cases are discussed by Erickson in this paper. The subtle and exact use of language in the preceding quote needs to be studied carefully.

Erickson and Rossi (1981) devote an entire chapter to ideomotor signaling in hypnotic induction and therapy. There is an excellent historical section, a discussion of ideomotor methods, case studies, and exercises. As in many areas of psychotherapy, Erickson seemed to have been first in not only seeing the practical applications of an approach, but also in exploring and extending its use.

1. The Chevreul Pendulum

The French chemist Chevreul (1854) was the first to report on systematic studies involving the ideomotor use of pendulums. Hence, the device is named after him, although the use of the dowser's forked twig or pendulum undoubtedly preceded Chevreul's work. There is evidence that Chevreul called attention to this phenomenon as early as 1833. Chevreul correctly interpreted the ideomotor movements setting the pendulum in motion as being the result of minute muscle movements caused by unrecognized (or unconscious) thoughts of the subject. It is that direct access to the unconscious that makes the use of the Chevreul pendulum and ideomotor signals so powerful.

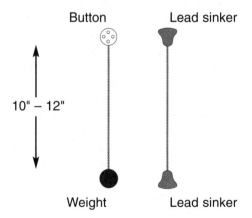

Figure 10.1

The pendulum itself is made from any light object such as a lead sinker used for fishing, a nut or a bolt, or marble or plexiglass sphere that is attached by thread (nylon dental floss is excellent). We have made "fancy" pendulums using small multi-faceted crystals that are used as jewelry pendants. The thread is about ten inches long. It is useful to have the thread terminate in something that is easily grasped between the fingers, such as a button. We have found that the cheapest way to make a Chevreul pendulum is to use the lead weights available in stores selling fishing tackle. Figure 10.1 shows two designs.

In practice, the Chevreul pendulum is used to obtain (unconscious) responses to questions posed by the therapist. The two standard responses that are sought are "yes" and "no." Other possible responses are "maybe" or "not now" or "I don't know" or "not willing to answer" or "not willing to answer now." Of these possible responses, it is only the last that we recommend as being the most useful. The unconscious mind is lazy and given a choice would prefer to respond with the ambiguous or delaying responses.

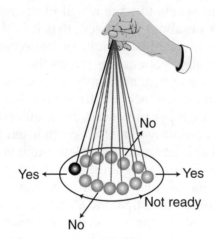

Figure 10.2

Besides, if you refer to Figure 10.2, there are only a limited number of definitive movements that a pendulum can make. These are: back and forth, left and right, and some circular movement—either clockwise or counter-clockwise. Thus, it is useful to limit the client to three unambiguous movements and use only three responses: yes, no, and not-willing-to-answer-now. (The last response *implies* that a response may be forthcoming later.) Typical movements are one direction for yes, a movement ninety degrees apart for no, and some kind of circular movement for not-willing-to-answer-now. The top thread holder is held between the thumb and forefinger of the dominant hand (preferred), with the elbow supported on an arm rest or a knee or braced against your side if standing, or on a desk. As the operator, you can specify a particular motion for each response. It is generally better to let the person "pick" their own responsive motions. You may wish to reread Erickson's comments above to note how he prepares a client for these responses.

The art in successfully using the Chevreul pendulum is in the sequencing of the questions. The game of "twenty questions" is the paradigm for this work. When working with the Chevreul pendulum the client can be in the waking or trance state. Generally, you start with the client in the waking state. As you proceed, a light trance is usually induced, for the questions force the client to focus inwardly. Eyes may still be open, but unfocused, and the pendulum seems to have a will of its own! This can be reinforced by talking about the "fact" that it is the unconscious that controls the minimal muscle movements necessary. "You need pay no attention at all to your arm as it rests there comfortably, and whatever movements appear are okay, and you need pay no attention at all as the movements come from your unconscious mind (from within, from deeper memories, from quiet/caring parts of yourself), and it is certainly okay for you to listen to me with one part of your mind and let another speak through your fingers, and I wonder how much you are going to learn for yourself today?" There are parallels in the way an attorney cross-examines witnesses and police investigators structure questions. As an exercise, you can write out several series of questions designed to elicit particular responses or memories or changes, and then study them to determine how many can be left out and how few you can use. Remember to design questions that will elicit yes, no, or I am not-willing-to-answer-now responses.

Cheek and LeCron (1968, pp. 99–100) gave the following verbatim transcript of working with a middle-aged woman with a chronic cough. They used the Chevreul pendulum and the "yes" and "no" responses reported below were based on pendulum movements:

Q1: Is there some emotional or psychological reason why you have this cough?

A: Yes.

Q2: Does the cough serve some purpose? Is there some benefit from the cough?

A: No.

Q3: Are you identifying with someone who in your childhood had a similar cough?

A: No.

Q4: Is organ language involved? Are you trying to cough up something, some idea or memory which is unpleasant, trying to get something out of your system?

A: No.

Q5: Is there a fixed idea working in your inner mind that makes you cough?

A: Yes.

Q6: Is there more than one idea involved?

A: No.

Q7: Is that the only reason why you cough?

A: Yes.

Q8: An imprint or idea has to have an origin. Is there some past experience when this fixed idea developed?

A: Yes.

Q9: Is there more than one such incident?

A: No.

Q10: Let's find out when it happened. You've had the cough for many years, ever since you can remember. Did this past experience take place before you were ten years old?

A: Yes.

Q11: Was it before five years old?

A: Yes.

Q12: Was it before three?

A: No.

Q13: Was it when you were three?

A: No.

Q14: When you were four?

A: Yes.

Q15: Is the cough associated with some illness?

A: Yes. (The patient then verbally volunteered that she had had a bad case of whooping cough at that age and had nearly died from complications.)

Q16: Was this whooping cough the experience we are trying to locate?

A: Yes.

Q17: Did someone say something at that time that set up this imprint or fixed idea?

A: Yes.

Q18: Was it one of your parents?

A: No.

Q19: Was it a doctor?

A: Yes.

Q20: What was the doctor's name? Answer verbally.

A: I don't know. (verbally)

Q21: Does your inner mind know his name?

A: Yes.

... The client slipped spontaneously into hypnosis and she obviously regressed to four years old and the time of her illness. She verbally told of being ill, her mother crying, and hearing the physician say, "She'll never get over this." The imprint was obviously this message. The operator told her while she was still in trance that she had recovered from the illness of which the cough was a major part. The imprint, however, in effect forced her inner mind to carry out the idea of "never getting over this." The operator then asked more questions.

Q22: Now that you see why you have continued to cough and since you really did get over the illness, do you think that the false idea the doctor planted in your mind need continue to affect you?

A: No.

Q23: Can you now be free of the cough permanently?

A: Yes.

... Follow-up showed that the client had indeed permanently given up the cough.

Cheek and LeCron (1968, p. 101) summarize the process as follows: "... explanation of the possible causes, search with the questioning technique, spontaneous development of hypnosis, age regression to the experience, reorientation and 'mopping up' by establishing that the symptom could be terminated." This is obviously a rapid and elegant procedure. In this case, the operator had some information about the details of the problem, but it is also possible to carry out this type of intervention as pure process in the form of "secret therapy." In addition, the process can be more rapidly done using finger signals. (See next section.)

Some detailed comments on the preceding transcript follow since it is worth additional study. Q1 establishes that there is an inner cause to the problem. Q2 concerns secondary gain, which always needs to be checked. Q3 asks about significant others in childhood as a cause, and in one question covers several aspects. In Q4 the important role of "organ language," discovering if there is some literal or metaphoric meaning to the symptom, is explored. Remember that children, in particular, understand words more literally than adults. Q5 focuses on establishing that it is indeed some inner message or idea that is the cause. (Always double check!) Q6 checks on the number of causes, and this is confirmed as singular in Q7. Finally, Q8 refers back to the original presuppositions about an inner imprint experience and establishes this as the cause. Q9 confirms just one such experience. Q10 through Q14 narrow down the year of the experience. (An efficient search procedure is to halve the time period each time.) It is generally not necessary to narrow down the time finer than the year of origin, although knowing the season or holiday or special event may be significant. Q15 confirms the association of the symptom with an illness. Note that the operator can always ask for a *verbal* response or clarification at any point in the process. Q16 confirms the actual illness. Q17 through Q21 are used to discover who was the significant deliverer of the imprint message. It is impressive that, within the asking of twenty or so questions, the core of the problem is reached, and that with a few more questions, one can obtain a *permanent* resolution. Between Q21 and Q22, additional verbal responses are solicited to fill out the background. Q22 is cleverly designed to lead to a resolution based on knowledge of the origin of the problem in the past, since this was really in the past and no longer appropriate or relevant. Q23 affirms the solution and seals it for now and the future. The theoretical orientation and psychotherapeutic system used by the therapist is important in terms of the specific questions they ask. You need to be careful to keep your particular bias as to etiology, for example, out of the questioning— *or* do it knowingly. Are the questions you use designed to elicit the responses that you want to hear or which conform with your system, or are they sufficiently open to allow other possibilities?

2. Finger Signals

Finger signals are generally to be preferred to the Chevreul pendulum since the responses are both more definitive and rapid. Larger body movements, such as raising a hand or arm or head nodding, may also be used. However, these latter movements involve larger muscles and can be intrusive. It is best to utilize the most economical and simplest movements of fingers on one hand. Some practitioners prefer to specify the hand (preferring the dominant one) and the specific fingers for the yes, no, and not-willing-now responses. This has the advantage of a consistent set of signals. It is also easier to watch one hand with direct or peripheral vision. The client is generally asked to not pay conscious attention to his/her fingers. The client's position may be so structured as to make direct viewing of their hand difficult, if not awkward. If the client's eyes close, then visual observation is precluded.

In many ways, you will get only as far in one session as the presuppositions or priming or seeding you have done either at the beginning of or prior to the session. Contrast the following two opening statements: (1) "Some of my clients have occasionally responded well to using their fingers, so we might as well give it a go." (2) "Finger signals are easy to learn, and all of my clients find the experience interesting. In fact, they are frequently surprised as to how fast they can change and get what they came here for." Again, we suggest reading Erickson's preparation of clients. If you are going to imply anything, why not imply the ease and success and naturalness of the process? Therapy using finger signals starts *before* the actual use of the method. Younger clients enjoy the "game" aspects of finger signals. If finger signaling leads to spontaneous age regression, then this game/mystery aspect automatically comes into play.

Some observations and comments will be made before outlining a general procedure for finger signaling. First, it is rare that finger signals give false information—the body's automatic system generally prefers not to give an answer at all to giving a direct lie. Use the speed of response as an indicator of willingness to respond. When there is a delay in responding, you can ask directly about what is going on in the client at that moment. Give the client an "out" by reminding him/her of the third response. Sometimes, responses are minimal—there may just be vibratory movements in the finger(s), or a very small movement. Again, you can ask for that movement to be verified or amplified. Remember that, if finger movements are truly automatic and outside awareness, you need to *tell* your client what the response to a particular question *was*: "Your yes finger has now lifted—let's explore this further." Questions always need to be simple, clear, unambiguous, and capable of one of these three responses. One of the hallmarks of the unconscious mind is that it tends to respond *literally* to questions. A no response to "Was there a single initiating experience for this particular behavior?" can mean that there was more than one such experience or that there was none. A follow-up question is indicated. Avoid compound questions or questions involving interpretation. You can always ask direct questions inviting a verbal clarification such as "Is there anything more you need to know to get the comfort you want?" or "Is there anything you wish to tell me verbally, now?"

The following is an annotated outline for the use of finger signals in hypnotherapy:

1. Establish Rapport: this is the bottom line in all therapeutic work. How can the client follow your lead if they don't trust you? Hanging up a shingle is not enough. We recall a friend who reported on his initial meeting with an ENT doctor. The doctor's first comment while shaking hands was, "I hope you are not *afraid of surgery*." This was before any examination was done! (Would you wish to continue with this doctor?)

2. Information Gathering: there is always a minimum amount of information needed about the client. In addition to the essential "What can you do for them / what have they come to you for?", certain "mechanical" information such as age, marital status, siblings, phone numbers, employment, hobbies, etc., are needed. Note the difference between asking a goal-oriented question versus a "why" or analytical question. Start your therapy with the information gathering.

3. Presuppositions/Priming/Seeding: presuppose comfort and ease and speed of resolution and positive outcome.

Presuppose your competence and experience. Presuppose their interest, concern, sincerity, and learning ability. Some schools of therapy presuppose "no gain without pain" or "you first have to go through the pain." Is this part of the therapist's belief system or really true? Discuss automatic responses in a general way to establish a "yes" set to this kind of phenomenon. People nod their heads and shake hands automatically, do they not? A thorough preparation at this stage will make the rest of the work flow more smoothly.

4. Establish Signals: establish the "yes," "no," and "I-am-not-willing-to-answer-now" signals. These signals should be practiced in the sense of giving the client many easy opportunities to give *unambiguous* responses. Age regression may be tried at this point. Clients generally slip into a trance at this stage. You can assist this by suggesting, "You may find it easier to respond with your eyes closed, and by becoming even more comfortable as I continue to ask these questions."

5. Nature of Problem: one presumes that, since the client is coming to the hypnotherapist, the presenting problem is psychological or emotional in nature and that its *origins* were also psychological. However, it is always worthwhile asking, "Is the origin of what you have come here about organic or physical in nature?" What if the client's body "knows" that the origin is in some hormonal imbalance, neurological disorder, cancer, or other physical impairment? While in a trance state, automatic responses may arise from unconscious biological information. At any rate, it is important to check on this possibility and, if necessary, refer to the medical profession. For some presenting problems checking on "organ language" may be important.

6. Secondary Gain: "Does this problem serve any purpose?" "Is there some benefit from having this behavior?" Always check for secondary gain. If it is present, you will need to deal with it immediately. "Assuming your problem is resolved today, would it then be okay to deal with that benefit or purpose immediately?"

7. Origin of the Problem: ask if they know when this particular problem started. (It is better to start with "when" than "why.") If the response is "no," you can ask if it started in a particular event. Another "no" here would lead to asking, "Did the problem slowly build up over time?" A "yes" leads to "Do you know when this build-up started?" Since all difficulties must have started at some point in time, once that is established, you can ask, "Is it okay to go back to that point in time?" With a "yes" you can ask them to do that. With a "no," you ask "Is there something you need that will let you go back to that time *safely*?" (You may need to expand at this point on possible options for safety. Some of them are: (1) take a protector or guide or helper back with you; (2) take the present-day more resourceful and knowledgeable you back with you; and (3) go back inside some protective time capsule through which you can safely observe those earlier events.)

8. The Originating Experience: ask, "Are you willing to describe to me in words what went on back then to that younger you?" If "yes," then have them do so. If "no," you can ask if there is something else they need to do so that they are comfortable and safe in describing that earlier event. If "yes," elicit the safety factor. If "no," ask if it is okay for them to just review the event safely internally (from a distance) without verbalizing. Build in whatever safety factors are needed for them to access, observe, and review the originating experience. In traumas a second level of dissociation may be required.

9. Knowledge Can Cure: ask, "Now that you know how all of this started way back then, are you willing to let go and not let it bother or trouble or influence you any more?" If "yes," let them just go ahead and let go. If "no," ask about specific events that need to be resolved. Also, ask if there is anything else that is needed. Then, proceed to deal with these other related and significant circumstances.

10. Connected Changes: presuppose that "letting go" of that earlier controlling circumstance or imprint has consequences not only for their present and future existence, but also on how they remember and view, as well as feel, about what they experienced since that original experience. Ask, "Are you willing to review your life since that time, noting how your perceptions of events and feelings about yourself have also changed?" If "yes," have them do so. If "no," imply that they will find useful new knowledge about themselves and their past at appropriate times.

11. Future Pacing: "Would you like some time, now, to review how what you have done today will change your present and future life?" If "yes," have them do so (you may wish to comment at this point on how *fast* the mind works). If "no," suggest that they can do so in comfort by themselves over the coming days and weeks. A special application of using the future is to have the client imagine they are standing in front of a blackboard, and that on the blackboard is written the date when their present problem has been completely resolved to their satisfaction. Ask if there is a date written on the blackboard. If there is, they can just read it to you. If not, ask if there is something specific that needs to be done to get a concrete date. Then, go on from there.

12. Secondary Gain: if needed, go back and deal with the secondary gain at this time. "Now that the problem has been resolved to your satisfaction, can you think of some more appropriate benefits or more sensible purposes that will replace the old ones and work with your new behavior(s) or feelings?" Access, reinforce, and anchor these new more appropriate interpretations or benefits.

Cheek (Rossi and Cheek 1988) has made use of ideomotor signaling for a variety of health-related problems. (Note that the late Cheek was an obstetrician and gynecologist.) Since Cheek was convinced that there was an imprinting during the birth experience, he has developed a method to access the labor and birth experience. To quote (Rossi and Cheek, 1988, p. 420):

Please orient your mind back to the moments before you are born. Babies are able to hear sounds transmitted through the mother's abdominal wall and the fluid in the uterus for several weeks before birth. Pay attention to the sounds as well as your feelings during labor. Notice how your head feels, whether it wants to move in any direction. When you are at the moment you feel the pressure of labor is starting, your yes finger will lift. Each time you feel or hear something important, your no finger will lift. When you know you are outside breathing for the first time, your I-don't-want-to-answer finger will lift.

Cheek goes on to explore the birth experience using finger signals to lead the client to talk about what they have heard and felt, how it has impacted their life and, most important, how their *present* awareness and understanding of those events has changed their life now. A kind of "forgiveness" occurs for (inadvertent) past hurtful, harmful, or limiting statements or actions by significant persons present at the moment of birth. Skeptics, of course, can doubt the "reality" of such memories, but Cheek's procedure has helped many people.

Cheek (1989) has used a projection technique with finger signals to discover primary traumatic experiences. He has the client imagine that he/she is standing in front of a full-length mirror and that there are tiny colored Christmas tree lights in different parts of his/her body which register sensations. The client is then told that the lights show by their color and intensity the *meaning* of the sensations in each place. Then, the client is instructed to "see" the light in the middle of his/her forehead which represents the feeling within his/her head and mind. Was this a good and healthy color? (Note that the colors and intensities have to be calibrated individually for meaning.) Then, systematically, each part of the body is checked (scanned) as to the color and intensity of the lights there via finger signals. Traumas or ailments or disease are then accessed via the finger signals and amplified upon eliciting appropriate verbal comments. If a current physical ailment is uncovered, this can be referred to and checked by a physician. Psychological blocks, limitations, difficulties, and traumas are dealt with using the aforementioned procedures.

Cheek was the foremost practitioner and trainer of the use of finger signals and those interested in their use should study his work. Certainly, listening to his artistry on an audiotape is a pleasure.

Ideodynamic finger signals have been used successfully in working with multiple personalities. In (or out of) trance, you can work with two personalities at the same time by having one personality give responses on one hand and the second personality responding on the other hand. Since there is usually a "dominant" personality present, this one can be kept on one hand while relations with the other personalities are explored using the second hand. This procedure lets you have access to two of the personalities at the same time, and this can lead to effective psychotherapeutic work.

3. Automatic Writing and Drawing

Automatic writing and drawing are both ideomotor manifestations of hypnotic phenomena that can be effectively utilized to help clients. It should be noted, however, that, despite a long history, they are little used in practice. Wright and Wright (1987, p. 109) are correct when they write, "However, effective responsiveness to dissociative writing or drawing procedures takes a much longer period of training on the part of the client." Not only may a training period be needed, but the operator needs to have materials and a convenient arrangement for their easy use available. Of course, the client needs to be prepared for these procedures in the usual expectational ways. On the other hand, Erickson sometimes *surprised* his clients into writing or drawing. Automatic writing and drawing may not be a part of your daily practice— they should be kept in reserve for clients where other methods haven't worked, e.g. surprising a client, helping a client disclose in a hidden or secret way, and for those clients who either express themselves best through a pen or who have difficulty verbalizing.

Erickson (1961) has written that he became interested as early as 1923 in automatic writing but, primarily at that time, in its use as an induction technique. This was successful, but slow and cumbersome. His other papers on this subject appeared in 1933, 1937, 1939b, 1939c (with L.S. Kubie), and 1940 (with L.S. Kubie). A paper on the use of automatic drawing was with Kubie (1938). Interested readers should consult these papers for details. In Erickson and Rossi (1979) in the exposition of Case 12, the authors give a detailed analysis of the use of automatic writing.

We consider the best illustration of automatic writing to be that given by Erickson and Rossi (1976) and will present some of the relevant dialogue between Erickson and his subject. This will be followed by some general comments about how to use automatic writing and drawing:

S: Now I have been trying for two years to automatically write something, and I can't get it. How do I go about getting?

E: Do you want to get it?

S: Yes! I wouldn't have been trying this long if I didn't want to.

E: Ever try writing with your left hand?

S: I don't think I have.

E: Ever try writing backward with your left hand?

S: I don't think I could.

E: You probably couldn't do that. Are you willing to find that out?

S: Yes.

E: Really?!

S: Writing backward with my left hand?

E: No, to find out. To find out.

S: How do I do this? How do I set it up?

E: You don't set it up. You don't need to. Just find out. Just find out. Do you mind if J takes your cigarette? Just find out. (S's eyelids begin to blink slowly.) That's it, close your eyes. And just close your eyes and sleep more and more deeply. And now what I'd like to have you do is to wonder about that writing. I'd like to have you get the feeling that you have written it. But just the feeling that you have written it, just the feeling. ... And the only question is, when will you do it? ... You can write that material without ever knowing what it is. ... And writing is one thing and reading is another. And knowing what should be written is a third. And concealment of the writing from the self is another thing. And keep right on because you are interested. ... Now you recognize, of course, that this automatic writing, don't you? ...

In the preceding excerpt, the ellipses indicate where we have left out parts of Erickson's statements. As an exercise, you can fill in with your own words what you think would be most effective at those points. As another exercise, you can reread the above, putting in pauses and emphases wherever they are needed. Finally, you can check, for your own learning, what Erickson really said, and the commentary thereon in the original paper. A student attending one of Erickson's lectures on hypnosis approached him for help as described in the following case summary (O'Hanlon and Hexum, 1990, pp. 157–158. Originally described in Erickson and Rossi, 1980, Vol. III, pp. 158–176):

Nervous Doodling

A 24-year-old college student attended one of MHE's lectures on hypnosis in which MHE discussed automatic handwriting and the possibility of the completely separate functioning of the conscious and unconscious. She sought his assistance for a recent depression and the development of an uncomfortable habit of doodling nervously. He had her prepare for doing automatic drawing by having her unconscious work on the problem before the next session. She came in and proceeded to relate the story of a recent novel she had read while at the same time drawing two pictures, one that reproduced much of the recent type of doodling she had been doing and a second that combined elements of those pictures into a more coherent drawing.

It gradually unfolded that she had become more and more annoyed and distant from her close girlfriend and that she had some matches from a local hotel that somehow reminded her of the picture she had drawn and of her annoyance with her friend. Through MHE's questioning of her unconscious through automatic handwriting and through suggestions that her unconscious would give her the information she needed, she realized that her friend had been having an affair with the patient's father. She was angry and brought the friend in to see MHE and to confront her with the realization. Her friend admitted it and the patient forbade her to visit the house. She severed their friendship. She also realized that her father had been having affairs through the years, which was subsequently confirmed to MHE by the friend. The patient stopped her nervous doodling. The friend continued the affair with the father. The patient adjusted and was happily married at last contact with MHE.

In a most complex case (Erickson and Rossi, 1980, Vol. IV, pp. 163–168), Erickson used automatic writing to elicit the underlying reason for a social service student's promiscuous behavior.

She was a good hypnotic subject and a compulsive story-teller— Erickson had a hard time getting a word in edgewise. He finally exercised his authority and took charge.

> At the following session, as she entered the office, she was told emphatically, "Sit down, shut up, and don't you dare to open your mouth!"

It took much development work while she was in deep trance for her to be ready to divulge the reason for her behavior at the right time. Erickson gave her a typewritten page, and she was told in trance to underline, in a random fashion, the letters, syllables, and words that tell the reason. This sheet of paper was sealed until the time she was ready to learn the reason. The random underlines, when organized, spelled out "I want to f uck f author." The successful resolution was described by her and Erickson.

> She explained, "It was any man, every man, all the men in the world. That would include father. That would make him a man, not a grease spot under my mother's thumb. Now I know what I have been trying to do, and I don't have to any more. How horrible!"

> She reacted by further intense sobbing, but finally declared, "That's all in the past now. What can I do?"

> The suggestion was offered that she undergo a complete physical examination to check the possibility of venereal disease. To this she agreed.

> She completed her next year's training successfully and was not heard from until several years later. Then it was learned from a colleague that she was most happily married and was the mother of three children. Subsequent personal inquiry confirmed the happiness of her marriage.

This case is another example of Erickson's extraordinary persistence and devotion to his clients, as well as his use of a wide variety of techniques designed to elicit significant information, while at the same time protecting his client.

Automatic writing is most conveniently done with the client seated at a desk with a pad of paper and either soft lead pencils or felt-tipped pens ready to use. The writing should not require pressing or orienting the implements correctly. An alternative is to use a pad with a stiff back or a pad in a clipboard that the client can hold on his/her lap. A lap board can also be used. A desk or a table is preferred. The client can be encouraged directly or indirectly to write with the dominant *or* the non-dominant hand. The writing that appears may be backwards, vertical, mirror-image, upside-down, small, large, or all possible variants. The writing may be legible or not, and may be done slowly or rapidly. Generally, the speed picks up as the client does more writing. Aside from legibility, what is written (or drawn) may in all likelihood be cryptic or symbolic. The client's aid will certainly be needed for proper interpretation. Note that this can be done with the client in or out of trance, as the individual circumstance warrants.

One of the authors (TLS), while beginning his clinical internship fifteen years ago with feelings of insecurity, was involved in intense study and writing a summary when he noticed his hand automatically finish a paragraph and continue to fill up the page. This was a strange, but comfortable, feeling. As he observed the automatic writing in bewilderment, he heard an unknown pleasant nurturing fatherly voice talking to him. The voice alleviated his insecurities and gave him confidence about being a neophyte psychotherapist. The fatherly voice reminded him of his varied past learnings and about those who had confidence in his abilities. This voice spoke knowingly with authority and confidence. It also said, "Remember, I will be with you!" The automatic writing was a written narrative of the voice's message. This serious psychology student knew that it was not God or an auditory hallucination, but interpreted it as the "voice of the unconscious." Two years later he became acquainted with the work of Erickson and became a serious student of hypnosis. He now knows that it was a dissociated experience called "automatic writing" brought about by an intensely narrow focussing of attention and an unconscious response to self-doubt, i.e. a spontaneous autohypnosis. Indeed, this voice was not only right, but has occasionally returned in troubled times offering comfort and nurturing. However, for whatever reasons, the automatic writing has never returned.

Automatic drawing while the client is in trance can be done with the client's eyes closed or open. In the latter case, the client can be provided with an assortment of drawing implements of different colors. Interpretations of drawings should be done by the client, generally in the waking state. Of course, there is an overlap between automatic drawing and the field of art therapy. When someone is focused on the drawings that art therapists request, they will generally be in a light trance. They can go deeper as their absorption in the drawing increases. Asking someone to draw may be used as an induction.

Other "automatic" artistically related processes include sculpting in clay, playing in sand, and constructions with blocks or other objects. Family "sculpting" using dolls may occur in trance states. There is lots of room for experimentation and many ways to help clients uniquely.

4. Rossi's "Fail-Safe" Use of Hands

Rossi has described in detail (Erickson and Rossi, 1981, pp. 126–38; Rossi and Cheek, 1988, pp. 38–41) and with two videotapes of demonstrations (Rossi, 1982, 1983) the hypnotic experience of moving hands described by Weitzenhoffer (1957) for rapid thera-peutic work. The use of "moving hands" is ideomotoric and the language used is an effective demonstration of the double-bind technique. In that sense, Rossi describes his particular approach as a "fail-safe" induction procedure with an (almost) foolproof hypnotherapeutic approach (at least in his hands!). The following is reproduced from Rossi and Cheek (1988, p. 39).

Box 11: Moving Hands Accessing of Creative Resources

1. Readiness signal for inner work

a. "Place your hands about six to eight inches apart, and with great sensitivity, tune into the real or imagined magnetic field developing between them [therapist demonstrates]. If your creative (healing) unconscious is ready to begin therapeutic work, you will experience those hands moving together all by themselves to signal yes."

[Pause. If hands do not move together, continue with the following.]

b. "But if there is another issue that you need to explore first, you will feel those hands being pushed apart to signal no. In that case, a question will come up in your mind that we can deal with."

2. Accessing and resolving problems

a. "As your unconscious mind explores the sources and important memories about [whatever problem], one of those arms will begin drifting down very slowly."

[Pause. When one arm does begin drifting down, continue.]

"That arm can continue drifting down very slowly so that it will finally come to rest on your lap only when you have completed a satisfactory inner review of that problem."

[Pause after arm has come down to rest on lap.]

b. "And now your other arm will begin drifting down all by itself as your unconscious explores all the therapeutic possibilities for resolving that problem in an ideal manner that is most suitable for you at this time."

c. "When your unconscious has resolved that problem in a satisfactory manner, that arm will come to rest in your lap."

3. Ratifying problem-solving

a. "Does your unconscious want to let your head nod yes all by itself to ratify the value of the therapeutic progress?"

b. "When your unconscious and conscious minds know that they can continue to deal with that problem in a satisfactory way, you will find yourself stretching and coming completely awake as you open your eyes."

The content of the above-quoted material can be productively studied in a variety of ways. First, you can outline the flow of suggestions, marking all of the presuppositions that are built in. Go over the statements indicating which words and phrases you would mark for special emphasis by pauses or intonation. Notice the compact use of language, its permissive nature, and the coverage of almost all possible responses. It is almost as if the client is being channeled in one direction to help him/herself, but using their own unique resources. This procedure is an almost perfect example of the use of process versus content. The entire procedure is enhanced via the kinesthetic and physiologic use of hand and arm movements. These serve as anchors and reinforcers. You do not have to even believe in "magnetic" or other forces for this process to work. Of course, the client almost automatically slips into a trance state following their focussing on their hand movements. Language can be interspersed, if needed, to enhance eye closure, depth of trance, relaxation, and resolution of the presenting problem. For example, "And you can continue to work on this problem bringing it to an even more satisfactory resolution." "And you can bring into play whatever additional knowledge and resources or changes you need, now, to achieve the health/resolution you desire, safely, surely, and simply."

C. Other Ideodynamic Methods

For completeness, we need to mention the other ideodynamic phenomena of ideosensory and ideoaffective responses. *Ideosensory responses* are sensory phenomena like tasting, smelling, touching, hearing, and seeing what arises from the operator's suggestions. Talking about eating pizza will result in a client's "tasting" a pizza. Rossi talks about this as "state dependent learning." People go back to their senses and actually relive, feel, and sense what it is you are suggesting. This is why you do not ask someone who has recovered from a heart attack about the experience. The body will automatically retrieve the physiological states (to varying degrees) that occurred in the original incident. Sufficient time from an event weakens some of these associations. However, it is best to use dissociation in some way if it is important to access such memories.

See chapter 13 on the arts as hypnotherapeutic metaphors. In some ways, *any* artistic activity involves ideomotor movements, particularly when the person's attention is narrowly focused.

In a similar way, ideoaffective responses are triggered by suggestions or environmental stimuli. The NLP model of phobic responses is that a visual-external stimulus triggers a visual-internal memory which then triggers the kinesthetic component which results in severe panic or anxiety. Such stimuli should be used consciously by the therapist and with great caution.

D. Summarizing Ideodynamic Methods

People respond ideodynamically all the time. In this chapter, we have given you ways to recognize those responses and use them to help your clients effectively and efficiently. Certainly, studying the way that Cheek uses finger signals or Rossi moving hands to work with clients in single sessions is eye opening. Ideodynamic methods provide rapid access to trance states and problem resolution. The Chevreul pendulum works, but is cumbersome and slow. You should convince yourself of its reality, and you can use it as a convincer for some clients of the existence of unconscious thoughts and motoric control. Finger signals are easier to use and with practice will find a place in your repertoire. Automatic writing and drawing can be saved for special circumstances and clients. Rossi's elegant use of moving hands is worth studying, both as an example of ideodynamic methods, and also as a brilliant use of effective hypnotic language.

Exercises

1. The various ideodynamic methods described in this chapter should be practiced to develop the skills involved. You should convince yourself initially of the reality of the Chevreul pendulum. Verify for yourself and others if it moves to indicate the three requested responses of "yes," "no," and "I am not willing to answer now." Work with many test subjects to test the Chevreul pendulum. It is always useful to have a third person available to you as an observer and someone who can whisper suggestions to you and take notes.

2. Practice with finger signals can be done in dyads and triads. How "deep" a trance is needed to use finger signals? Experiment with this. Does a "spontaneous" trance develop? How can you facilitate this? Since the essential part of using ideodynamic methods has to do with the series of questions asked, write out for yourself several series of questions that might be used with different clients. Then use these questions in practice sessions. Record your sessions so you can learn

from the tapes about the language patterns and the questions that you use. You might wish initially to memorize the patterns of questioning used by LeCron and Cheek.

3. You can also test the use of the Chevreul pendulum and finger signals on yourself by putting yourself into a light trance or a relaxed state. We find this quite useful for personal work.

4. Experiment with automatic writing and drawing. Which of your clients would most benefit from these automatic processes?

Chapter 11

Basic Metaphor

Rubin Battino, M.S.

31 Another parable He put before them, saying, "The kingdom of heaven is like a grain of mustard seed which a man took and sowed in his field; 32 it is the smallest of all seeds, but when it has grown it is the greatest of shrubs and becomes a tree, so that the birds of the air come and make nests in its branches."

34 All this Jesus said to the crowds in parables; indeed He said nothing to them without a parable. 35 This was to fulfill what was spoken by the prophet: "I will open my mouth in parables, I will utter what has been hidden since the foundation of the world."

Matthew 13

A. Introduction

All of the great religious leaders of the world taught with parables (definition: a comparison; specifically a short fictitious narrative from which a moral or spiritual truth is drawn), stories, and metaphors. They taught in this way because stories of any kind are inherently engaging, if not entrancing. People like to make *connections* to what they already know, to their own unique experiences. In the *constructionist* theory of learning, people build upon their present knowledge and understanding—stories and metaphors and analogies help people to make those connections and bridges.

Perhaps the most common request of a child is to "tell me a story," and we never seem to outgrow our need for and our fascination with stories. Just think of the variety of stories we are hooked on: fairy tales, romances, westerns, novels, science fiction, adventures, mysteries, ghost and occult, history, biography, Hasidic tales, nursery rhymes, soap operas, sitcoms, myths and legends, sagas, and movies of all kinds. All cultures transmit their heritage via myths and legends and rites and rituals. Some of these stories contain mysteries and riddles (like Zen koans, parables, and Hasidic tales) which further engage the listener by involving him/her in finding answers or solutions. The oral tradition is particularly powerful since each listener must translate the teller's words into their own images, sounds, senses, and experiences. In this sense, radio is a much more powerful medium than television with its fixed images. How many times have you seen a movie based on a book you have read and been disappointed because the movie did not match your internal images, or the actors, your internalized characters? (In fairness, there are occasional book-based movies which are so well done that they transcend the written word.)

Since stories are so compelling, how can they be used in psychotherapy, and in hypnotherapy, in particular? It was said of Erickson that he never answered a question straight when he could respond with a story (or stories). Certainly, the four published volumes of his seminars, workshops, and lectures (Rossi, et al., 1983, 1985, 1986, 1992) are replete with examples of Erickson's responding to questions by telling stories and, in particular, telling about individual cases. In this sense, it is difficult to distinguish between a case and a parable! The great Yiddish writer and Nobel Laureate, Isaac B. Singer, once commented on the difference between his writing and "modern" novelists in the following way: Singer said that he let the *stories* of his characters carry the meaning and essence of their lives rather than go inside their heads and tell us directly what their thoughts and feelings were. Singer was a storyteller, and his writings were the richer for that. Erickson was a storyteller, and the therapy he did was the richer *and* the more effective for that. Erickson was a teacher in the "old" tradition and taught by the examples of cases and stories.

In this chapter we will discuss the basic elements of storytelling as a therapeutic approach. Within the field, this has come to be described as *therapeutic metaphor*. Before beginning, we will briefly note relevant references aside from Erickson's published works. Gordon's book (1978) was perhaps the first to systematically discuss the structure and use of metaphor for psychotherapeutic work. It contains a good set of references, but no index. Lankton and Lankton (1983, pp. 245–311) provide a thorough and system-atic approach to the use of metaphor in psychotherapy and hypnotherapy, with many examples. A second book by the Lanktons (1986, pp. 153–217) has metaphors specifically oriented for use in family therapy. A third book by the Lanktons (1989) is specifically devoted to "tales of enchantment" and contains many detailed metaphors with particular applications for adults and children. O'Hanlon (1987) has a relatively brief, but good, description of the use of metaphors. Wallas's two books (1985, 1991) contain well-written metaphors with an indication for the intended use of each story. An example is "The Seedling," a story for a client who had been abused as a child. Combs and Freedman (1990) give stories and case studies illustrating metaphorical strategies. Rosen (1982) has collected the teaching tales of Erickson in a fascinating volume that includes commentary on the tales. Mills and Crowley (1986) have written a book specifically with therapeutic metaphors for children (see chapter 13). There is an accompanying audiotape. Havens and Walters' (1989) book on hypnotherapy scripts gives complete scripts for metaphors in various categories like: affirming the self, alleviating unwarranted fears, developing spontaneity, and improving performance, as well as five "general purpose" metaphors. Finally, we single out Frankl's "Man's Search for Meaning" (1959) as an extraordinary example where the *story* of one man's search for meaning has had profound effects on its readers. Indeed, certain writings like Frankl's may be considered to be bibliotherapy via metaphor.

Zeig has given eight reasons for the value of anecdotes (or metaphors) in therapy. They are: (1) anecdotes are nonthreatening; (2) anecdotes are engaging; (3) anecdotes foster independence—the person needs to make sense of the message and then come to a self-initiated conclusion or a self-initiated action; (4) anecdotes can be used to bypass natural resistance to change; (5) anecdotes can be used to control the relationship; (6) anecdotes model flexibility; (7) anecdotes can create confusion and promote hypnotic responsiveness; (8) anecdotes tag the memory: "They make the presented idea more memorable." Anecdotes are also respectful and gentle.

B. Basic Metaphors

The Greek roots for the word metaphor mean to "carry over" or "to transfer." A dictionary definition states: "A figure of speech in which a word or phrase literally denoting one kind of object or idea is used in place of another by way of suggesting a likeness or analogy between them." So, one idea or object is linked to another via the *implication* or *suggestion* that the two are related or connected in some way. A common understanding of metaphor is that it is storytelling. Yet, the key word above is "suggestion," i.e. a story by itself is just a story which may or may not be entertaining. For the story to be therapeutic in some way, the therapist must imply indirectly or directly that there is something of significance in the story for the client. This implication will trigger a trans-derivational or inner search for unique significance. For many people, the mere telling of a story is sufficient to start an inner search because of a general cultural expectancy that stories have "points" or meaning. This attitude has been behaviorally instilled in literature classes and in religious training. To be on the safe side, the therapist can always be explicit: "Many of my clients find special personal significance, and even useful directions, in the stories I tell. I wonder in what ways these stories will help you/teach you/offer interesting possibilities to you." We have used the plural above since you want to be redundant and provide many opportunities for your client to "carry over" or make connections. You can tell several related or unrelated stories, or nest several stories within the initial story. If you are not now a natural storyteller, where do you begin?

Using a metaphor involves four parts: (1) gathering information; (2) constructing the metaphor; (3) delivering or relating it; and (4) providing some kind of closure. These elements of a metaphor are commented upon in this section.

1. Gathering Information

Two kinds of information are needed before constructing appropriate metaphors. The first is about the presenting problem, and the second is related to obtaining sufficient personal information so that the metaphors can be tailor-made. These two aspects will be discussed separately.

a. Information about the Problem

In a chapter on "negotiating the problem," Cade and O'Hanlon (1993) give a useful list of questions designed to clarify the presenting problem. The questions are followed by some commentary.

(1) *When* does the problem occur? Are there any patterns or regularities in the occurrence of the problem, e.g. only on weekends, in the evening, at midnight, etc.?

(2) *Where* does the problem occur? Is there a pattern as to particular locations where the problem occurs or does not occur? Is it never at work and only in the kitchen, for example?

(3) What is the *performance* of the problem? What would an objective observer see when the client had the problem, e.g. specific stances, movements, speech, gestures, actions? If I had your problem, how would I act to reproduce it?

(4) *With whom* does it occur? When you have the problem, are you alone? With specific others? Does the "audience" change? How do these potential others interact with you?

(5) What are the *exceptions* to the rule of the problem? Are there times when the problem does not occur? What is different about those times/location/environment?

(6) What does the client (or clients) do differently, or what activities are prevented, *because of the problem*? In other words, in what specific ways does the problem affect their lives in terms of activities they are involved in or avoid?

(7) What does the client *show in the session* that is related to the problem? Many therapists believe that it is not possible for a client to talk about a problem without reliving it at the same time. Talking about a state recalls all the physical and mental memories associated with that state.

(8) What are the client's *explanations* and frames regarding the problem? How is the problem perceived from the client's unique perspective and history? This is an important check to keep your guesses and possible projections at bay.

(9) What are the client's or others' *attempted solutions* regarding the "problem"? You need to know what has already been tried so you don't fall into the trap of doing "more of the same," and also to gain some insight into the client's problem-solving approaches.

(10) How will we (and others) know when we get there? What *objective* tests and behaviors will be available so that you know the problem is resolved? Stating behaviors that others can observe concretizes the client's difficulties into a solvable problem because the outcomes are known. These outcomes must be realistic.

Identifying what, to the client's mind, has stopped them in the past gives you clues to their connecting strategies. However, you should avoid dwelling on impasses and spend more time in the search for the *exceptions* which house the seeds of solutions. Also, although it is useful to know how the problem progresses, *it is more useful to know how the problem abates*. After all, the severest migraine does wax and wane and finally abate. *How* did the abatement occur?

It is useful to gather as much information about the problem as possible. In studying Erickson's cases, it is clear that he frequently spent a very long first session in just getting acquainted with his client, in obtaining a detailed history. Experience will dictate how much information about the problem is needed before moving on. You could probably obtain most of the information implied in the ten questions listed above in fifteen to twenty minutes, if you keep the client on track.

b.   Idiosyncratic Background Information

Everyone is unique and the more personal and idiosyncratic the information you have about the client, the more accurate the connections you can make between their problem and the metaphors you use. Is the client a devout or a lapsed Catholic? What are the client's hobbies; talents; profession; upbringing; rural/urban/suburban background; travels; age/sex/marital status/birth order; education; and work? You wouldn't generally tell a metaphor about farming to a lifelong city dweller, and vice versa. Metaphors make connections between this and that, so you need to know the "this" in the client's experience. When dealing with children, for example, it would be important to know what is shown on children's television and what are current popular children's books. There are some "standard" or "universal" metaphors that can be adapted to many clients, but it is better to use specifically tailored metaphors. People learn based on their experience.

2. Building the Metaphor

The Lanktons (1983) are systematic in their construction of a metaphor and start their process with an awareness of six areas in which to find evidence of change before considering treatment complete. The six areas to check for desired outcome(s) are (p. 87): (1) bonding and age-appropriate intimacy; (2) self-image enhancement; (3) attitude restructuring; (4) social role change; (5) family structure change; and (6) enjoyment of life. Their condensed outline (p. 92) for developing an individualized metaphor for each client is:

(1) Listen to the problem as offered.

(2) Guided by the six areas of desired outcomes, list dramatic themes that are part of the current and desired situation.

(3) Construct metaphors that parallel those themes.

(4) Design appropriate general outcomes.

(5) Arrange the outcome to create suspense or mystery.

We can envision two extremes in using metaphors with clients. On the one hand, we might have a "natural" storyteller who intuitively can create or relate highly relevant stories on the spur of the moment. There are such "naturals" out there. As an aside, we recall a childhood friend who naturally and unknowingly spoke in profundities—his utterances were made to be immortalized in needlepoint! By contrast, the other extreme is the systematic and conscious design that the Lanktons use, and with which we agree. Clients deserve your conscious concern and involvement. The starting point is the conscious development of appropriate metaphors—after much experience in their use, many of the steps and checks will become part of your automatic responses. Remember that it is almost always permissible to take a "timeout" (which you are devoting to the client's benefit) to consult with colleagues or to develop the metaphor (or other intervention) on your own. If you use a time-out, remember to "seed" relevant thinking on the part of your client.

In the following outline for the construction of a metaphor, we draw upon the steps developed by Gordon (1978) and by Lankton and Lankton (1983).

Outline for Metaphor Construction

a. Gather Information: this was dealt with in some detail earlier. For the metaphor to be meaningful, it needs to have elements uniquely connected with the client's life. A sailing metaphor won't work with someone who doesn't swim and is prone to seasickness. A city dweller may have no knowledge about growing fruits and vegetables. Knowledge of hobbies is quite useful. Who are the significant persons with whom the client is involved? What are their inter-relationships? What events are characteristic of the problem? In what ways does the problem progress? Determine in *behavioral and objectively verifiable* terms what outcome(s) the client wants. It is always useful to know what has been tried in the past. Are there any particular things that "stop" the client from making the desired changes? (Reiterating some of the gathering of information aspects is our way of emphasizing the importance of this step.)

b. Outcomes Guide: using the Lanktons' six areas of desired outcomes as a guide, *list* the *dramatic* themes that are part of the current and desired situation. Stories are inherently dramatic. To be effective, the potential dramatic components need to be elucidated *and* connected to the desired outcomes.

c. Construct/Adapt the Metaphor: the metaphor needs to parallel the six areas in some way. You may wish to list the areas and the parallels with the metaphor. What is the context or setting of the metaphor? How much detail about this setting will be significant? To be too specific defeats internal searching and the client's filling in of details (radio vs. TV). Who will populate the metaphor? The inhabitants need to be sufficiently isomorphic with the significant persons found in the gathering information step. Generally, it is better to avoid the use of animals or extra-terrestrials, unless they are specifically indicated. Children, for example, may better identify with animals or super-heroes or fairy tale characters than adults. The Wookie or Yoda in *Star Wars* may be perfect as a character. In general, the simpler the tale, the better. (See the next chapter for comments on multi-embedded metaphors for a more complex construction.) Match the level of complexity to your client and, perhaps, their level of "resistance." Stories need to have beginnings, middles, and ends. Consciously design them into the metaphor. In particular, design in appropriate *general* outcomes. We deliberately indicate the plural here since you want to give your client *many choices* to select from. The choices need to be connected to the client's desired outcomes. It is worthwhile noting Talmon's observation (1990) that, when clients on follow-up were asked to identify statements that their therapist made that were particularly helpful, the therapist frequently did not recall making that statement or in that way or that it was particularly significant!

Creating new and unique metaphors for each client can be time-consuming and even intimidating. Hence, it makes sense (see below) to have available a set of adaptable "standard" metaphors. For example, the theme of a person or plant or animal growing up can be adapted to many situations. The construction of a house, computer program, play or novel, or organization has many parallels.

d. Drama/Suspense/Mystery: good stories are dramatic, and that characteristic is bolstered by suspense and mystery. Whodunnit? What will happen? and when? and to whom? and in what ways? The "tease" for these elements needs to be planted early in the metaphor. Humor, of course, can always be incorporated. The word play of puns, oxymorons, and homonyms is also dramatic. In Shakespeare's tragedies, the most dramatic times are invariably preceded and set up by a scene involving comic relief. A study of play and story construction would not be amiss.

e. Reframing: to a great extent, the value of telling a story lies in the reframing inherent in the story. Tales are told, and the outcomes are new perspectives and choices. With this in mind, the metaphor can contain consciously designed reframes of the presenting problem.

f. Closure: metaphors may be told with the client in the waking or the trance state, although the telling of a good story invariably invokes some level of trance in the listener. So, the client will need to be reoriented to the present time and location at the end of the story. Where indicated, amnesia for the metaphor may be induced by direction or by the indirection of a non sequitur or distraction at the end of the metaphor. Although a story may have a verbalized "moral" or punch line, it is rarely necessary to emphasize the "point" of the story. The effectiveness of metaphors is primarily at the unconscious level of internal searches and discoveries and choices.

Once the metaphor has been constructed, and it can be written out or memorized, then it must be told. The next section discusses the factors involved in the delivery of the metaphor.

3. Delivery

The impact of a metaphor is directly related to your skill as a story-teller. The same story read by an amateur or a gifted actor has quite different outcomes. A "natural" storyteller has an advantage, but storytelling skills can be practiced and learned. A basic element is to be aware of the pacing and leading and rapport-building skills we have written about earlier. Pacing, amongst other things, means paying exquisite attention to your client for physiological and postural and verbal feedback so you can adjust your metaphor in terms of the client's responses. Taped metaphors and the reading of metaphors (prepared by you or others) can be effective, but not as effective as a "live" session. Experienced story-tellers and comedians and speakers, for example, are all flexible in their delivery and are adept at "reading" their audiences. (As an aside, we are certain that you have all noticed the difference at conferences in the reception of prepared addresses which are read, and those speakers who work from notes.) Another example involves lecturers who use overhead projectors and who are in constant visual contact with their audience versus those who write on blackboards and must be continually turning to make contact. You must observe to be able to pace and lead.

Audiotapes "designed" to do this, that, or the other require the listener to continually adjust what is heard to his/her own needs. Since everyone is so singular, it is important in the use of any metaphor or induction or intervention or audiotape to explicitly give the client *permission to modify* what they hear for their own individual purposes. Why not make use of the nature of verbal interactions?

If you are aware of your client's preferred representational system (auditory, kinesthetic, visual), then you should make use of this in the design of your metaphor. Matching a representational system adds accuracy and validity to the metaphor. At the same time, you can *cross over* to other representational systems within the metaphor to enhance and enlarge your client's experience. For example, a visual person who has a sexual dysfunction problem would probably benefit from crossovers to the kinesthetic, along with embellishments in the auditory and the olfactory. When you are in doubt about a preferred representational system, then be sure to include all three in your metaphor and *observe* their impact.

Voice quality is an important part of delivery. A harsh, grating, or squeaky voice will incur negative reactions in most people. A well-modulated voice with a range of volume and delivery is certainly more effective. It is important to match in some way, or ways, your clients' speech patterns. It is also important for your delivery to be congruent with the content of your metaphor. Unless you have some conscious reason to do otherwise, you do not talk about exciting things in a flat monotone.

We have written almost endlessly earlier about language forms. In the delivery of a metaphor, you will need to use all of your language form skills. These include: empty words, connecting words, analogical marking, temporal marking, embedded commands, quotes, ambiguity, paradoxical language, puns, oxymorons, lack of referential index, clang associations, unspecified verbs, exaggeration, nominalization, etc. You may wish to review language forms before attempting metaphor construction.

You can certainly use anchors in the telling of metaphors. Just as you may have a "hypnosis" chair in your office, you may also have a metaphor chair. Your way of sitting or tilting your head or your voice quality may be used as an anchor to indicate that it is story-telling time. (What anchors did you use with your children for this?) Within the metaphor certain words or images may be used as leitmotifs or anchors. Auditory, kinesthetic, and visual words may be used to lead the listener to certain desired states. You've grasped that in a sound way as you've been picturing it, haven't you?

C. Some Sample Metaphors

Good sources of therapeutic metaphors are: Buber (1975), Combs and Freedman (1990), Gordon (1978), Haley (1973), Havens and Walters (1989), Kopp (1971, 1972, 1983), Lankton and Lankton (1989), Mills and Crowley (1986), Rosen (1982), and Wallas (1985, 1991). Fairy tales, myths, legends, movies, novels, and family stories are also good sources on which to build. If you can, you should design your own metaphors. To help you, we are going to present a number of "standard" metaphors that can be adapted to many circumstances. We will *italicize* key words and phrases in the stories. You can use them as a kind of scaffolding on which to build your own metaphor. In fact, we will start with a construction metaphor. (The exercises at the end of this chapter will help you further.)

1. Construction of a Building

Have you ever been a sidewalk supervisor, watching a skyscraper being built? They always dig so far down to *construct the foundation*. And isn't it interesting that you first have to *clear a site*, and then remove so much dirt and rubble *before you can begin*? What a *wonderful balance* since there is always someone who wants clean landfill—one person's waste or excess is another person's need. As water seeks its own level, the foundation needs to be waterproof or with a way to pump out the excess fluid. I am always surprised at how deep foundations need to go—*to rise above* the level means to *build solid* and deep supporting structures. To *be grounded* applies to buildings, as well as people. To *be rooted*, to plants as well as people. The framing may be steel or reinforced concrete. Foundations must be concrete and *solidly based*. As the skeletal frame rises, it almost seems so airy and insubstantial. Yet all the stresses and strains are calculated with *safe margins* of error—to be economical you don't want to overbuild more than is necessary *for your security* and safety. It is in the interlocking and *interconnecting* of all of the structural elements that the *strength* comes from. The whole is *much more* than its parts, yet each part has a part to *play together*. What kind of walls should this building have? Some buildings are almost transparent, some you can see out of, but not in—mirroring the outside world; some have solid substantial sealing walls, and some *have a balance*. There are so many ways to skin a building, *what is your facade like*? And that's *just the outside*. How many rooms and what shapes, and is there enough room? And you always need to provide places for storage and *ways to get in and out*. What kinds of doors? And how do you roof and cover and *protect the insides*? And all those simple but *important lines to the outside world*, with water and sewage and electricity and communications. So many details when you *build something*. And when a building is completed, that is *only the beginning of its life*. Many buildings have built-in ways to *ease remodeling, adaptability* in steel, *changing* within concrete, *expanding* rooms and vistas. And how will you build the skyscraper of your life?

Commentary—Many of the statements used above can be adapted to building a house rather than a skyscraper. You still need foundations and utilities and framing and walls and windows and doors and a roof. But you must first lay the foundations.

2. *Growing Corn*

One of my son's favorite books was about a kernel of corn. We had read that story so many times that he knew if I made the slightest mistake in reading—children have such *good memories* for *pleasant* things, and *know so much more* than you give them credit for. Corn is so good to eat, and did you know that each kernel carries within it the *seed to grow* a whole stalk? We started out with two kernels of corn, each in its own jelly glass full of potting soil. Sometimes a kernel will not grow, and we can be sad about that one and rejoice with the other one—so we always planted two kernels—*you need to be prepared for life*. The potting soil was broken up and dribbled into the glass so it would provide such a soft, *receptive* bed for the kernel. We enjoy the *soft* moistness of the soil.

Now it is time to *plant your seed* and wonder just how soon the *roots will descend* and the stem *rise*. Gently make a hole with a finger, about one inch deep; put in the kernel pointy end up, and cover it with loose soil. Add the *right amount* of water. And, in a few days, *knowing how* we do not *know how* it knows what it knows, the *kernel opens* and a small tendril *reaches out, ready for growth*. And did you know that it grows down and around as much as it *grows up*? The roots start spreading and reaching out to *build a strong* foundation. The higher you grow, the stronger your roots must be. One day, one day that magic moment comes when the stem first bulges the soil, then *breaks through to the light*, ready to *assert itself, ready to grow, ready to rise* to its natural height, *reaching for the sun* and the moon and the stars. We watch and watch while it grows, seeing some of the roots against the side of the glass while the stem *stretches itself upward*.

When it has outgrown the glass, we transfer it to a larger pot with *more nourishing* soil and *so much more room to grow*. At each stage of its growth, the corn from the kernel needs *just the right amount* of room and nourishment and light. The sun *shines its light of energy* on the green-growing plant. And carbon dioxide from the air and water in the soil and nutrients in the soil combine together in the light to *make more growth*. Just the right amount of *each* nutrient is used so unknowingly and so accurately *to balance and grow*. In its thankfulness, the plant gives us oxygen.

We *prepare a sunny spot* in the garden. *Always be prepared*, and transfer the growing plant so it can now be on its own and *sink its roots* even deeper, *find stronger foundations, reach even higher, differentiate* and *grow* new kernels of corn, *new ears*, what does an ear of corn hear? And each new kernel in this sturdy, tall, being proud of *growing on its own* plant, has a tassel that *awaits fertilization* from another plant. So, the corn *depends on its neighbors*, friends, and relatives to *become fully mature*, to be able to *bear its own fruit*. The corn *enjoys the sun*, is washed and nourished by the rain, *feels its roots* firm in the ground, sways to a passing breeze, *realizes itself*.

The time comes to pick the corn which the plant *lovingly gives us* so that we may *be nourished*, too, and *continue the cycle*, the endless cycles of growth, nourishment, death, and rebirth when we save some seeds for next year, *looking ahead*, preparing for more kernels of corn, and *more growth*. The corn bears fruit by giving and sharing to *continue itself* in whatever new ways are available in the endlessly interesting variety of life. Who would have thought a kernel of corn knew so much?

Commentary—The growing of plants provides many opportunities for interspersal and embedding messages. The previous metaphor concerned a kernel of corn, but other plants are available for particular clients. A sunflower follows the sun and hangs its head and brightens a field and replenishes itself and feeds birds and stands tall. A tomato has its firm, round, red nourishing tangyness, a love apple that was once green. A rose has its beauty and its aroma and its thorns for protection. A potato or carrot or beet or radish does its growing underground in a protected environment until it is ripe and ready to emerge. Grapes grow in bunches hanging down, and bananas in bunches standing up. There is lots of soil here for fertilization—match the plant to your client.

3. *Learning Basic Skills*

There are *so many ways to learn* and so many things that *you have learned already* and forgotten how you learned, and even, sometimes, forgotten what you've learned. It is said that elephants *never forget*. It is also said that *people never really forget*, that somewhere, somehow, in some way, in all those nerve endings, everything important you've ever learned or experienced is stored. Yet, isn't it just wonderful, remarkable, how *your mind protects you*? How certain problem memories are *just hidden* or *stored away* to return at *safe times* for *new understandings* and learnings? Or how some can just be *safely locked up* or buried or hidden in ways that they will never ever come back to bother you? Just safe and secure permanent storage with *no effect at all* on your present and future life. Who said, "It is never too late to *begin anew*, or to *have a happy childhood*, now?" Memories are so interesting.

Sometimes when I am riding my bicycle I wonder just how it can *stay up* on just those two thin wheels. Oh, I know the physics. Yet, those odd, old thoughts do come through, but they do not stop me from *balancing* and *riding safely*. One of the great achievements of my life, which happened when I was 53, was to *learn to ride* a bicycle without hands! Imagine, after 40 years of riding, I *learn something new*! And, all of these automatic, useful things that *you do for yourself* are really different from that story of the centipede— you remember when it was asked how it kept those hundred legs moving without tripping that it confused itself and got all tangled up—you can really think about automatic things like riding a bike or writing *without confusion*, and that *thinking can teach you new ways*, riding hands-free, or whatever makes sense to you.

As I think about riding, writing sounds so similar, and I wonder or wander about words. Can you write in the *right way* about a rite? That is different than having written correctly about a ritual. There are *so many ways* to do the same thing, and some of them make so much *more sense*, do they not? Did you have the same trouble I did when learning the alphabet and forming letters? An O is much like a Q; an H is almost the same as an A—there is the bar, but the other two lines tilt differently; an F has two bars and an E three, but do they point left or right? If they point down, that is like an M, isn't it? A B has two bumps and a D just one; and a U is so much like a

311

V. And keeping them on a line! And some of the lower case letters had pieces that went below the line. So hard to learn, or was it? Did you think about it at the time or *just enjoy the learning* and the discoveries and the new skills that are *so automatic now*?

There is *so much that you know*, but may not know that you know. So many useful things that you *do so automatically* to *take care of yourself*. So many more useful things, attitudes, *ideas to learn*. And, in looking back, the learnings which took time then are so simple and automatic now, so much *a part of you* that you can *continue to wonder* how much more, how soon, *enjoying the moment* and the process, both *looking forward* and back, and being here now. *So many ways to learn*.

Commentary—The learning metaphor can be generalized to many areas. We used learning to ride a bicycle and forming letters in the preceding metaphor. What other early childhood learnings can be adapted? There is learning to: crawl, stand up, walk, speak, sing, write, read, count, do arithmetic, spell, type, drive a car, use a computer, use a telephone, cook, clean, dress, tie a shoelace, court, make love, tell time, wash yourself, shave, comb hair, make a fire, study, take tests, exercise, and, of course, getting along with others. Learning to get along with others can be subdivided into: parents, siblings, relatives, friends, adults, police, teachers, medical professionals, salespeople, car mechanics, et al.

You can suggest that your client regress or time travel or move back or imagine an earlier time, or you can (better) *just talk* about that particular learning experience and your client will *naturally* access that earlier time and state. When you talk about how you learned to ride a bike or write, not only do you automatically access that younger you, but you take your client with you to her/his similar time. Unless you are consciously or metaphorically reminded about how much you already know, it does not enter conscious awareness. However, recalling other times of learning can seed new learnings.

4. Weaving

A number of years ago I received a small loom and a book about weaving as a birthday gift. Before that gift I had not thought much about cloth and how it was made. Now, I started to inspect the clothing I wore with an eye to how the cloth was made. How were all those individual threads *woven together* to *cover, comfort,* and *protect* me? What *surprises* and *wonderment* were in store for me! How the ordinary can *be so magical* when you *really look at it,* when you see and touch and feel and smell it! I know that some cloth is printed, but that is another whole story—about mordants and dyes and chemicals and patterns, ways of imprinting and *making fast.* Some things you have to *wait to learn* about, leave for another time, when they become really important.

Since I could see only so much with the naked eye, I got out my magnifying glass. With that I could *see the individual threads* that made up the whole, just moving through each other in such regular array. With a stronger lens I noticed that there were little irregularities that were not visible to just my ordinary eyes—but, how wonderful the overall effect was; *one I didn't notice*; one I *could live with.* Sometimes, *you can look too closely* at what is in front of you and miss the importance of *the bigger pattern,* the designs of life, if you will. That is so, is it not? (I even remembered getting excessively annoyed over some minor thing my wife did today— it was really trivial.)

I was particularly interested in examining the corduroy pants I was wearing. To a person as naive as I was, weaving a flat cloth was simple, but how do you weave something with bumps and ridges, ups and downs, and have it *stay together*? Well, I studied and studied that corduroy cloth and never did figure it out until I made a small swatch myself—*some things you just have to do for yourself*—I still have that swatch around to remind me how the *threads of life can be woven* into *such interesting patterns,* ridges and valleys *into a sturdy fabric.*

So, I learned about weaving. And, I soon discovered that the most important part was the *planning,* the preparation, the setup. *You really need to know what you are doing in advance. Pick the pattern,* study it, *dress the loom* with the warp, the long threads bound to their beam, the *foundation* for all of the rest, *getting the threads of your life in order and tied down so you can create.* And the warp or ends move through the heddles with their eyes held securely in their harness. Depending on how complicated the pattern, you may need several harnesses, almost like harnessing up several horses to pull a heavier load.

And the shuttle carries the weft or woof or filling—there are sometimes *so many ways to describe the same thing*, are there not?— through the shed, that *parting of the threads*, to let the shuttle pass. And, after each pass, the beater *firms up* the weft against its fellow threads, sometimes firmly, sometimes loosely, *depending on your purpose*. And *how tightly* do you pull to make the edges of the fabric, the selvedge? For every filling thread *turns around in its own special way*, leaving smaller or larger gaps around its edges, *all under your control, so many choices*, so many ways to *weave that fabric of your life*—tighter or more open, ragged or even, firmer or looser, ribbed or flat, complicated or simple, colorful or plain—knowing that *you can vary the pattern* section by section, patch by patch, even minute by minute to suit your needs.

And *it's all connected* even though sometimes a thread breaks. If you knot the ends together or add a new thread, *the break can be mended*. And you can even make that knot, that mending, *part of the pattern*. Persian rugs and mosaics always have one deliberate mistake that the artist incorporates since only Allah is perfect and *we are ever so human* and mortal. *That mistake may not be visible* to a casual observer, but the creator of that rug or mosaic knows it is there and that is sufficient. The knowledge of *one deliberate flaw can mask so many natural ones*, and that is right, isn't it?

The last task is *tying off* or ending the weaving in such a way that *it will not unravel*, sealing the edges so that the fabric is *secure within its own boundaries*. And, the fabric may be an end in itself to hang on a wall or cover a table. Or, it may be used to cut to another pattern to sew together an article of clothing, *something useful made out of whole cloth*.

Looking at and feeling and listening to the movement of a piece of cloth, a weaving of threads and color and texture and pattern to create something that *is more than the original parts*, to make a whole around the holes between the threads, you can *continue to wonder* and marvel at the *changing patterns* in the fabric of your own life—what looms in *your future*?

Commentary—The weaving metaphor lends itself to variations in any artistic or utilitarian process involving a step-by-step creation of a whole from parts. These variants, chosen to pace and lead your unique client, can be: sculpture in any medium, painting or drawing, pottery, woodworking, origami, sewing, building models, needlework (Mills and Crowley, 1986,) use a leitmotif of learning to crochet in their book), basketry, and nest-building. (This is being written in the spring while I watch some robins tease pieces of string off last year's tomato lattice.) It is, of course, important for the storyteller to have some familiarity with the vehicle for the metaphor.

5. *Treks to Gurus, et al*

Erickson once said, "We all begin to die from the moment we are born. Some do it faster than others. All we can do is enjoy life." There is a special wisdom in Erickson's words, a profound under-standing of *life* that *can change you* as the *meanings penetrate* and make connection with *your own individual needs*. But, sometimes you are not ready to *receive such wisdom*, and all you know inside is an aching *yearning for answers*, for directions that someone wiser than you can impart. There is a feeling, a need for outside guidance. And so you *set off on your journey* to find a guru, a master, a wise man or woman or ...

You can set off on a blind search or ask the way to the mountain, the hideaway, where the guru dwells. And *some people give you false directions*, and does that really matter if you don't know where you were going, now? How much can you learn by going in the wrong direction for a while? Is it true that there is *no such thing as failure*, only feedback? Only other, perhaps *more interesting ways to learn*. Sometimes, you can make your own way, research the possibili-ties, find the right path, *rely on your own judgment*. Do you always need to know exactly where you're going, or why?

And, some journeys can be long, and some can be short, and some can be just average. On your way, *what baggage are you carrying* with you? Is it old? Is it heavy? Is it useful? How much do you really need to get along, to *get where you want to go*? How much can you *shed right now*? Of that excess baggage, how much will you give away, store for later use, or just *discard forever*? It is so much easier to *travel light*.

You have finally found the guru you have been seeking and, as you expected, he (she) lives way up a mountain in a secluded cabin in a secluded glen. As *you ascend*, you think and think about what specific questions you would like to ask. Will the guru be receptive or just put you off with riddles or Zen koans? As you get closer, your inner turmoil and discomfort increase—so many questions, so many fuzzy ideas: Who am I? What am I? What should I do? Where am I going? What is the meaning of life? What is *the meaning of my life*? Does *clarity* always come out of confusion?

At last you come to the secluded glen and there is the guru, quietly sitting in a chair, reading, eating an apple. What were you expecting? He looks so average and normal. Is being just not not being? You approach and are invited to eat an apple. What does this mean? What does he/she mean? Is there anything special about this apple? Does he/she already *know what I want*? You eat, and then you chat about this and that. You stay for supper. You stay overnight. After breakfast you leave and, in *some unspoken way*, some unfathomable way, answers and directions and *solutions have grown within you. They were there all the time* and the very normalcy of the guru and his/her house in that quiet secluded glen were all that you needed to *find your own way*, for *most of the doubts to disappear*. What a wonderful discovery—you can *live an even more interesting life* with the certainties balanced by some doubts to add impetus and challenge. And *some risks are safe* and some are not and some are just risky.

It is not always what you see with open eyes that is the most important. The hidden messages, the cloudy images, the vague feelings *can all teach you* just as well. This particular journey is over. Where will your next one take you?

Commentary—Treks to gurus lend themselves to endless moralizing, adages, and maxims. Match them to your client. But, better still, devise the meeting with the guru to tap your client's own inner and unique resources. Metaphors are just another way for people to connect with what they already know about themselves and their relationships, and what they can do now for themselves.

Variants include: a "hero's journey"; providing a guide of some ilk; magical or mystical elements; a directive guru; endless obstacles, both external and internal; and journeying with a significant other.

6. Erickson Metaphors

Erickson was famous for his storytelling. Rosen's collection (1982) is replete with many of Erickson's favorite teaching tales. We will just reproduce four of them here. You are urged to read the entire collection and to listen to the many audiotapes available from the Milton H. Erickson Foundation. Remember, Erickson would have been the first person to urge you to develop your own stories and match them to your unique client. The following is to give you a sense of Erickson's tales. Rosen's book also contains commentaries.

Being Six Years Old (p. 162)

I received a letter from my daughter-in-law last week in which she told me about her daughter's sixth birthday. The next day she did something for which her mother reprimanded her, and she told her mother:

"It's awfully hard to be six years old. I've only had one day's experience."

He Will Talk (pp. 58–59)

A lot of people were worried because I was four years old and didn't talk, and I had a sister two years younger than me who talked, and she is still talking but she hasn't said anything. And many people got distressed because I was a four-year-old boy who couldn't talk.

My mother said, comfortably, "When the time arrives, then he will talk."

Scratching Hogs (p. 59)

One summer I sold books to pay my way through college. I walked into a farmyard about five o'clock, interviewed the farmer about buying books, and he said, "Young fellow, I don't read anything. I don't need to read anything. I'm just interested in my hogs."

"While you're busy feeding the hogs, do you mind if I stand and talk to you?" I asked.

He said, "No, talk away, young fellow, it won't do you a bit of good. I'm not going to pay attention to you; I am busy feeding the hogs."

And so I talked about my books. Being a farm boy, I thoughtlessly picked up a pair of shingles lying on the ground and started scratching the hogs' backs as I was talking. The farmer looked over, stopped, and said, "Anybody knows how to scratch a hog's back, the way hogs like it, is somebody I want to know. How about having supper with me tonight and you can sleep overnight with no charge and I will buy your books. *You like hogs.* You know how to scratch 'em the way they liked to be scratched."

Whistleberries (pp. 151–152)

One day a college girl passed flatus loudly in the classroom while writing on the blackboard. And she turned and ran out and went to her apartment, drew the blinds, and ordered her groceries over the telephone and collected them long after dark. And I got a letter from her saying, "Will you accept me as a patient?"

I noticed the Phoenix address that she gave and I wrote back, "Yes, I would." And she wrote back, "Are you really *sure* you *want me* as a patient?" I wondered about it—and I wrote back, "Yes, I *would* like you."

It took her about three months, and then she wrote me and said, "I would like an appointment with you after dark. And I don't want anybody to see me. Now, please don't have anybody around when I come to your office."

I gave her a ten-thirty appointment, and she told me about passing flatus loudly in the classroom and running out of the room and confining herself to her cabin. She also told me that she was a converted Catholic. Now, converted Catholics are always so ardent; and I questioned her, "Are you *really* a good Catholic?" And she assured me she was. And I spent a couple of hours with her, questioning her about her goodness as a Catholic.

And then in the next interview, I said, "You say you are a good Catholic. Then why do you insult the Lord; why do you make a mockery of him? Because you are. You ought to be ashamed of yourself—making a mockery of God and calling yourself a good Catholic!"

She tried to defend herself.

I said, "I can *prove* that you have little respect for God." I hauled out my anatomy book, an atlas, showing all the illustrations of the body. I showed her a cross section of the rectum and anal sphincter.

I said, "Now, man is very skilled at building things. But, can you imagine a man being sufficiently skillful to build a valve that contains solid matter, liquid matter, and air—and emits downward only the *air*?" I said, "God did. Why don't you *respect* God?"

Then I told her, "Now, I want you to demonstrate earnest, honest respect for God. I want you to bake some beans. They are called whistleberries by the navy. Flavor them with onions and garlic. And get in the nude and prance and dance around your apartment, emitting loud ones, soft ones, big ones, little ones ... and enjoy God's work."

And she did that. A year later she was married and I made a house call to check up on her. She had a baby. And while I was visiting her, she said, "It's time to nurse the baby." She opened her blouse, exposing her breast, and fed the baby and chatted casually with me. A complete change of reference.

Exam Panic

Now, as for the lawyer, all I did for him was to make him think Arizona was a nice place to live, and that the law examination was awfully unimportant; so he had no anxiety, no fear. He only had to write one little trickle of information at a time. Anybody can do that. And I've treated quite a number of lawyers in the same way—and medical men in the same way—by giving them a feeling of mental peace, of confidence and of self-assurance.

A woman had flunked her Ph.D. examination over and over again. Her committee knew that she could pass, and yet she always went into a panic and blanked out everything. So I had her sit in with a class where I told about the lawyer and she went into a trance listening to the case about the lawyer. After I finished the report she awakened. I dismissed her and she went back to her home state. A month later she wrote to me: "I passed my Ph.D. exam with flying colors. What did you do to me?" (Erickson laughs.) I didn't do anything to her except tell her about that lawyer. (Zeig, 1980, pp. 63–64)

Bedwetting and Baseball

Now, another bedwetter: Ten-year-old Jerry had been wetting the bed every night for ten years. He had a younger brother, eight years old, who was bigger and stronger than he was, and the eight-year-old brother never wet the bed.

And 10-year-old Jerry was ridiculed. His parents whipped him and he would go without his dinner. They belonged to a very narrow church. They had the congregation of the church pray aloud that Jerry would quit wetting the bed. They humiliated Jerry in every way. He had to wear a shield that covered his front and back and was held together by straps saying, "I am a bedwetter." Jerry had been given every punishment that his parents could think of and he still wet the bed.

I questioned them very carefully. I found out that they were extremely religious and belonged to a narrow church. I told the parents to bring Jerry over to my office. They did. The father had him by one hand and the mother had him by the other hand and they dragged him into my office and made him lie face down on the floor. I sent them out of the room and closed the door, and Jerry was yelling and screaming.

Now when you yell, you eventually run out of breath. I waited there patiently, and when Jerry paused his screaming and took another deep breath, I screamed. Jerry looked surprised. I said, "It was my turn. Now it is your turn." So Jerry screamed again. He paused for another breath and I took my turn screaming. He and I took turns screaming and finally I said, "Now it is my turn to sit in the chair." And Jerry took his turn sitting in the other chair. And then I talked to Jerry.

I said, "I know that you would like to play baseball. And do you know something about baseball? You have to coordinate your eyesight and your arm movements and your hand movements and have your body balanced. It's really a scientific game. You have to play it by coordinating, working together—your eyesight, your hearing. And you have to get your muscles set just exactly right. In football, all you have to have is bone and muscle and you just crash your way." His eight-year-old brother played football. (Erickson laughs.) We talked about the science of playing baseball and Jerry was delighted with the way I described the complicated things involved in playing baseball.

And Jerry also, I knew, played with a bow and arrow. I showed him how, in playing with a bow and arrow, you had to use your strength exactly right. You had to use your eyesight exactly right. You had to pay attention to the wind, to the distance, the right elevation in order to make a bulls eye. "It's a scientific game," I told him. "A regular name for a bow and arrow is archery, a scientific name for bow and arrow shooting is toxophily." And I praised Jerry for being so good in baseball and in shooting the bow and arrow.

And the next Saturday, Jerry, without an appointment, came in and had another talk with me about baseball and archery. He came in the next Saturday voluntarily without an appointment. On the fourth Saturday that he came in, he said triumphantly, "Ma can't break her habit of smoking." That's all that was ever said. Jerry had broken his habit. (Erickson laughs.)

And throughout the rest of his years in grade school and high school, Jerry usually dropped around to have a weekly visit with me. We discussed various things and I never once said the word "bed wetting" to him. I just talked about what he could do.

I knew Jerry wanted to have a dry bed. I gave him praise on muscular coordination, visual coordination, sensory coordination and he applied it elsewhere too. (Erickson smiles.)

You treat patients as individuals.

(Zeig, 1980, pp. 110–112)

The story that Erickson told the construction worker (O'Hanlon and Hexum, 1990, pp. 182–183) helped him over his fear of heights, but on a second occasion, his stories did not help the client's impotence.

Fear of Heights and Impotence

A construction worker had a fear of heights and sought MHE's help after his wife had seen MHE for fear of dental procedures. There were deep holes in the construction site where the man was currently working and he was afraid he would have to quit his job due to the fear. MHE had him come in on the weekend so as not to interfere with his job. He put him in trance and told a lot of stories. One story was about a tribe of American Indians who had no fear of heights. Another was about the time MHE's son had broken his leg and found as he recovered that he was afraid to get off the couch. The son had finally gotten off the couch by gradually getting his feet closer and closer to the floor. Another story was all about the experiments MHE had done investigating psychological and physical changes in people in trance when he changed the locus and movement of his voice.

MHE then told the man that our fear of heights is a natural thing and one of the least recognized components is that our unconscious minds recognize the slight differences in the echo of sounds in holes and at heights. He recommended that the man investigate this at the holes at his construction site to find out for himself. The man thought the stories were not helpful to him, but he found himself intrigued by MHE's idea about sound differences. He started investigating by making sounds at different distances from the holes and discovered it was true. By doing this he got over his fear of heights and was able to keep his job.

Later, the man sought MHE's help for his impotence. He had developed impotence after having flu and a long fever. MHE saw him once, told him a number of stories and dismissed him, telling him, "I'm sure you'll work it out." The impotence never improved.

D. Summary

In this chapter we have provided a basic foundation for the theory, construction, and use of metaphors. If you are not a natural storyteller, you might wish to add this powerful change agent to your repertoire. One simple caution is to be wary of going overboard on metaphors—there are other ways to help your clients! There is an old story about a group of people who had heard the same treasured old jokes so often that they simply numbered them to save time. A newcomer observed the hilarity resulting from a member saying "six" or "nine" and tried his hand by saying "twelve." No one laughed. When he asked why, the answer was, "your *delivery*." Practice makes ...

In the next chapter we will present some advanced metaphoric approaches, and in Chapter 13 we discuss the arts as hypnotic metaphors.

Exercises

1. Go through the five general metaphors presented in this chapter and:
   a. Read them aloud practicing your delivery.
   b. Tape your reading of these or other metaphors and listen to your delivery.
   c. Go through each metaphor in this chapter marking out those words and phrases that are particularly significant to you. Do this with a certain client in mind. Which phrases or words have special meanings for you personally?
   d. Consider just *how* you would mark out particular words and phrases. Will you use loudness, pauses, accent, voice focus, pitch, or rhythm for this purpose? Can you calibrate your client as to which style of marking is most effective?

2. Gathering Information: How do you go about gathering sufficient information to construct a relevant metaphor? Make a list of the kinds of information you feel are needed. Be exhaustive in preparing the list, knowing that you need not use all of the items. Do you feel comfortable taking notes during a session?

3. Constructing the Metaphor: With a particular client in mind, construct *several* metaphors that will work with that client. Pay attention to: story line, suspense, key words and phrases, how the story is populated, isomorphism, closure, and future-pacing. There are suggestions in the commentaries about variations on the themes presented. Pick some variations that match your client.

4. Delivery: Practice delivering the metaphors. It might be easiest at the outset to read someone else's metaphor (see the references) into a tape recorder several times, *playing* with your voice dynamics. Listen to the way Erickson and other master storytellers told their stories. You may even wish to get some training in acting or voice to improve your skills. However, the act of listening *consciously* to how others tell stories can tell you a great deal. You can subvocalize along with them. If you have young children, you have a built-in audience for practicing!

5. Closure: How do you end a story? Punch lines and morals are good exits, but to be most effective it is generally wise to *distract* your client at the end so that he/she has an amnesia for the story or parts of it. Again, *listen* to how experienced storytellers end their tales.

6. Pick one particular word or phrase that your client uses and build an instant metaphor incorporating that word or phrase. Practice this in dyads or triads.

7. How would you use the Erickson metaphors presented in this chapter? Would it be okay to just read an appropriate one on occasion? Can you adapt any of Erickson's teaching tales (see Rosen, 1982) to your style?

8. How would you weave in commonly known myths, fairy tales, legends, nursery rhymes, and children's books into your practice?

9. Make your own list of "standard" metaphors that you find flexible and easily adaptable. Write out five of them with markings and with particular clients in mind. Practice with colleagues or in a study group.

10. Renew your acquaintance with traditional stories by re-reading them. How many themes can you find in *The Wizard of Oz* or *Huckleberry Finn*, for example?

11. Consider the practice of taking a "time-out" to prepare a metaphor. Unless you are very skilled, taking a time-out is a good idea, and some therapists do this routinely.

Chapter 12

Advanced Metaphor

Rubin Battino, M.S.

The subject of the advanced use of metaphors will be treated in two parts: multiple embedded metaphor in this chapter, and the arts as hypnotherapeutic metaphors in the next chapter. For the former, we rely heavily on the detailed development by Lankton and Lankton (1983, pp. 247-311). You first need skills in the use of basic metaphor before attempting the more complex procedures outlined in this chapter and the next.

A. Introduction to Multiple Embedded Metaphor

The use of multiple embedded metaphor can be classified as a confusion technique or as an overload technique. The basic process is to tell stories within one or more other stories. A character in story one tells a story and a character in that story tells another story. Or several characters in story one tell other stories. Or you may say that the story you are telling reminds you of another one, and then something in that story reminds you of ... The level of complexity needs to be adjusted to each client's needs. Each story can make multiple "points" in that the client finds many potential solutions to his/her problem(s). In fact, this is a way to deal with several problems at one time. Metaphors trigger unconscious inner searches. The use of multiple embedded metaphors tends to create amnesias for many of the areas explored. This is useful in that it keeps the conscious mind from sabotaging the solutions generated in the inner explorations. Such amnesias can, of course, be seeded as part of a story line.

You do not need to be "polyphrenic" or a multiple personality to keep control of the different stories, but you can help yourself by using notes or anchors (say, with your own fingers) to know which story you are relating. You can always use a time-out to design a multiple metaphor. There is nothing wrong with using notes in your client's presence—you should have already seeded in their mind that the notes are a simple aid for you to *help them* even more effectively. Assuming your client goes into some depth of trance with eyes closed, consulting notes is not a problem (unless you make lots of paper noise!).

Erickson did not have a systematic way of telling stories, he simply told a multitude of stories carefully chosen to relate to solving the client's problems. Lankton and Lankton (1983, p. 311) give a logical explanation for the development of therapeutic metaphors for use in hypnotic trance. They offer the following steps for developing and implementing therapeutic multiple embedded metaphors:

1. Engage the conscious and unconscious attention of the client.

2. Retrieve and help build the necessary experiential resources.

3. Direct hypnotic work at the core of the neurotic bind.

4. Link the resources to the immediate social and practical concerns in the client's world.

5. Facilitate generative change by associating the changes to perceptions and images which the client will encounter in the next stage of social development beyond that in which s/he is currently engaged.

This is a useful model for thinking about the process of change and how to facilitate it with trance work.

The Lanktons (1983, pp. 247–311) use a seven-step model for metaphoric work. The seven steps are: (1) induction; (2) matching metaphor; (3) metaphors to retrieve resources; (4) direct work on the core issue; (5) linking resources to social networks; (6) ending the matching metaphor; and (7) reorienting to the waking state. Information gathering must precede these seven steps. They give several case examples along with transcripts and commentary illustrating their approach. This chapter in their book is well worth studying.

Our structure for a multiple embedded metaphor using three stories is:

1. **Induction:** this can be a formal induction or a conversational one, or the induction can be incorporated as part of the first story.

2. **First Story Begins (A):** this follows the basic metaphor formula and matches the client's problem in some isomorphic way(s). Pacing and leading is involved as the metaphor parallels the client's concerns and background.

3. **Second Story Begins (B):** the second story grows out of the first story in some way, e.g. a character in story one tells a story. The purpose of the second story is to stimulate, access, and retrieve resources within the client that are pertinent to solving his/her problem.

4. **Third Story Complete (C):** again, the third story grows out of the second story in some way. You can parallel the development of the second story or use a new approach. The purpose of the third story, which is told to its completion, is to work directly on the problem. This "direct" work involves hints and ideas and actions within the story that would stimulate new or different feelings, thinking, and behaviors. Indirectly, the story shows how to solve the problem. The story may emphasize support systems, imagery, words and phrases, and interesting new actions or behaviors.

5. **Second Story Ends (B):** connection is made back to the second story whose ending links the ideas and resources from the third story to the desired outcome. Also, the resources earlier elicited in the second story are reiterated and connected to outcomes. Future associations and actions are connected to resources. The second story can end with a punch line or reinforcer.

6. **First Story Ends (A):** connection is made back to the first story. The continuation of the first story reiterates earlier themes with an attempt to consolidate and continue (future pace) gains. The desired outcome may be modeled in some fashion.

The ending can be logical or have a surprise. A closing memorable, profound, or wise statement can add weight to the story. It can also have an amnesic effect. The ending provides closure for the collection of stories.

7. **Reorientation:** the client is reoriented to the present in a way that is consciously chosen to induce amnesia for one or more stories, or with positive injunctions to remember and continue the work of change that is already in progress.

There is much conscious effort on the therapist's part to construct and interweave the stories. The pattern suggested above is A-B-C-B-A as indicated by the letters. Depending on your skill, more stories can be added, or you can crosscut between the three stories for added effect. (A related skill to the multiple embedded metaphor is writing a computer program with the use of a flow chart to indicate the interconnections and dependencies of the parts.)

B. Two Transcripts of Multiple Embedded Metaphors

We will illustrate the use of multiple embedded metaphors by two cases—each case will be described and then a transcript provided. (Note that the first transcript of "Fred" is read by RB on a CD/audiotape which accompanies this book, available separately.)

Case 1 – Fred

The client, Fred, is thirty years old and works as a computer programmer. He has been married for three years to Elise who works in an office as an administrative assistant. His presenting complaint is a sudden onset of premature ejaculation that has continued for several months despite everything they have tried. Fred was raised by a single mother who was soured on men. He spent considerable time with her parents who were very rigid and controlling. Fred is an avid cyclist and health nut. Elise likes to cycle but is not addicted to it. They both enjoy dining out and going to movies and the theater. Their goal is a satisfactory sex life and increased intimacy.

1. Induction

There are so many ways to count, are there not? And you can count forwards and backwards and by twos or threes. I suppose that you can readily count in binary or octal or hexadecimal. And the Romans counted with Is and Vs and Xs, and do you recall what letters they used for fifty and one hundred and one thousand, as you continue to feel even more comfortable? And on what number will your eyes comfortably stop all that blinking and completely close? Let's just count randomly from twenty on down. Twenty, nineteen, twelve, and why aren't twelve and eleven uni-teen or bi-teen or two-teen—you could have had two more years as a teenager. Sixteen, nineteen, nine, and four; three, two, ten, and one. That's right, make every number count, almost like a random number generator throwing out especially significant numbers in some closed loop. That's right. Thank you. Closed and rested and breathing so easily, and wondering with one part of your mind "What's next?" "Can I still be surprised?" And ransom is so similar to random, and what will be ransomed?

2. Start of Story 1

I remember vividly a friend telling about an especially good dinner she had recently with her husband. She was surprised that they almost closed the restaurant, talking and tasting and eating for hours and hours, and the time flew ever so slowly for her—she could remember and taste almost everything. You know, she unconsciously licked her lips and chewed and swallowed while she told me of that meal. She remembered vividly the number of times her husband smiled and reached out and touched her. They even played footsie under the table which was fortunately in a corner and had an especially long table cloth. Being touched in a public place was both daring and exciting even though, of course, they had to hold back, waiting for a more appropriate time, later.

3. Start of Story 2

One of the things they talked about was going to the movies, and that reminded me of movie going, from being taken as a kid to that enchanting dark place where you could be alone with all those other people being privately part of something larger, accepting in its own way, moving into that dark place and just feeling you could stay there forever. As you grow up, you experience movies in different ways. It is different going out with the guys than with your first date, sharing popcorn, a drink, sitting close, wondering whether you can hold her hand, feel her fingers and palm—not knowing when to stop—arm around shoulder, head touching your head, going too far too fast, secretly, casually feeling the swell of her breast.

And everyone eats popcorn differently. Some people just stuff it in by the handful, never really tasting. I think you need to slow down. My second girlfriend taught me that, how to really slowly enjoy one piece of popcorn at a time, slowly putting it in the mouth, slowly tasting, savoring, until it melts slowly all by itself in its own time, and, somehow, it never seems too long, or long enough, that feeling. She also taught me to listen and enjoy the sounds of eating and the visual delights of eating, just drinking in with eyes and ears and nose.

4. Story 3

I still remember a special feature I saw with girlfriend number two. It was a short thing on race walking. Boy, did they look funny up on that screen. But, I got curious and went to a meet. A man there, his name was Dave, told me about race walking. I can almost hear him talking.

"... I started out learning how to do this correctly later in life. It took so much control, so much holding back and letting go in just the right way. The key to control is really in the mind. You just need to slow each step, each movement down, until it is so natural. That straightening out of the leg and holding it that way just long enough, then swinging out and down, making contact solidly, moving forward, balanced, even, breathing naturally, all parts in coordination, setting up the next swing and movement, holding and releasing, breathing, smelling, enjoying the sound—you can almost hear your bones as they move so smoothly, and bones are so hard and permanent, aren't they? And, the next movement, and the next. And pretty soon it's time to end. You've come such a long way, enjoying the slow beats and pulses, coming to that finish line and over it and through it, almost not knowing when to stop, the body moving so automatically, continuing the build-up of those feelings. Even when I'm walking fast, I enjoy the slow rhythm of my body."

I learned a lot from Dave. There are so many interesting ways to enjoy your body.

5. End of Story 2

I was just thinking that the very smell of popcorn carries me right back into a movie theater. There can be so much anticipation. And, sometimes, the movie doesn't start right away, and I need to almost consciously say to myself, "Slow down, make the popcorn last." Maybe save some for the big scenes, although sometimes they are so exciting that you stop eating and make the popcorn last even longer. Just drawing it out and not even noticing how long you were so excited, so involved, looking, listening, smelling, touching, tasting. A kind of slow revelation comes over you in a rush at the end. But, then, you know you can do this again and again and again. There is food for thought, and so many ways to learn.

6. End of Story 1

My friend's memories of that special dinner got all confused in her mind with the eating scene in "Tom Jones." To her mind, that was the most sensuous thing she had ever seen on the screen. That slow touching, eyeing, smelling of the food, the eye contact as they each slowly savored each bite, making each morsel last as long as possible, the completely intimate involvement with each other and each different piece of food, eating with their fingers, sensuously sensing, touching, lasting, listening, tasting, chewing, eyeing, wiping, then reaching for another piece to enjoy, another movement, slowing it agonizingly even slower, enjoying each move, until at last, a great gushing orgiastic relief in each other and the food. What a movie, what moves. My friend was ecstatic in her memories, such long-lasting memories. And there were many more, she assured, many more to come, too.

7. Reorientation

I'm always amazed at how much you can learn from such simple things, such simple stories. And, you can know, now, that whatever special meanings these tales have for you will be there for you when you need them, when the time is appropriate. Some learning is fast, and some is slow, but new ways are built from old. There is so much that is temporary, that seemed permanent when it first popped up, but takes its place in history as just another interesting episode, something that was out of control then, but fits in right now. Just one more slow step in the rhythm of life.

When you are ready, take a few moments to consolidate what you've learned, and then counting in some random way from one to twenty, come back to this room, here and now, feeling ever so rested and yet energized, with a few deep breaths. Thank you.

Case 2 - Judy

Judy is a thirty-five year-old, third grade school teacher who came to see me after she had been divorced for one year after a four-year marriage. She complained about "panic" and "anxiety" attacks, particularly on days when she "confronted" or even had any dealings with an authority figure. She recently met a man she liked, but found herself unable to be comfortable in his presence or open about herself and her needs. She considered not seeing him again because of the way she berated and criticized herself afterwards. He seemed "serious" about her. Judy indicated that she had a hard time showing affection, except to young children. In the previous session, while in trance, she told of a traumatic experience when she was ten years old. Her older brothers had thrown her into the deep end of a swimming pool to teach her how to swim. A friend's mother "rescued" her while her father looked on. The brothers were only mildly scolded. She has conscious memories of the event and forced herself to become a "master" swimmer, even though, deep down, she still fears the water. Judy wants a "normal" life with a husband and children and no more fears. In addition to swimming, her hobbies include reading and knitting. She is well-known for the toy people and animals she knits as gifts.

1. *Induction*

There are so many ways to learn. Some seem easy, and some seem hard, and some occurred so simply and naturally as we were growing up that it is difficult to tell now how we learned then. There are so many things you learn as a child, some by a seeming osmosis, and some by the endless repetition that children enjoy so much. They will say a new word over and over and over until it is learned and that case is closed. So much practice, and the more you practice, the more confident you get, so that old doubts and fears just simply disappear. And you can close your eyes now as you drift back to an earlier time, perhaps when you were three or four or five or six, and learning letters.

2. Start of First Story

My teacher, Miss McDougal, told us stories about each letter and how it was formed. There were so many mysteries about those black lines. How could they mean anything? The capital printed letters were the easiest, and yet could be so confusing way back then. It's so much easier now when you can forgive yourself and maybe the parents or relatives who pushed you when you weren't ready. Now, I understand that deep down they loved me and wanted what was best for me, even if they made mistakes then.

And it is so much like an A—just two vertical lines and one connecting one. Miss McDougal said that H was like a line between two trees or two people standing tall, but holding hands. The A was two trees that bent to meet at the top, or like a tent with a line across the middle, or two people leaning to touch heads facing each other and holding hands. We giggled at the last one, but tried it anyway. Sometimes you have to try new or funny or scary things in order to learn, don't you? An O was like an open mouth, and a Q, one with your tongue sticking out on the side. We liked doing that one.

Oh, there were so many letters and so many stories and so many ways to learn. And just when I had mastered the capitals, along came the lower case; and then the script capitals and the script lower case. Was learning something new hard or fun then? There were even times I felt I was over my head for a while, just a short while.

We even sang songs about the letters—like remembering the alphabet. And, how did that go?

3.   Start of Second Story

One of my best friends in class, Norman, grew up to be a singer. I remember having lunch with him not so long ago. I'm a curious person and asked him lots of questions about singing. How are you going to learn unless you ask or try? So, I asked. People really like to talk about what is important to them.

Norman told me how surprised he was to learn how physical singing was, how much effort it required, and how much control it needed. He recalled a lesson where he was singing so hard that he almost fainted, he was out of breath, and his teacher had to almost pull him out of his scared state. Norman was so immersed in his singing that he forgot to breathe properly. That was an important lesson for him. Breath control is so important, and your body position, and how you hold your head. And so much practice, relating one part of the body to another, and keeping that internal rhythm, getting each note just right and at just the right time, reaching out with his voice and making contact in a sound way with his world and the people in it, relating one note at a time. I learned a lot from listening to Norman.

4.   Story Three

He told me his wife, Mabel, liked to make comparisons between her weaving and his singing, and it wasn't just weaving a song from notes strung out on a melodic line. A foundation had to be created first. The melodic themes and the warp lines prepared to receive the patterns of threads. An intricate weaving of your life together in new and interesting connections, reaching out one thread at a time, one pass through the shed, filling in, changing, returning for another pass, beating the threads firmly and strongly against each other, being surprised sometimes at how normal all this change and growth seems, just one stroke, one thread, one touch, one contact, one thread, one line, one note at a time. And, how colorful should the new weaving be? How complicated? How varied? What new connections dared? How strong? How much testing? Singing is one note at a time and weaving is one thread, and sometimes sounding a new note is so important, sometimes running that one new thread changes the whole pattern. It doesn't take much daring to change one thread, or does it?

5. End of Story Two

Norman likes Mabel's weaving and the way they go together. He sometimes keeps a small swatch of one of her weavings in his pocket when he sings as a kind of protection or lucky piece. He says his singing soars even higher when he has that connection, that memory, that good feeling. He knows deep down that loved ones can make mistakes and forget and maybe even not protect at crucial times, but that connection helps him to understand and forgive and move on and remember his capacity to love. He notes that sometimes, when he is not paying attention to particular notes, but paying more attention to the pattern, he sings better. You can sometimes look too closely at patterns, and it is better to let yourself go in the bigger symphony to better sing your song.

6. End of Story One

Norman once recalled how hard it was for him at first to learn to read music—all those funny lines, and what did they mean? Notes are related to sounds, and letters are related to sounds. Miss McDougal had us sounding out the letters and making sing-songs of them. English is such a funny language—sometimes a C sounds like an S and sometimes a K. There are so many rules and exceptions, and which ones do you follow, when, to make meaning in your life? Forget irrelevant things, and remember and do important ones. Forgive and forget what happened long ago and is no longer important. When you are in the swim of things, knowing your strengths, breathing so regularly, smooth rhythms of movement, sliding forward, knowing that in some areas there is always a lifeguard present, knowing your limits and being willing to test, to try. And, what surprises await you as you sing your song, write your life, swim towards your goals? Life provides little setbacks here and there so we can learn even more.

7. Reorientation

You can, even now, sit back and take a minute or so to put into perspective what you've learned today and how it relates to your future. What will you be doing differently soon? What changes that have already started will you be continuing? People have so many more strengths than they think. Take a minute now to consolidate for yourself, remembering to be gentle. ... And, in your own way and time, take a deep breath or two, and blink your eyes, and stretch, and come back to this room, here and now, wide awake and maybe even wondering. Thank you.

C. Erickson and Joe the Florist

This is one of Erickson's most famous cases and the full details are available (Erickson and Rossi, 1980, Vol. IV, pp. 268–274). We will summarize the case here, but include the complete transcript including his highlighting in italics, the especially emphasized interspersed parts.

Joe was a florist who was intensely devoted to his work, but also a good husband, father, friend, and member of the community. A growth was removed "too late" from the side of his face. He couldn't speak. Erickson was informed that Joe did not like the word "hypnosis." Joe probably did not know why the family wanted to introduce him to this other doctor. He was in severe pain. The segment quoted below is only one part of what Erickson said.

Joe the Florist

Joe, I would like to talk to you. I know you are a florist, that you grow flowers, and I grew up on a farm in Wisconsin and I liked growing flowers. I still do. So I would like to have you take a seat in that easy chair as I talk to you. I'm going to say a lot of things to you, but it won't be about flowers because you know more than I do about flowers. *That isn't what you want.* [The reader will note that italics will be used to denote interspersed hypnotic suggestions which may be syllables, words, phrases, or sentences uttered with a slightly different intonation.] Now as I talk, and I can do so *comfortably*, I wish that you will *listen to me comfortably* as I talk about a tomato plant. That is an odd thing to talk about. It makes one *curious. Why talk about a tomato plant?* One puts a tomato seed in the ground. One can *feel hope* that it will grow into a tomato plant that *will bring satisfaction* by the fruit it has. The seed soaks up water, *not very much difficulty* in doing that because of the rains that *bring peace and comfort* and the joy of growing to flowers and tomatoes. That little seed, Joe, slowly swells, sends out a little rootlet with cilia on it. Now you may not know what cilia are, but cilia are *things that work* to help the tomato seed grow, to push up above the ground as a sprouting plant, and *you can listen to me, Joe,* so I will keep on talking and *you can keep on listening, wondering, just wondering what you can really learn,* and here is your pencil and your pad, but speaking of the tomato plant, it grows so slowly. *You cannot see* it grow, *you cannot hear* it grow, but grow it does—the first little leaflike things on the stalk, the fine little hairs on the stem, those hairs are on the leaves, too, like the cilia on the roots, they must make the tomato plant *feel very good, very comfortable* if you can think of a plant as feeling, and then *you can't see* it growing, *you can't feel* it growing, but another leaf appears on that little tomato stalk and then another. Maybe, and this is talking like a child, maybe the tomato plant does *feel comfortable and peaceful* as it grows. Each day it grows and grows and grows, *it's so comfortable, Joe,* to watch a plant grow and *not see* its growth, *not feel* it, but just know that *all is getting better* for that little tomato plant that is adding yet another leaf and still another and a branch, and it is *growing comfortably* in all directions. [Much of the above by this time had been repeated many times, sometimes just phrases, sometimes sentences. Care was taken to vary the wording and also to repeat the hypnotic suggestions. Quite some time after the author had begun, Joe's wife came tiptoeing into the room carrying a sheet of paper on which was written the question, "When are you going to start the hypnosis?" The author failed to cooperate with her by looking at the paper and it was necessary for her to thrust the sheet of paper in front of the author and, therefore, in front of Joe. The author was continuing his description of the tomato plant uninterruptedly, and Joe's wife, as she looked at Joe, saw that he was not seeing her, did not know that she was there, that he was in a somnambulistic trance. She withdrew at once.] And soon the tomato plant will have a bud form somewhere, on one branch or another, but it makes no difference because all the branches, the whole tomato plant will soon have those nice little buds—I wonder if the tomato plant can, *Joe, feel really feel a kind of comfort.* You know, Joe, a plant is a wonderful thing, and *it is so nice, so pleasing* just to be able to think about a plant as if it were a man. Would such a plant *have nice feelings, a sense of comfort* as the tiny little tomatoes begin to form, so tiny, yet so *full of promise to give you the desire to eat* a luscious tomato, sun-ripened, it's so *nice to have food in one's stomach,* that wonderful feeling a child, a thirsty child, has and can *want a drink, Joe,* is that the way the tomato plant feels when the rain falls and washes everything so that *all feels well.* [Pause.] *You know, Joe,* a tomato plant just flourishes each day *just a day at a time.* I like to think the tomato plant can *know the fullness of comfort each day. You know, Joe, just one day at a time* for the tomato plant. That's the way for all tomato plants. [Joe suddenly came out of the trance, appeared disoriented, hopped upon the bed, and waved his arms; his behavior was highly suggestive of the sudden surges of toxicity one sees in patients who have reacted unfavorably to barbiturates. Joe did not seem to hear or see the author until he hopped off the bed and walked toward the author. A firm grip was taken on Joe's arm and then immediately loosened. The nurse was summoned. She mopped perspiration from his forehead, changed his surgical dressings, and gave him, by tube, some ice water. Joe then let the author lead him back to his chair. After a pretense by the author of being curious about Joe's forearm, Joe seized his pencil and paper and wrote, "Talk, talk."] Oh yes, Joe, I grew up on a farm, I think a tomato seed is a wonderful thing; *think, Joe, think* in that little seed there does *sleep so restfully, so comfortably* a beautiful plant yet to be grown that will bear such interesting leaves and branches. The leaves, the branches look so beautiful, that beautiful rich color, *you can really feel happy* looking at a tomato seed, thinking about the wonderful plant it contains *asleep, resting, comfortable, Joe*. I'm soon going to leave for lunch and I'll be back and I will talk some more.

Erickson went away for a while. On his return, Joe was eager for him to continue talking, and communicated with him by handwritten notes. Erickson continued using the tomato plant metaphor, but emphasized the flower this time. Joe did well and required little pain medication, and actually gained some weight. After lunch, hosted by Joe, Erickson gave "a long monologue ... in which were included psychotherapeutic suggestions of continued ease, comfort, freedom from pain, enjoyment of family, good appetite, and a continuing pleased interest in all surroundings." These suggestions were interspersed in a multitude of topics. Joe survived in reasonable comfort for about three months after Erickson's initial visit.

D. Commentary

The two transcripts by RB provided above are aids to preparing your own transcripts for multiple embedded metaphors. The exercises which follow provide guidelines for trying out multiple embedded metaphors. One of the important messages you can get from reading the Lanktons is how *consciously* they design their interventions. You would do well to do likewise.

Exercises

1. Make copies of the multiembedded metaphors for the two cases presented earlier. (a) Go through each of these verbatim

transcripts and indicate the language forms used. Would you use different language forms or word patterns? (b) Go through the transcripts and indicate which words or phrases you would mark out and how you would deliver them. (c) Make a tape recording of each transcript practicing your delivery style. Feel free to "play" with your delivery. You might record one sentence in three or four different ways. How do you sound to you? (d) Share this practice with the transcripts with someone else so you can get feedback.

2. In addition to Rosen's book (1982), there are many transcripts of Erickson telling stories and talking to clients and giving lectures and demonstrations. Go through several of these and carry out the same exercises indicated in (1) above. How frequently does Erickson use multiple embedded metaphors versus simple, straight stories?

3. Study the way the Lanktons (1983) present multiple embedded metaphor. Carry out the exercises in (1) using the metaphors in Lankton and Lankton (1989). Do the same with Wallas (1985, 1991).

4. Since the best way to learn about multiple embedded metaphors is to make up your own for particular cases, develop five cases based on your experience (or imagination) and: (a) write out case histories including relevant information; (b) plot out one or more multiple embedded metaphors for each case; (c) write out the metaphors, indicating by underlining or parenthetical comments just how you would deliver significant words or phrases; (d) tape your metaphor, practicing various ways of delivery and marking; (e) share what you have done with others for feedback; (f) rewrite your metaphor using what you have learned.

5. To help create multiple embedded metaphors, we provide several cases as potential examples. Go through steps 4(b) to 4(f) for each case. Feel free to flesh out or add details to each case.

   a. First Practice Case—A 33-year-old male psychologist who was recently given tenure, has panic reactions about speaking at professional meetings. He needs to do this to keep up his professional standing. He is always very well prepared for these professional talks and rehearses them beforehand. He is married with two small children, not his own. Although he panics and gets tongue-tied, he somehow muddles through the talks. He has no difficulty giving lectures in class. His hobbies are playing a musical instrument, reading, and traveling.

b.   Second Practice Case—A 39-year-old single woman who was divorced eight years ago, no children, is having trouble completing her master's thesis in social work. All of her course work and research have been completed and she is actually part way through writing the thesis. She is facing a statute-of-limitations deadline, but desperately needs to complete the thesis so she can keep her job. Her hobbies are singing in a chorus and skiing and cycling when she can.

c.   Third Practice Case—A 56-year-old housewife has such a fear of heights that she cannot go above the ground floor in buildings. One grandchild lives in a high-rise apartment. There are no children at home. Hobbies are square dancing with her husband 2-3 times per week, sewing, church, housekeeping, gardening.

d.   Fourth Practice Case—A 42-year-old woman discovered that she was sexually abused as a child when she went to see a therapist about being depressed. It was elicited that the abuse occurred over several years and was done by her older brother. She is married and has several teenagers at home. She works part-time in a supermarket. Her hobbies are sedentary and include playing cards, knitting, cooking, and watching television.

e.   Fifth Practice Case—A couple who have been married for thirty-two years are consulting you about marital problems and a possible divorce. A single daughter in her mid-twenties lives with them. The presenting problem by the wife is an uncommunicative husband and, by the husband, a "frigid" wife. They fight frequently. She has a temper, and he retreats. They used to like camping and ballroom dancing.

Chapter 13

The Arts as Hypnotherapeutic Metaphors

Rubin Battino, M.S.

A. Introduction

Mills and Crowley (1986) have written a book that is primarily about the use of metaphors with children. In the last two chapters they explore what they term "artistic metaphor," or the use of art as metaphor. Although the methods they write about are primarily in the use of art media such as drawing, clay, sand trays, etc., one can expand this concept to *all* of the arts as hypnotherapeutic metaphors. This expanded idea would include: drama and psychodrama, musical instruments, voice, dance, movement, sculpture, body and family sculpture, writing, poetry, storytelling, and rituals. Gilligan, for example, has certainly raised the use of rituals to an art form. One might even consider the Lanktons' use of ambiguous function assignments as art, or Erickson's and Haley's use of ordeal therapy. In their work, Mills and Crowley also use cartoons, puppets, and a board game developed with the child called a "resource board" game.

The Mills and Crowley model for the use of art generally involves three steps, as in the "pain-getting-better-book" they use for children. The child is asked to draw: (1) how the pain looks right now; (2) how the pain looks "all better;" and (3) what will help picture one change into picture two. Bernie Siegel, in his work with people who have life-threatening illnesses, uses drawings extensively. Typically, he asks people to do four drawings (which all may be on the same page): (1) yourself; (2) your illness; (3) your treatment; and (4) your immune system eliminating the illness. His instructions are rather open-ended. We particularly like his use of the word "eliminating," since this is a rather vague descriptive which allows for individual choice. Contrast this word with "killing" your cancer.

We would like to generalize the pioneering work of Mills and Crowley and Siegel (and many others) into an eight-step process for each of two classes of clients: those who have emotional / mental / psychological / habit / behavioral problems; and those who have "physical" health problems of some sort. These two classes will be dealt with separately below with suggested language and commentary for each step. Remember to adapt your use of language (including representational systems) to each client's unique model of the world.

The model, which is described separately for each class of client, involves the same eight steps: (1) the "normal" you; (2) your present state; (3) treatment; (4) desired state; (5) your inner healing resources; (6) change process; (7) maintenance and future orientation; and (8) review and ratification. For a particular client you may not wish to use all eight steps, and it may make sense to alter the order. A client may wish to do the drawings over a period of time or at one sitting. A single drawing may incorporate several steps in a comic strip fashion or some other way. Follow-up may be done by having the client repeat the entire set of drawings at a later time (or times), or just repeat particularly relevant drawings.

The following set of instructions is for both classes of clients and may be reproduced.

Instructions for Drawing on Your Inner Healing Resources

You can literally "draw" on your inner healing resources by doing drawings or pictures. Bernie Siegel has shown the benefit of this for people with life-threatening diseases, and the field of art therapy has shown its value for people with a great variety of personal problems. The following instructions use an eight-step model for making connection with your own inner healing resources. The eight steps are: (1) the "normal" you; (2) your present state or condition; (3) your treatment(s); (4) the "desired" you; (5) your inner healing resources; (6) the change process; (7) maintenance and future orientation; and (8) review and ratification.

You can do the drawings in any medium and on any kind, size, color, or shape of paper. Some people like to use scented felt-tipped pens, others crayons, some pen and ink, and some pencil. Pick the drawing implements that make sense to you. You can choose different colors of paper and you can certainly make cut-outs or do collages. Although the instructions given here are for drawings, you may wish to carry out the instructions in some other medium like clay or sand or dance or singing or acting. (If you use a "non-permanent" medium, you may wish to record your actions on videotape for later review.) Feel free to express the requested drawings in line and color and shape and form and words. Some people use "balloons" as in comic strips to give voice to people and/or things in their drawings. Others just add words or phrases in appropriate places. You may wish to caption each drawing and/or write out a brief explanation on the back. Each drawing should be numbered and dated. Some people put all the drawings on a single sheet and others make several drawings for each step.

You do not need to be an artist for this kind of work to be of benefit. Although you may have difficulty in accurately depicting your feelings as well as you might wish, the important thing is to simply *represent* in some appropriate way that *makes sense to you* the material in each step. Stick figures, for example, are as expressive as anatomically correct drawings. Some people spend a lot of time making the drawings, while others do them very rapidly. The bottom line is that each drawing should be done in such a way that it is an expression of *your* inner feelings and physical states. Remember, this is for you, and you can certainly have fun exploring yourself in this way. It helps to date each drawing on the back. After you complete each drawing you may wish to write some comments on the back.

B. Eight-Step Model for Clients with "Psychological" Problems

First, we assume that you have established rapport with your client and also established that the difficulty they have come to consult you about is emotional or mental or psychological or behavioral, i.e. something suitable for a mental health professional. Although the following illustration is based on drawing pictures, it can be generalized to any mode of artistic expression that suits your client. In fact, for some particular clients, it may be useful to repeat the process in several modalities. We like to use a set of colored felt tip pens and an artist's sketch pad. (Some sets of these pens are scented with different related odors for each color.)

Preparatory Comments — You do not have to be an artist in order to make drawings that can be of use to you. It is not the quality, detail, or accuracy of the drawing that matters, but just your willingness to use line and shape and color to *represent* your feelings and images. RB once took a course in art therapy where he was the only class member who had no background or training as an artist. However, his stick figures and blotches of color were as meaningful to him as the more representational drawings his colleagues could render. Does what you draw in whatever way you do it carry the sense and feeling you wish to communicate? Although you may feel frustrated from time to time (RB was) at an incapability to exactly render inner images, remember that whatever you draw still carries with it your unique feelings and meanings. Whatever you draw must be you and yours. The drawings may be completed in the office or the client can do them at home following a written set of instructions.

Instructions for Clients with "Psychological" Problems

1. **The "Normal" You** — For picture one, draw yourself or some appropriate representation of yourself that you consider to be the "normal" or "healthy" or properly and comfortably functioning you. This may be you before this particular problem started, or it could be you right now when you are functioning normally in between the times your problem creates difficulties.

Comment: Picture one establishes a baseline for the rest of the pictures. The wording also seeds the idea that the problem is not occurring twenty-four hours each day at the present time (a solution-oriented therapy approach).

2. **Your Present State** — Picture two is a drawing of you at the present time showing you in your actual problem state, i.e. how you think you appear or look when you are experiencing the difficulty. Put in the picture all those elements or feelings that truly represent that problem for you. Individual colors or shapes may have particular meanings for you.

Comment: Picture two establishes the nature and reality of the presenting problem. Since the very act of drawing this state will vivify it, you need to carefully observe your client and, if necessary, add any dissociation or distancing that might be necessary. Depending on the nature of the problem, it may be important to have your client do the drawing from a safe, protected, dissociated position. The directions seed the use of color. You can also add comments such as "The picture may surprise you" or "Really let your imagination/feelings go in drawing this picture."

3. **Treatment** — For picture three make a drawing of the nature of the professional treatment or help I or others are giving you. The drawing can be as specific as it needs to be. It is certainly okay to include relevant words in the drawing. Colors and shapes may be important.

Comment: It is useful for both the client and you to know how he/she views the treatment process. This sets another kind of baseline.

4. **Desired State** — In picture four make a drawing of yourself that shows you *completely free* of the problem. Add whatever details or words that will clearly, soundly and solidly indicate to you that the "you" in that drawing is functioning in a desired way. The "you" in the drawing should be specific and realistically attainable. In addition to today's date, indicate directly or symbolically a date beyond which this desired change has already occurred. This is the date by which you have already become the "you" that you desire to be, and put this problem behind you. Certainly, that you in the picture may have already looked back and laughed or chuckled at how you were stuck now.

Comment: In the NLP technique of working with submodalities (see Bandler, 1985 and Andreas and Andreas, 1987), the client works with two internal pictures. The first is the present state and the second is the desired state. By behavioral practice, picture one is converted into picture two using variations in submodalities to bring about and install the change. In this process, NLP practitioners consider it important that picture one be experienced in an *associated* state and picture two (the desired one) in a *dissociated* state. The latter increases perspective and motivation. In the model presented here, you may wish to consider using directions to make picture two (safely!) more associated and picture four dissociated. Please note that there is more inherent dissociation involved in drawings than there is in mental images.

It is important that picture four include as many realistic and specific details as are needed to give it credibility, as well as desirability. For example, the date by which the change *will have* already occurred needs to be explicit and not just a month or weekday, but a full date. Change *will have* already occurred by a specific date of the client's choosing.

5.   **Your Inner Healing Resources** — It is well known that the body and mind have many inner and automatic healing resources that are continually available to keep you healthy. Many problems seem to clear up all by themselves. In picture five, make a drawing or representation of all the different inner resources you have available to help heal or resolve your particular problem. These may be thoughts, feelings, memories, things you've done for yourself, ideas, an ability to relax or meditate or focus your attention or make images or whatever feels right to you that you already have inside of yourself. This could even be ways of caring for yourself that you have incorporated or learned from others and might involve others. You may wish to make separate drawings for each inner resource.

Comment: We know that "time" heals many problems. Why not use those resources *now* rather than wait for them to be used at some future time? Remember, the very act of identifying inner healing resources activates them!

6.   **Change Process** — Now that you have a completed drawing of the "you" that exists after change has occurred and you know your inner healing resources, it will be useful to make a drawing of just how that change or changes occurred. So, in picture six, represent in some relevant way all those things that you did to make those changes. You may actually be surprised by the strength and ingenuity of your inner resources, and how you draw them. Any relevant contributions by other people can also be indicated.

Comment: The actual things that your client projects as *having done* to have brought about change may be quite different from the "professional" treatment given in picture three. This step gives the client permission to use his/her uniqueness and inner resources to design specific strategies that they "know" on some deep internal level will work for them. Notice the use of language forms in this and the preceding steps that *presuppose* change.

7. **Maintenance and Future Orientation** — There is one more important picture that needs to be drawn. Picture seven is a representation of all of those ways of feeling, being and doing that will *continue* to ensure that you not only maintain the desired state you have already attained, but that you will continue to change and evolve in ways even more beneficial to you. Again, put in the picture actual drawings or representations of what you will have done to keep moving comfortably, safely and healthfully ahead.

Comment: The process of change does not stop with a single event; it needs to continue into the future. This is described as "future-pacing" by NLP practitioners and is an important part of any change work. This change, this desired you, is only the beginning.

8. **Review and Ratification** — Now that you have completed the drawings, take some time to review them. You may do this review by yourself or with your therapist. As you look at each drawing in turn, you may wish to add some descriptive or relevant words. You can get the "big picture" by looking at them all together. In your own words, you may tell the therapist as much as you wish about each drawing, the parts of the drawing, and any special significance they have to you. Please be sure to *not* tell your therapist anything you do not wish to reveal at this time. These are *your* drawings, and what they mean to you is the most important thing about them.

Comment: This review is needed to *ratify* and consolidate the change process depicted in the drawings. The review serves to validate the predicted changes as having already occurred! You need to be especially careful about offering any interpretations about the drawings. These are your client's unique drawings, and any interpretations you offer are only (educated) *guesses* as to the significance of the drawings. There are some art therapy practitioners (and others) who like to interpret "universal" symbols. We are reminded of Joseph Campbell's comments about mandalas (circular drawings common to many cultures) which we paraphrase here, "It is not surprising that mandalas appear in almost all cultures—after all, their environments presented them with an endless series of circular objects." Elicit *your* client's *unique* interpretations.

C. Eight-Step Model for Clients with Physical Health Problems

The preliminary set of instructions is the same for this class of client as for the preceding. Bernie Siegel (1986, 1989) has, as already noted, used art therapy in his work with patients who have cancer and other life-threatening diseases. The title of Furth's book (1988), "The Secret World of Drawings. Healing through Art," implies that art may be used as a medium to help people heal themselves. His book contains many illustrations of this with reproductions of clients' art work. Furth gives practical guidelines for the use of drawings to help people. His work should be studied before attempting to use art as a therapeutic intervention since his comments, cautions, and advice are quite advantageous.

Ethically, and for your own and your client's legal protection, you need to be certain that any client you work with who has physical health problems is under a physician's care. If you are using the eight-step model described here, it would be well to do it in consultation with your client's physician. Bernie Siegel, for example, considers his work to always be a *partnership* with the medical profession. (A client would just get the instructions without the commentary which is given here for the reader.)

Instructions for People with Physical Health Problems

1.   **The "Normal" You** — For picture one, draw yourself, or some appropriate representation of you that you consider to be the "normal" or "healthy" you. This is probably you as you were before having this particular health problem. Use color, shape and line liberally.

Comment: This establishes the self-image of the healthy condition for reference. Captions or descriptions are always useful.

2. **Your Present State** — Picture two is a drawing of you in your present physical condition, indicating the particular health problem, its location, its extent, and how you feel about it. Colors or shapes may be important for you to show just how you look and feel now. The picture may indicate how you think you look to others or to your doctor. You can make different drawings for the several aspects of your current physical state.

Comment: How does the person perceive him/herself? For some people, it is even more important to draw how they *think* others perceive them. It might be useful in that case to have a picture 2A (self-image) and 2B (what they think others see). Drawing themselves in this way may be the first opportunity they've really had to be *objective* about their illness—it provides some perspective, some reality, and both some connection and distancing. Some clients may need assistance to make this drawing in a safe, dissociated state, since the act of drawing may vivify physical and emotional feelings associated with the condition.

3. **Treatment** — For picture three, make a drawing of the treatment or treatments your doctors or other health providers have prescribed for you. This picture can be in several parts or several different pictures. Include drawings of treatments that have been described to you, but which you haven't yet received. Use colors, shapes and written words to allow yourself maximum expression, and to make your drawings as accurate as possible. You don't have to be a trained artist to express yourself. This is your drawing, and there are many ways to express yourself in your own unique way.

Comment: Some dissociative help may be needed here. It is significant how the client perceives his/her own treatments. (Wouldn't it be interesting to have the relevant helping health professionals from receptionists to technicians to nurses to GPs to specialists do similar drawings—the whole set of seven—for a particular person?)

4. **Desired State** — In picture four, make a drawing of yourself that shows you, perhaps from different perspectives, as you are

when you will be free of this particular health problem or problems. This is a picture of yourself with the problem completely in remission or cured. Add whatever details or words or colors or shapes or lines that indicate most clearly and directly how you would look at this healthy time, so that anyone looking at the drawing would know just how healthy you are and how far along you have progressed. This "desired you" that you draw, in whatever way that you do the drawing, should be specifically and realistically attainable. (That is, you can't regrow an appendix or a limb.) Indicate directly or symbolically the date *after which* all this has already occurred for you. The "you" in this picture looks back at your time of ill health and has almost forgotten what that was like for you back then.

Comment: One obvious caution here has to do with realistic expectations. At age seventy you may have your cancer go into remission, but you will still be seventy years old. A mastectomy can't be reversed, but a woman can lead a normal, healthy and active life free of cancer. Yet the client can be encouraged to be more optimistic than statistical expectations—if only ten per cent have severe problems with radiation, then ninety per cent do not! If only ten per cent have complete remissions, why can't your client be one of the ten per cent? Expectations are endlessly important and effective, so why not see glasses as half full rather than ...? The desired state should be sufficiently and specifically appealing to be very motivating and activating.

5. **Your Inner Healing Resources** — Over the years you have developed many ways of taking care of yourself. We may call them your inner healing resources. These are the ways that you (mostly unconsciously) take care of yourself. For example, you don't have to tell a cut finger how to heal—your body does this automatically, even reproducing the fingerprints. In this picture, put representations of all of those inner healing resources that have helped you overcome difficulties in the past, and that you expect will be available to you for overcoming present or future problems. Represent these inner healing resources in whatever ways make sense to you using color, shape, line, form, and words. These resources can include feelings, thoughts and memories, or an ability to relax or focus your attention or make images. Use whatever feels right and that you already have inside you. This could be a "good" heart or

a deep religious faith. You can use resources that you've read about or learned from others that feel right for you. You may wish to make separate drawings for each inner resource.

Comment: The body does automatically maintain itself. Some call this homoeostasis. There is an abundance of biofeedback built into the body and monitored by the brain which has the capability to influence changes on the cellular level both neuronically and via chemical messengers, many of which it can synthesize itself. (See Rossi (1993).) Again, the very act of identifying inner healing resources activates them. There is much power in simply naming things.

6. **Change Process** — Now that you have completed a picture of the "you" that is well and happily functioning after this health problem has been surmounted, you can make a drawing of just how that came about—what did you do and what did your physicians do (or not do) that helped bring about such good health? Which inner healing resources were used? Were there changes in your lifestyle? your employment? your relationships with others? your relationships with significant others? your diet? your exercise program? your hobbies? your mental state? meditation? relaxation? guided imagery? religion? faith?, or ...? that had a significant impact on your health? How have your personal dreams and hopes changed, and how many have you realized or are currently working towards? Put these things in the picture from the perspective of having already made those changes that were significant for you. You may actually be surprised at what you did and how you draw those actions. Also, indicate any relevant contributions from other people.

Comment: The wish is frequently the prelude to the reality. Just conceiving that something has changed and the mechanisms for that change can actually activate the process of change. In a way, this step gives the person permission to dream *and* to change.

7. **Maintenance and Future Orientation** — Picture seven is a representation of all of those ways of feeling, being, living, loving and doing that will *continue to ensure* that you not only maintain the desired state of health you have already attained, but continue to keep you well and healthy into the future. Put into this picture

drawings or representations of what you will have done to maintain and improve your health in comfort and in safety. Be as specific as you can. Do not be too surprised at what some of these activities or states may be.

Comment: This is the "HMO" (health maintenance organization) part of the eight-step process. Life goes on beyond individual health crises. How can health be maintained and ill-health be prevented? Build this into the process so that your client can continue without you—shouldn't this be the goal of all helping professionals?

8. **Review and Ratification** — Now that you have completed the set of drawings, take some time to review them. You may wish to share these drawings with someone else or just keep them for yourself. As you look at each drawing in turn, you may wish to add some descriptive words. In your own words, you may tell a supportive friend as much as you wish about each drawing, the parts of the drawing, and any special meanings or significance that come to mind. Please be sure to *not* tell this friend or helper anything you do not wish to reveal at this time. These are *your* drawings. Others may guess at the meanings, but the really important meanings are your own. You can get the "big" picture by looking at them all together.

Comment: A review is needed to *ratify* and consolidate the change process shown in the drawings. The review can validate the predicted changes *as if* they had already occurred! Resist the temptation to offer interpretations because it is effectively impossible to do so without leading your client. *These are their drawings, and only their interpretations are valid.* If you feel you must lead, do it cautiously and therapeutically, e.g. "And this can symbolize how your inner healing resources can continue to help you in the future?" The reviewer facilitates the client's finding his/her unique meanings in their drawings. Based on your experience, interpretations may be offered tentatively.

D. General Comments About the Eight-Step Process

The matter of *interpretation* of drawings or dreams or other projective media is an important one. To some extent, we still operate

with the Freudian inheritance of the analyst analyzing or interpreting what the client says. Without being a clone of your client,
all you can really offer is educated guesses (based on your experience) about the significance of particular statements or drawings.
With all we have written (and is in the literature) about the importance of presuppositions and suggesting and leading and seeding,
you need to be very careful in the review process to not impress
your ideas on the client—you are a *facilitator*. Each client is unique
and their drawings are unique and should be treated as such. On
the average, certain symbols and shapes and colors may appear to
be part of some "universal" language—but isn't it simpler and
safer to just *ask* your client for his/her interpretations? You can
lead them in general ways, "Does this part of the drawing have
any special meaning for you? There are eight branches on this tree.
Does that have any significance? The feet are missing on this
person—that's interesting, isn't it? There seem to be a lot of strong
colors in this drawing. Everything is rather small, isn't it?"

Furth (1988) suggests a number of things you can consider about
drawings. That is, you can ask your client what the following
mean to them:

(1) initial impression of the whole picture;

(2) size of the drawing in relation to the size of the paper;

(3) vertical or horizontal;

(4) color;

(5) shapes;

(6) direction and amount of movement;

(7) placement of objects;

(8) number of repeated objects;

(9) missing items;

(10) amount of detail;

(11) words;

(12) symbols;

(13) any "odd" portions;

(14) relative size of objects and people;

(15) from what perspective;

(16) people and their relationships and positions;

(17) any barriers within the picture;

(18) borders or lack of them;

(19) what is central or predominant;

(20) shape distortions;

(21) shading;

(22) how edges are used;

(23) appropriate to season;

(24) extensions, e.g. objects drawn in the hand of a figure;

(25) drawing extended to back of paper;

(26) underlining;

(27) erasures or cover-ups;

(28) lines across top, bottom, or side;

(29) transparency of certain barriers (walls);

(30) degree of abstraction;

(31) filled-in versus empty; and

(32) colors out of place.

You can ask the client to *become* particular parts or objects in their drawing so that they can give voice to that part, or act out what they see/feel/hear/say as that part. *The above are ways you can lead your client into giving his/her own interpretation.*

So far we have only written about one art form for the eight-step process. There are obvious extensions to sculpting in clay, working on a sand table, doing finger painting, dancing, singing, miming, and positioning your body as a representative sculpture. For the last four items, it would be important to make a videotaped record as your client goes through the first seven steps in the process. Puppet play can also be used. In a group setting, the client can serve as the playwright and director to set up a psychodrama for each step. The projective method needs to match your client's predilections (utilization principle).

The relation of these projective art forms to hypnotherapy is that they all involve a limited and focused attention on the client's part. When a person is engrossed in drawing or singing or acting, he/she is necessarily in a hypnotic state and his/her unconscious mind is more accessible. This means that the artistic output is more representative of unconscious states than conscious states. This yields a potentially truer "picture" of the client's problems and ways of resolving those problems. Like ideodynamic methods, art can be a useful shortcut to the unconscious and change.

Exercises

1. Go through the five practice cases presented in Chapter 11 and devise approaches using any of the arts (or several) as an appropriate intervention. You may add details to the cases as you wish.

2. Write out five cases and indicate how using the arts as hypnotherapeutic metaphors would be useful for them. Would you use all eight steps for each case?

3. Try the eight-step model yourself for a behavioral or psychological problem, and also for a health problem. Use as many different arts as you can. Which approach works best for you?

4. Make a checklist of nonleading questions that you could use to help a client interpret his/her drawings or artistic output.

5. Practice using the eight-step model with as many friends, colleagues, and clients as you can. Write out the speeches you would use with each step. Do this for several specific clients.

6. How many of the arts have you tried yourself? When will you make time to try more?

7. Consider the two cases presented in Chapter 12. Would you use one of the arts for either case? Which art medium would you choose?

8. Develop your own set of instructions for each of the two general classes of clients. Develop sets of instructions for artistic media other than drawing.

Chapter 14

Utilization of Hypnosis

Thomas L. South, Ph.D.

A. Introduction

Effective hypnotherapy relies on adequate communication of ideas and understandings to the hypnotized person at both the conscious and unconscious levels. Thus, communication needs to be presented to meet the client's personal needs, learnings, and experiences so that there can be an acceptance and a response to suggestions with a feeling of personal satisfaction. To illustrate the therapeutic use of hypnosis, the following presentations are offered to give the reader ideas of how to use the techniques in this book.

B. Common Habits

Since most people think of weight loss or smoking cessation when the topic of hypnosis is mentioned, these topics will be covered in the following sections. These consumers usually hold the false belief that hypnosis can cause them to lose weight or stop smoking and are looking for magic. Remember, there is no magic, and clients should be made aware of this. The only way to lose weight is to use more calories than are consumed. Period. The best way to stop the complex behavior of smoking is to change the smoker's attitude and to replace all the smoking cues with other behaviors— a much more difficult task than weight loss. However, both can be successfully achieved if the client is sufficiently motivated to follow homework assignments or if he believes in the magic of hypnosis. As repeatedly stated, hypnosis is a special form of communication where the subject has suspended the conscious mind by redirecting its focus of attention. Hypnosis is a therapeutic technique to aid individuals in accomplishing their goals.

1. Obesity

During the information-gathering session, the therapist ought to ask specific questions to obtain the antecedent stimuli and environment that contribute to eating behavior. These questions can seed behavior change. Many overweight individuals are not aware of the extent of their food intake—especially when watching TV or socializing with friends. Calorie-counting or food groups are not necessary when utilizing hypnosis; this is not to discredit the importance of nutrition. Hypnosis is a cognitive behavioral technique. Thus it relies on utilizing motivation to change attitudes about eating, as well as eating behavior. For example, if a person eats any place or at any time as most overweight people do, the therapist restricts the time and place of food consumption, e.g. only in the kitchen and never while being idle (such as watching TV). Eating behavior needs to be isolated as only *one* activity in a specific place and at a specific time.

Notice that in the two following presentations eating attitude is changed at the *beginning* of the induction. Positive imagery is used with cooperative clients while negative imagery is designed to be used with resistant clients. These inductions are generic and fit the general overweight population. Certain changes should be made to pace individual differences in eating behavior, but the slowed hypnotic eating process should not be changed because it is considered to be the crux of the induction, i.e. the steps involved in preparation to eating and the actual consuming behavior. These scripts and modifications of them have been successful with every client seen who was motivated to lose weight in six to eight one-hour weekly sessions, with follow-up sessions at two to three week intervals. Most clients had achieved their desired weight loss or had terminated treatment after the halfway mark and had confidence that they would use self-hypnosis to reach their goals.

Positive Imagery

I'm going to talk to you, so sit back comfortably in your chair and close your eyes. Let yourself begin to relax. Feel your muscles relaxing. Your mind relaxing. Allowing your body to slow down. Your mind slowing down. The time slowing down. We have lots of time. And as I continue to talk to you, you can become more at ease, more peaceful with yourself. Calm and relaxing. Now, it will seem that nothing is happening to you, but you will be doing the work. And that's all right. Become aware of your breathing. So take a deep breath and slowly exhale. Take another deep breath and feel how much more relaxed you are becoming. Feel the rise and falling of your chest. As you feel your body relaxing, take another deep breath and slowly exhale and breathe out all those tensions of the day. Gradually feeling yourself becoming more relaxed and not distracted by any outside noises, because they are not important. The only important thing is the activity of your unconscious mind. Now, in the past, you have come to think of yourself as a heavy, overweight individual. Maybe feeling unattractive to others, or even to yourself, from overeating or eating certain foods with the consequence of gaining weight. So what I want you to do now is to eat less and enjoy your food now. And we all like to enjoy our food by eating less.

What I want you to learn is that eating can be an art. You can learn how to eat as a gourmet and, contrary to popular belief, most gourmet eaters, if not all gourmet eaters, are slim or well-built individuals because they take care of themselves and really enjoy eating food. So, when you use those techniques, the techniques of eating as a gourmet, eating as an art, you can enjoy eating your food more and obtain pleasures from eating that are greater than you have ever imagined possible.

And this is how you can enjoy eating food more than you ever have in the past. Eat only at meal times, and when you eat focus all of your attention on your food. Do not watch TV, or read, or talk on the phone, because those things have nothing to do with eating and enjoying your food. And there is no need to engage in conversation unless it is absolutely necessary. People don't like to be bothered while they are eating for this distracts from enjoying food to the fullest. And, before you begin eating your food, spend a few moments observing your food. Take the time to notice the colors, the shapes, and the textures of the food before you. Focus your attention on those colors, textures and shapes. Study what you're eating. The different shades of the colors, the different types of textures, the various shapes of the food. Probably something that you have never done. Know what you're eating. Inhale deeply and enjoy the aromas of the food. Really enjoy the smells of the various foods. And when you are ready to begin eating, take only small bites of food, and only put small portions on your fork or your spoon; or take very small bites of those foods that you hold in your hand such as small sandwiches. Focus your complete attention on the food that you are eating. While you're focusing all of your attention on the food, your thoughts won't be able to wander. Become aware of all your taste buds that are on your tongue and how they are stimulated by each tiny bit of food so that you can really enjoy the taste of your food. Then, chew your food many times and move your food around in your mouth with your tongue so that you can savor the flavor of the food before finally swallowing it. And, by doing this, it will satisfy all the taste buds on your tongue and give you greater pleasure from your food. And enjoy each mouthful to the maximum. You can really learn to enjoy each bite of food. Each time you swallow, focus your attention on all the feelings and sensations in your stomach.

As you continue eating, let yourself become aware of an ever increasing feeling of fullness, a fullness in your stomach. So that when you have finished your meal, you will feel comfortably full and completely satisfied—completely fulfilled. Since you have enjoyed every mouthful and you're aware of each bite of food, you can feel completely satisfied until your next meal. That's right. And as you were focusing on all the subtle tastes of each bite that you take and the feeling of fullness in your stomach. Each time that you swallow, tell yourself that time is slowing down. And there's lots of time. Every second can feel like it's stretching out. Every second can feel like five seconds or ten seconds or 25 seconds. And five seconds can feel like 20 seconds. And 15 seconds can feel like 30 seconds, 45 seconds or 48 seconds, 50 seconds. Notice how, as you eat, there's so much time between each bite that you take. As you chew your food slowly notice how you feel as if every second is a minute and there's so much time. As if everything is in slow motion. When at last you have finished your meal, you can feel comfortably full and satisfied. That's right. As if you had been eating for hours. So, instead of giving up food, you can become a gourmet eater by learning to enjoy food to the utmost. You can do this by first becoming aware of the colors, textures, shapes, and amounts of your food. And then by only taking small bites of food into your mouth, and totally focusing on your food, and all those subtle flavors as you chew your food several times slowly. Moving the food ever so slowly within your mouth with your tongue as if in slow motion.

In addition to totally focusing on your food and eating as a gourmet, there is yet another aspect that is an integral part of the enjoyment of food. This important aspect is hunger. You simply cannot totally enjoy food if you are not really hungry when you begin to eat. If you are not really hungry when you begin to eat, your hunger will really be satisfied with the first few bites of food. It will be satisfied with the first few bites of food. Then, after that, you will not be able to truly enjoy eating your meal. Your meal will simply be finished out of the habit of a feeling of fullness in your stomach. When you eat when you're truly hungry, hunger helps us enjoy our food. However, whenever you feel hungry and it's not time for you to eat, you can tell yourself several things such as, "My body is now using up some of that excess fat, that excess weight that I really want to lose." You can tell yourself that "When it is time to eat this feeling of hunger will help me enjoy it to the utmost." So, starting today, whenever you feel hungry, you can have a feeling of real joy. An inner feeling of deep satisfaction because, whenever you feel hunger, you will know that you are accomplishing your goal of losing weight.

You can feel those clothes becoming looser and looser. You may not notice it at first or know exactly when you began losing weight. You won't know exactly how much weight you're losing in a day because sometimes we lose six ounces or eight ounces or 12 ounces and it doesn't register on a scale. And, I don't know, but you may feel your clothes feeling looser in your shoulders before you notice the looseness around your waist. And it might be interesting to discover where that looseness is going to be first. You'll just have to wait and see.

It's also nice to discover new things about ourselves. It may take several days or a week, or ten days to two weeks before you actually notice yourself losing weight. Noticing the difference in your body. So, now, picture yourself slender and attractive, standing in front of a mirror, or standing on a scale noticing the difference in your appearance. Standing there more slender and more attractive and noticing yourself reaching the desired weight. Reaching your goal. Standing there with good feelings and very happy, realizing that you can achieve your goal, but you don't know exactly when, but you can see yourself standing there feeling very proud of your achievements. Of accomplishing what you set out to do. Notice how healthy and vibrant and alive you feel as you realize your full potential of your unconscious mind. Whenever you feel like eating something that you're not supposed to eat or eating at a time other than meal time, picture yourself healthy and trim. Tell yourself that you don't want that food. That you don't need that food. You have no need to eat at this time, and see yourself losing weight. See yourself slender, attractive, healthy and in control of your own life. Feel the true, inner deep satisfaction—the inner security—in your inner confidence in yourself. Knowing that you can control the amount of food that you eat and in this way you can take control of your life and other things.

So relax and tell yourself that you're on a road that will lead to a new you—a more attractive, a more healthy, energetic and alive you. Feel those feelings now. Feel an overwhelming feeling of confidence and security now rising up from within you. Now realize that you have taken control of your life. You will no longer allow yourself to be the victim of fattening, disgusting, tasteless food, but you're going to enjoy your food more by eating less, and eating as a gourmet, and really enjoying your food.

Now, I want you to positively picture yourself eating healthy food in moderate amounts and feeling yourself losing weight, clothes feeling looser, feeling those pounds melting off your body. You might consider some moderate exercise. Feeling healthier and taking great pride in your new experience. Hear your friends complimenting you on your new glow of health and new appearance and the relationships with your loved ones improving. Now just continue to relax. Enjoy these pleasant feelings of relaxation and comfort. In a moment you will gradually open your eyes and awaken, but not yet. At my signal begin counting backwards from 20 to 1 and at the count of 1 open your eyes and become completely awake. Start counting now.

The purpose of the following presentation is to assist overweight people from being tempted to eat undesirable foods that keep them from achieving a desirable weight. It utilizes an individual's own abilities of visualization to accomplish this goal. It is designed to help individuals who have a history of not being able to follow diets or who have poor impulse control towards foods.

Negative Imagery

I'm going to talk to you. As I talk to you, nothing will be done to you. So just settle back in your chair and close your eyes. Take three deep breaths and feel yourself slowly relaxing. That's right. Now, I know it may seem that I have done nothing because you will be doing the work. As I continue talking to you, you will notice that you will feel more and more relaxed. That's right. Just like that. You know that you know the difference between reality and fantasy. But you also know that we can imagine things so vividly that they seem real and that they can have a dramatic effect on our lives. So now you can keep your eyes closed, or gradually open them still feeling comfortable and relaxed. There's no need to move. Just make a decision whether to close your eyes or keep them open.

You know that we all have dreams. Some we remember and some we don't. Sometimes, we have unconscious dreams at night and other times we have dreams during the day called daydreams. So, with your eyes open or closed, picture yourself at a fast-food restaurant, looking at the assembly line production of quarter pounders and cheeseburgers that have been lying there under warm light to keep them warm, knowing that hamburger spoils faster whether it's cooked or uncooked under warm light. And micro-organisms grow and breed faster under warm light than any other place. See restaurant help perspiring. Their foreheads, their armpits drenched with perspiration and mopping this sweat on their clothes. Sneezing and coughing and wiping snot on their hands before handling your order. The sweat from their foreheads and chins rolling and dripping onto the hamburgers and buns. Knowing that teenagers are irresponsible about their work habits, and that they don't always wash their hands after being in the restrooms and wiping their hands on their uniforms. They pick up meat that has fallen on the floor where people have been walking with the same shoes that they wear in the public restroom. No matter how clean the restaurant is before they started working, roaches in droves, disgusting, dirty roaches crawling all over the floor and on the sides of the walls and on the counter tops before the sun comes up. Employees picking the hamburger off the floor and placing it in a hamburger bun with roach eggs, thousands of them hatching, so small that you can't even see them, eating the micro-organisms that are growing and spreading on the surface as well as throughout the meat. Then see them crawling out of the meat and onto the bun leaving a trail of dirt, slime and defecation all over the bun and the hamburger and a trail on the cheese with their six legs moving and antennae waving in the air telling other disgusting roaches what they have found. And flies with their ugly, beady eyes landing and rubbing their front legs preparing to eat the bun. See flies laying eggs, and maggots and other larvae hatching from these maggot fly eggs, boring holes through sandwiches and crawling over it with disease and disgust. You know that employees with good sense never eat in the restaurants that they work in because they know these things.

Now see that uncooked meat that has been lying out all day, thawed and mushy with these micro-organisms and roach and fly eggs being placed back into the freezer to be served yet another day to some unsuspecting customer, such as yourself. Now see, the fast food restaurant's trucks that have broken down on the highway with the freezer unit shut off due to power failure on a warm day. The meats and cheeses are being spoiled long before they arrive at their destinations. Picture where these trucks have come from. Warehouses.

Picture these warehouses realistically. They are dirty, filthy places with rats, roaches and termites, where these foods are stored in boxes. Rats chewing the boxes open and partially eating the contents. Dirty, disgusting diseased rats from sewers with ugly faces. Big, beady eyes and whiskers, urinating yellow urine on the boxes and into the boxes of food and defecating all over the various foods. Slimy round black and green mushy stools. Vomiting all over, mixed with saliva seeping into the food, and drying until you can't tell it was there. Roaches crawling into those openings where germs flourish and spreading these germs throughout the warehouse.

Knowing that when you eat these foods at a fast-food restaurant, you don't know if what you're eating is disgusting gristle or little round rat bones or gritty, granules of suet or dirt or whatever. You know it makes no difference whether you go in and order from inside or at the drive-thru window, the food is the same. You don't need to imagine swallowing this material and having it slide down into your stomach and being stored in your body. You know the precaution of cooking pork well-done so that tiny microscopic hookworms don't get into the muscles of your body. Now, you can picture these negative things, that they may or may not be true all the time, any time you are tempted by those undesirable foods. You can refuse to eat them. You know the difference between fantasy and reality.

Now, I want you to positively picture yourself eating healthy foods in moderate amounts and losing weight. Your clothes feeling looser. Feel those pounds melting off your body. Feeling healthy and good about yourself. Taking great pride in your new experiences of weight loss, seeing your friends complimenting you on your glow of health and physical appearance, your relationships closest to you improving, and feeling their pride in you. See yourself reaching your desired weight and having good feelings of success in your accomplishments, knowing that you can achieve more with those feelings and new learnings. Now, close your eyes and continue for just a few moments longer and really enjoy these pleasant feelings of relaxation and comfort. Knowing that you have experienced a lot today. Now count backwards from twenty to one and completely awaken feeling quite rested as if you have had several hours of restful sleep.

2. Smoking

The following script has successfully been used with about 50% of those clients seeking hypnotherapy to stop smoking. It was modified here to fit the general population, but the original version was a spontaneous induction while working with an excellent hypnotic subject who was highly motivated to quit smoking because her retired physician husband had just undergone triple by-pass heart surgery and had to quit smoking to live. The hypnotic session was a "one time shot" because she came from out-of-state and her husband was being discharged from the hospital the following day. The session lasted 90 minutes. Three months later she called to report that she had quit smoking that night without any difficulty and still had no desire to smoke.

Since the following script is general and is suitable for all smokers, it should be changed to meet individual needs and any other idiosyncrasies of the client.

Stopping Smoking

Just relax and settle back into your chair. Close your eyes. That's right. You know that hypnosis is a form of relaxation, but it can also help alleviate the temptation of smoking. So, not only will you become more relaxed, but the self-destructive impulses that you experience will also subside to the point that they will no longer be a major influence, and you can gain more control over your life. As I continue talking to you, you can find yourself becoming more and more relaxed. And my voice can become that of a friend, a relative or someone else known to you. Or you don't even have to listen to my voice, for your unconscious mind will hear it. And you really don't have anything else of importance to do. You already know something about the unconscious for it has been protecting you in your dreams. It has let you forget unpleasant experiences, memories that your conscious mind can't remember. It has awakened you every morning. It has helped you remember some of your most pleasant experiences. And it will continue to help you and guide you with any problem or need that you might have. You can respond to challenges in life. These are opportunities to grow in strength and maturity rather than reacting to them and being upset by them. You know that you can permit obstacles to control your mind to the point where they are uppermost in your mind and become the dominating factors in your thought patterns. By learning how to cast them from

365

your mind, by refusing to be subservient to them, you can rise above obstacles that you ordinarily let defeat you. If you follow these instructions and practice what I'm going to say on a daily basis, you can experience an amazing experience within yourself. You will be able to assume control over circumstances in your life rather than continuing to be directed by them.

We all learn many habits early in our lives, and those habits that are good are kept and they become important aspects of our lives. Those that hinder us from enjoying life with those closest to us are given up. Now, you know that this habit of smoking cigarettes is a nasty, dirty, disgusting habit that you want to give up and leave behind with the other bad habits that you have overcome. Like most habits, the habit of smoking occurs in the early years—those teenage years. Those years of defiance, rebelliousness towards conforming. Smoking usually begins in the company of friends—other teenagers. Smoking is usually done out of peer pressure to conform. It was an acceptable behavior at that time in our young lives, but you have matured since those teenage years. You have become an adult with adult understandings. You have had many other experiences since then that have changed your life, and you no longer need to let the decision of an irresponsible teenager continue to run your present adult life and ruin your present state of health. That teenage part of you that decided to take the risk of breathing toxic gases and accepted smoking regardless of the cost to your health is in the past now. So, now, as an adult, it is no longer acceptable and you need not accept the irresponsible decision of a teenager. An adult outgrows these childhood behaviors just as you no longer play in a sandbox or play with childhood toys or believe in Santa Claus. As we grow older into mature adults, we re-evaluate earlier decisions that were once made and leave behind those self-destructive habits and those impulses that we really no longer need or appreciate.

Now, to help you re-evaluate that earlier decision, I would like to tell you a story about a woman who came for hypnotherapy to stop smoking. She had been smoking for a long time. She had quit smoking before for weeks and even for months at a time, but she had decided, now, that she had been smoking long enough and wanted to retire from smoking. She went into a trance—a very relaxing, very comfortable trance. She remembered those times that she had quit smoking. She didn't know exactly how she had quit smoking. She only knew that she had the ability to quit smoking. Everyone who smokes knows that they can quit smoking for 15 minutes, for 30 minutes, for 35 minutes, for 60 minutes. And anyone who can quit smoking for 60 minutes can quit smoking for five more minutes and five more minutes and for five minutes at a time, any time. She realized that she could quit for five minutes and five more minutes, and before she realized it, 90 minutes had passed and then two hours and four hours and six hours and eight hours, and 12 hours was a half day, and then she realized that several days had gone by. She visualized in a trance every cell in her body—all the nicotine in the cells of her body was being eliminated from every cell in her body by the exhaling of all those poisons. As she exhaled, she felt all those poisons leaving her body for good. She could see green and yellow smoke coming out of her body into the air until she finally saw white transparent smoke being exhaled and knew that all those toxic gases had been eliminated and she could breathe in fresh air and experience her lungs clearing up. I told her this story.

A young man in the Navy came to see me. He wanted to quit smoking and, when he was out at sea, he heard over a loudspeaker the commander's voice bellowing, "The smoking lamp is out. The smoking lamp is out. The smoking lamp is out." Now, feel that smoke being forced into your lungs against your body's will. That feeling of gagging, that feeling of nausea in the pit of your stomach and those tearful eyes. Your body is telling you something about that experience. That nasty tar and nicotine that was invading your lungs was the desire of an irresponsible teenager. Now, you've learned later in life that making a re-decision as an adult, making firm decisions as an adult, is the key to changing behavior. You have made the right decision by re-evaluating those earlier decisions and you're no longer willing to risk your health for anyone. You have the inner resources and capabilities to overcome any bad habits that you choose. So make a commitment now to yourself that you need not accept a decision made by an irresponsible person, and visualize and experience all the addicting nicotine leaving every cell of your body—being exhaled from your body and eliminated. The lungs are clearing up. The body is healing itself. You're breathing more comfortably. Re-experience the pleasant sensations of breathing clearer—breathing cleaner—fresh air. Enjoy these good feelings that come with having an adult's control over your life. And those closest to you admiring and feeling very proud of you.

There are other needs that require to be fulfilled. You can become more aware of your health, about living and really enjoying life more with those closest to you.

It's nice to discover that we can alter our lives in ways that can help us accomplish our goals. By gaining more control of our thinking and feelings and by changing our attitudes and behaviors, we can change the direction of our health.

Now, you can slowly awaken at your own pace feeling better than you have for a long time.

C. Medical Conditions

There are a variety of ways in which the guided imagery approach can be effectively used in connection with medical treatment. The two following medical conditions are examples of the implementation of this approach.

1. *Hypertension*

After an induction, proceed as follows:

Now, visualize what high blood pressure is. Visualize as best you can—a diagram, a medical chart or actual pictures of the blood cells in the body. See the little muscles in the walls of the blood vessels tightening down so that they cause much higher pressure than necessary for the blood to be driven through. Now, see yourself taking whatever medication your doctor has prescribed for relaxing those little muscles in the blood vessels. Your heart is pumping evenly with less resistance, and blood is flowing smoothly through those blood vessels. Now, see rich, red blood cells full of oxygen and nutrients flowing through these blood vessels throughout your entire body—healing, healing any damage to these tiny muscles—constructing and repairing them—making them stronger and healthier. See them becoming stronger and healthier and more relaxed. The more relaxed you are becoming. That's right. You can continue to become more and more relaxed knowing that your body is healing itself. You're getting stronger and healthier as you continue to take your prescribed medication and continue to relax.

Now transport yourself to any place you choose. A nice quiet place only known to you. It can be your private place away from all the tensions of the day as your body continues to heal itself. You can go to the woods and sit under a tree. See the sunlight streaming down through the branches. Feel the warmth of the sun as it caresses your body. Enjoy these experiences. By frequently visiting this private place, you can have a more relaxed life.

When we look back at our childhood, most of us can remember many experiences. Many experiences were positive and had a beneficial effect on our lives. However, some were not beneficial. For example, if children see their parents arguing, they may feel that expressing hostility is bad and make a decision that pleasing and cheerful behavior is appropriate no matter what their real feelings are. And this can make life a strain and very stressful.

Some children may make an early decision that they are responsible for the feelings of others. So they feel that it is their responsibility to help them feel better whenever others are unhappy.

Those decisions in childhood may have been the best decisions at the time and enabled them to get through difficult situations. But, now, they may no longer be appropriate in adult life since circumstances are different. It's nice to discover that we can alter our lives in ways that can decrease the stress in our lives. By gaining more control of our thinking and feeling, we can change our attitudes and behavior. We can change the direction of our health. So, see yourself becoming more relaxed when dealing with life's difficult and unfortunate events. See yourself doing this exercise at least once a day. Most people feel relaxed the first time they use this technique. But since relaxation is something that can be learned and improved upon, you will find that you will enter into increasingly relaxed states as this process is repeated with practice.

Then awaken.

2. *Arthritis*

Following an induction, say:

Life is full of variety because life is full of opposition. There is darkness at night. There is light during the day and in between there is dawn and dusk and ever-changing shadows. There is working and there is resting, and there are many options for balancing the time. There is pleasure and there is pain and varying degrees of both in our lives. We can live a constructive and more meaningful life, if we choose to be less miserable.

If you think back through time, you can probably remember many small ailments in your life such as colds or headaches that occurred when you were tired, overworked, under stressful circumstances or emotional stress. You have probably said many times that you caught a cold because you were run down, meaning not only physical fatigue, but also emotional depletion.

Serious ailments such as heart attacks, ulcers, high blood pressure and arthritis have been observed to follow periods of overwork, or tension, or just pushing the body and mind too hard. These problems tend to occur when the body has reached its upper limit of tolerance and the signals of the situation have been ignored.

Anyone who has had an ulcer is aware of how it acts as a feedback device for an emotional overload. The pain from the ulcer is most likely to occur when they are tense and anxious.

So, now, visualize a pleasant, quiet place to rest and relax, such as sitting in the shade of a beautiful tree next to a stream, surrounded by the beauty of nature. Feel a gentle breeze against your face. Hear the sound of water as it rushes over the rocks in the free-flowing stream. Enjoy these pleasant experiences knowing that you can return frequently, and enjoy the experience of relaxing.

Now, in this relaxed state, picture your hands and any other arthritic joints in your body. See the joints very irritated and having little granules on the surface. See your round, white blood cells coming in and cleaning up the debris. They're picking up the little granules and smoothing over the joint surfaces. See rich, red, healthy blood cells coming in with nutrients and oxygen to aid the white blood cells. They're nurturing and healing the joints as the white blood cells carry away the debris. See the debris being flushed, safely, from your body through the liver and kidneys and eliminated in the urine and stools. See the white blood cells smoothing over other joint surfaces of your arms and legs, carrying away any debris until the surfaces become smooth and glistening. See healthy tissue growing over and replacing deteriorated dead cells, helping the normal cells grow in health. Feel yourself growing in health as your arthritic symptoms progressively decrease. See yourself having more energy, and feeling increasingly comfortable as the pain symptoms disappear.

Whenever you are experiencing pain, picture the army of white blood cells flowing into that area and soothing the pain. Whatever the problem, give your body the command to heal itself. Visualize your body becoming healthier and healthier. See yourself active and doing what you like to do, free of joint pain.

See yourself participating in your own recovery by doing this imaginary exercise at least once a day for several weeks and noticing the difference in how you feel. If the symptoms return, you know that you are overloading your system and, by once again practicing this exercise for several weeks, you can diminish them by continuing this technique.

Then awaken.

These imagery techniques used during trance have proven to be quite effective with other medical conditions. The therapist should always gather as much detailed information as possible in order to effectively pace and lead the client. For example, this author has used this approach to alleviate purging during chemotherapy treatments in cancer patients. Gather information regarding thoughts about the treatment, the details of the waiting room, the treatment room, medical procedures and the conditioned response to specific stimuli, e.g. colors, hypodermic, and time. After one treatment, the client can give all this information upon questioning. Before trance and during trance, it can be suggested that the red lights and hazardous warnings in the waiting room can be triggers causing them to relax because of their familiarity, and can trigger a light trance. Entering the treatment room can cause a deeper trance, and the syringe can produce a profound trance as soon as they purge into the already placed bedpan. The suggestion for a profound trance is suggested because they have to sit still for hours as the chemicals steadily drip into a vein. Suggestions are then given to continue relaxation and to remain in a somnambulistic trance for the following week in which the stomach is completely relaxed, and that light foods, e.g. soups, Jell-O, etc., will begin to taste better. The initial purging could not be extinguished, but consequent purging was eliminated in six patients after four sessions. This is just one other example of the use of this powerful approach.

D. Pain Management

Although pain is a subjective experience that seems involuntary and uncontrollable, it is also a psychophysiological experience. There are psychological, physiological and neurological learnings, associations, and conditionings that make it possible to control and even abolish it. Pain is especially susceptible to hypnosis because it varies in its nature and intensity, and also acquires secondary meanings. It can be transient, recurrent, persistent, acute or chronic. Since pain consists of past remembered pain, the present pain experience, and anticipated future pain, two-thirds of the pain can be relieved quite quickly with suggestions of amnesia and pseudo-orientation of time. It is also quite possible to diminish or completely alleviate the present pain in many situations—no matter what the physiological cause—with a variety of hypnotic techniques. However, it must also be remembered that there should be no attempt at using hypnosis for pain relief unless the individual is under the care of a physician or the hypnotherapist understands the cause of the pain. Hypnosis does not "cure" pain, and the individual should be examined by a physician for the underlying medical condition before trance work is initiated for pain control. Although there are a variety of effective pain control techniques, only two of the author's favorite techniques will be presented. (These should not be attempted by the novice.) Five relevant references are: Erickson, Hershman, and Secter (1981); Barber and Adrian (1982); Melzack and Wall (1982); Hilgard and Hilgard (1994); and Barber (1996).

1. Glove Anesthesia

Although the induction can be done in any creative manner the hypnotherapist chooses, including the hand lying in a person's lap or resting on a bed, the author suggests practicing this technique utilizing the Extended Hand Induction (Induction #8) in Chapter 8. After the subject's hand is in a cataleptic posture, the wrist of the extended hand is lightly grasped with the thumb and forefinger until there is a gradual firm grip. After the hand is extended, the hypnotherapist might begin this way:

> I'm going to grasp your right hand like this. And you can feel the pressure being exerted on your wrist as I cut off the blood flow to your hand. I can feel the throbbing in your wrist as the blood circulation is being cut off, and your hand can begin to feel numb. That's right. You can close your eyes now. Maybe you will begin to feel a tingling sensation first in your fingertips before the tingling sensation in the palm of your hand. (Therapist lightly touches the fingertips and gently feels the palm with the fingers of his other hand.) You can keep feeling those tingling sensations until there is no more

feeling in the hand as it becomes more and more numb as the circulation has been cut off. We have all had the experience as children of sitting on our hands, and without our awareness the hands become completely numb and anesthetized. And when we were children playing in the snow, our hands became numb without our awareness just as your hand is becoming cold now—more and more cold the number it becomes. (The therapist monitors the coldness of the hand as an indication of the degree of anesthesia. This comes with experience, and you can judge when the hand has satisfactorily become anesthetized.) The hand will continue growing more and more numb after I release your wrist, and your hand will feel completely anesthetized. (Therapist gradually releases the wrist and it remains cataleptic.)

Commentary: This concludes the glove anesthesia technique. This can obviously be quite useful if a person has pain in the hand for whatever the reason. However, this is far too limiting for such a grand and useful technique. During a glove anesthesia demonstration I was conducting at a workshop on advanced pain management, a physician remarked, "I know how to do that. Is that all you're doing?" While I thought that she was being inconsiderate of the subject who was in a trance, I responded in a hypnotic voice, "And do you know the many uses of glove anesthesia and how powerful it is? And I wonder how numb your hand is becoming," and reached for her hand as she was sitting close to me. She extended her hand. I grasped it with my thumb and forefinger and told her to close her eyes. Now I had two individuals experiencing glove anesthesia!

The beauty of this simple technique is that the anesthesia can be generalized to any part of the body by contact with the anesthetized hand or by the anesthesia or numbing sensation spreading from the hand to any part of the body that cannot be touched by the hand. After the cataleptic position and glove anesthesia is achieved, suggestions for movement can be given, just as in hand levitation, to any part of the body that can comfortably be reached. As the hand is moving, suggestions can be offered similar to this:

When the hand touches the other hand, feelings of numbness can spread into that hand and keep spreading into that hand until it, too, becomes completely numb. And after both hands become completely numb, they can drift down until they touch your stomach. And, then, as you slowly move them across your abdomen, feel that numbness spreading from your hands into your abdomen. Maybe you first feel a tingling sensation on the surface of your abdomen and, as your hands make circular motions, that numbness begins to spread across your abdomen. And, as it spreads, you can feel that numbness penetrating into your abdomen—deeply penetrating—deeper and deeper, as it spreads across and deeper into your abdomen as it completely relaxes. Now, feel it spread around your body and through your body until your abdomen becomes completely numb. Now, feel it spread—(up into your breasts or down into your buttocks and into your thighs, etc.). And when you awaken, but not yet, those soothing sensations of pleasant, comfortable numbness can remain in your abdomen even upon awakening and your abdomen can remain numb and in a trance after awakening. And you can enjoy these good feelings for the rest of the day and while you're asleep tonight, and awaken in the morning with your abdomen still in a trance for as long as your unconscious mind sees fit and your body warrants these good feelings. Now, awaken by slowly and gradually opening your eyes. That's right. How do you feel?

Do not discuss pain, for it may undo the trance work and be a suggestion to trigger the pain response. Talk about good feelings and other pleasant topics. Transferring glove anesthesia has been successfully utilized by this author to abolish dental pain, mastectomy pain, and obstetrical procedures (South, 1988), such as a hypnotic saddle-block for amniocentesis and in combination with natural and caesarean births, as well as other uses.

For two recent review articles on the application of hypnosis to pain management see Chaves (1994) and Chaves and Dworkin (1997). We quote here a relevant section from the second paper (1997, p. 367):

> No form of psychotherapy, or any single component of multimodal therapies for chronic pain, hypnosis included, has yet proven relatively superior in any definitive fashion. When symptoms seem to have outlived their usefulness, then any form of psychotherapy appears efficacious, whether it be behavior therapy using hypnosis for systematic desensitization or psychodynamic hypnotherapy using hypnosis to uncover the "true" meaning of unconscious defenses. It remains the case, substantiated by increasingly better psychotherapy outcome research, that psychotherapy seems effective for removing a wide range of physical, behavioral, emotional,

and cognitive symptoms, sometimes superior to pharmacological methods over longer time periods and sometimes established as more efficacious than biomedical interventions. The general consensus seems to be that cognitive-behavioral and behavioral therapies are better suited for physical symptom removal.

2. *Multiple Embedded Metaphor*

The following is a script to demonstrate how the conversational method can be utilized within the context of a multiple embedded metaphor (discussed in Chapter 12). Notice that the metaphors are within a traditional counting induction. This method has been successfully used to alleviate pain in private practice clients:

Now, I'm going to talk to you. And as I talk to you nothing will be done to you. And I know it will seem that I have done nothing. You may feel that nothing has happened at all except that of a feeling of profound relaxation. And that's all right. So just settle back in your chair, close your eyes and get as comfortable as you can. Now take a deep breath and slowly exhale. Take another deep breath. Now feel how relaxed you are becoming. So, once more take another deep breath and slowly and gradually exhale, and as you exhale breathe out all the tensions of the day, and gradually feel yourself becoming more and more relaxed as I talk to you. That's right. And as I talk to you, you need not be distracted by any outside noises because they are not important. The only important thing is the activity of your unconscious mind.

You know that you have a conscious mind and an unconscious mind. And that your conscious mind is what you use in your everyday transactions, and your unconscious mind holds your vast storehouse of memories and wishes and everything that you have done. It is the part of you that dreams at night and helps you remember the things that you want to and need to remember. It helps and guides your conscious mind through the day. And it has abilities and capabilities that are out of your awareness, but you can have faith in your unconscious mind, that it will help you and give you the ability to do anything reasonable that you request.

And your conscious mind doesn't have anything of importance to do right now. And it can think about anything that it wants, while your unconscious mind listens to my voice and can learn a great deal more than your conscious mind, and help your conscious mind deal with anything that happens to be bothering you at this time.

Now I'm going to begin counting backwards from 20 to 1 and as I count you can feel yourself becoming more and more relaxed, and with each number that I count you feel yourself becoming deeper and deeper relaxed. Now I'm going to begin the count: 20—19—18, beginning to feel more relaxed, 17—16—15. That's right, more and more relaxed. That's right. And notice how much more relaxed you are becoming. And as you become more and more relaxed, I wonder if you can sense the different places in your body that feel more relaxed than others. Perhaps you feel your shoulders and neck becoming more relaxed than your legs while one hand feels lighter than the other hand. I don't know. And it really doesn't matter. It doesn't matter at all. Maybe you feel one arm becoming more relaxed than the other arm. I don't know. I wonder if this restful relaxing feeling is already beginning to spread and flow down throughout your entire body. From your forehead into your facial muscles, down through your neck across your shoulders, down through your back, your abdomen, and down through your legs. That's right.

14—13—12—11—10. Now you can visualize a nice quiet place. A place known only to you. Away from all the tensions of the day. A place in the woods, so calm and serene. As you visualize yourself walking through the woods, you can see the trees and leaves, the sun shining down through the branches as you look for a place to sit down by the stream and, while sitting on the creek bank and under the shade of a tree surrounded by trees, you can feel a gentle breeze and smell the moisture in the air as you see the ripples on the surface of the water and the water splash over the rocks and hear the faint sound of a waterfall not far away. And enjoy these experiences as you become more and more relaxed.

9—8—7—6—5. And, resting in the forest, you can take time to reflect and remember something that you have forgotten in your early childhood when you just went to school. You had to learn the alphabet and, at the time, it seemed to be a big insurmountable task. You had to learn to differentiate between an A and a B, a C and a D, an O and a Q, and a V and a W, and you ate lunch at home or at a cafeteria, and you can recall those experiences.

9—8—7—6—5. And you probably remember what you had for breakfast but not what you had for breakfast today, last week, a month ago. And sometimes you have forgotten what the day is, have you not? And you have forgotten the day that you may have been working in the yard and cut your finger or skinned your hands, and didn't realize it until you had come into the house and began cleaning up. It wasn't important and not relevant to what was going on. It had nothing to do with reaching your goal. And you have a very good memory to forget unimportant things that you would rather forget and really don't matter.

4—3—2—1. And you know a lot about remembering to forget unpleasant experiences that are not important for you to forget. And you've learned a lot about relaxing by learning how to relax. And you can feel how really relaxed you are right now. That's right. And you can become even more relaxed by practicing relaxing by reaching this profound state of relaxation and, the more you practice it, it can become an unconscious habit to enjoy and feel good about these new learnings and accomplishments. And whenever you feel tensed or stressed you can unconsciously take several deep breaths and feel yourself becoming more and more relaxed as the relaxation spreads and flows throughout your entire body. Now visualize yourself sitting at home or at the office and as you are sitting there, becoming more aware of the heaviness of your body in the chair as you feel yourself growing more and more relaxed just as you are right now. That's right. And any time in the future when you feel tired, fatigued, tensed, or have any discomfort, just sit down and let the experience of sitting be a cue to relax. Now feel good about yourself for learning how to relax at will. That's right.

Now, in a moment, I'm going to count back up to 20, one number at a time, and as I count you can know that you have had a very enjoyable experience, and each time you practice this you will get better and better at building an unconscious habit of relaxing.

1—2—3—4—5. And just as you have remembered to forget when you've skinned yourself in the yard, you can forget any sensation that is linked with an unpleasant situation or experience. And you can learn to remember to incorporate all of your experiences with pleasant experiences. That's right.

6—7—8—9—10. And learning the alphabet was a permanent learning, but at the time you didn't know that it was a permanent learning. You didn't know that you were forming permanent images in your mind. And when you learned script, it, too, seemed to be a difficult task, but, without knowing it, you were once again forming permanent images in your mind that would be very useful. And you remember all of these learnings that will last a lifetime. Every time you print or write you do it with an unconscious learning.

11—12—13—14—15. Sitting there reflecting by the stream and getting ready to leave this very peaceful and restful place. You know that, when you enjoy yourself, an hour can seem like a matter of minutes or minutes can seem like several hours. And you can see yourself getting up and preparing to leave. You know that you have learned many things today and you can discover that you have learned things that you didn't realize that you were learning. And that you have done good work and you can have a sense of pleasure in knowing that you can return to this private place and reflect any time that you have a need to feel restful and relaxed. And it will be nice to discover when your unconscious will use these new learnings. It may be today, tomorrow, or sometime next week. And your unconscious will guide you and protect you and only give your conscious what it feels will be useful to you to know, at its own pace, in its own way.

Now, in a moment, you will awaken from this very pleasant restful state as I continue to count and you will only remember what you will need to know. And you may think that nothing at all has happened, but you will feel completely refreshed and relaxed as if you had had several hours of restful sleep. And at the count of 20, you will open your eyes and gradually feel wide awake and alert. And your body can feel as if it has just had a very refreshing nap.

16—17—18—19 and 20. Wide awake and refreshed.

(This terminates the Hypnotic Induction Analgesia Procedure.)

E. Surgery

After mastering the use of hypnosis in pain management, this author had the opportunity to use hypnosis to prepare clients for pending surgeries. After successful utilization with an obstetrical patient, hypnosis was used successfully to alleviate the anxiety experienced before surgery. The following script was used with an elderly religious woman having great anxiety, due to her age, about another surgery. Although the script is presented verbatim to demonstrate specific pacing and leading to meet her individual needs, it can be modified to meet the unique needs of any client. This presentation begins after a preliminary trance induction similar to the ones on the preceding pages:

You already know something about the unconscious. For it has been protecting you in your dreams. It has let you forget unpleasant memories that your conscious can't remember. It has awakened you every morning and it has helped you remember some of your favorite passages from the Bible, and it will continue to help you and guide you with any problems or needs that you might have, such as this inconvenient operation that you are about to have. You have been in a hospital before. It is an unfortunate inconvenience but a necessary inconvenience that will help you in the long run. And you know that this is true. Just like the other inconvenient operations that others that you know have had to have due to unfortunate circumstances. And they, too, were able to effectively cope with them, for they knew that they would only be inconvenienced for a short period of time.

So now let your unconscious mind help prepare you for this upcoming event by letting you realistically visualize what will probably happen this coming week. You will probably go to church on Sunday and enjoy the service and talk to the other parishioners who are your friends, and they and the minister will pray for you. You will then come home and enjoy a pleasant Sunday knowing that you are a good Christian woman and that the Lord will take care of you. And you can have a good night's sleep and wake up feeling refreshed and well-rested, reminding yourself of your faith in the Lord, and knowing that you can do all things through Jesus Christ who strengthens you. And you can feel peaceful knowing that you will be well taken care of. If you only have the faith of the grain of a mustard seed, you know that the Lord will be with you.

Now see yourself saying your evening prayers and feeling good about yourself. And waking up feeling quite refreshed and rested, as you feel now. You may feel somewhat apprehensive, but this is normal—and nothing to concern yourself about, for this is the body's way of meeting the demand of the operation.

See yourself being taken to the hospital with someone who is very close to you and who really cares about you, knowing that your husband will also be well taken care of during your absence by a close member of the family.

At the hospital you will be required to fill out some papers and have some tests taken such as a blood test, x-rays, or whatever is required. And then you will be assigned a room. Now, see yourself in your room reading the Bible and other materials that you have brought with you. Knowing that you have faith in the Lord, and that your husband is being well provided for by those who love him. And you can relax. Relax by taking several deep breaths and thinking these thoughts and relaxing. And then having a restful sleep.

In the morning you will be prepped for surgery, and be given an anesthetic before and probably during the operation, and the Lord's hand will be guiding the doctor's skills, and you know that he is a good doctor for he has operated on your daughter, and delivered your granddaughter, with whom you have found such delight and pleasure.

When the anesthetic wears off you may feel druggy and not yourself, but only for a short time. You will probably feel some discomfort, but if it becomes more than you want to bear a nurse will give you something for relief. And once relieved, you can once again become more relaxed and rested.

And, as you rest, you can reminisce about past pleasant experiences that you have enjoyed and take great delight in them. You can listen to the tape that you have, or you can continue to read the Bible and other materials that you've brought.

Now, see yourself enjoying the company that you will be seeing, and feeling yourself healing and becoming stronger every day, and looking forward to coming home and resuming your life. And feel at ease with yourself, knowing that this is only a temporary inconvenience and will soon be over, and feel good about yourself for having effectively coped with it.

Now, you can awaken yourself by counting backwards from 20 to 1, and awaken feeling completely refreshed and rested as if you had had several hours of restful sleep. Begin counting.

As a follow-up to preparing an individual for surgery, hypnosis can also be used to aid in the healing process as well as managing pain after surgery. Personal experience has shown that individuals can heal in about half the time that healing normally requires, e.g. about four weeks instead of six weeks. However, follow-up care and instructions from the physician should be followed. Modifications of the following script have been successfully used with clients having eye surgery, mastectomies, and other cancer related surgeries, as well as obstetrical procedures. Notice that the healing suggestions are similar to the section on medical conditions but are more general. However, the suggestions can be made more specific. The following presentation is to be used as a guide and begins after the preliminary trance induction.

Now, while you're in this very relaxed state, visualize your body healing itself. See rich, red, healthy blood cells flowing through your body, carrying nutrients and oxygen to aid the white blood cells, and to nurture and heal your body, going to any part of your body that needs repair. See the white blood cells smoothing over these areas and healing your body. See healthy tissue growing over and replacing deteriorated dead cells, helping the normal cells grow in health. Feel yourself growing in health. See yourself having more energy and feeling increasingly comfortable.

Whenever you feel any discomfort in your body, picture the army of white blood cells flowing into that area and soothing the discomfort. Whatever the problem, give your body the command to *heal itself*. Visualize your body becoming healthier and healthier. And see yourself active, doing what you like to do. See your purpose in life being fulfilled, your relationships with people becoming more meaningful.

See yourself participating in your own recovery by doing this exercise at least once a day for several weeks, and noticing the difference in how you feel.

And it's nice to discover that we can alter our lives in ways that we can resolve our problems by gaining more control over our mind and our body in the direction of our health.

No one knows how long it will take. I don't know, and you don't know how long it will take before you begin to notice yourself feeling healthier. It may be today, tomorrow, or some time during the next two weeks, because you don't know which alternative your unconscious will choose to let your body recover.

So just continue to relax and enjoy these pleasant feelings of complete relaxation and know that, any time you choose, you can return to this pleasant relaxed state. For in a moment you will awaken yourself by counting backwards from 20 to 1, and you will awaken knowing that you have successfully completed this exercise in participating in your own recovery. And you will feel completely refreshed and relaxed, as if you had had several hours of restful sleep. Begin counting.

F. Phantom Limb Pain

A student referred her out-of-state elderly father for one hypnotherapy session to help him with multiple difficulties in his later life. He was a newly retired skilled laborer. His leg had been recently amputated due to poor circulation that resulted in blood clotting in the leg. He was still sore from surgery, and was in physical therapy to learn how to balance himself with a prosthesis, and was having difficulty balancing himself on parallel bars. He was a proud man who had become dependent on his supportive wife, and was frustrated with believing he was useless and a burden to others. He felt forced to retire because he had become legally blind and could not fine tune tools anymore, as well as being dependent on family members to drive him places and read to him. He had also been a musician and had played several instruments when he was younger. He and his wife were quite religious and had a deep faith in the healing process. He had never been in psychotherapy and knew nothing about hypnosis. He only came to the session at his daughter's request. Although he was doubtful about hypnosis helping him, he did appear to be open-minded and willing to give this "young doctor" a chance to help him.

He was wheeled into my office, and introductions were made by his daughter. She then left. This young hypnotherapist (TLS) was nervous due to the expectations of the student and the desire to succeed with this likeable elderly man. Thus about a 20 minute interview was initiated to establish rapport and obtain necessary information for the trance work which then lasted approximately two hours. The formal hypnotherapy began with the floating hand levitation induction (Chapter 8) and was followed with guided imagery to the beach since this was a favorite vacation for him. Following the imagery work was the Early Learning Set (Chapter 7) incorporating learning the alphabet. Following this long-forgotten learning experience was a description of how a baby learns to walk. A detailed description was given of how a baby has to learn balancing one day while holding onto a chair, shifting weight to balance the body on two legs (not feet); and about the numerous times a baby has to fall down and get back up in order to learn to walk for the first time; and how he already had the programming for walking, but had to modify that already acquired learning in a new way. Then he was told anecdotes of how one forgets names, places, and car keys, from my own personal experience, and finally about injuries obtained while working on a car, e.g. cuts and scrapes on the hands, but being too busy to notice it. This amnesia technique proved to be effective in alleviating the soreness from the surgery and the fitting of the prosthesis. This was followed by a story of how another patient successfully learned how to balance himself and walk with a prosthesis. Further pacing and leading suggestions were offered with another metaphor regarding how callouses gradually grow on a farmer's hands as he begins hoeing a garden until the palms and fingers became hard and pain is no longer felt, and hoeing becomes easier. Guided imagery similar to the medical conditions scripts regarding circulation and the body healing itself were then offered. His frustration was then addressed by reminding him of how difficult and frustrating it was to learn how to play the piano, but that he had succeeded, and that he could use that ability to overcome the frustration of learning to walk with a prosthesis. A support metaphor was then used to remind him of the pride he had in his wife whom he could depend on. The trance work was terminated with guided imagery taking him to the beach before awakening.

The student informed me that her father returned feeling much better and had no difficulty learning to walk with the prosthesis.

G. Respirator Phobia

A fireman was told by the Chief of the Fire Department that hypnosis could possibly help him. He had been a fireman for about five years, and the Chief wanted to retain him but would have to let him go if he could not wear a respirator. During a fire drill, he had spontaneously developed a respirator phobia. Further discussion revealed that he had had asthma as a child and he remembered how afraid he had been each time the doctor put him on a respirator. He kept remembering the doctor's big hands and how helpless he felt. He reported that he was afraid of not breathing and dying.

During the second session, he was easily placed in a trance utilizing the floating hand induction. He was instructed to quickly review everything he knew about respirators at my signal and in 20 seconds he would be told to stop. He was then told:

> Now. Begin at the beginning. And go all the way through quickly. With a tremendous rush of force skipping nothing. Including everything. And reach a complete understanding of everything about respirators. Stop. You now know you understand. You no longer need to fear. You don't even need to remember when you awake. But your unconscious now knows and will continue to know, and to completely understand, and give you the ease that you want. And each time you put on that respirator you will become more comfortable. You will become more relaxed. Now, see yourself at home. And as you put on that respirator you're going into a trance. And you know everything there is to know about respirators, and you're walking around the house feeling comfortable. Now see yourself at work. The fire alarm rings. You quickly grab your gear, especially your respirator. You're at the scene fighting the fire and you hear a baby crying from inside about the same age as your youngest child. And, without thinking about it, you quickly put on your respirator. See yourself courageously fighting smoke and fire, coming to the rescue of that small child. And you came out of the building carrying that child. You saved his life. By your courage and your life-saving respirator. And your fellow firemen are cheering you on. Your respirator and you. You and your respirator. Now awaken with the good feelings.

A week later this fireman called and told me that he was cooking supper for his children. He was holding his youngest and wearing the respirator.

H. Impotency

This individual was in his early thirties, and had been employed as a machinist for fourteen years. His wife had died of cancer after ten years of marriage. He reported that, during the last five years of marriage, "Everything I did was seldom right and not enough." He became impotent when she died. He was presently attending a community college to further his education and had no difficulty meeting women but was unable to have an erection. There was a woman who lived down the street who wanted a relationship with him and frequently invited him for dinner, but he only wanted friendship. Overall, he was thought to be an over-achiever and tried too hard. After the sixth session, he reported that he was beginning to enjoy sex again and terminated the sessions.

The following are parts of the hypnosis script that this author believed was instrumental in solving this problem.

1. First Session

Before you go into a trance tonight, I'd like to ask you some questions. I've been wondering about how you maintain your impotence. Now, I'd like you to look at that spot, and I'm going to talk to you. That's right. And slowly close your eyes.

Think about what impotence is. ... What keeps you feeling that way? ... You felt helpless. ... And you do the same thing over and over and then you feel the same way. ... I wonder what you kept telling yourself while you were married and since her death and what you keep telling yourself now. Now, these thoughts and images have been trying to escape and you have held onto them. It's time to let go, now. ... Now, see a good time when you enjoyed sex when you were younger. Do it now. ... And I want you to keep seeing these images throughout the week.

2. Second Session

I want you to relearn something that you haven't thought about for some time.

When you get hot, different parts of your body become flushed with blood and become swollen and hard. The harder you try, the harder they get. And you don't know when it will subside.

You can isolate different parts of your body and they can feel flushed with blood and become hard. And you have to figure out how to release that tension. You can leave the office with a tingling sensation in your hand. Knowing that you know a lot without knowing that you know.

3. Third Session

Now, I want you to go into a trance. ... That's right. Now, I'm going to talk to you.

We have learned that our nose gets harder in the winter time. And people don't use it. I want you to relearn something that you haven't thought about using. When you get hot, different parts of your body become flushed with blood and become swollen and, until you learn that, the harder you try, the harder it gets. And you don't know when it will subside.

You can isolate the different parts of your body, and they can feel flushed with blood and become hard. And you have to figure out how to relieve that tension. When we blush, we don't know how to turn it off. The harder it becomes, the more turned on your body becomes. Now, awaken with a tingling sensation in your hand. I wonder what else will happen and I wonder how embarrassed you can be when you can't stop blushing, but it is nice to be surprised.

4. Fourth Session

Now, I want you to go into a trance. ... That's right. And you can remember your past trance experiences. ...

I want you to relearn something else that you haven't thought about using. When your nose gets harder, we learned this in the winter time—people don't use it. When you get hot, the different parts of your body become flushed with blood and become swollen. And the harder you try, the harder it gets. And you really don't know when it will subside. You don't know when you will find relief.

And when we blush, we don't know exactly how it got turned on. And don't know how to turn it off.

5. Fifth Session

Look at that spot and go into a trance. That's right. That's right.

I think it would be interesting to attempt this as soon as possible. You have had a complete physical and know that you can relax. You have a fear about getting involved with a woman because it could lead to marriage, and one has to protect his possessions. Just because friends have remarried quickly and have gotten divorced doesn't mean it always turns out that way until we know the reasons they got married. There is no reason why this will happen to you. You are expected to fulfill your needs after two years. All your life, you've been helping others and trying to meet their needs by working overtime to support your family, and it has not always been successful.

You are a very achieving type of person, who likes to accomplish things in life. You get satisfaction out of working. You have a lot of experience working with a screwing machine. You have experience with tools. You have worked on a production line. And you have been able to sustain *long hard* working hours in the past. And because of that you have been able to sustain it in the present and can continue to do so now.

You can't get away from working hard and long with screwing and production machinery. You have been working with screwing machines and production for nineteen and a half years in a general machine tool room. And you're capable of learning new things— new ways of thinking about things—new ways of doing things. You are going to the community college to gain new learnings and don't know exactly what you are learning and will continue to learn.

You've learned in a book how hypnosis can induce a post-hypnotic suggestion that a person can get an erection by fluffing up a pillow and then consummate the sex act with a woman. Now, you know the power of hypnosis. You can recall a time many years ago when you were a teenager and observed how a post-hypnotic suggestion was employed very successfully.

You also know that very attractive women are difficult to please. They expect more than other women who have pleasant personalities. And you know this from experience just as you know from experience that there are many traits that make a man. Traits that you admire such as honesty, integrity, and good honest communication and sharing. You know that no one performs to their potential all the time, and you don't have to perform up to someone's expectations. Sometimes we have good days and sometimes other days are not as good. And, on those days, you don't have to perform at all. And, on some days, your performance is average and that's all that is expected, but that is satisfactory. And you need not feel obliged to give any more than your body is willing to give at that point in time, and any other point in time, on some days you don't have to perform at all.

And just like a car. On some days, when you start a car, it's sluggish. The motor has to run for a while before it gets going, and the more the motor runs, the better it gets. And you can tell when it has been running enough—when it's hot enough. And, when it is ready, you can put it in gear. And when it gets going, it goes fine. Now, I want to shift onto something else.

You know that you have no problem finding a sex partner, and there are many women who are willing but unattractive to you. You are only willing to go to bed with those women who have pleasing personalities. You are not expected to please them all the time. Sometimes, you are simply not in the mood. But other times, you are in the mood, and spontaneous sex can be very enjoyable.

So, I want you to see yourself with a woman who is attractive, but not pretty. A woman whom you know who has a very pleasant personality and who really enjoys your company. Who really likes you for who you are. Who likes your honesty, wit and humor. Someone who you can be comfortable with. I want you to see yourself with her in a very comfortable setting. You are talking to each other and having a good time. Now, see the two of you embracing one another and, maybe, some sexual foreplay. I don't know. This woman really likes you and accepts you the way you are. She is happy with anything that you can give her because, no matter what you give, it is you she wants to be with. She is happy with whatever you can give her at the time, and you don't have to do anything. And, as your body is responding to her touch and her body to yours, you can feel very good about yourself for responding to her responding. But I don't know how *you're going to reach a climax*. I don't know what *you're going to do*. Because after you get warmed up, you have to drive and drive before you reach a climax. I don't know *when you will climax*. And she doesn't know when *you will reach a climax*. The first few minutes seem like a long time, and five minutes seems longer, and ten minutes seems even longer, and, the harder you try to reach a climax, the *harder it becomes*. After fifteen minutes, you hope you can reach a climax in twenty-five minutes. But it will probably be between twenty-five and thirty minutes until you stop. That's right. And you can wonder how long it will take next time, and how hard it must be, as you feel yourself completely satisfied, as you look into her happy face. Now, simply relax.

And, now, I want you to know that you have accomplished things today, and that you will accomplish many other things in your life. But you don't know yet what things you will achieve or exactly how you will achieve them.

You don't know exactly what makes a car sluggish one day and exactly what makes it run smoothly another day. But you do know how screwing machines and tool machines work, and you can control the outcome of these machines. And you can't get away from working hard just as you have been working hard here today. You have learned much about yourself today. But you don't know when your unconscious mind is going to use these new learnings. I don't know if it will be tonight. It might be a Saturday or a Sunday night. Monday is the beginning work day and Wednesday is the middle of the week, and Friday is a good finish. Now, we are finished here today and you can awaken by counting backwards from twenty to one.

I. Ejaculatio Praecox

Erickson entitled this case "Psychotherapy Achieved by a Reversal of the Neurotic Processes in a Case of Ejaculatio Praecox." The patient was a 38-year-old single man who had suffered from premature ejaculation since his first attempt at sexual relations when he had been 20 years old. This experience had frightened and humiliated him. He had not attempted sexual intercourse again for several years. All of his attempts had ended in failure.

The successful therapeutic procedure utilized by Erickson follows:

> Therapy was begun by inducing a light trance on the patient and impressing upon him, most tediously, that the "light trance" was a most important measure. Its purpose, he was told repetitiously, was to ensure that he had both a conscious and an unconscious understanding of the fact that a deep hypnotic trance would settle once and for all time whether or not he could ever succeed in sex relations. Two hours of repetition of these general ideas resulted in a deep trance, but no effort was made to give him an awareness of this fact. An amnesia, spontaneous or one indirectly suggested, was desired for therapeutic purposes.

> Then, as a posthypnotic suggestion, he was told that he must, absolutely must, get a wristwatch. If at all possible, this wristwatch should have an illuminated dial and illuminated hands. Absolutely imperative was the fact that the watch should have a second hand. The second hand, it was stressed over and over, would be absolutely necessary.

> A second posthypnotic suggestion was given that he must, and could, and would thenceforth sleep with a night-light at his bedside so that he could tell time to the very second at any time during the night, since he must, absolutely must, and would wear his wristwatch whenever he should happen to be in bed.

> Solemn promises in relation to these demands were secured from the patient with no effort on his part to question the author's reasons for his various insistences.

It was then explained to him that he would continue his "useless inviting of girls to spend the night" with him. To this he also agreed, whereupon it was emphasized that only in this way could he find out what he "really really really would want to learn."

The next posthypnotic suggestion was presented most carefully, in a gentle, yet emphatic tone of voice, commanding, without seeming to command, the patient's full attention and his full willingness to be obedient to it. This suggestion was a purportedly soundly based medical explanation of the expectable development, on an organic physiological basis, of his "total problem." This was the fact that his premature ejaculation, by virtue of body changes from ageing processes, would be diametrically changed. The explanation was the following posthypnotic suggestion:

Do you know, can you possibly realize, can you genuinely understand, that medically all things, everything, even the worst of symptoms and conditions, must absolutely come to an end—*but not, but not, I must emphasize, not in the way a layman would understand?* Do you realize, do you understand, are you in any way aware, that your premature ejaculation *will end in a failure,* no matter how long your erection lasts, no matter how long and actively you engage in coitus, you will fail to have an ejaculation for 10, for 10 long, for 15 long minutes, for 20, for 25 minutes? Even more? Do you realize how desperately you will strive and strive, how desperately you will watch the minute hand and the second hand of your wristwatch, wondering, just wondering if you will fail, fail, fail to have an ejaculation at 25 minutes, at 25½, at 26, at 26½ minutes? Or will it be at 27½ minutes? (This last said in tones expressive of deep relief.)

And the next morning you still will not believe, just can't believe, that you won't fail to have an ejaculation, and so you will have to discover again, to discover again, if you really really can have an ejaculation, but it won't be, it can't be, at 27½ minutes, nor even at 28, nor even at 29 minutes. Just the desperate hope will be in your mind that maybe, just maybe, maybe at 33 minutes, or 34, or 35 minutes the ejaculation will come. And at the time, all the time, you will watch desperately the wristwatch and strive so hard lest you fail, fail again, to ejaculate at 27 minutes, and the 33, 34, 35 minutes will seem never, just never, to be coming with an ejaculation.

And now this is what I want you to do. Find one of the girls you are used to. Walk her to your apartment. When you come to the corner at 8th, even as you turn right (all of this was said with the utmost of intensity), try so very hard to keep your mind on the conversation, but notice that you can't help counting one by one the cracks in the sidewalk until you turn into the court way and step upon the board-walk. With complete intensity you are to try hard, very hard to keep your mind on the conversation, but keep desperately counting the cracks, the cracks between the boards, the cracks under you [to the unsophisticated, slang often gives opportunities for double meanings], all those cracks all along the way to your apartment until it seems that you will never never never get there, and what a profound relief it will be to enter, to feel comfortable, to be at ease, to give your attention to the girl, and then, and then, to bed, but not the usual—but the answer, the real real real answer, and from the moment you enter [pause] the apartment [pause], your mind will be on your wristwatch, the watch that, as time goes by, can, at long last, bring you the answer.

Quickly now, keep all that I have said in your unconscious mind—locked up, not a syllable, not a word, not a meaning forgotten—to be kept there, used, obeyed fully, completely. You can even forget me, all about me—just obey fully— then you can remember just me and come back and tell me that the wristwatch was right when it read 27½ minutes and when it read 33, 34, and 35.

Arouse now, completely rested and refreshed, understanding in your unconscious mind the completeness of the task to be done. The patient aroused, seemed puzzled, and departed hurriedly. (Erickson and Rossi, 1980, Vol. IV, pp. 351–353.)

Three days after the last session, the patient excitedly telephoned Erickson. He made an appointment and gave a detailed account of having coitus with a woman. He married and was still having good sexual relations with his wife after seven years.

J.   Menstrual Function

That menstruation may be precipitated, delayed, interrupted, or prolonged by strong emotional stress is a common observation. While menstruation appears to be an involuntary biological function, the mind has the ability to alter its duration, its timing, emotional stress, and any accompanying physical discomfort.

The following two cases by Erickson show how menstruation can be controlled through hypnosis.

Case 1

In "Control of Physiological Functions by Hypnosis," Erickson gave the following account of a woman in her thirties who had irregular and painful menses:

Painful Menses

Each period resulted in daily severe headaches, vomiting, gastrointestinal disturbances, and actual invalidism for five days; no invalidism the first day and no invalidism the last day. She wanted medical help, but she did not want psychotherapy. However, she consented to go into a trance to please me. I was perfectly willing to be pleased. A deep trance was induced in her, and she was instructed that on any Saturday night she chose, she would have a dream in which she would telescope time. In the dream she would experience a whole week's menstrual invalidism; that is, the dream would seem to last five whole days. She would be invalided, she would dream that she was vomiting, having diarrhea, cramps, and everything else that went with her past history; but that she would sleep soundly and wake up the next morning rested, refreshed, and energetic. Moreover, she would awake with an amnesia for the dream experience, and the dream experience itself would result in a satisfactory menstrual period later.

Two weeks later she was surprised to find herself menstruating without any difficulty, without an invalidism, with no pain, no discomfort. She came to me and asked me what I had done, what had happened. She had had a lifelong experience of having painful menstruation, and here she was feeling like a queen—perfectly comfortable, perfectly at ease. Why didn't she have cramps? What was wrong? In the trance state she knew exactly what I had done, but consciously she had no awareness whatsoever of it. Since then, and that was several years ago, she has had no painful menstrual periods whatsoever. Everything has gone along perfectly all right. She is regular in her menstruation and has no pain, no discomfort, no distress. I think that she can readily come under the heading of controlled physiological functioning. The measure was indirect, but the history certainly warrants the belief that if I hadn't done that sort of thing, she would have continued to have painful menstrual periods. (Erickson and Rossi, 1979, Vol. II, pp. 182–183)

Case 2

This case was taken from "Psychogenic Alteration of Menstrual Functioning: Three Instances." The second case will be quoted here. Erickson gave the following account of a woman who used autohypnosis to alter her menses as follows:

Altering Menstrual Function

An artist's model with a regular menstrual cycle and a history of profuse flow in the first few days was offered an unexpected assignment in nude posing on the second day of her period. She had had previous unsatisfactory experience with intravaginal tampons and was about to refuse the assignment when she recalled her previous experimental work with a physician interested in hypnosis and psychosomatic medicine. This led her to accept the assignment with the intention of employing autohypnosis, with which she was experienced, to inhibit her menstrual flow. A telephone call to this writer confirmed her in her intention, but no helpful advice could be given to her except that she should rely upon the capacity of her unconscious mind to function competently.

Shortly before reporting for work she developed an autohypnotic trance and in some manner unknown to her conscious mind she inhibited the flow from 7:00 p.m. until her return home at 11:00 p.m., after 2½ hours of posing in the nude. She employed no precautions; and, as she explained, she "forgot" her period "both psychologically and physiologically." "I didn't remember after I came out of the autohypnotic trance that it was my menstrual period, and I didn't recall that fact until the flow steadily resumed as I was preparing for bed. I just forgot it as completely physiologically as I did psychologically. I still don't know how I did it."

On another occasion, where the values of the situation were significant, this same young woman discovered that her regular menstrual period would intervene and bar her attendance. Again she consulted this writer, who explained that the appearance of the menses was often temporarily altered by various physiological forces, and hence, in view of her past experience in inhibiting menses, she might try the experiment of delaying her period. Instead, because she thought it the safer procedure, she induced her period 10 days early.

Subsequently, she postponed her period experimentally for 10 days, beginning the period of delay the day before her period was to begin, and after the usual molimina had indicated that the menses were about to begin. (Erickson and Rossi, 1980, Vol. II, pp. 208–209)

K. Summary

This chapter has been presented to demonstrate how one can masterfully use hypnosis in various ways to assist individuals with varying requests and needs, including medical conditions. Remember, these presentations are offered as guides. You are only limited by your own creative minds and mastery of hypnosis.

Exercises

1. What other common habits would yield to the type of interventions described in this chapter?

2. Read through the detailed scripts in this chapter highlighting the language forms used.

3. Read through the detailed scripts in this chapter and indicate how you would deliver them, i.e. which words or phrases would you mark out for special delivery, and where would you put in pauses.

4. Develop your own detailed scripts for the conditions described in this chapter. Tape them and critique your delivery.

5. Are there any conditions in your experience that would require different approaches to the ones described here? What would you do differently?

6. Would you feel comfortable using the strong negative imagery in the script in this chapter?

7. Are there any other medical conditions that make sense to treat in these ways? (Always in conjunction with medical personnel.)

Chapter 15

Ericksonian Approaches in Medicine

Sandra M. Sylvester, Ph.D.

A. Introduction

Those of us who have chosen medicine as a way of life want nothing more than to be a healer. But, in order to be a healer in another's life, we first must be willing to go on a journey along an uncharted path. And we must go alone.

The journey may be long or short. It may hold one overwhelming crisis, or a series of little obstacles or annoyances. It may hold the greatest fear of all—that of facing death—or little "scaries" that cause a spontaneous gasp as each one occurs.

In the manner in which each of us responds on the journey, one decision at a time, we learn to live in balance with the rhythms of nature and the universe. It is then that we feel expansion and contraction, solidity and emptiness, substantiality and insubstantiality, begin to separate. We learn that nothing exists without its opposite. There is nothing that does not change in order to be permanent. We learn that opposites, although different, complement each other, that continuous movement occurs between them: just as when night reaches its final moment, day dawns and when day reaches its zenith, the light fades into night.

All of nature has this continuous movement. The earth moves around the sun, causing the movement and flow of one season into another, producing annual rhythms. The earth rotating on its axis, the flow of day and night, causes Circadian rhythms. The hormonal rhythms of one and one-half to two-hour fluctuations cause Ultradian rhythms. (Rossi, 1994; Rossi and Nimmons, 1991) It is these rhythms in nature that are the underpinnings of the spontaneous hypnotic trances that occur in 90 to 120 minute cycles, and are the basis for the use of clinical hypnosis in healing. (Rossi, 1994)

B. The Use of Clinical Hypnosis in Medicine

Clinical hypnosis has been widely used in medicine, particularly for childbirth; for pain management; for controlling unconscious and autonomic processes such as gag reflexes, thumb-sucking, enuresis, hypertension, etc.; for stress management in anxiety, cardiac care, and auto-immune diseases; and to augment the healing process (Hammond, 1990). Interest in clinical hypnosis has been varied between periods of great interest to periods of little interest. The most common reason for not wanting to use hypnosis is the perception that it takes too much time and that drugs work faster and more reliably. This may be due to the fact that hypnosis, as it has been traditionally used in medicine, has been *done to* the patient instead of something the patient *does himself or herself.*

Central to an understanding of hypnosis and hypnotherapy is the idea that in order for hypnosis to be effective, periods of self-hypnosis (or centering, or meditation) are best incorporated into daily life. This can be accomplished in a formal way by setting aside 20-minute sessions spaced throughout the day; or informally, utilizing what Erickson referred to as "naturalistic" trance, and Rossi refers to as Ultradian Rhythms which occur, wave-like, in 1½ to 2-hour patterns, throughout the day (Rossi and Lippincott, 1993; Rossi and Nimmons, 1991). In this way, self-hypnosis can be practiced on a daily basis. All too often we think of hypnosis as a learned skill; however, knowing "about" hypnosis or knowing "how to do hypnosis" is not enough, it is the actual "doing" that is important.

In using hypnosis for medical problems, are we then saying that all medical problems are "psycho-somatic"? In Western medicine we continue to struggle with unlearning a Cartesian vocabulary where the body and the mind were artificially dichotomized 400 years ago. Scientific evidence supports the concept that the body and mind are two aspects of the same whole (Ader, 1993). Eastern medicine and philosophy has always held this notion of the body/mind as indivisible and inseparable (Eisenberg, 1993, and Kaptchuk 1983). In fact, the vocabulary does not exist in Eastern cultures to separate the two. The application of clinical hypnosis to medical problems assumes the body/mind to be inseparable.

Milton H. Erickson, M.D., through his own experiences in dealing with polio and the multiple complications consequent to polio, used his own illness as an opportunity for self-knowledge and self-awareness (Sylvester, 1993). He always assumed that the body and the mind were inextricably connected even before Hans Selye linked psychological stress and physical disease (Selye, 1956); Robert Ader linked psychological classical conditioning with the physical immune system (Ader, 1981); Candace Pert linked physical opiate receptor sites and endogenous morphines (Pert, 1993); and David Felten connected the information systems of the auto-immune system and the information systems of the nervous system (Felten, 1993). In fact, Erickson designed treatment protocols by utilizing the patient's emotional needs and building upon the patient's own psychophysiological resources in assisting him in achieving health through self-empowerment (Erickson, 1983). Erickson delighted in the fathomless possibilities of the human spirit to maintain hope, to reinterpret sensory stimuli, to resolve symptoms (Erickson, 1986).

C. Applying Hypnosis to Medical Problems

In discussing the application of clinical hypnosis to medical problems, a three-step process will be described for designing a hypnotic approach to medical patients. This will be followed by three brief case histories illustrating the application of this process.

In applying clinical hypnosis to medicine, it is well to note that any patient coming to any doctor has anxiety. In the presence of anxiety, normal human dependency needs come into play. This anxiety state induces a trance state recognizable in the following hypnoidal behaviors: far-away expression, glassy-eyed stare, smoothing of facial expression, lag in responsiveness, preoccupation, inward focusing, repetitive movements such as nodding/shaking head, and slow deep respirations. If the physician is aware of these indicators of trance, these can be used to help the patient by presenting constructive ideas or suggestions, softly, slowly, vividly; interpreting what is happening, teaching the patient how to respond, what to expect. Seize this moment of rapt attention by giving positive suggestion.

A Three-Step Process

Step one: Through interviews with the patient, come to know what the patient's understanding of the problem is. This is Erickson's utilization of the patient's world view: attending to the patient's words, concepts, knowledge about the causes, progression, and regression of symptoms (knowing how the patient views improvement vs. worsening of his condition), etc. Also, learn what the patient feels *passionately* about, what gives *meaning* to that particular patient's life.

Step two: Reframing the patient's view into one where he controls what he can control, and gives up trying to change what he cannot. Sometimes, if a professional just hints to a patient that something is possible, the patient will make it so.

Step three: Designing a therapy with measurable gains.

Many references are available which give samplings of inductions used for specific purposes by experienced clinicians (Hammond, 1990; Klippstein, 1991). This chapter will discuss the concepts involved in designing hypnotic interventions as an adjunct to medical treatments, rather that give specific therapeutic inductions. Three brief case studies will be offered as illustrations of the concepts involved.

In the past, when a search for organic causes of a disease or a dysfunction could not be found, a patient was told, "It is all in your head." Today, we view this differently. Since the mind is inextricably intertwined with the body, what is "mental" cannot be separated from what is "physical." Every disease that affects the body affects the body/mind, just as each and every attitude, fear, and belief affect the body/mind.

1. *Patient 1: MS patient, Priscilla*

Priscilla, a 35-year-old married female, came to her physician with vague symptoms of muscle weakness and disturbances of vision. She was subsequently given a diagnosis of MS. Priscilla used self-hypnosis and meditation to build serenity and calmness. She used an image of warm oil flowing down her body and washing away stiffness and weakness. She used this meditative technique for two years, and went into remission for 12 years.

This year she began to re-experience symptoms of MS when her leg "quit working" while she was on a walk with her husband. She was told by her physician that, with this flare-up, she had crossed over the line which separated benign MS from the active form. She talked about riding her bike and falling over because, when she went to slip her foot out of the toe clips, her leg wouldn't work. She was frightened in dealing with the diagnosis of a chronic, progressive, debilitating disease for which there is, as yet, no established treatment or cure. She wanted to do the hypnotic work she did 10 years earlier, because she attributed this to "making the MS go away."

Besides wondering about the course of the disease, she is concerned about the following aspects of her life: "Will I become a burden to my family?" "How long will I be able to maintain my independence?" "Will I be the exception and beat this disease?" "How can I stop myself from "awful-izing" every time I notice a muscle twinge or weakness?" "Should I share my fears with the significant people in my life, or should I try to be positive with others and handle my fears alone?"

We discussed the fact that the MS patient is on an uncharted course. For the most part, as far as traditional medicine is concerned, there is no known treatment or cure for MS, and there is no predictable pattern for the progression of the disease for an individual patient(Scheinberg, 1983). So Priscilla would have to become an expert in her own care. It is only through her personal experience that she will learn what works and what doesn't work for her. She already knows that stress exacerbates her symptoms. The task is to avoid panic. For panic sets up the underpinnings of voodoo death (Cousins, 1981).

Therapy, Priscilla decided, is not so much building muscle and strength, as it is in re-educating the nervous system to build new neurological communication networks to regain a sense of balance. We designed a hypnotherapeutic approach. This included relaxation together with practicing balancing techniques to explore the question, "How do I stimulate my nerves to build new connections?" trusting that nerve stimulation will, in turn, stimulate the muscles.

Discussion—Maintaining *hope* in the midst of a disease with no known treatment or cure is critical. It is also true that we are just beginning to learn to tap into the resources of the body/mind. Medical literature is full of interesting cures attributed to "misdiagnosis" or the placebo effect. Teaching the patient skills so that she can be an active participant in her treatment gives her a goal with achievable results. Meditative techniques calm her mind, remove panic and reduce stress. Balancing techniques retrain the nervous system, enabling her to fully use the intact neurological functions that she does have, and learn neurologically to compensate for those which have been lost.

2.   Patient 2: Acute pain patient, Phyllis

Phyllis, a 50 year old with a congenital vertebral malformation and scoliosis, had back surgery to rebuild an unformed vertebra and stabilize her scoliosis. The patient became very active in seeking out this surgical repair. She did personal research so that she had a thorough understanding of the procedure involved. She interviewed other surgical patients who had had the same procedure and questioned them thoroughly regarding the post-operative course of recovery. She measured herself against the other patients and concluded that she would do just fine. Her understanding of the surgery was that she would have bone scooped from her pelvis and grafted onto a vertebra. Then her body would grow bone from the graft to form half of a vertebra which had never formed genetically. She would also have a titanium rod inserted to stabilize her spine.

This particular patient was a gardener. She and her husband were in the process of completing a private garden with mountain views. She had personally selected all the plants. She learned to recognize the signs of a plant that was setting out new roots and was establishing itself in the garden. Likewise, she could recognize plants that did not form roots and were withering, and was replacing these. She knew intimately the process of planting plugs of ground cover that would grow and spread out to fill in bare spots.

Phyllis began to realize that she could use the same process in her recovery that she saw unfolding in her garden. She would have a plug of bone, which, like her ground cover, would grow and spread to fill in the "bare spots." She was reminded that plants take a whole season to grow and set out roots. And that one could not rush a natural process. She used this visualization to prepare for surgery.

After surgery, her surgeon told her she was very fortunate because her bones were strong. Phyllis said that this was true, her bones were strong and that she would grow bone and heal very well. Phyllis has had an uneventful recovery. Her post-operative pain has been minimal. Her disposition has been cheerful. Because of her successful recovery, Phyllis is extremely self-confident and is putting her renewed creative energy into her professional work.

Discussion—A highly motivated and resourceful patient follows minimal cues and is off and running with very little input needed from the outside. This patient had a passion for growing things. This passion led her on a very productive path for her recovery. The analogy of growth in a garden also helped her develop the patience she needed as her body sent out new growth, one cell at a time.

3. Patient 3: Cancer patient, George

The following case discusses two very different medical approaches with the same patient. Dr. S., an oncologist, is concerned with the quality of life of the patient. His approach is holistic, treating the body/mind. Dr. W., a radiation oncologist, is concerned with the progression of the disease process. He is more focused on the body, rather than the quality of life of the whole person. He is a scientist, looking at what medicine can do to prolong life. One of their patients is George.

George is a 58-year-old British man with metastatic renal cancer. Two and a half years prior to his symptoms and diagnosis, George retired from his own business as an international chemical engineering consultant to live in a motor home and spend quality time with his wife, exploring the United States, bird watching, and fishing. It was in his fishing boat, while vacationing in Washington

State, that he became symptomatic with renal disease. Within one week of his diagnosis, he had his left kidney removed. X-Rays revealed metastases, too numerous to count, in his lungs. However, the surgeon in Washington mentioned to George that in the case of renal cell cancer, when the primary site is removed, there can be a shrinking and disappearance of the secondary sites. (The life expectancy for George's type of cancer was approximately 6 months. Treatment in such cases is palliative.)

After 2 months' post-surgical recovery in Washington, George and his wife returned to New Mexico, so that George could have one oncologist oversee his care, develop a treatment plan, and follow him. George knew about the cancer in his kidney, which he felt was taken care of because the diseased kidney had been surgically removed. He saw the X-Rays of his lungs. He believed that he would recover and the cancer in his lungs would regress. George told his oncologist, Dr. S., that he had been troubled by depression in the past and was worried that he was becoming depressed while dealing with his cancer. Dr. S. talked to him at length about England and his own interest in fishing. Dr. S. told him that he did not think George would become depressed, because his depression had been so horrible that he would never allow himself to suffer such a depression again. He told George that George, himself, would do whatever it took to avoid depression. George thought that Dr. S. was correct. His depression was horrible. He did not want to become depressed. He felt relieved that he would not become depressed again. Dr. S. told him to do whatever he wanted to do as his strength permitted and to go on his planned trip to England.

After returning from a wonderful trip to England and Ireland, George noticed a rapidly growing, painful lump, at the site of his removed kidney. His oncologist, Dr. S., told him that was no problem, they could radiate the lump. George had a course of radiation which lasted 5 weeks. During this time, George stayed with us at my home and helped us design a very complex remodeling project. George said he dreamt about the project and would wake up at night with a new idea that he would sketch out the following day. X-Rays after his radiation revealed that the lesions on his lungs were getting remarkably smaller. In fact Dr. S. could not even see the lesions until George's wife pointed them out.

However, both George and Dr. S. concluded that they were indeed getting much smaller. Dr. S. told George that he was in the "lucky" 2% of the population who had regression of lung metastases. The tumor receded, the pain lessened, and George began slowly to regain his strength and hope. Dr. S. told him to go fishing. George continued to go fishing, he continued to explore new and beautiful places in the United States. With his wife, he took longer and longer hikes and built up his strength. He came back and checked-in with Dr. S. every two to three months. Both Dr. S. and George concluded that George in fact was doing quite well, and the quality of his life was indeed improving.

One year post-surgery, after many U.S. explorations *and much fishing*, plus another trip to England to see his newborn grand-daughter, George, on a visit to Dr. S., mentioned some discomfort in his ribs. Dr. S. said not to worry. If the discomfort continued, they could spot radiate his ribs if necessary. Two months later, on X-Ray, George had some problematic areas in his ribs, so they gave him a short course of radiation.

The irony is that, in the process of accepting life as it is, George felt more alive and was able to live more fully—even when facing death. For George, as for each of us, being healed is not the same as being cured. Being healed is the process of becoming whole, physically and psychologically. Healing can take place even as the body weakens. Healing comes from embracing life as it is—joy, anger and pain included. In working with any patient, it is impor-tant to note this distinction between cure and healing.

Discussion—George is now 1½ years post-surgery. This has been quality time for George. He has currently lived three times longer than expected and is still going strong.

T.X. Barber viewed hypnosis as a state of heightened suggestion, a state in which individuals give full credence to statements they hear about themselves and their capabilities. George was never formally hypnotized. He did receive positive suggestions for recovery from his oncologist and was deeply involved in a design project that totally occupied his waking thoughts and dream states. As his health improved throughout the year, he actually played a major part in the construction of this project.

In the year and a half since being diagnosed with renal cell cancer, George has caught approximately 200 trout and 138 salmon. He has been to Europe three times. He has explored Arizona, New Mexico, and California with his wife. He has spent quality time with a childhood friend, his family, and American friends. He has designed and helped build a complicated and intricate remodeling project. He has designed and built improvements in his motor home. He has hiked about 300 miles, seen thousands of birds, added 20 birds to his life list, and tamed a feral dog.

D. Conclusion

Healing is a process of becoming whole, even though a cure may not be possible. In nature, we are born, we grow, we mature, and we die, just as the seasons unfold in a year.

If illness is accepted as a change in the rhythm of life that can hold out new learnings and new challenges, then we can learn from illness as a teacher. Hypnosis and meditation help us to slow down enough to savor the experiences of life.

Chapter 16

Ericksonian Approaches in Dentistry

James M. Auld, B.D.S., Dip. Soc. Sc., Msc

A. Background

Dentists generally are caring people constantly working in a stressful environment. Of all health care professionals, they are the only ones who routinely perform potentially painful treatments in a very sensitive area of the body and have many of their patients experiencing significant anxiety during treatment. It would be extraordinary if this was not reflected in the behavior of the dentist, both in the interpersonal relationship with a patient and in the dentist's internal responses to the situation.

Given this environment, the dentist has several choices. The first (and worst) is to dissociate from the interaction and depersonalize the patient so that "only" the teeth are being treated. The second is to use drugs to sedate patients to a state where they avoid their stress; this is undoubtedly effective for the patient, and probably reduces the stress for the dentist, but introduces other risk and dependency factors. The third is to learn the psychological or interventional skills necessary to teach patients how to change their attitudes. A side effect of this is to give the dentist very powerful tools for his/her own stress management and personal development.

Hypnosis courses conducted by various professional and lay organizations have been for many years a favorite way of gaining these skills. This training has usually been confined to the use of traditional hypnotic techniques. But, as these traditional techniques can be quite time consuming and many dentists are reluctant to charge an appropriate fee for this time, they are not widely used. To facilitate treatment with hypnosis where this was indicated, many rapid induction techniques evolved, and dentists also became aware of the power of indirect suggestion in the clinical relationship. This enabled "hypnosis" to be used while dental treatment was in progress—a case of working with your mouth as well as your hands!

Dr. Erickson's work with indirect hypnosis provides the theoretical background against which these empirical techniques could be formalized and better understood. One of his students, who later became a close associate, is Dr. Kay Thompson, a practicing dentist in Pennsylvania. I would like to acknowledge here the influence Dr. Thompson has had on my thinking and practice since we first met in 1979. Kay's teaching dispersed the fog and enabled me to see clearly the things I had been groping towards. Much of what I present here was originally suggested by her, and some of the wordings of suggestions may be almost verbatim, as I have absorbed her words and not found a better way to express them. I sincerely thank her for the guidance I have received over the years, and hope I am able to add something to her teachings.

The principal authors of this book have described specific techniques in some detail, so the focus of this chapter is on the practical applications of those techniques as I use them. Even though different countries such as the USA, Canada, the UK, and Australia share a common language and may have similar mixtures of ethnic origins, their cultures are still very different, and there are significant differences in the use of language, some of which are quite subtle. You are certainly aware of differences within sub-groups of your own culture, so please recognize and compensate for the slight incongruities which occur because I write from an Australian perspective. Please also note the synonymous use of patient and client, surgery and treatment room, and other small linguistic aberrations!

B. Anxiety Control and Stress Management

Anxiety control and stress management start from the time patients enter the office. The front office staff can be trained to assess a patient's level of anxiety as he or she is welcomed. This assessment consists of noting skin color (flushed or pallid), heart rate (observed in the carotid artery), strength of cardiac contraction (tremor in voice when speaking), degree of sweating (upper lip), respiration rate, and muscle tremors. Obviously, allowance must be made for extraneous factors in making this assessment—the heat of the day, recent physical exertion, etc. In talking with the patient the *words* the patient uses to frame answers are particularly noted as these will often indicate fear which the patient may be unwilling to admit consciously.

Appropriate action by the staff varies from chatting for distraction, to providing a newspaper or magazine and discussing some topical news, to escorting the patient to a private waiting room and "visiting" with them until they are needed.

It is often the simple things which are so important. For example, never ask a patient, "Would you like to come in now?" This only prompts them to think of all the reasons they wouldn't like to! A nice use of the "yes set" is to say to a patient as they enter the treatment room, "Please come in, sit down, and relax." Since the patient is in the process of complying with the first two, it is difficult to reject the third. If a patient responds with, "You must be joking!" or something similar, you have a perfect opportunity to discuss their anxiety/fear without having to broach the subject directly.

Much of the discomfort patients experience during a dental visit is produced within themselves. The release of large amounts of endogenous adrenaline as part of the "fight or flight" response can cause acute anxiety, and this reaction may be triggered by the paired associations of past treatment and the particular environment (in your office or other offices). A powerful stimulus for this is the characteristic smell of a dental surgery. Now, I know your surgery doesn't smell, Doctor, but what do you notice when you visit any of your colleagues? I know I have a totally different experience entering my own rooms as a "Doctor" than I do as a patient visiting an associate! You are probably aware that the sense of smell connects directly to the primitive brain and is therefore the most powerful sense in terms of memory recall.

The *sound* of an air turbine is also quite disturbing to many patients. I recall a patient who, even under sedation, would experience physical pain in her teeth at this sound with the handpiece nowhere near her mouth. (She had some other serious psychological problems as well, but resisted any attempts at referral for counseling.) Insulating the waiting room from treatment area sounds is an excellent practice.

1. A "Regression" Approach

This idea can be discussed in *general* terms with a patient along the lines:

> You know that when you feel threatened your body responds by releasing adrenaline. This speeds up your heart and makes it pump harder so that more blood gets to the muscles, and it speeds up your breathing so that you get the extra air you need, and it cuts down the circulation in your digestive system so that there is more blood available for the muscles. All this is part of the "fight or flight" response which can be life-saving, but can be uncomfortable in circumstances where neither of these actions is appropriate. The result is that you may often feel extremely anxious without really knowing why, other than that it was associated with a dental visit.
>
> Then, at a subsequent visit you would remember that earlier feeling of anxiety and anticipate it occurring again, so making the situation worse. But, if you go back far enough there must have been a beginning.

All the above can be used to develop rapport and fixate attention, so that you have set the scene for the following. You can now use a slower pace and a softer voice tone:

> When you think back to when you were a child of eight or six or seven or ... and remember the house you lived in then ... how big and bright the rooms are ... and there is that big table you all sit around for meals ... and how high you have to reach to touch the doorknobs. And that wonderful smell when you come home from school and Mom's been baking ... cupcakes or cookies (or biscuits) ... and there is that big old tree you play under with your friends ...

Notice the change of tense, from past ("think back," "remember" and "lived in") to present for the remainder. The implication is "be there!" i.e. regress to that age. You either need to obtain information about their early life *or* use words that are more generic than specific.

> But when you ... go back now ... and look at that house, the rooms are not so big and bright, and that table is pretty ordinary, and the doorknobs are just normal. But none of these things have changed, only the way that you look at them has changed.

Re-orientate to the present with memory of the regression.

> The memories that you have of events that happened a long time ago are recalled in the way that you experienced them then. Now that you are a grown (wo)man, with a vast wealth of experience of life and all the personal strengths developed over the years, you can take a different view of these events and put them into their true perspective. You can also recognize that you have all those resources you had forgotten to remember you had learned in the past to now apply to the present and the future for your own benefit next time.

Recover resources and relate to the present, finishing with some slight confusion and a positive statement.

Many patients will enter a spontaneous, eyes-open trance during the above. This is readily identified by fixated vision, respiration changes and lack of movement, and can be utilized for further suggestions, if desired. It can be very therapeutic to simply allow a patient to remain in this state for several minutes while you practice your own relaxation. There is a reprocessing of past memories and a reorganization of resources, and sometimes this takes a while. The trance can be terminated by using a conversational voice and saying, "And isn't that a good feeling?"

2. *Remembering How To Relax*

A patient will sometimes say, "I can't relax," or will appear very tense. This is a perfect cue to use the following technique. It does rely on having access to a patient's right hand, which is usually accessible for a dentist.

> I want you to let the muscles of your fingers and your hand relax completely. Just let them go so that your hand feels like a bag of sand, completely relaxed and loose. In a moment I'm going to lift the first finger just a little. I don't want you to assist in any way, just let me lift it, let it happen. Then when I let it go, just see how readily it drops back to the armrest; you don't have to do anything, you don't even have to think about it, just let it happen.

The index finger is lifted clear of the armrest using as little contact with your own fingers as possible. As you slip your finger away, the patient's finger should drop as though made of rubber. If there is resistance, or control of the return movement, this should be drawn to the patient's attention and the exercise repeated until this can be done successfully. It may take three or four attempts to achieve this.

> Now I'm going to do the same thing with several fingers, and I want you to do exactly the same thing as you did before, ... just let it happen (etc.).

When this exercise is successful, usually fairly quickly, continue with ...

> You've learned to relax those fingers very well. Now I want you to let that feeling spread to the rest of your hand. I'm going to lift your wrist a little, and I want you to just let it be completely limp and loose. Don't do anything to help it, let me do the lifting (etc.). When I let go, just let it drop back to the armrest, just as heavy as lead, completely limp and loose (etc.).

Again, this exercise is repeated until successful. The amount of wrist lift should be only enough to lift the tips of the fingers clear of the armrest. If the fingers curl under and prevent a "clean" drop, the tips of the fingers may also be supported.

> Now that you've learned again how to let that part of your body relax, just let that learning spread to the rest of your body and let it feel just as comfortable as your arm does now. And you can continue to enjoy that wonderful feeling of relaxation and practice that new learning the whole time you are here so that you will never forget it again.

Many patients will exhibit signs of trance; those who do not, enjoy a marked sense of relaxation and a loss of muscle tension. The technique seems to work by having the patient focus on their kinesthetic sensations to the point that awareness of other inputs is diminished. For most patients the good feeling which ensues is so different from what they usually experience that they are quite prepared to continue this work to keep their sense of comfort. Looking at it another way, when they are assured and convinced that they have control, they are quite prepared to use it.

On the topic of "control" the following can be used in conjunction with the above to reinforce what has happened:

> Control is an important issue for many people. One of the worst things they can imagine happening is losing control in public, and crying or swearing or in some other way "disgracing" themselves. They spend so much time fighting to maintain control that they don't have any time left to focus on other things which might be more appropriate in the particular situation. When you really have control, you don't have to worry about keeping it because you can get it back any time you want it.

3. Arm Catalepsy

A variation of the above can be used as a direct or indirect induction technique. It is easiest to perform if the patient is seated with elbow support available, but this is not essential. Take the patient's wrist lightly between your thumb and first or second finger, with your hand above the patient's, and with her fingers hanging downward. Your contact is light and should give an impression of hesitation or tentativeness. It is most important that the patient is supporting the weight of her arm and that you are not holding it up in any way. It is an advantage to have your arm supported, too, as you will need quite fine muscle control later. Introductory verbalizations vary, but for an anxious patient it might be:

> You appear very tense, and seem to be having trouble letting go of all that muscle tension. Let me show you a good way to learn about relaxation.

As you take hold of the wrist and "pick up" the arm:

> Just hold your arm up so ... and let your fingers relax, just let them hang limp and loose.

At this point you should not be supporting the arm at all, just touching lightly on the lateral surfaces of the wrist. If it tends to droop when you "let go," repeat the above with more emphasis on "hold your arm up." It can sometimes be helpful to use your other hand to do the "lifting" so there is a further implication for the patient to do the "holding" when you change hands, the second hand being then perceived as a guide only.

> Watch your fingers carefully ... they will sometimes twitch a little as all the muscle fibers relax and the nerves quieten down ... just like when you're going off to sleep and a leg or arm jerks ...

Attention is focused on the fingers. One hand is used to stabilize *very lightly* the position of the patient's arm. Your other forefinger is now used to "bump" the patient's fingers, just lifting each a fraction and ensuring it is hanging loose. You are ostensibly looking for any residual muscle tension, but the "bumping" reinforces the patient's feeling of looseness and rubberiness by stimulating the proprioceptors in the attached muscles. Draw attention to any twitches, and a quasi-logical explanation can be given if the patient's knowledge is adequate. This also serves as a distraction for those analytical types who will try to analyze just what is happening!

> The tension in the muscles is maintained by a continuous stream of nerve impulses, and as these reduce in number so the muscle relaxes; but as it relaxes it stretches and so triggers small reflex contractions to control that relaxation, but as the relaxation progresses so that rubbery feeling gets more and more intense. ... (etc).

All the above should take no more than two or three minutes. At this point "bumping" should stop. Note the deliberate use of "the" rather than "your" in the following; this is to assist with dissociation.

> Now that the fingers are completely relaxed, let that feeling spread to the back of the hand ... all the way to the wrist and the forearm ...

From here on the suggestions are slowed and timed so that they are matched with the patient's exhalations. At the same time, the fingers used to "hold" the patient's wrist are moved very slightly so that there is a constantly varying contact. (This was adapted from Erickson's "handshake induction.") There is some unconscious confusion generated about what is holding, but it is done very gently so that the patient is not aware consciously of the changes. The objective is to break contact with the patient without her being aware that it has happened. Eventually there is contact only with the hairs on the sides of the wrist, and then only the sensation of warmth through proximity of your fingers.

> Let the feeling spread up the arm ... that's right ... all the way to the elbow ... and even further ... up the arm ... all the way to your shoulder ... And feel how it spreads from there ... all the way down your chest ... with each breath ... you can feel that spread ... deeper and deeper down ... to your diaphragm ... to the muscles of your tummy.

This can be continued for as long as you feel is necessary, but it is not usually longer than the above takes to say. By now the patient will be exhibiting classic signs of trance, with or without eye closure. Eye closure is not important.

> And isn't it interesting how the hand can sit up there all by itself, a part of you but apart from you? And that can be a very interesting kind of learning experience.

From this basic induction, which usually takes no more than four minutes, you can continue into anything else which is appropriate. Examples follow.

3. Sand Bucket

> Can you imagine you have a child's sand bucket hanging from the hand ... (lightly draw your finger over the back of the wrist) and that you're going to fill it slowly with sand. With each scoop of sand you place in the bucket it will get heavier and heavier, and the arm will begin to be pulled down harder and harder [more and more]. I don't know what color your bucket is, or how big your scoop is, but I can see the hand beginning to move now ...

Suggestions as above are continued as appropriate, along with whatever other suggestions you wish to insert. For example:

> The heavier the arm gets, the more deeply relaxed you will become, but the arm will only come all the way down when you have reached the appropriate degree of relaxation. Your conscious mind may believe a particular level of relaxation is appropriate, while

your unconscious or inner mind will continue until the right level is reached. Just let it happen ...

4. *Balloon Technique*

Can you imagine you have a big lighter-than-air balloon attached to your wrist here? (Touch the skin lightly.) And with each breath it is getting bigger ... and bigger ... (timed to exhalations). I don't know what color your balloon is ... but isn't it interesting to see ... how the color changes ... as the balloon gets bigger ... and bigger ... and you can feel it beginning to ... lift your arm up higher ... and higher, lighter and lighter. And as your arm gets higher ... and higher ... so you become deeper ... even more deeply relaxed ...

I wonder if your arm will come all the way up to your face, or only a part of the way, or if it will rise up high in the air or only as high as your shoulder? (Binds of comparable alternatives.) You may be very curious how high your arm will rise (presupposition), but your unconscious, your inner mind, will let it lift as high as is necessary for you to learn what it is you need to know (conscious-unconscious dissociation).

With the arm in a suitably high position this can be further utilized as a deepening technique as follows:

That balloon has developed a small hole, one that's just big enough to cause it to deflate slowly. As it starts to shrink you can feel the weight coming back into your arm, and it will slowly start to move back down, but your unconscious won't let it come all the way down until you really know what it is you need to know. You may be curious what this is right now, but your unconscious is the part of you doing the exploring, the discovering and the learning, and it may not let your conscious mind know just what that is just yet. Just be content to let it happen in its own way ... in its own time, and be curious, very curious ...

5. *Analgesia*

The cataleptic, dissociated hand is usually quite analgesic. A few suggestions can potentiate this effect which can then be readily demonstrated to the patient. Some "trance logic" can then be used to "concentrate" the numbness and to transfer it to the desired region.

> Isn't it interesting how the hand can be a part of you yet apart from you? ... and while you know consciously that it's there, it's as though it isn't there and it really doesn't matter what happens to that hand there because it's so far away. You can feel some pressure, some tightness, but even when I pinch the skin on the back of the hand it doesn't hurt. Just feel the tightness ...

The skin can be pinched quite firmly, even twisted hard, without the patient showing any signs of feeling it. If there is a reaction, you can repeat the pinch on the other hand and ask the patient to note the difference. I have never encountered a patient who did not experience a considerable difference in feeling between the two hands. This is usually a positive confirmation of trance for a patient and will reinforce other suggestions.

> You can use that numbness in other places, too. Just imagine the numbness being focused and concentrated in one or two fingers ... feel it flowing into those fingers ... (etc.) And when that has happened, your arm will lift slowly up to your face ... but not until your unconscious mind is ready ... your fingers will touch (place where analgesia is required) ... and all the numbness will flow into that area leaving it feeling very, very different, and your fingers and hand returning all the way back to normal. Even as your hand goes back down, that numbness will increase more and more so that (the area) will remain comfortable for the whole time you are here and for (as long as is appropriate after the appointment).

C. Pain Management

Pain is a danger or warning signal; it has a protective effect allowing the painful area to be rested and given time to heal. If pain continues for long periods, it interferes with normal function by causing loss of sleep and irritability, and often spreads to neurologically adjacent structures.

Acute pain in general dentistry is usually confined to the emergency patient requiring treatment of trauma or infection. Unless there is a specific reason to use hypnosis, such patients are more appropriately treated with local anaesthetic because of the pre-existing state of anxiety and the immediate surgical intervention which is usually necessary.

Chronic pain falls into two categories: appropriate and inappropriate. "Appropriate" pain is that present after surgery or similar treatment; this is the [possible] pain you warn the patient about before treatment and before they leave the surgery. "Inappropriate" pain is that where the patient has to contact you following treatment because normal healing is not progressing. See Thompson (1976) for "a clinical view of the effectiveness of hypnosis in pain control" for her first published paper on pain control, which she has elaborated on in later papers.

1. *Appropriate pain - pain facilitates healing.*

After any treatment, such as the one you have just had completed, there is always some level of possible pain. Pain is a warning or danger signal. This is your body's way of ensuring that you are really aware of that region and giving it the protection it needs so that it has the very best chance of healing in the quickest possible way. When you have some pain like that, you can really focus in on the part affected and supply it with lots of nerve energy to facilitate healing. The area becomes warm and flushed as the blood supply increases, and the local temperature rises. This provides the best supply of nutrients and ability to fight infection that the body can give.

"When everything that can be done, and should be done, has been done, there is no longer any reason for the pain [continuing discomfort]. You can be pleasantly surprised how very comfortable it will be as long as normal healing is progressing." (Note: This is a typical Kay Thompson statement.)

2. *Inappropriate pain - pain interferes with healing.*

That pain you are experiencing really is a terrible nuisance. Pain is a danger or warning signal your body uses to tell you that something is wrong. When that pain continues longer than appropriate, it starts to interfere with healing because you are putting so much extra energy into controlling the pain that you don't have any left to help with the healing. Now that we have checked the painful area and treated the problem, it will ease.

"When everything that can be done and should be done has been done, there is no longer any reason for the pain. You will be pleasantly surprised how very comfortable it will be as long as normal healing is progressing." (Kay Thompson style.)

In both of the above there is an implicit suggestion that some pain will return if healing is not "normal," so that both you and the patient are protected.

What is "normal" healing? We each have an expectancy of how healing will progress in ourselves, based on past experience and the present "set" created by the environment in which we find ourselves, most importantly including the people and personalities involved. Sometimes healing is influenced so much by our expectancies that it can be significantly slower than is possible.

There are many examples of "accelerated" healing in the literature, several to be found in Kroger (1977), but a well-known example from the Ericksonian literature is that of Robert Pearson, described by Rosen (1982, p. 174 et seq.). Pearson was operated on for the open reduction of a depressed skull fracture on a Thursday; by the following Wednesday all that remained was a hairline scar. Pearson had a very strong desire to attend a convention, and so healed in the time available.

If a patient asks how long something will take to heal, resist the temptation to predict healing time based on "normal" expectations. It is far better to suggest that healing is dependent on how well the patient looks after the injury, and how much time and effort they are prepared to invest in helping the healing happen. This changes the perception of healing from a passive involvement to one where the individual has active control over their body's responses. You can even suggest how "surprised" they may at the rapidity of their healing.

D. Muscle Control

Some patients have difficulty opening their mouths wide enough and long enough for certain procedures. Any induction procedure can be used, and the following suggestions are given:

> You have become so relaxed that it is increasingly difficult for your jaw muscles to keep your mouth closed. It is just as though a weight is attached to the tip of your chin, becoming heavier and heavier with each breath. You might like to try to keep your mouth closed as long as you can, because then you will become even more relaxed,

and it will be so much more comfortable for you when you finally let go, and can let your mouth drop open. As those muscles let go and your mouth opens all the way, it is just as though the muscles are made of rubber, and your jaw can fall all the way open quite effort-lessly, quite comfortably, and it can stay that way just as long as we need it to do so.

When a rest is indicated, the following can be suggested:

It's time to stretch those relaxed muscles and just feel how good it is to stretch and relax. Just stretch and relax, so that in a few minutes your mouth can open again so easily and comfortably.

E. Gagging

In my experience this is almost invariably associated with an impression-taking procedure. The patient should be shown the impression tray with the seal at the back to "stop the material escaping." A supine position seems to be an advantage, perhaps because the tongue seals the pharynx more easily. I believe it is important to describe the flavor, etc., of the impression material, and also to demonstrate the viscosity, showing how stiff it is and how difficult it would be for it to run where it is not wanted. There is no "induction," but the following is said very quietly, intensely, and timed with the patient's breathing:

Just breathe comfortably ... letting your chest rise and fall ... feeling the muscles in your tummy relax ... and all the muscles in your chest relax ... each time you breathe out. Focus completely on your breathing ... keeping your tummy muscles nice and loose ... nice and relaxed ... listening to your breathing ... and feeling the muscles of your chest ... relax with each breath.

An occasional difficulty is encountered with new oral appliances, particularly dentures or orthodontic retainers. Most frequently this is related to excessive thickness in the posterior border of the appliance rubbing on the dorsum of the tongue, particularly the lateral aspects. Careful trimming, thinning and polishing of these areas and explaining the cause of the problem to the patient will usually allow tolerance to be developed.

The patient who cannot be helped by the above is probably in need of more extensive therapy. These problems may relate to traumatic childhood experiences, even as young as one or two years of age. Childhood tonsillectomy, endoscopy and choking on food have all been encountered as causes of adult gagging which is resolved by "reprocessing" of the early memories. The techniques used are similar to those for dental fear described earlier, but with deeper levels of trance and more explicit age regression. There is a significant possibility of abreactions, so this should be undertaken only by those prepared and trained to deal with the consequences.

F. Bleeding

It is well documented that bleeding can be controlled by hypnotic means. There are films showing a person in trance bleeding only in alternate inches from a scratch down the arm, another showing a hemophiliac having a lower premolar tooth surgically removed with hypnosis as the only anaesthetic and no transfusion or plasma concentrates needed. Finally, there is a film (Milton H. Erickson Foundation) of Dr. Kay Thompson bleeding and not bleeding on command from a cannula inserted in the dorsum of her hand.

A "clinical" trance is not required in a clinical setting to achieve some practical results. After tooth removal these suggestions can be made:

> I want you to bite firmly on this pad, and you don't want to waste any blood, so just let the socket fill and then turn off the bleeding.

Many patients will give you a strange look at this point, which is your cue for:

> Didn't you know that you can control the blood flow around your body? Just think of what happens when it's summer, and you run around so much that you feel your tongue stuck to the roof of your mouth and your hands and cheeks feel as though they're glowing. What's happened? All the blood vessels in your skin have opened up to let the blood near the surface so that excess heat can be radiated away. And what happens in the winter when you've stayed outside longer than you should have, and your ears and cheeks and fingers are so cold that you can hardly feel them? Those same blood vessels

have closed right down so that you don't lose the heat that your body needs to keep inside.

All this has happened without your being consciously aware of it, but your body knows how to do it. All you have to do now is to lie back and let it happen. Just let the socket fill with blood once and then turn off the bleeding.

Beware of your wording and the hypnotic virtuoso! Following an extraction, a Filipino woman who had expressed concern about bleeding was told, "You won't bleed while you are biting on this pad." The implication was recognized but ignored at the time. On checking a short time later, the socket was found to be bone white, with no bleeding at all—a very literal following of my instruction. The suggestion was made, "Of course you do need to bleed just enough to fill the socket, so that healing can be as rapid as possible," which she also faithfully followed. No deliberate attempt had been made at any time to induce trance in this patient, but her cultural background undoubtedly contributed to her literal responsiveness.

G. Amnesia

Suggestions of amnesia can be effectively used before and during long or difficult procedures. With the patient in a trance of whatever depth, and involved in pleasant hallucinatory surroundings, the following suggestions can be made:

You can remember the [that] way in the past you have experienced time going so slowly when you had a difficult or unpleasant chore to do, and the way time just seemed to fly when you were away on that wonderful holiday, or enjoying a good party. So, while you're enjoying where you are, you might be pleasantly surprised to realize later just how fast time has passed, or maybe you just won't remember all the things you experienced, only the important ones, or maybe you will only remember to forget all the things which are unimportant; perhaps you will forget to remember anything which is only partly relevant and just keep the best parts.

Similar suggestions can be repeated during the procedure to enhance the effect. Another technique is to use an "embedded metaphor." Typically this can be a long and involved "shaggy dog" story, with parts of it being interspersed with the treatment. The patient focuses on the story and accepts more easily the suggestions about forgetting the irrelevant experiences (the treatment). (See Chapter 12 on advanced metaphor.)

H. Sensory Modification

This is useful where local anesthetic has not been one hundred percent effective for cavity preparation, and the patient is still experiencing some pain. Attention is drawn to the feelings of cold—this is present because of the water spray—and suggestions are made about the way very cold areas become numb and lose their normal sensitivity, in fact the colder it becomes, the less they will feel.

It can be used effectively where restorations are required on deciduous teeth by telling a story about ice cream, or "slushies" or similar confections, and coupling the parts about eating to the periods of drilling. This does not require a deliberate trance state, but obviously will be more effective if one is present.

I. Salivation

With a relaxed patient salivation is not much of a problem, but where salivation persists the following can be offered:

> Having so much saliva present is really a nuisance to both of us, but can you imagine how those old-time explorers would have liked to have a mouth as wet as yours when they were out in the desert with no water and really had to conserve every drop of moisture?

Follow here with a description of how dry and dusty the desert is and how your body and mouth feels under such conditions. Remember to reverse this when you are finished!

J. Oral Habits

All dentists are asked by worried parents at some time to assist with their child's finger or thumb sucking habit. The "*The Collected Papers of Milton H. Erickson*" (Erickson and Rossi, 1980, Vols. I–IV) describe two techniques which can easily be incorporated into your practice.

The first accepts the habit, and raises it to a conscious performance task, with the parents and siblings enrolled as "enforcers" to remind the child which finger is TO BE sucked, rather than admonish that sucking cease.

> Which finger (thumb) do you suck? Why that one? Have you tried the others? You might be really missing out on something worthwhile if you haven't tried ALL the others as well. I'll tell you what, I'll help you with a program so you can really get to find out which one is the very best one to suck!

At this point the child's hands are placed on a clean sheet of paper and the outline of the hands traced on it.

> Now, this is your present finger, and today is Monday, so we'll label this finger Monday, the next one Tuesday... (etc. for both hands). This has to go up on your notice board at home where everyone can see it, because you're going to need some help! You can continue with your present finger today, but tomorrow you have to suck your Tuesday finger, and only your Tuesday finger! Then, on Wednesday it's your Wednesday finger, and so on until you've tested them all to find out which one really is the best.

The second procedure works well with younger children by appealing to their sense of self esteem. Assuming you have a child of four, you might say:

> Tommy, you're four years old and your mother has asked me to get you to stop sucking your finger. That's silly, because everyone knows that it's all right for a little four-year-old boy to suck his fingers. And it's all right, right up until the time you turn five, because all big boys of five have stopped sucking their fingers; they've had all they need by the time they become big boys of five. So you just go right on sucking your fingers and enjoy it while you can, right up to your next birthday.

K. Summary

Dentistry is a wonderful environment to utilize indirect hypnosis: your patient is supine, is unable to respond, and is willing to accept any help you can offer with their stress. It's also a great help to maintain the dentist's sense of humor and sanity!

There are many practical applications of hypnosis in dentistry, but the most commonly used is undoubtedly that associated with relaxation and stress management. A comfortable patient is easier to work on, will accept your prescribed treatment more readily, and will tell the world about you. As you become aware of the many opportunities to use hypnosis and suggestions in your everyday work, you will practice the verbalizations most comfortable for you. With time you will use these quite naturally (unconsciously) and be surprised at the changes in your work, your environment, and your life.

Exercises

1. Practice the arm catalepsy induction—it sounds easy (and it is), but it does require a sensitive touch and careful observation of the patient to know to what stage the patient has progressed. This comes only with practice. (You can't fail if you don't state your objective, so don't be anxious about practicing.)

2. Develop your vocal skills so that you can communicate effectively with voice tone as well as with words. This added level of meaning is very powerful. Cultivate a quiet, soft voice, with plenty of tonal expression. Learn to use pauses effectively so that the patient becomes curious ... about what comes next. This facilitates the inner search process and lets the patient wonder whether they found the answer themselves or whether you provided it for them.

3. Highlight those phrases in this chapter that you think will be particularly useful. Practice using these phrases until you develop, and are comfortable with, your own "automatic" phraseology.

4. Practice the pain control inductions. Work with other dentists in a study/practice group.

5. Write out and/or tape record your own hypnotic/suggestive interventions using the ones in this chapter as a model.

6. If you are not a dentist, ask your dentist if he/she is willing to be trained in these interventions, and then do so.

7. For further study see the following in vol. I of Erickson and Rossi (1980): ch. 7, pp. 168-176; ch. 8, p. 177 et seq.; ch. 10, p. 259 et seq.; ch. 20, p. 412 et seq.; and ch. 22, p. 452 et seq. In addition, reading the books by Rosen (1982) and Yapko (1990) will be helpful.

Chapter 17

Hypnotherapy with Special Populations

Rubin Battino, M.S.

A. Introduction

Erickson appears to have worked with whoever walked through his office door, although the literature shows that there were occasions when he turned clients away or refused to work with them. In particular, he refused to work with people who were attempting to manipulate him, or who clearly had no interest in changing, or those he perceived he would not be able to help. His early work was with institutionalized patients in the era before drug therapy. Considering the range of clients he dealt with, it is not surprising that he did much pioneering work in child psychology, and in working with couples and families. In his time (and now!) you might consider his work with "resistant" clients also to be pioneering.

The principal authors of this book have had wide experience in the field, but felt it advisable to have three experts write on the special subjects of medical and dental applications, and substance abuse. Our expertise is evident in the chapters we have authored. In this kind of "catch-all" chapter we comment briefly on the utility of using hypnosis for various populations and types of problems. The next chapter deals with substance abuse. An excellent resource for locating Erickson's work in specific areas is O'Hanlon and Hexum's book (1990). Hypnotherapy with people who have life-threatening diseases is the subject of Chapter 19. Examples of dealing with habits are in Chapter 14, along with case studies on a variety of presenting symptoms and situations. Working with institutionalized people is beyond the scope of this book. Yapko (1988) has written extensively about working with depression.

B. Family, Couples and Children

In the development of psychotherapy, the early model was to work singly with individuals, since the focus of interactional problems was perceived to be the individual. Gradually it was discovered that more effective therapy could be done by working with couples, single families, and finally with extended families. That is, the "system" within which the individual functioned needed to be taken into account. However, in recent times we have come almost full circle back to the idea of working with individuals, but with a different focus. The individual can function as a "change agent" within the larger system. If the new behaviors of this change agent are cleverly chosen and carried out consistently, then perforce the system must change to accommodate him/her. This is central to the effectiveness of the "miracle question" as used by de Shazer (1985, 1988, 1991, 1994) and his colleagues: the client imagines how life would be different after the miracle has occurred. Once these changes have been envisioned, then it is almost anti-climactic for the person to start behaving in ways to bring about the changes. The client knows his/her spouse or family so well that the expected behavior changes in them are almost certain to occur.

This development from individual to systems and back to individual work means that the flexible therapist is free to work with whatever grouping of individuals makes sense or is possible (the utilization principle!). Of course, hypnotic work can be done with couples or families via group inductions. Also, one or another family member may be hypnotized in the presence of the others, and hypnotic language can be used at any time.

Children are generally readily hypnotizable. Since children are closer to story-telling than adults, and tend to have more unfettered imaginations, the use of appropriate metaphors is particularly effective with them. Erickson cured a ten-year-old boy of bed wetting by talking about the muscular control involved in archery and playing baseball. Wallas (1985, 1991) has published a large number of metaphors suitable for children or families.

In the history of the development of family therapy, Erickson's contributions are largely overlooked. Yet he was working with children and couples and families long before such work got labeled. In effect, this was part of his utilization philosophy—you work with whoever walks through the door and use their strengths and history to help them. We give four examples of his work here.

Mother Sits on Johnny

E: Oh yes, Johnny was a very, very brilliant seven-year-old boy. One spring he decided that he would demonstrate his omnipotence. Mother was divorced. Mother is a school teacher. Johnny had a sister a year older than he. Sister is well-behaved. One day at school Johnny defied the teacher. I think Johnny's brighter than that teacher was. Johnny did a good job. And Johnny decided to defy the whole school. Then to defy the neighborhood. His mother, when she brought him in to me said, "He's a hell-raiser. I've got no authority, nothing at all, the last straw was reached the other night when in the middle of the night, Johnny got up and took a metal ashtray and battered a hole in the wall, knocking plaster off and the laths off. Johnny says he's going to show me that he's going to be the toughest hoodlum in Arizona." And Johnny said, "That's right. An old man like you can't do anything at all about it. My mother can't." So I said, "Well, you really mean that? You think you can win?" Johnny said, "Yes, I can." I said, "Then you're not afraid of what your mother will do, are you?" Johnny said he wasn't the least bit afraid of what mother did. I said, "Well, you're not afraid to have me give your mother advice?" "Give her all the advice you want." So I asked Johnny when the tug-of-war should occur. I said, "Today is Friday, tomorrow is Saturday. That would be a really good day to take your mother to the cleaners if you can." He said, "I can, and I will." So I talked to the mother. The next morning mother awakened him and said, "Let's wait until after breakfast. I'd like you to have a good breakfast." Johnny threw the eggs on the floor and said, "I want bacon." Mother prepared the bacon. He threw some more stuff on the floor. The mother let him get a good breakfast. Then mother picked up a glass of water, a couple of oranges, a couple of bananas, and put them on the bookshelf right along side their telephone. Johnny wondered about that. Mother went to the bathroom. Mother weighs 160 pounds. Johnny was age seven. Mother came back from the bathroom. All of a sudden Johnny found himself flat on the floor, mother sitting on top of him. Beside the telephone. Johnny yelled, "Get up off me." Mother said, "I haven't finished thinking things out yet." Johnny kicked and struggled, but it was 160 pounds on a seven-year-old. After about an hour, Johnny said, "I'll be good." Mother said, "Are you sure?" Johnny said, "Yes." Mother said, "I have not yet learned how to believe you." Johnny raged and kicked and yelled obscenities and profanities. He tried to get out from under that 160 pounds of weight and couldn't. (Laughs) So after a while he sobbed and said, "I'll be good." Mother said, "You know, you told me that before, and then you kicked up a worse fuss than ever. So I have not yet learned how to believe you." Johnny said, "I'm thirsty." Mother said, "Well, I put my water right there where it's handy for me, and she reached up on the shelf and took a drink of water. (Laughter) The telephone rang. His mother reached up and took the telephone and answered her call. Johnny didn't even think of yelling into the phone. It took him by surprise. His mother was ready. About noon his mother said, "Well, Johnny, maybe you'd like to have a rest from your learning. Of course, I've got bananas here, and I've got oranges here. I've got sandwiches here. For *my* lunch, if you don't want to take a rest from learning." Johnny said, "I'd like my rest." Mother said, "Well, can we start again at one o'clock?" He started to yell and scream. So she continued sitting there. Johnny took just one session.

H: That was a good one.

E: His mother had sandwiches, bananas, oranges, milk, water, the telephone. A handy book to read. She gave him a rest by letting him roll over on his back. Gave him another rest by letting him roll over on his tummy while she sat on him. He tried to bite her bottom. She said, "Dr. Erickson told me to put on my tightest girdle and lots and lots of petticoats." Johnny came in to see me. He said, "Some kids can learn, can't they." That's right. Some kids can learn. But that mother was absolutely desperate.

H: Well, how did you persuade her not to give in at the crucial point?

E: I pointed out to her that if she gave in at a crucial point, she was whipped—and the child was whipped. He was already a neighborhood threat, and a neighborhood nuisance, and she was going to have to move out of that neighborhood. The neighbors would not tolerate it anymore. She had just, about a year before, purchased that new house. (E = Erickson, H = Haley. Haley, 1985, Vol. III, pp. 135–138)

Barbara's Too Big Feet

I regard hypnotic techniques as essentially no more than a means of asking your subjects (or patients) to pay attention to you so that you can offer them some idea which can initiate them into an activation of their own capacities to behave. The best way to illustrate this point is by way of a clinical example. Barbara was a 14-year-old girl who had been failing in her adjustments at school and had developed serious behavior manifestations. She said her feet were too big, so she was not going to go to school, church, or out of the house. She was not going to talk to anybody. Her mother, who was my patient and a good hypnotic subject, consulted me about her daughter's problem. The mother described how Barbara's behavior had been going on this way for two long weeks, that Barbara had been secluding herself in the home, not talking, and was most unresponsive. I told the mother I would make a house call, and that she was to go along with whatever I said. She was not to discuss the visit beforehand with her daughter.

When I arrived at the home, I took out my stethoscope and said to the mother, "I think that the first thing I ought to do is examine your chest. So will you please take off your blouse and bra, but call your daughter in here to act as a chaperone and have her bring a towel." The girl of course could not refuse to come in; she had to come in to act as a chaperone. That was the first thing that I got the girl to do for me. It seemed to be so innocent, so appropriate, so right, but I was getting a response from her. I carefully examined the mother's chest, all the while with Barbara standing there beside the bed in her bare feet, with a sullen look on her face. Finally I got up from where I had been sitting, stepped backward, and brought my heel forcefully down on Barbara's toes so that she let out a yell of pain. I turned to her, seemingly very irate, and said: "If you had only grown those damn feet big enough for a man to see, you wouldn't get them stepped on." *If you could grow those damn feet big enough for a man to see, they wouldn't get stepped on.* Barbara looked at me, first in a frightened way, and then all of a sudden the smuggest smile I ever saw came over her face. She turned and walked out of the room. On the way out she said, "Mother, can I go to the show?" Barbara went to the show that day, she went to Sunday School the next day, and returned to school the next Monday. It was the end of her symptomatology.

What had I done? I had asked Barbara to respond. I also made her respond by stepping on her toes. I did it in a totally unexpected way. Then I took the idea that her feet were so big that she was ashamed to be seen in public, and in a horribly impolite fashion, I convinced her that I honestly felt that her feet were very small, and that she was remiss in not having grown them larger. Could I have ever told Barbara that her feet were of normal size, of a good size by just pointing it out to her, by measuring her feet, by showing her that she had feet no larger than her classmates? Barbara needed therapy, she needed to stop secluding herself. It was to get Barbara in some way from within herself to make response-behavior that would be corrective of her situation and her condition that I proceeded as I did. *Hypnosis is essentially that sort of concept, i.e. a way to offer stimuli of various kinds that will enable patients in response to those stimuli to utilize their own experiential learning.* I helped Barbara reorient to the size of her feet rather than to *ideas* about the size of her feet. Hypnosis facilitates exceedingly effective learning that would be impossible otherwise except by prolonged effort and therapy. (Erickson and Rossi, 1980, Vol. II, pp. 315–316)

Dawdling

The parents of a boy named Jimmy complained to MHE about the amount of dawdling the boy did over breakfast and in putting on his socks in the morning. Despite their exhortations to hurry, he typically took two hours to do either task. MHE recommended that the parents spend a week emphasizing that Jimmy was a boy who liked to eat slowly. At the end of that week, on Sunday, the parents were to cook the boy small pancakes, one at a time, beginning with 15-minute intervals between each, touting it as the perfect solution for someone who liked to eat slowly but preferred his pancakes hot. They were to keep increasing the interval, until the boy was yelling at them to hurry. It took Jimmy less than a week to consistently beat everyone in his family at finishing his breakfast.

Jimmy was invited to a party. On the day of the party, MHE suggested, Jimmy's mother should lay out some socks without holes in them. She insisted that Jimmy spend two hours putting them on, as usual. Jimmy pleaded and begged to be allowed to put them on faster, because he did not want to miss the party. She remained firm, telling him that she believed he enjoyed dressing slowly that morning and she still believed it now. Tomorrow, he might tell her something different and she might believe him, she said. The next day, Jimmy told his mother he liked to dress fast, but she insisted he did not have to. (Case summary from O'Hanlon and Hexum, 1990, pp. 230–231)

In-Laws and Ulcers and Vomiting

E: I remember a woman who couldn't stand her in-laws visiting her three or four times a week and she developed a stomach ulcer. She had a stomach pain which incapacitated her at work, in her own family relationships, and in her social relationships. My statement was, "You really can't stand your in-laws, but you *can* stand church."

H: You can stand what?

E: Church.

H: Oh.

E: "You can stand the card games with the neighbors. You like your work, but you *really* don't like your relatives. They're a pain in the belly. Why not have the pain in your belly every time they come? It ought to be usefully developed; they certainly can't expect *you* to mop up the floor if you vomit." (Laughter) She hears that statement, "They can't expect *you* to mop up the floor if you vomit when they come." What did she do? She vomited when they came, and she weakly and piteously had them mop up the floor.

H: (Laughter) Did they come back again?

E: She would hear them drive in the yard, she'd rush to the refrigerator, and drink a glass of milk. They'd come in and she'd greet them, start talking, get sick to her stomach, and vomit. She had her wherewithal, she just wasn't sure if she had the wherewithal to vomit.

H: And she did this every time they came?

E: They quit coming. They started calling up to find out if she was well enough. "Not today, not today, not today." Then she might say, "I think I'm all right today," but unfortunately she made an error.

H: Now that's teaching her to handle them in a weak way and helpless way, isn't it?

E: As long as she wanted to be helpless and have a stomach ulcer, fine—go along with her. The relatives got sick and tired of mopping up that floor. (Laughter) She had her way, and she saved all her pain in the belly for their visits and had her own satisfaction. It is an awfully good stomach she had; it could throw the relatives out. (Laughter) That reversed pride.

H: Pride on the usefulness of the stomach you mean?

E: The goodness of it, and the usefulness and the effectiveness.

H: She gave up the stomach ulcer?

E: Oh certainly. She didn't need to keep it. So much simpler to vomit and make them clean up the mess. After they stopped coming for a couple of months she invited them to come over *for the afternoon.* They came warily. She could control them. After they'd been there the afternoon and she wanted them to leave, she merely had a distressed look on her face and her rubbing on her abdomen. They were very ready to leave. She hadn't asked them. Why should they mop up the floor again? (Laughter) Was it a weak way, or was it a strong way? Anyway, the relatives were whipped by it.

H: It was weak in the sense that it inflicted the punishment without taking responsibility for the punishment, and her husband couldn't get mad at her for inflicting punishment on his relatives because this was a helpless thing she was doing.

E: But it was a strong thing when she kept that glass of milk handy in the refrigerator. That was deliberate, intentional. (E = Erickson, H = Haley. Haley, 1985, Vol. I, pp. 45–46)

C. Other Populations

In this section we will briefly touch on other populations for which Ericksonian methods are useful.

1. *Multiple Personality Syndrome*

Erickson (1980) in an unpublished paper written in the 1940s discussed "The Clinical Discovery of a Dual Personality." To give some sense of his understanding of this syndrome, we offer the following quotations from his paper:

> At all events my findings do indicate that multiple personalities are not necessarily rare, even though no definitive conclusions can be offered concerning their actual frequency. (p. 262)

> In all these cases the discovery was essentially an accident. (p. 263)

> Hence, I would stress as an adequate measure of discovery for multiple personalities any procedure of systematic clinical observation that would permit the recognition of different sets and patterns of behavior integration and a determination of the interrelationships or lack of interrelationships between various organizations of behavior reactions. (p. 263)

Foremost among the various misunderstandings prevalent about multiple personalities is the belief that they are more or less unintentionally built up by the hypnotist and hence are artifacts. ... In my own hypnotic work I have, as an experimental approach to personality problems, attempted over a period of years to build up new personalities in hypnotic subjects, only to realize the futility of such attempts. ... Nevertheless, a careful analysis of the material actually available on these topics in the literature will enable the earnest student to reach a satisfactory realization that multiple personalities constitute something of a different character from special hysterical states. (p. 264)

Another serious misapprehension is the common but mistaken belief that multiple personalities can occur only in highly neurotic persons and that the secondary personalities are necessarily destructive and vicious in character. My experience is contrary to this belief. (p. 265)

The following quote is an excellent summary of the clinical nature of multiple personalities:

To proceed with the question of what actually constitutes the clinical nature of the dual or multiple personality is a most unsatisfactory task. One must make the simple, dogmatic, and not satisfactorily informative statement that the person with a dual personality actually possesses two separate, distinct, independent personalities. Each of these personalities derives from a single, total experiential background that serves each of the personalties in a markedly different fashion. The dominant, ordinary, or primary personality has the richer background of reality experience, and nearly all contacts with reality belong to it. The secondary personality, however, has the richer background of intellectual and emotional knowledge commonly held by passive, observant, nonparticipants. Thus, there is a dominant personality that has actively participated and shared in the major portion of all contacts with reality; out of this experience a personality complete with its various attributes is derived. The second personality, however, except for a limited number of reality contacts unknown to the other personality, has usually not shared actively to the same significant degree in reality contacts and has largely observed reality only in a passive fashion. For the secondary personality the experiential background is largely a matter of intellectual and emotional understandings acquired passively through the proxy constituted unwittingly by the primary personality. Out of this background of chiefly passive experience the secondary personality, also complete with its various attributes, is derived. (pp. 265–266)

Of particular interest in relation to the nature of the dual personality are certain primary characteristics. First of all, the ordinary personality is totally unaware of the secondary personality. Even when confronted with adequate proof, there is a marked tendency to reject such proof as pure invention or as having some other explanation. ... A second characteristic, ... is that the second personality tends to know all about the first personality, or, if such knowledge is lacking, has ready access to it. ... However, certain items of information of a minor type are not available to the second personality. (p. 266)

In the remainder of this paper Erickson discusses the case of a 24-year-old woman. The following article with D. Rapaport (1990), an unpublished manuscript written in the 1940s, discusses the results of projective and psychometric tests and two different dual personalities. This work clearly shows the distinctly different personalities. Erickson and Kubie (1939) discussed the clinical treatment of an obsessional phobia via communications with an unsuspected dual personality. By the use of hypnosis secondary personalities may be accessed and worked with to relieve symptoms or to bring about an integration of the personalities. Sometimes, ideomotor finger signals may be used to access both personalities at the same time with each personality responding to questions with a different hand.

2. Retarded and Geriatric Clients

In general, it is difficult to hypnotize people with low I.Q.s since their attention span tends to be quite short. However, hypnotic language may be useful in the development of new behaviors. Incremental changes can frequently be induced. Some of these same observations may be made in working with the elderly. Erickson would probably get them to do something, and then work around that activity.

The following case of Erickson's (Zeig, 1980, pp. 285–286) is not really a geriatric one, but his way of dealing with a lonely, single, older woman can be generalized since he found a simple way for her to focus her life and give it meaning:

The African Violet Queen of Milwaukee

Now I'll tell you another story. Ralph told me, "My mother's sister lives in Milwaukee. She's 52 years old. She never got married. She's independently wealthy. My aunt has only one interest in life. She goes to the Episcopalian Church on every possible occasion. She has no friends there. She never speaks to anybody. She slips out at the end of the sermon very carefully. She likes me and I like her, but for the last nine months she's been horribly depressed. She has a house-keeper come in every morning and a maid that comes in every morning. They stay all day and do the cooking, the housekeeping and the shopping. She pays the yardman for keeping up the lawn and for shoveling the sidewalk in the wintertime. The housekeeper manages everything.

"My aunt sits around reading her Bible and going to church. She has no friends. She and my mother have quarreled, and they won't speak to each other. I feel too incompetent to visit her very often. I have always been fond of her and now I know she has been profoundly despondent for nine months. On your next trip to Milwaukee to lecture, will you call on her and see what you can do for her?"

I called one evening. The housekeeper and maid had left for the day. I identified myself very carefully. She was very passive, and I demanded a tour of her home. She was sufficiently passive to permit me to have a guided tour. She led me from room to room.

I looked around very carefully at everything. In the sun room I saw three adult African violets of different colors in full bloom, and a potting pot in which she was propagating another African violet.

Now, you know, African violets are very delicate plants. They are very easily killed by the slightest amount of neglect.

When I saw those three African violets of different colors I said, "I'm going to give you some medical orders, and I want them carried out. Now you understand that. Will you agree that you will carry them out?" She passively agreed. Then I said, "Tomorrow you send your housekeeper to a nursery or a florist and you get African violets of all different hues." I think at that time there were 13 different hues of African violets. I said, "Those will be *your* African violets and you are going to take good care of them. That's a medical order."

435

"Then you tell your housekeeper also to purchase 200 gift flower pots and 50 potting pots and potting soil. I want you to break off a leaf from each of your African violets and plant it in potting pots and grow additional mature African violets." They propagate by planting the leaf.

I said, "And when you have an adequate supply of African violets, I want you to send one to every baby that's born in any family in your church. I want you to send an African violet to the family of every baby christened in your church. I want you to send a gift adult African violet to everyone who is sick in your church. When a girl announces her engagement, I want you to send her an African violet. When they get married, I want you to send African violets. In case of death, you send a condolence card with an African violet. And the church bazaars—contribute a dozen or a score of African violets for sale." I knew at one time she had 200 adult African violets in her home.

Anybody that takes care of 200 African violets is too busy to be depressed. (General laughter.) She died in her seventies with the title of "The African Violet Queen of Milwaukee." I saw her only once. (Erickson laughs.)

3. Traumas

Under traumas we consider post-traumatic stress syndrome and sexual/childhood abuse. The hypnotherapeutic intervention generally follows the same pattern for dealing with traumas since their origin was typically a number of years in the past, and that much (if not all) of the traumatic circumstance(s) has been lost to conscious memory. While in the trance state (the deeper the better) the traumatic experience(s) may be *safely explored with amnesia provided* until it is wise to slowly and safely have this repressed material come to consciousness. The trance state provides a degree of dissociation and distance to work safely through this older, difficult material. The unconscious can be asked directly about when it would be appropriate to divulge this material to the conscious mind and in what way. The client must be protected at all times! The ethical therapist must be careful to not ask "leading" questions so as to avoid any possibility of confabulation, or the creation of false memories. On the other hand, a "helper" or "guide" or authority figure may be introduced to the client in the trance state, with the implication that this person will be able to help the client achieve freedom from the trauma in a safe and secure and realistic manner that takes the client's present circumstances into account. The work of Yvonne Dolan (1991) with clients who were sexually abused as children may be taken as a model.

4. Phobias

Erickson's favorite method of working with phobics was to get them to "violate" their phobia in some small way. This is an incremental approach wherein the apparent involuntary behavior of the client is slowly made more voluntary. This approach may be considered to be a progressive process of desensitization. If you can take two steps out of your house and nothing bad happens, then three steps would also be safe. As in dealing with pain control, it is important to not completely remove many phobias. There are some snakes that are poisonous, there are some closed spaces that should be avoided, there are some aircraft one should not board, and there are some heights which are dangerous.

Phobias can also be successfully dealt with by using trance states. (The comments in the previous section on traumas are relevant here.) The origin(s) of the phobia can be safely explored in trance with protective amnesia, if needed. Since phobias typically have their origins in real events, trance can be used to: (1) reframe the *meaning* of the event; (2) dissociate feelings from the fearsome physical responses; and (3) provide a "helper" if that makes sense.

Here are two of Erickson's cases dealing with phobias in similar, but different ways:

Erickson's Closet

Another patient had claustrophobia. She couldn't bear to be shut up in a small room. Her mother had punished her as a child by putting her in the outdoor entrance to the cellar, closing the door, and then clicking her heels as she walked down the street, deserting the girl. She had clicked her heels on the sidewalk, making the girl think she was going far, far away.

And the girl grew up with an absolute phobia for small rooms. So I asked her to sit in the closet of my office.

She said, "I'll only do that if the door's wide open."

I said, "Suppose instead of having the door wide open, it lacks one millimeter of being wide open?"

And she agreed. She stayed in the closet with the door wide open, except for one millimeter. And then, we worked up to two millimeters, three millimeters, a centimeter, half an inch, an inch. And how open did she have to have that door?

So she stood in the closet and slowly closed the door. I waited to see when her panic would develop. She found she was comfortable even when the door was only a half an inch open and she kept her hand on the door knob. Finally, she closed it and found out she could live and breathe in that closet with the door closed, as long as she had the doorknob in her hand.

Then I suggested she might try looking through the keyhole. Since she could see outside through the keyhole, she didn't have to hang on to the doorknob any longer. (Rosen, 1982, pp. 134–135)

Lying in Ditches

In a quite different approach, Erickson resolved a fear of traveling for a young man who insisted that he wanted only that one problem solved. The young man could only drive a car on certain streets, and he could not drive outside the city limits. If he drove to the edge of town, he became nauseated, and after vomiting, he would faint. Driving with friends did not help. If he kept going, he would only recover and then faint again. Erickson required him to drive to the edge of town at three o'clock the next morning, wearing his best clothes. It was an untraveled highway with wide shoulders and a sandy ditch running alongside. When the young man reached the city limits, he was to pull over to the edge of the road, leap out of the car, and rush to the shallow ditch beside the road. He was to lie down there at least fifteen minutes. Then he was to get back into the car, drive one or two car lengths, and repeat the lying down for another fifteen minutes. Repeating this again and again, he was to continue until he could drive from one telephone pole to the next, stopping at the first evidence of any symptoms and spending fifteen minutes on his back in the ditch. Under protest, the young man followed the procedure. He later reported, "I thought it was a damn-fool thing you made me promise to do, and the more I did it the madder I got. So I just quit and began to enjoy driving." Thirteen years later, he still had no problem in driving his car. (Haley, 1973, 1986, pp. 69–70)

5. *Panic/Anxiety/Hysteria*

These responses can be considered to be variations of traumatic reactions and the interventions discussed above would be reasonable to follow. Reframing is important not only to put the problem in perspective, but to change that perspective. Providing a dissociation in trance between emotional states and physiological reactions often works. The solution-oriented emphasis on finding exceptions to or exceptions of expected behavior opens the door to change via a reframing of daily activities.

The following case (Haley, 1985, Vol. I, pp. 81–82) could be considered under the headings of paradox or anxiety:

But I'll Die Tonight

On January 1st one year, I got a patient who told me that he was going to die that night from heart failure and he'd be dead in the morning. I said, "All right, call me up tomorrow morning and tell me you are dead." (Laughter) He called me up at 11 o'clock in the evening and told me he was dying. I said, "Well, you don't know at what time, but I want to be notified tomorrow morning." I got my call in the morning, "I didn't die last night, but I'll die tonight." Every night he called me at 11 o'clock to tell me he'd die that night. In February he called in the morning, and I said, "Yes, you tell me that you will die tonight. If I remember correctly, you told me January 1st that you would die that night, but you didn't. You told me January 2nd that you would die that night, but you didn't. This is February 1st and you tell me you'll die tonight." February 2nd he called me up and said, "I'm dying tonight." I said, "Yes, you're telling me you'll die tonight. You told me on January 1st that you'd die that night. You told me January 2nd you'd die that night. You told me January 3rd that you'd die that night. You told me January 4th that you'd die that night. But you didn't. You tell me you'll die tonight. You told me you'd die January 1st, but you didn't. You told me January 2nd, but you didn't. You told me you'd die January 3rd, but you didn't. You told me you'd die January 4th, but you didn't. You told me on January 5th, 6th, 7th, and 8th that you'd die, but you didn't." (Laughter)

By March he said, "Goddamn it, I don't care about what I said last January about dying." I said, "I do. I had to take those calls every night, and I didn't believe a one of them." In April he said, "I was mistaken in January, in February. I was mistaken in March, but I am going to die tonight." "Call me tomorrow morning." In May, "I think I'm going to die tonight." "I know, you thought that you'd die in January, you were sure you'd die in February. You were positive you'd die in March, you had some doubts about it as April started going by. This is May. Call me up, will you?"

Erickson handled stage fright in a concrete manner (Gordon and Meyers-Anderson, 1981, pp. 139–140):

Stage Fright and Colored Towels

A couple of years ago I got a Christmas card, it said, "I want to thank you for the *excellent* time I spent with you in 1959. I know I should have written before ... I kept putting it off. Now, I spent *three hours* with you and life has been *glorious* ever since." He was a very wealthy man. He had been trained as a concert pianist. He had a private auditorium of his own and the first public concert he gave, or rather he WANTED to give, he got stage fright and was unable to walk out on the stage. And while he was here in those three hours in 1959, I explained to him ... oh, he had kept on practicing the piano. In all the ten years having elapsed since the first attempted public concert he managed to allow ONE friend to be present in the auditorium. He couldn't stand to have TWO of his friends to be an audience. And when he came to me I said, "Well, your problem is very simple. I want you to buy a stack of colored towels ... red, green, blue, purple, flowered and so on. When you get home, you very carefully spread them out across the stage floor, and save the 1st two for the piano seat, and the last towel you put on top of the piano. Then you send out invitations for a piano concert and have the entire auditorium filled. And when it comes time to go out on stage, you stop and look at the first towel ... do you want to FAINT on that one, or would you prefer to faint on the second one?" So he moved down to the second and had the same debate—should I faint on this one or on the third? He got to the piano bench ... he knew it would be very awkward to FAINT on it, so he SAT on it. And he considered fainting on top of the piano, but didn't see his way clear. So he played his concert. Now I think that is *therapy* because it took ALL his fears and anxieties and put them in a concrete *form* and located them on a *towel* and it was a matter of WHICH towel. And he went down the row of towels and each one he passed over ... he HAD to play, he

COULDN'T use the towels. He's been playing as a concert pianist ever since.

6. *Meaning*

Frankl (1959) has found that about twenty percent of his clients (this appears to be a general finding) have significant difficulties with finding *meaning* in their lives. Logotherapy was specifically developed to help these people. The search for meaning may also underlie many other presenting problems. Hypnosis can help with respect to pseudo-orientation in time, or assisting the client to find (internally) a guide or guru who provides direction and/or meaning. Since the significance of a lack of meaning is frequently overlooked, it is important to always consider this dimension. Finally, it is not unusual that a successful resolution of any set of presenting problems results in a renewed interest and meaning in life.

D. Summing Up

This chapter has provided a brief overview of working with special populations. Again, you may wish to refer to Erickson's collected papers or the guide to his cases prepared by O'Hanlon and Hexum (1990). Other hypnotherapists like Yapko (1988) and Dolan (1991) have written about specific populations. Remember, it is not the trance state per se that helps clients to change, but what you do while they are in trance.

Exercises

1. Make a list of all of the special populations you can think of and write out the characteristics of those populations. Then, indicate your preferred mode of dealing with those problems. If these involve using trance, then indicate what you would do in the trance state, e.g. the metaphors that might be appropriate.

2. Think of a specific case and figure out how you would use that person as a "change agent" in a couple or a family. Can change agents work in larger institutions such as schools or businesses? Is it ethically responsible to do this?

Chapter 18

Ericksonian Techniques in Substance Abuse

Leon S. Segal, M.A.

A. Introduction

1. Ericksonian Techniques and Substance Abuse

No magic exists in applying Ericksonian techniques and philosophy to treating substance abuse patients since they, like other mental health patients, portray the same problems, conflicts, and illnesses. The only thing which separates them is that their addiction to chemical substances is the primary treatment focus. Although other issues and illnesses may be involved, the goal is to minimize, control, and eliminate substance abuse or dependency. The substance abuse therapist deals with the patient's denial and, to a point where they accept therapy and develop the motivation to change behaviors, beliefs and lifestyles. Patients must recognize the negative consequences and catastrophes that have brought them to treatment and the need for recovery. *Together* with the drug therapist, the patient must structure a recovery program.

Therapists use the same Ericksonian techniques used with other patients in other contexts, except they are directed to the specific needs of substance abuse. The whole arsenal of techniques: trance work, reframing, paradoxical interventions, metaphors, secret therapy, and utilization can be applied.

2. Definition of Substance Abuse

Portenoy and Richard Payne (1992) say, "Current definitions of addiction, which have been developed by addiction specialists, characterize it as a psychological and behavioral syndrome in which there is a drug craving, compulsive use and other aberrant drug-related behaviors, and relapse after withdrawal." They go on to say that, in addition to the craving, there is a psychological component, which involves rumination about the drug and an intense desire to secure its supply. In other words, there is now a *drug consciousness*.

Drug abuse occurs when a patient uses illicit drugs or alcohol on a regular basis and begins to encounter negative consequences as a result of its use; e.g. Drive While Intoxicated, family conflict, loss of income and employment. The abuser uses drugs outside of societal and cultural standards, i.e. abusers get into trouble. Dependency occurs when the compulsive use of, and obsessive focus on, drugs is coupled with an increasing physical dependence. As the physical tolerance increases, the amount of drugs consumed increases to satisfy the *physical* cravings. By this time, the patient has a lifestyle dominated by drug seeking and related behaviors.

As the physical addiction takes hold, deterioration of other aspects of the patient begins. Character and moral deterioration permit drug users to do things they never dreamed of doing before entering into their addictive state. Thinking becomes distorted. Lying, stealing and manipulation become easy. Driven by the need for drugs, internal boundaries and inhibitions dissolve. It becomes easier to commit crimes and other aberrant behaviors. Drug dependents no longer use drugs or alcohol to "get high" or for euphoric pleasure. True drug dependents use drugs in order to avoid pain or discomfort and to "feel normal."

Deeper into dependency, the physical body begins to erode and decline. Personal hygiene slips. Medical conditions related to drug use may occur. Because drug use covers pain, the patient may not even know that physical conditions exist. Problems with interpersonal relationship arise, support systems break down, family relations are strained, and friends are lost. Patients keep on using drugs to solve basic life problems, *if only temporarily*.

3. How Addiction is Introduced

Addiction and abuse of various non-drug substances and experiences surround us. We are addicted to food, TV, chocolate, gambling, relationships, work. It is a way we use to solve a problem, feel good, or get something we want or think we need. In all cultures, there is also a desire to change consciousness in some way.

A major factor in the drug recovery program is the physical detox which involves much pain and suffering. This often drives patients back to drug use. One way of handling this is to *reframe* the pain: they must learn that "PAIN IS BEAUTIFUL" i.e. *pain means the body is healing itself*, cleaning out the toxic substances, promoting health and recovery.

Most drug dependents begin using drugs as adolescents or pre-adolescents. Pressure to conform to group mores in order to gain acceptance is very strong. During any point in the life cycle, a person may become vulnerable to experiences or conditions which can precipitate drug abuse or dependency. Drugs contain the magic power to suppress feelings of inadequacy, raise low self-esteem or deal with crushing depression.

4. Problems Related to Drug Treatment

Most patients come to treatment for reasons other than wanting to become drug free. Almost every drug dependent patient has attempted, unsuccessfully, to stop using drugs alone. Since most patients don't really want treatment, motivation and breaking through elaborate denial systems are the therapist's first problems. Before treatment can begin, the patient must go through the stage called *surrender*. Here the patient must admit a problem exists, and that the problem belongs to him/her. The patient must also admit his/her life is out of control and something must be done. This is when the patient has committed to treatment.

After the therapist obtains this commitment, then treatment can begin. Together, the patient and the therapist must accomplish a physical, mental and social detox. Physical detox, something patients most dread, is the easiest to accomplish. It can take between forty-eight hours to a few weeks or months. More difficult to accomplish is the mental detox. After years of drug-using behavior, patients develop corresponding *drug lifestyles* where almost everything revolves around finding and using drugs.

The third detox *which must be accomplished* is the hardest, the social detox. The patient's support system is primarily drug dependents who are involved in drug lifestyles. A major task for the therapist is to help patients overcome their fear, shame, or guilt about drug use and make contacts with non-drug using others who will accept them and not undermine recovery. AA and NA and other such 12-step programs serve an important function in providing such contacts.

Once surrender occurs and the patient is willing to face the reality that their choice is between recovery or death, then the therapist may begin to work with the real issues: grief, abandonment, co-dependency, trauma, abuse.

B. Ericksonian Techniques as Applied to Drug Addiction

There is a drive toward health and personal empowerment which patients, even the least healthy, have. The Ericksonian philosophy works toward effecting self-empowerment and change, by (a) *Utilization*—identifying some characteristic behavior, such as anger, resistance, defiance, guilt, pain, rage or low self-esteem, to use as a resource; and (b) *Using Client Resistance and Defiance*—resistance to treatment can be used to involve a patient with treatment.

Lovern (1991) outlines an elaborate and sometimes risky dance between the therapist and the patient to utilize resistance and defiance. The "dance" begins *by making sure the client is defiant enough*. From the beginning to the end of this interaction, the therapist *provokes* patient defiance by doing or saying things and acting in provocative and obnoxious ways in order to elevate the therapist as a source of defiance. Lovern suggests:

> To ensure defiance, the therapist can make him or herself easier to defy. That is, the therapist can behave in an arrogant, impudent, rude and demanding way, offering a tempting target for defiant resistance.

To use this strategy, the therapist must have the support and cooperation of other resident patients or group members. Upon identifying a patient who shows defiance, the therapist begins a conversation about this patient to another patient while the defiant patient is in the room, pointing out how the defiant patient is "one of the sickest I've ever seen." The therapist and assisting patient play a game of good cop/bad cop which culminates in the therapist betting the assisting patient a cup of coffee that the defiant patient is not man enough to show up the next day for the treatment session, and, if they do show up, the person will not have the guts to participate.

Another Lovern tactic is to *predict a patient's relapse* after leaving the hospital. One particular patient had to take a long bus ride to return home. The therapist predicted, that sometime during that journey, the patient would get off the bus, buy liquor and relapse. Using this strategy requires a high degree of sensitivity, training and supervision. Therapists should still be able to be gentle, soft, and understanding when needed.

1. Using a Client's Anger and Rage

One residential client heard that his wife, whom he left in another city, had taken up with his best friend. He was enraged. He said goodbye to the therapist, saying he was returning home the next day in order to kill them both to satisfy his honor. "That's not revenge," the therapist told him. "If you really want revenge, you want her to suffer for a long, long time. When you kill her, it's all over for her. She doesn't suffer. You suffer. You go to prison, and she's dead. How can you *really* make her suffer?" The patient decided the way to really make her suffer was for him to succeed, remain in treatment, get off drugs, go back to work, make lots of money and then go home. Once there, he would have a new car and clothes, flash money as he laughed at her, showing her what she was missing.

2. Utilizing Low Self-Esteem and Self-Hate

In one classic case (Haley, 1985, Vol. I, pp. 110–113), an alcoholic aviator came to see Dr. Erickson carrying a scrapbook with clippings of all his accomplishments, seeking treatment for his addiction. Erickson immediately accused him of coming to see him under false pretenses, calling him a "dirty, filthy, foul-smelling, unshaven bum who had no right to any respectable man's scrapbook." Dismissing him sharply, Erickson predicted that he would get drunk anyway as soon as he left his office. A few months later, the man returned asking for help again. Erickson told him he was going to give him a dressing down, and did so for the next three hours. The man left the office and started taking control of his life. He joined a gym, started working out, and getting into good shape. He joined the Air Force and became a captain. By confronting and attacking him, Erickson was being honest and showed genuine concern. The man responded to this and changed. Had Erickson acted otherwise, it would have been phony.

3. Trance Techniques

In order to "hook" the patient into treatment, the therapist must help them "feel good" quickly. Putting the patient into a trance state and teaching him self-hypnosis builds rapport and provides a tool to obtain relief without using drugs.

Most patients arrive for therapy in an upset state. Being offered an opportunity to relax and lift some stress is inviting. A successful trance experience demonstrates to patients the possibility of self-empowerment. The trance state can be used to deal with pain, depression, anxiety and relapse.

One technique the writer developed—the "Segal Sure-fire Method"—is very useful with all patients, especially resistant patients. Begin by explaining that most clients resist going into trance because they fear losing control to some outside agent. Next, inform the patient that he/she has control at all times. The patient may open his/her eyes at any time. They can then *look around, take a deep breath, and drop into a deeper state of relaxation.* Anytime the patient desires to test control, he should open his eyes and then drop into a *deeper* state. If the patient doesn't test, the therapist will suggest the patient do it. After a trance state is achieved, teach the patient a variety of self-induction techniques and encourage them to create new and personalized techniques.

In trance, the therapist teaches patients how to increase and enhance positive memories and feelings. By anchoring these images to a finger squeeze, or other body part, one can recall them as needed. The NLP "swish technique" (Bandler, 1985; Andreas and Andreas, 1987) is very useful where the positive image is superimposed upon the negative image and replaces it.

Another enhancing technique is the "photo album." Once the patient has an *image* which generates positive energy, give him a *"positive* photo album." The first picture in the album is that energized image. Suggest the patient review his life to find other positive memories to fill at least twenty pages, responding with an ideomotor signal when the picture is installed. The album has a hundred or more pages. Any time the patient wants to relax or feel good they can look at the album. One technique which works well in pain control is to re-create the pain and *then* learn how to control it. Another pain control technique is to ask the patient to symbolize or visualize a particular pain, conflict or problem as fire, chains, pins and needles or whatever images come to mind. Next, the patient *visualizes an antidote* such as water to put out the fire, a bolt cutter to cut the chains, or a magnet to pull out the pins and needles. As the symbol for the pain dissolves, is destroyed, or shot off into the sun, it can provide a feeling of relief and control.

4. Adding Cognitive Approaches

Sometimes one can combine hypnotic technique with a cognitive therapy approach to discover a client's distorted beliefs to help them alter, modify or change the distortions. They can then begin to use more realistic beliefs which help to achieve personal goals in a more satisfactory manner.

A variation of this is to *"program* a client with new parents" when coming from a dysfunctional family or abusive childhood is an issue. The therapist has the client review all the women they have known, and choose one who most clearly approximates the *ideal mother*. Sometimes a client can make up a composite parent by taking desired characteristics from a group of people the client likes and using their desired traits.

5. Reframing

Reframing is a valuable tool in working with drug dependent clients. For instance, one reframing technique the therapist can use is to reframe the clients' years of drug abuse as a *training period* for the rest of life, i.e. using their negative experiences for a positive base such as becoming a drug counselor. Women who have suffered incest, rape or sexual molestation can use their experiences to work with other women who have suffered in these ways.

By spending years in criminal activities drug dependants learn many *transferable* skills which can be used in the legal marketplace. *Criminal skills may be reframed to legitimate job skills.* By having clients develop a job description for a mugger, armed robber or prostitute, they can identify skills to find work they can, and probably like to do. One former prostitute, now a successful car salesperson said, "Drug dependents are all manipulators. For me, selling cars is easy and fun." We can see how usable skills are embedded in illegal trades. Muggers who know how to intimidate people make excellent bill collectors, rental agents, and security guards. Burglars who climb up roofs unafraid of heights make excellent roofers, gutter repair workers, TV dish installers, and house painters. Prostitutes who are experts in personal relationships provide companionship more often than sex. They are good in health care, as hostesses, and at sales work. One prostitute who liked to give massages went on to get trained to give real "massages" and made a fairly good living at it. Shoplifters know how to steal from stores and can work as security agents, teaching clerks to spot shoplifters.

One client had a difficult time finding a job. We told him, "Forget about getting a job. You're in business for yourself!" We explained that he could make money from salvage, by picking through trash and picking out metals, paper and cardboard. The client liked the idea and now makes fifty dollars for two hours work a day. If he wants to work more, he can make more.

One drug dependent, who never held down a regular job in his whole life, got an idea to start a business using what he had learned in hustling drugs. He began a fruit basket service for people who wanted to remember hospital patients, mourners, and people celebrating festive occasions. He visited a local supermarket and found out where they put together their fruit baskets and watched how they did it. He also found the source of supply for the baskets, and where he could buy the fruit wholesale. Next, he practiced making up the fruit baskets till they looked quite professional. Lastly, he went to funeral homes, churches and benevolent organizations and gave out cards. He created a business out of thin air.

Reframing is the gentle art of turning lemons into lemonade. Part of the learning process for a patient is to learn that "getting high" is okay. There are alternative ways of generating their own internal drugs or stimulating their pleasure centers such as the practices of: the Yoga masters of India; the Tibetan monks who chant; joggers; Native Americans who go on vision quests; and Christian mystics who fast and meditate.

It always shocks patients when you ask them to state the *positive gains* they obtained from their years of drug use. They respond with traits such as resourcefulness, ability to focus on a goal, and solve problems creatively, a high degree of social awareness, ability to influence others, and the ability to survive under difficult circumstances. One patient observed, "If we were as motivated to make money and invest it as we are in chasing drugs, we'd all be multi-millionaires." Thus the clients' years of drug abuse can be reframed as a *training period* for the rest of their lives.

6. Dealing with Denial, Resistance, and Procrastination— Some Metaphors

As with all clients, the demons of denial, resistance and procrastination have to be dealt with, too. Drug dependent clients are as terrified of changing as anyone else. To handle resistance and help clients step out of the Egyptian river (De Nile!) that's holding them back from recovery, various methods are used. Metaphors are a powerful tool in order to embed important messages into patients' unconscious minds. At different points in the treatment process certain messages need to be planted for different reasons. A sample of different metaphors follows, the first story helps show patients that they do have a choice to live or die:

The Philosopher and the King

Once there was a king who had a wise philosopher living in his kingdom. The king hated the philosopher because, every time the king wanted to trick the philosopher and make him look like a fool, the philosopher turned the tables and made the king look like a fool. This time the king hit upon an idea to trick the philosopher so the king could have him killed.

The king commanded, "Bring me my philosopher." The guard brought in this old man with a long white beard.

"How can your humble servant be of assistance to you, oh mighty king?" asked the philosopher.

"See this?" the king shot back, showing the old man a tiny bird in the middle of his palm. The king folded his hand around the bird and put it behind his back.

"Now, wise philosopher," the king growled at the philosopher, "is the bird alive or dead?"

The philosopher thought fast. If he said "alive" the king would squeeze the bird to death and then kill the philosopher. If he said "dead" the king would show him the bird lived and would kill him.

The philosopher thought deeply for a long moment. A smile broke out on his face and the old man said, "As you wish, great king. The result will be whatever the king wishes."

Along the same lines, another metaphor gives the directive to the client to take responsibility for his/her life and recovery:

The King Who Sought Personal Empowerment

Once a king commanded his advisors to tell him something that would empower him, help him overcome obstacles in his life, help him to achieve goals, and energize him to move forward. The advisors told him everything they knew, but he rejected it all, saying he had heard it all before. "Yes, yes," said the king, "you've told me all these things already. Tell me something new that will really empower me."

Finally, the advisors told him about an old wise man who lived in a cave on top of a mountain on the other side of the world who knew everything and could answer his question. The advisors cautioned the king that the journey to see the man was long, tiresome, and dangerous. One had to travel across stormy, turbulent oceans, cross burning deserts, tramp through snake-infested jungles, cross rivers with piranhas and other man-eating creatures, and finally climb a high mountain that even the guides refused to climb.

The king insisted that he still must go despite the advisors' protestations. So he went on the voyage, traveled the oceans, crossed the deserts, tramped the jungles and rivers, and climbed the mountain till he found the cave.

Inside, the king saw an old man with a white beard, wearing only a loincloth, staring into the fire. The king began to talk to the old man, but he stopped the king, telling him he already knew why he was here and would soon answer the question.

After a long period of silence, the old man looked at the king and said, "If you want to achieve your goals, overcome obstacles, empower yourself and move forward in your life, everyday in the morning, every night, and several times during the day, you must say this, "IF IT'S TO BE, IT'S UP TO ME. IF IT'S TO BE, IT'S UP TO ME."

This story can help when the therapist wishes to emphasize the importance of the social detox and how patients must separate themselves from others who still use drugs lest they get pulled back into a relapse:

The Snake, the Envelopes, and the Ax

Once a man heard about a snake who had a secret formula which helped a person become wealthy, healthy, and achieve one's life goals. The snake's secret was hidden in one of five envelopes. The seeker had to choose one of the envelopes. If the person chose the correct envelope, then they received the secret formula. If the person chose the wrong envelope, then the snake could do to the person whatever it wished to do.

So, the man told the snake he wanted to play the game and take a chance by choosing an envelope. He opened the envelope and found it was empty.

"Now," said the snake, "I can do to you whatever I wish." And with that, the snake grabbed an ax and whacked off the man's arm from the shoulder down. Smiling, the snake asked, "Do you want to play again?"

Of course, the man did, and chose another envelope. Again, he was the loser and lost his other arm from the shoulder down.

The snake offered him another turn, saying that there were only three envelopes left. The man chose another envelope, and this time lost his leg.

With two envelopes left, the snake told the man, "You have an excellent chance of choosing the correct envelope." The man took the bait and lost again, losing his other leg. As he lay there in a pool of his own blood, the snake said, "To show you no hard feelings, I'm going to open the last envelope and read the message to you. This will show you my kind and generous nature. I'm going to share the secret formula anyway." So, the snake read the formula to the man: BEWARE WITH WHOM YOU DO BUSINESS.

The following metaphor is particularly useful to help patients deal with crisis situations in their lives. It helps develop patience and maturity:

The Old Man, His Son, and the Horse

Once in the poorest county of a poor country there lived a man and his son. They were considered very wealthy by all their neighbors since they owned a horse and could plow their field with its help. One day the horse ran away. The son came crying to his father, "Oh, father, what's to become of us now our horse has run away?"

"Son, we don't know if this is good or if this is bad. We must wait to see what will happen."

Three days later the horse returned, bringing two other wild horses with it. "Oh, father, day of joy." The father replied, "Son, we don't know if this is good or if this is bad. We must wait and see what happens."

A few days later, the son tried to ride the horse and was thrown off, breaking his leg. The son cried to his father, "Father, curse the day those horses came. See, now I have a broken leg."

The father said to him, "Son, we don't know if this is good or bad. We have to wait and see what happens."

A week later an officer came through the county, rounding up cannon fodder for the king, picking young boys to fight in a war the king was planning. The officer said, "You go, you go, and you go," pointing to all the young men. When he came to the old man's son he said, "You can't go. You have a broken leg."

7. The "No Treatment Treatment Technique"

One technique for allowing the client to take responsibility for treatment we might refer to as the "No Treatment Treatment Technique."

A client came into a counselor's office at a residential treatment center terribly upset. This client had been making the grand tour, spent time in about five different local area drug programs, and "failed" each one. He had been through all kinds of therapies, treatments and groups. At this latest program, things were "laid back." This bothered him.

He began yelling at the counselor, "When does the therapy begin? What kind of treatment program is this anyway? Where's the help?"

The counselor immediately told the client that if he did not like their services he could be referred elsewhere and, if he had any complaints, he should express them. Then the counselor said to the client, "You are the treatment. The recovery is within you and not within the center. I don't have to tell you what to do to get off drugs. You already know that yourself better than anything. You would probably do just the opposite anyway just to spite me. In other words, you got yourself into this. You have to get yourself out of it. You have to become RECOVERY. You have to learn everything you can about recovery and do those things that are meaningful to you and that make sense and that work. I am a resource, I can answer questions, make referrals, lend you books, act as a listening post, but I cannot organize and do your recovery. That's something you have to do for yourself!"

With the responsibility for recovery placed directly upon the shoulders of the client, he started responding, figuring out a plan, attending meetings, changing his behaviors, and detoxed himself.

One detox was completed when a client was handled using a somewhat opposite approach. This client was afraid of going to prison since his case was soon pending. This client was told, "The way for you to avoid going to prison is to become *straight*. Do the things that straight people do: get a job, go to church, get a haircut, shave, wear clean clothes, smell nice, go to Little League ball games and picnics. Watch what straight people do and do whatever they do."

The above discussion does not provide a definitive summary of all possible techniques applying Ericksonian principles to drug dependent clients. It is merely a sampler of some of the things which can be and have been done.

Chapter 19

Hypnotherapy with People who have Life-Threatening Diseases

Rubin Battino, M.S.

A. Introduction

Erickson's philosophy about life and death can best be summarized in the following quote (Zeig, 1980, p. 269):

> Because we all start dying when we are born. Some of us are faster than others. Why not live and enjoy, because you can wake up dead. You won't know about it. But somebody else will worry then. Until that time—enjoy life.

This is the statement of a realist and the statement has built-in presuppositions and expectations. "Some do it faster than others." And, the key word in the last sentence is "enjoy." Joseph Campbell's advice is to "follow your bliss," Lawrence LeShan's is to "sing your song," and Erickson's is to "enjoy." They are all different ways of saying the same thing. We are also reminded of Wyschogrod's observation, "Life poses a peculiar problem, to become who you are." All of these quotes are relevant to working with those who are in severe pain, those with life-threatening diseases, and those who are dying. (Some prefer the word "deathing" to "dying.")

Starting with the work of Elisabeth Kübler-Ross some twenty-five to thirty years ago, Americans have become more aware and open to issues of death and dying. How can the Ericksonian hypnotherapist help with these natural processes? Certainly, in reviewing Erickson's work we can cite the classic cases of Joe the florist and the tomato plant metaphor (see Erickson and Rossi; 1980, Vol. IV, pp. 268–275; Haley, 1973, pp. 301–306; Zeig, 1985, pp. 41–43), and the woman with the hungry tiger under her bed (Erickson and Rossi, 1979, pp. 138–139; Zeig, 1979, pp. 188–189), amongst others. Erickson used stories, time distortion, dissociation, displacement of a symptom, and imagery among other interventions to help the dying. Much of his work had to do with controlling the severe pain with which terminal cancer patients struggle. In this chapter, after briefly discussing the work of several others, we will present material this author has been developing in areas like the use of self-image, guided imagery, and unfinished business.

The psychologist, L. LeShan (1977, 1989) has worked with terminally ill patients (mostly cancer) for several decades. In his work he has shown the efficacy of "traditional" psychotherapy in alleviating the distress caused primarily by unfinished business and denied personal dreams. Some of his patients have had remissions, presumably as a result of his interventions. He was able to help most of his patients die in a more comfortable state with themselves and others. The Simontons (Simonton, Simonton, and Creighton, 1980) started the use of guided imagery, relaxation methods, and group work to help cancer patients. Norman Cousins (1979) wrote movingly about how getting involved in your own treatment and your personal approach to your illness can have a profound effect on its course and your life. Frankl (1959) has written extensively about coping with life's travails. Rossi (1986) and Rossi and Cheek (1988) have applied Ericksonian hypnotherapeutic methods to healing and have provided a scientific basis for this work in their summary of research in the area of psychoneuroimmunology. David Spiegel and his colleagues (1989 et seq.) have unambiguously demonstrated the effect of group psychotherapy in helping people who have cancer. In their seminal study they reported that psychotherapy lengthened by one and one-half years the lives of women who had metastatic breast cancer, while reducing their anxiety as well. This work has since been replicated in several studies.

To a large extent, this chapter has grown out of the work of the author in facilitating a Bernie Siegel style ECaP (Exceptional Cancer Patient) group for over seven years. Siegel has written three books (1986, 1989, 1993) which explore in different ways the impact of a person's attitude on the course of their disease. Siegel has been quite influential in spreading the word about personal involvement. Typically, ECaP groups end with a "relaxation" or guided imagery or healing imagery meditation. Such meditations involve hypnotic states. The effectiveness of these states can be enhanced by the knowledge and use of hypnotic language. Siegel makes extensive use of drawings to which we have devoted a separate chapter. Hypnotic skills are particularly useful with the dying who are frequently comatose or semi-comatose in their last days. One comment that Bernie Siegel has made about the word "dying" is important, "You are either alive or you are dead." "Dying" is an attribution made by others who judge that a person may be close (days, weeks, or months) to death . In the last hours (typically 12–36) of life, one may say that a person is "actively dying" since well-recognized physiological changes occur during this period. But, you are either alive or dead!

Finally, several cautions need to be mentioned. This work with the terminally ill is best done with the knowledge and cooperation of the person's medical team. The person's overt permission is always required. It is also wise to work with and have the permission of the family. This work can bring with it unusual strains (and rewards!), and you should be prepared by having a colleague or friend available for your own support.

B. Self-Image

How you feel about yourself and your illness can have a profound effect on your health and the course of the disease. There are those who believe (supported by anecdotal evidence and some studies) that certain "personalities" or character traits make one more open to cancer. There is good evidence that stress can depress the immune system. One theory about the onset of cancer states that we always have some aberrant or cancer cells in our bodies. The immune system can normally rid the body of these abnormal cells. However, in times of high stress (however caused) the immune system can weaken and the cancer cells proliferate and overwhelm it. So, it might make sense to state that we actually bring about cancer by our life-style. The problem with this theory is that *only a small percentage* of those who live stressful lives actually get cancers. In terms of self-image it is truly self-defeating to "blame" yourself for your cancer. There appears to be a certain amount of capriciousness to life and the onset of a given disease. It is best to start with the fact of the physical diagnosis, without blaming yourself, and then to go on from there.

In your particular case your life-style *may* have been a contributing factor. So, the physical diagnosis can be considered to be a *gift* or an *opportunity* to assess your goals in life and your life-style. Ken Wilber (1993, p. 51) puts it this way, "Since nobody knows what caused your cancer, ... why don't you try this. Why don't you use your cancer as a metaphor and a spur to change all these things in your life that you wanted to change anyway. ... And don't change them because you think they caused the cancer—that will make you feel guilty—change them simply because they should be changed in any event." Bernie Siegel tells (on some of his tapes) of a lawyer with cancer who never liked practicing law and who loved playing the violin. This man, under the pressure of his cancer, gave up the law for his violin. This particular story has a happy ending with the disappearance of the cancer and a career as a violinist. The basic importance of this story is that if *one* person can turn around his life this way, that we all have the *potential* for such personal transformations. As an Ericksonian hypnotherapist you need to be aware of these *potentials* so that in working with clients with life-threatening diseases you can enhance and strengthen their immune systems. (We will write about this more in the section on unfinished business below.)

Ericksonians are adept at working with expectations. One beautiful example of this is the observation, "Cancer is not a sentence, it is simply a word ..." This observation, in effect, de-nominalizes the word "cancer" and gets it out of the realm of being a "death sentence." After all, no one gets out of life alive, and being alive is already a "death sentence." What do you do between *now* and that inevitable *then*? It is the function of the therapist to provide choices and to access dreams and expectations to help make the choices realizable. Most people who are diagnosed with cancer are not aware of the many choices still available to them. They may need permission to obtain second or third opinions, or to fire their doctor(s) if they feel they are not getting proper support, or their questions answered. One friend fired her doctor after being brusquely told that she needed surgery and that he was scheduling it for after he returned from vacation in two weeks! You may have a physician who is generally recognized as being competent, but you should also know that outcomes of treatments are affected by *how collaboratively* and *with how much trust* those treatments are chosen. As a therapist you can guide these expectations, making your client aware of how his/her involvement in the treatment process can affect its outcome. A friend who was preparing himself for surgery by doing some self-hypnosis was surprised by the suggestion that he could prepare a list of "hypnotic" suggestions, and ask his surgeon to use them appropriately during the surgery! Taking control of one or more aspects of your treatment can have profoundly beneficial effects. An Ericksonian can coach a client in pre- and post-operative relaxation, control, and healing-enhancing techniques.

Erickson had a life-long interest in anthropology and effectively used his knowledge of other cultures in working with his diverse client population. If you are going to work with the dying or those with life-threatening diseases, then you need to be sensitive to the cultural background of your clients. Is a disease and its treatment "hot" or "cold," "evil" or "good," "natural" or "unnatural," "fated" or "random," "divinely caused" or "environmental"? You need to work within and with an understanding of your client's belief system—Erickson's utilization principle. In Erickson's classic case with Joe, the florist, Erickson used his knowledge of growing things to pace and then lead Joe to comfort in his final days. If you use metaphors, they need to be constructed with an awareness of how a particular client approaches severe disease and death.

C. The Role of Guided Imagery

Simonton et al. (1980) pioneered the use of relaxation and guided imagery for working with cancer patients. Guided imagery, or healing meditation, is typically preceded by instructions for relaxation. Earlier workers typically used progressive relaxation, but Ericksonians will find indirect suggestion and expectation easier and faster to use. It is well-known (e.g. Benson, 1975; Rossi, 1993) that relaxation not only has profound physiological effects, but also enhances the immune system.

Achterberg (1985) has written a scholarly work on imagery in healing, tracing its roots through various cultures. She gives a table (p. 152) listing the use of imagery in psychotherapy for some thirty different therapeutic approaches. Her book also contains transcripts for imagery work. She emphasizes that there is an important distinction between disease and illness. A *disease* is considered to be the physiological malfunctioning of the body, e.g. a broken leg or an ulcer or a cancer or a hormonal imbalance or a stroke. An *illness*, by contrast, is concerned with the psychosocial and cultural responses to a disease. Thus, disease is physical and illness is attitudinal. There are, of course, links between the two. The field of psychoneuroimmunology has illuminated these connections on the biochemical and neurological levels (see Rossi, 1986, 1993, e.g.). We also make a distinction between *healing* and *curing*. The word "healing" relates to the sociocultural and spiritual abatement of an illness, becoming whole and in harmony (as in the Navajo sense). The word "cure" relates to the physical aspects such as the disappearance of a disease.

The book by Achterberg, Dossey, and Kolkmeier (1994) explores in depth the use of rituals in healing. These rituals involve three phases (pp. 22-31): separation, transition, and return, which are described in detail in the book. The authors also distinguish between several types of imagery: (1) *receptive imagery* consists of those images that just pop up or flow through the conscious mind and which are not deliberately caused; (2) *active imagery* is consciously and deliberately constructed; (3) *concrete imagery* tends to be biologically correct, and people generally prefer to start with such images; (4) *symbolic imagery* is the person's unique replacement for the concrete images and tends to be more powerful; (5) *process imagery* signifies a systematic step-by-step imagery which is directed towards a specific goal; (6) in *end state imagery* the final or healed state is imagined; (7) *general healing images* involve events, persons or things such as a healing presence or light or color or power animal or an inner/outer guide; (8) *drumming* at the rate of 3–7 beats per second appears to aid imagery work; (9) *preverbal imagery* appears to exist at the interface between inner experience and conscious expression, i.e. there is more of a "body" connection; and (10) *transpersonal imagery* is not confined to a single person's body/mind, but is a mode of communication from one person to another (through unknown and invisible pathways). This book is replete with many examples of healing imagery for a truly astonishing variety of concerns. The authors generally recommend starting with concrete imagery and later shifting to person-specific symbolic imagery. There is an implication that the more *accurate* the image is, the more effective it will be.

Early work with guided imagery was directive in terms of suggesting highly specific images to enhance healing. In particular, following the concept of a "war" on cancer, the suggested imagery was oriented towards killing and destruction. A pacifist with cancer would justifiably object to this! In recent times imagery work has become more permissive and tied to the particular belief system of the client. Can cancer cells be gently smothered by *love*? Or just coaxed to gently leave? Suggestions are now more open:

> As you sit there calmly resting, just let your mind find some simple and natural way to heal those parts of your body that need healing. I just don't know what way or ways will feel just right for you, what images or words or sounds or feelings. They may be of special cells or chemicals or animals or helpers or spirits or objects. Just find your own special way or ways of helping and healing, now, easily and comfortably.

Note that, if you are working with someone whose primary representational system is auditory or kinesthetic, that you need to seed "imagery" (i.e. internal processing) that can safely use sounds and physical senses. An auditory person might "image" a song or a sound that would destroy or push out the cancer cells. A kinesthetic person's "image" might be a sieve that can be felt selectively moving through the body gathering up cancer cells for removal. The more specific your suggested images, the fewer people you will reach. Help them to find their own unique healing "image."

There are many imagery and healing tapes available. See the ECaP catalog (ECaP, 300 Plaza Middlesex, Middletown, CT 06457; 203-343-5950), for example. Also, see Naparstek (1994) which contains guided imagery scripts for many circumstances and conditions. She sells a variety of tapes (Image Paths, Inc., 891 Moe Drive, Suite C, Akron, OH 44310; (800) 800-8661.)

You can do direct hypnotic work for imagery using metaphors. Since many cancer patients are restricted in movement, a particularly effective use of trance is to take the person on a trip within their own mind, doing those natural everyday things they can no longer perform:

> As you lie there now, I know just how frustrated you must feel in not being able to get up and move around, to do all of those simple everyday things. But, you know, it would be okay, it would certainly

be okay to do those things within your mind, to just let your body lie there and within your mind to just get up, now, and move around. Gently and easily, within your mind, get up, move your legs over the edge of the bed, stretch gently, easily and simply stand, leaving your body back there. That's right. And, you can move off to another room, feeling, within your own mind, your legs moving ever so easily, and the floor under foot. Is it carpeted or wood or ...? This is your trip, and you can make it as real as you like. Are you moving to the kitchen or the living room or ...? Perhaps, within the privacy of your own mind on this trip, you may wish to use the toilet or take a shower or bath. That's fine. Go right ahead. And, when you've had enough of moving around, you can come back to this bed, here, and rejoin your body, having had such an interesting little trip. And, you know, you can do that as often as you wish, within your own mind, comfortably and safely. Thank you for letting me spend this time with you. Relax, rest, for now. Peace and love, and, love and peace.

D. Unfinished Business

One of the significant difficulties many dying people have to cope with is unfinished business. LeShan (1977, 1989) has worked for many years with dying people and has found that "straight" psychotherapy is frequently of great value. (Also, see David Spiegel et al.'s work.) Generally, this work has to do with resolving either unfinished business with family members or with unrealized dreams and hopes. After all, once you are dead, you can no longer work out relationships with family or achieve those old ambitions and dreams. Sometimes, this work can be so releasing that the disease disappears (as for the lawyer/violinist cited above) or greatly eased. The therapist is working with the "illness" and not the disease.

For many people in the last stage of their life it is difficult to acknowledge and work on the many unspoken and unresolved problems that center on relationships. There may be things they never said to loved ones—sometimes simple statements of love. This resolution work can be facilitated if the other person is present and the therapist works as a mediator. If the person is absent, then there are many choices such as: the Gestalt Therapy two-chair approach; regression to an earlier time to resolve the difficulties; metaphoric work; letter writing; and open talking. Some simple statements are, "I now forgive." "I (now) forgive myself for I didn't know any better (then)." The other side of forgiveness is to provide the person with an opportunity for "telling off" those people they never felt sufficiently safe or comfortable with to directly show anger or strong emotions. Such unspoken statements can fester. Once spoken or written these "negative" emotions can lead to forgiveness. If the person is comatose or semi-comatose, they can still be led through an unfinished business/forgiveness procedure. There is considerable evidence that the comatose can hear and respond—for example, you can always ask for physical responses and note tiny movements. Although deathbed confessions have their place, it is much better to do this work with unfinished business well in advance of death.

If the dying person has sufficient energy and awareness, a good life-ratifying thing to do is to interview them about their lives on audio- or videotape. This is an excellent vehicle for focusing on their life, and also for leaving a record for survivors. Drawings and writing also serve a similar function.

Joseph Campbell once reported overhearing a father in a restaurant state in response to his wife's query about why he was so hard on his son's behavior, "I don't see why I should let him get away with things—I've never done anything in my life I wanted to do." How sad! What happened to our childhood and teenage and young adult dreams? One of the important things we do in ECaP groups is to periodically give people the opportunity to talk about their dreams and hopes—What are/were they? Is there any way you can work to fulfill them today? What would you need? Most of the time these dreams and hopes embody rather simple and still attainable things. One woman we know was diagnosed in the summer as having a few weeks left to live. She was a young mother of three, and one of the things that particularly annoyed her was traveling in a small car with her family. Her husband promised her a van if she lived until Christmas. She got her van. Her next dream had to do with a trip overseas in the summer. (Sadly, she did not live long enough to realize this dream.) The expression of these hopes and dreams can have a powerful effect not only on the person's mental comfort, but also on their disease.

Giving someone permission to die is related to unfinished business. Death is natural and unavoidable. (Bernie Siegel has commented, "Don't do things so that you won't die—it doesn't work!") Yet, in the last days of life some people refuse to give up because they may feel they are still needed and cannot abandon their loved ones. This lingering, often in considerable discomfort, may be thought to be for the benefit of the survivors, but I have seen too many families live through prolonged strain and anguish to believe this. Everyone should die in their own time and in their own way. Yet they may be unaware that loved ones can indeed go on functioning without them. In trance work you can metaphorically remind the dying person of the seasons, and of the natural cycle of life and death, of how they did such a good job in raising and training self-sufficient children and spouses. In short, join them in their concerns and assure them that it is okay to die when they are ready. Although this message can be delivered directly, it is probably best to do so metaphorically. Of course, the family's permission is needed for this.

E. Bonding

The term "bonding" has been used in the context of male and female bonding. I use it for an approach in which I "bond" with the client and serve as the conduit for giving them whatever healing or change resources they need via the bonding anchor—this anchor is generally holding one or both hands. First, it is necessary to obtain the trust of the client, then permission to hold a hand. Next it is important to project in some congruent manner your deeply held belief that the connection through contact with you has the power to enhance and educate their own immune and healing systems. (For emotional concerns, the conviction is that they will be able to learn viable solutions via the contact, and that they will also be able to access their own innate resources.) The people I work with know my deep conviction that there is always hope, and that I believe in miracles. They also know of my belief that significant change can occur rapidly. You need to sit comfortably and close enough to your client to hold a hand or two, but where your hand is passive. Always ask for permission for this physical contact.

As an example of how this works, the following transcript is delivered using hypnotic language and voice control, but without a formal induction. This particular transcript was developed for a client with cancer. Prior to the delivery there will have been some preparatory informational work concerning psychoneuro-immunology, the nature of the immune system, and the effect of cancer on it. Generally, there is also some discussion about the nature and power of mind/body interactions:

Healing via Bonding

You should know that contact with my hand keeps you in touch with the present and with all of your strengths and knowledge. By the amount of pressure you put on my hand, you can control just how much strength and healing power you need from and through me. Please know that you can take as much as you need through me for I am only the channel for what you need, now. My body and my immune system can also serve as patterns for enhancing and strengthening your own immune system. Just continue to relax and breathe easily and calmly. That's right, softly and easily and gently. Paying attention to your breathing as you relax even further, feeling the support of that chair and your feet on the floor, and the comfort of the contact with my hand. And, through that hand you can begin to sense that some healing power and knowledge is moving into your body. Now, I don't know exactly where the cancer cells are, and we don't need to know—your body knows in some deep internal way where the healing work is to be done, and that's okay, isn't it? So, just let that healing power move into you through this contact, spreading through your body, moving precisely to just those places where it is needed at this time. And, that healing power, that healing knowledge, just, somehow, eliminates the cells that shouldn't be there. One at a time, working here and there. Then, faster, working on groups of those cells at a time, just as fast as your body can now accommodate the elimination of those cells. You may feel a special warmth or tingling or even mild itching in the parts of your body where this work is going on. Continuing to rest and relax. Breathing calmly and slowly, easily. That's right. Just as fast as your body can do that healing right now. A deep inner sense of where the healing is needed, where it is going on. Yes. And, at the same time, you know that your own immune system is getting stronger. Through my hand it is strengthening and learning just what to do and how to do it, cell by cell, part of cell by part of cell, molecule by molecule, the learning continuing until your own immune system can do this work by itself, stronger and stronger, faster and faster, healing, healthy, normally, naturally, easily, automatically. That's right, isn't it? Simply and easily. Just one cell at a time, as fast as is possible now. And, you know that this ability, this knowledge, is now a part of you, deeply imprinted in every molecule, every part of every cell, every cell, every nerve and tissue. All yours, now, and whenever you need it. At any time during the day you can take a few minutes, pay attention to your breathing, and let this healing power move through you, doing its work, and strengthening your own internal healing powers. Becoming part of you, now. Slowly and simply and easily and naturally. Yes. Yes. Yes ... And, when you are ready, you can return to this room, here and now, feeling ever so relaxed and refreshed and, somehow, full of energy. Thank you.

F. Fusion

The fusion approach is somewhat similar to the bonding approach. The main difference is that the client obtains healing knowledge from a projected healing image of themselves. The preparatory information again includes a discussion of psychoneuroimmunology, the nature of the immune system, and the power of mind/body interactions. It is explained that for whatever reason their immune system was caught unprepared and was overwhelmed by the cancer cells. Since aberrant or cancerous cells are being produced (from whatever causes) in us all of the time, our immune systems have been developed to rid the body of these irregular cells whose only function seems to be rapid reproduction. At some time in the past their body was perfectly capable of destroying these cancerous cells. They can also imagine that at some time in the future their immune system has cleansed their body of cancer, and is strong enough to continue to do so. The client is given the choice of being helped by their past perfectly functioning body or the cured one from the future.

It is useful to begin by establishing two anchors: one for contact with the present and the support of the therapist (holding a hand works well for this); and one for contact with their present day resources, knowledge, and strengths (this second anchor can be touching a knuckle once these resources have been accessed). The following transcript was also developed for a client with cancer, but may be adapted to other diseases or emotional difficulties:

Healing via Fusion

You should know that contact with my hand keeps you in touch with the present and with whatever support I can give you. Even though these are difficult times for you, we did talk earlier about some recent times when you really felt good about yourself, had a strong sense of control and understanding, even a sense of peace. Think about those times now; really get into that sense of "right now I'm feeling okay." That's right. (Set the anchor when you can tell that they have accessed this resource state.) Continue to breathe easily and simply and normally. You can imagine, now, that somewhere in front of you is that younger you, the you whose immune system is functioning normally and automatically and at peak efficiency. (Usually, they will have closed their eyes by this time, but this is not necessary.) As you look at your younger self, you can tell, you really know just by the way she is standing there, the way she moves and smiles, her stance, her attitude, that she is well and healthy, and that her immune system is strong and powerful.

As you continue to observe this younger healthy self, you notice that she notices you, here, now. She smiles, and slowly walks towards you. Then she reaches out and touches you, hand to hand, making firm contact. And you can feel her presence, can you not? Her strength and her health and vitality. And, now, an interesting thing begins to happen. Through your contact with her, hand to hand, touching, she starts to transmit from her body to yours the strength and knowledge and capability and effectiveness of her immune system. Educating, enhancing, strengthening yours. Atom by atom, molecule by molecule, part of cell by part of cell, cell by cell, tissue by tissue, organ by organ, bone by bone, fluid by fluid, nerve by nerve. And you may even feel, now, a warmth, a tingling, some mild electrical currents as this knowledge, this strength, from you to you, moves and suffuses through your body, permanently fusing, becoming one with your essence, and all your body parts and functions. Just feel these changes, now, as they become an integral, an integrated, part of you. So they can work and continue to work for you, within you, now, and this evening, and tonight, and tomorrow, and for as long as you need this extra help.

And now, within your mind, you can imagine and feel this younger you hugging you, merging with you, her knowledge and strength and abilities are yours. And, you thank her for this gift. You know the mind is remarkable, and any time you need this extra boost from yourself, you can just find a quiet place, and pay attention to your breathing, and just go right back to this time, her presence and her gift, feeling it filling you again. Yes. Yes. Yes.

Thank you for letting me share this time with you. And, when you are ready, you can return to this room, here and now, feeling ever so refreshed and energized. Yes. Thank you.

G. Secondary Gain

It is well known that secondary gains can play a significant role in maintaining psychological problems and physical disabilities. Becoming free of depression radically changes family dynamics. Becoming free of chronic lower back pain might involve: losing disability checks, having to go back to work, and losing sympathy and support from one's family. An alcoholic needs to find other ways to have a social network and to get family concern before becoming sober, or as part of the process. Can cancer and other life-threatening diseases involve secondary gains? The answer is a guarded "yes." This means that, if you are working with this population, then you must explore in some careful and gentle way the area of secondary gains. If it is clear that there appears to be a significant component of maintaining the disease related to secondary gains, then this can be handled via standard psychotherapeutic techniques. A particular malaise that can have significant effects on the course of a disease is connected with lack of meaning in life, a sense of hopelessness, and sense of no goal(s). This will be dealt with in the next section.

One of the paradoxical statements made by almost everyone I have talked with who has a life-threatening disease (this even extends to most support persons) is, "You know, in some ways having this cancer has been a blessing." This is a seemingly strange statement until they go on to explain that the cancer has taught them many things: the importance of really being in the present—touching, feeling, smelling, sensing, tasting, loving, caring, really seeing things, and living one day or one hour or one moment at a time. They now have a perspective on what is really important to them—trivia become trivia, relationships strengthen, society driven goals wane; and they become more intensely alive, packing lifetimes into days. They almost pity the rest of humanity with their humdrum routine existences, doomed to walking their treadmill until they just fall off at the end. This paradoxical response of people who have life-threatening diseases is a life-affirming way of coping, and you need do nothing but be an active and sympathetic listener, and *learn from them* the art of living one day or one moment at a time.

H. The Search for Meaning

The late Viktor Frankl's landmark book (Frankl, 1984) entitled "Man's Search for Meaning" has sold in millions and has inspired people worldwide. It is written about his experiences in concentration camps in World War II, and is one of the most impressive descriptions of the value of the human spirit in overcoming adversity. His basic message is that, although there are many things in our lives over which we have no control (like getting cancer), we always have the *choice* of how to respond to these adversities. People who have cancer, for example, invariably ask, "Why me?" "Why now?" "Why this particular disease?" These questions can rarely be answered, although those who are deeply religious can sometimes find comfort within the teachings of their religion. Frankl's response is to go beyond breast-beating to making choices and discovering meaning in the context of the new circumstances. He developed *logotherapy* as a specific psychotherapeutic approach to help people resolve this existential question about meaning. As an Ericksonian hypnotherapist you can build on Frankl's work and provide open-ended metaphors within trance work to assist clients to find meaning in their lives. You need to be cautious in doing this, following the client's interest in such endeavors (rather than impressing on them what you may think is best). You *offer* them the opportunity to do meaning work. Of course, this work may be done in collaboration with a minister or the family.

I. Preparing People for Surgery

One of the things I do is to prepare people for surgery. This is usually done in two sessions, but you should understand that my sessions are always open-ended and can extend well beyond two hours. The first session is mainly devoted to discussing the range of things described in this chapter incuding "mechanical" things such as queries about wills, living wills, durable power of attorney for health, financial and funeral arrangements (membership in a memorial or burial society—I am healthy, but have made all such arrangements, and so has my wife), if appropriate. Information is elicited about preferred imagery and ways to relax, as well as prior experiences with surgery and hospital stays. This first session typically ends with a relaxation as preparation for the second session and an audiotape. The client is also informed about evidence that patients can hear what is said in the operating room, even when they are fully anesthetized.

The second session is used for more information, listening to the client's concerns, and a thirty-minute hypnotic session which is similar in content to the audiotape which will be given to them at the end of the session. This tape is longer than my standard fifteen minute guided imagery for healing tapes, enabling me to cover all the necessary material, and to provide a longer time to be immersed in the soft calming environment of the tape. Typically, the hypnotic session is divided into four parts: (1) relaxation / induction; (2) pre-op suggestions (such as knowing when to go to her safe haven within her mind); (3) operation suggestions that incorporate the statements given to the surgeon to say (see below); and (4) post-op suggestions for rapid and comfortable healing. The suggestions are given in a way designed to have them function as post-hypnotic for the surgery experience. A certain amount of dissociation and time distortion (e.g. how surprisingly fast the entire experience will be) are built into the process. Then the client is given copies of a letter written to their surgeon. The client decides what is the best time to give this letter to their surgeon.

This letter is in two parts. The first part gives information relating to my work with the client (Mary) and information about my bona fides. The second part follows:

> There is a great deal of evidence that patients, even under the surgical plane of anesthesia, can hear things that are said in the operating room. It is felt that, if the surgeon (or an assistant known to the patient) makes encouraging and healing comments directly to the patient during the surgery, then this has a beneficial effect on outcomes and recovery. This has been both my personal experience and that of the people I have advised. To this end, you will find a brief set of directions and some simple statements that we hope you will be willing to say to Mary at appropriate times during the surgery. These statements need to be made only a few times, and should always be prefaced by using Mary's name so that she knows the message is directed to her; and ended with a "thank you" so that she knows the message is over. Mary has an audiotape to listen to in advance of the surgery.

The statements (note: they should be modified to suit the particular surgery) are:

1. Mary—please slow down (or stop) the bleeding where I am working. Thank you. (Note: Kay Thompson suggested that sometimes a little bleeding is necessary to clear the operating field.)

2. Mary—please relax your muscles in this area. Thank you.

3. Mary—this is going very well. Thank you.

4. Mary—you will heal surprisingly quickly. Thank you.

5. Mary—you will be surprisingly comfortable and at ease after this. Thank you.

6. Mary—your recovery will be very rapid. Thank you.

This preparation procedure has worked well for everyone with whom I have worked. One friend said that the hysterectomy she dreaded was "almost pleasant." Mary's comments are, "I was sure this works for other people, but not for me. It was after the first meditation you led me through that I was convinced this stuff would work. I found the imagery tapes so wonderful—always fell into the deepest sleep. By the time I got the surgery tape I was ready for it, and listened to it every day for nine days. I was listening to it for the three quarters of an hour when they were injecting the dye into me in the hospital. The tape worked—I was able to relax. I only felt nausea briefly afterwards. The anesthetist read the messages during my surgery. The head nurse was very impressed. I would recommend this highly and have told all of my friends ... "

J. Conclusions

Working with people with life-threatening diseases and the dying can be stressful, but also rewarding. The literature about Erickson's work shows him to have worked with many dying people, most frequently for pain control. Trance work is certainly useful for the control of pain and discomfort. However, the discipline involved in the use of hypnotic language particularly lends itself to working with this population. Since you may be working as much (or more) with the dying person's family, the use of subtle hypnotic language is even more important. (You may also be interested in a book the author is writing entitled "Guided Imagery and Other Approaches to Healing" (due early 2000). This book has grown out of a course he teaches and his volunteer work.)

Exercises

1. Familiarize yourself with the literature in this field starting with Kübler-Ross, Simonton, LeShan, Siegel, Frankl, Spiegel, Achterberg, and Rossi.

2. Visit an old age home, a support group for the seriously ill, an ECaP group, or a hospice. Learn by listening and observing. Consider volunteer work at these places.

3. If you have a friend or relative who is dying or has a life-threatening disease, ask their permission to use your skills to help them.

4. Attend seminars on death and dying and grief therapy.

5. Write out scripts for: guided imagery; pain control; unfinished business; permission to die; fusion; secondary gain; bonding; meaning; and preparation for surgery.

6. Do personal work on your own beliefs and feelings about death and dying.

7. Study the healing imagery in Achterberg et al. (1994) and Naparstek (1994). As an Ericksonian, how would you deliver a particular script and/or modify it to be most effective? Are the scripts too specific or not sufficiently specific?

8. Is guided imagery the same as hypnotic work?

9. Examine the literature on psychoneuroimmunology and mind/body interactions. Vol. II of Erickson's collected works contains his papers on psychophysiological processes. (Of course, Erickson also did much work with "terminal" cancer patients as illustrated in the famous case of "Joe the Florist.")

Chapter 20

Ethical and Legal Considerations

Rubin Battino, M.S.

A. Introduction

The various popular conceptions and misconceptions about hypnosis and hypnotherapy have resulted in a great deal of caution about the subject over the years. After all, the distinguished investigating committee of the French Academy consisting of Lavoisier, Guillotin, and Ben Franklin found Anton Mesmer to be a charlatan at the end of the eighteenth century! Hypnotism made a slow recovery that was curtailed again by the discovery of chemical anesthetics. A second resurgence, initially aided by Freud, was doomed when Freud turned against hypnosis in favor of his own discovery of psychoanalysis. It is only in recent times, due almost solely to the efforts of Erickson, that hypnosis and hypnotherapy have come back into repute. The American Society of Clinical Hypnosis was founded in 1957 by Erickson and others, but it wasn't until 1958 that the American Medical Association and 1960 that the American Psychological Association recognized hypnosis and hypnotherapy as acceptable procedures. The image of a Svengali or a Dr. Fu Manchu using hypnosis to have people submit to their wills still lingers in the public mind. There is a "dark" side to hypnosis that will be discussed at the end of this chapter.

The confusions about hypnosis and hypnotherapy which are still extant may be the reason that licensing by state authorities are either nonexistent or quite variable. After all, states find it much easier to license plumbers, hairdressers and electricians because there appear to be objective standards in those fields. If many helping professionals find it hard to accept hypnosis as a psychotherapy, how can the state be expected to regulate it! In Ohio, for example, counselors, social workers and psychologists are licensed. You are violating state law if you do "psychotherapy" without a license, yet anyone can do hypnotherapy. (Anyone can also do palm reading, mystical interpretations, astrological readings, phrenology, "advising," dream interpretation, and psychic healing!)

In this chapter we will attempt to offer some guidance on the ethical practice of hypnosis and hypnotherapy. The guidelines used by various professional societies will be presented and discussed. There will be a brief discussion of forensic hypnosis. We will present our recommended guidelines, and then discuss the "dark" side.

B. The Milton H. Erickson Foundation

The Milton H. Erickson Foundation, Inc. (3606 North 24th Street, Phoenix, AZ 85016-6500; (602) 956-6196) has relatively simple eligibility rules for attendance at their training programs, workshops or congresses. (The Foundation has a web page at **http://www.erickson-foundation.org** and their E-mail address is: **office@erickson-foundation.org**.) To quote from the announcement for the Spring 1993 Phoenix Intensive Training Program: "Eligibility: Open to professionals with master's degrees and above from accredited institutions and eligible students." A more complete statement of eligibility is found in the announcement for the Fifth International Congress on Ericksonian Approaches to Hypnosis and Psychotherapy (December 2–6, 1992):

> The Congress is open to professionals in health-related fields including physicians, doctoral level psychologists and dentists who are qualified for membership in, or are members of, their respective professional organizations (e.g. A.M.A., A.P.A., A.D.A.). The congress is also open to professionals with mental health-related degrees (e.g. M.S.W., M.A., M.S., M.S.N.) from accredited institutions. Applications will be accepted from full-time graduate students in accredited programs in the above fields who supply a letter from their department certifying their full-time student status as of December, 1992.

The Milton H. Erickson Foundation, Inc. is accredited by various professional organizations to provide CEUs (continuing education units).

There are over seventy societies and institutes worldwide that are officially associated with the Foundation. These groups maintain the same eligibility standards for membership and for attendance at their own training programs. The Foundation carefully investigates each potential institute and society before granting association status. Guidelines are being developed for the "certification" of training in Ericksonian hypnotherapy. But anyone with any kind of background may call him/herself an Ericksonian hypnotherapist and may conduct workshops or training with that descriptive. The Foundation can take legal action only if someone or some group claims association with the Foundation when, in fact, they are not associated.

C. Society for Clinical and Experimental Hypnosis (SCEH)

At the time of this writing (November 1998) the membership requirements are those indicated below. There are several categories of membership. The following membership requirements are quoted from the Application for Membership for the calendar year 1994–1995 and as far as I am aware where there have been no substantive changes since:

Requirements for Full SCEH Membership:

(a) D.D.S., M.D. or D.O., Ph.D. (Psychology) or Psy.D., M.S.W. (Clinical) of D.S.W. degree.

(b) Professional membership

(1) American Dental Association, American Medical Association, or the American Psychological Association;

or

(2) Clinical social workers who meet the graduate educational (M.S.W., D.S.W., Ph.D.) license and postgraduate supervision requirements of the American Board of Examiners in Clinical Social Work.

(c) Completion of one or more courses in hypnosis taught by recognized members of the above associations.

(d) Publication in a national or international scientific journal; presentation of a paper at a national or international meeting on the subject of hypnosis; evidence of competence in practice or research; teaching hypnosis on a regular basis at any recognized doctoral level institution; or participating as faculty for several recognized national workshops.

(e) Two sponsoring letters are required: certification of competence in practice and/or research commensurate with the above requirements by two professional sponsors. At least one such letter should be from a colleague in the community who knows the applicant and his/her work. If possible, one sponsoring letter should be from a member of SCEH. However, if you are not known by an SCEH member, both letters can be from professional colleagues.

Applicants for Associate Membership meet all of the criteria listed above with the exception of (d). All applicants are responsible for securing sponsoring letters.

The membership categories are: student affiliate, associate, full, and fellow.

The code of ethics of the Society is found in their bylaws. The full code may be obtained from the Society (128-A Kings Park Drive, Liverpool, NY 13090, (315) 652-7299). There are four ethical principles which are summarized and paraphrased below:

1. Principle I: a member of the Society should be a member in good standing of their own professional society, which also implies acceptance of the ethical and scientific standards of that particular society.

2. Principle II: members of the Society shall limit their clinical and scientific use of hypnosis to the area of their competence as defined by the professional standards of their own particular field. Members who encounter problems in the use of hypnosis shall seek the help of qualified specialists. Extending the use of hypnosis must be carried out with appropriate safeguards.

3. Principle III: no members of SCEH shall offer their services for public entertainment nor shall they collaborate or cooperate with lay or stage hypnotists. Members should not give courses in hypnosis to lay people or to anyone who is not a member of the Society or eligible to be a member. Society members may serve as consultants about professional standards. No member of the Society shall offer their professional use of hypnosis via newspapers, radio, television, or similar media.

4. Principle IV: members may make clinical and scientific use of hypnosis if it contributes to the welfare of patients and/or to the advancement of professional knowledge. Proper safeguards are to be used in research investigations and whenever a human subject is exposed to stress.

The Society maintains a Committee on Ethics and Professional Attitudes to oversee compliance with its code of ethics. A charge of an ethical violation may be initiated by anyone, whether a member of the Society or not. These charges are investigated with due protection of rights for all parties. Details of how such ethical violations are handled may be obtained from the Society.

The Society, which was established in 1949, publishes *The International Journal of Clinical and Experimental Hypnosis* and conducts annual workshops and scientific programs.

D. The American Society of Clinical Hypnosis (ASCH)

The American Society for Clinical Hypnosis (2200 East Devon Avenue, Suite 291, Des Plaines, IL 60018-4534. (847) 297-3317) states that applicants must meet the following standards for eligibility for Membership January 1997):

1. An M.D., D.D.S., D.M.D., D.O., D.P.M., Psy.D., or a Ph.D. or an equivalent doctoral degree with psychology as the major study, or a master's degree in nursing, in social work, psychology, marriage and family therapy, or mental health counseling.

2. Required degree shall be from a University or College accredited by its appropriate regional accrediting body.

3. A current license to practice in the state/province of residence.

4. Membership, or eligibility for membership, in a professional society other than ASCH or SCEH consistent with his/her degree.

479

5. Appropriate professional training and experience in clinical or experimental hypnosis.

To be eligible for *Associate Membership* only criteria 1-4 above are needed. To be eligible for *Student Membership* the following must be met:

1. A full time student with a minimum of 45 completed graduate semester hours or 60 completed graduate quarter hours; and shall be enrolled in a graduate program in active pursuit of a doctorate in (1) medicine (M.D., D.O., D.P.M.), dentistry or psychology; or (2) enrolled in a doctoral program where psychology is the major field of study.

2. Pursuing his/her doctoral degree at a University or College fully accredited by its appropriate regional accrediting body to give such a degree.

ASCH also gives certification in two categories: *Consultant in Clinical Hypnosis* and in *Clinical Hypnosis*. They may be contacted for additional information. ASCH conducts regularly scheduled training workshops and publishes *The American Journal of Clinical Hypnosis*.

E. The American Psychological Association

The APA "Ethical Principles of Psychologists and Code of Conduct" went into effect on December 1, 1992. This detailed fifteen-page document covers a great variety of areas within the field, but does not deal specifically with hypnosis or hypnotherapy. There is a resource person who may be contacted about psychological hypnosis. There are two categories of regular membership. A member must have a recognized doctoral degree in the field. An associate member must either have completed two years of graduate work in psychology at an accredited institution *or* an accredited master's degree in psychology plus he must have one year of acceptable professional experience.

F. Hypnosis and the Law

Although the practice of psychotherapy and, by implication, hypnotherapy is regulated by each state separately, the practice of "hypnosis" per se does not appear to be generally regulated. To be safe, you need to consult the licensing or certifying boards in your own state. For example, in California, licensed physicians and psychologists may practice hypnotherapy without *any* evidence of prior training, while licensed marital and family therapists are first required to take and pass a forty-hour course in hypnotherapy.

The topic of this section, hypnosis and the law, generally refers to interactions with the courts with respect to hypnotically refreshed memory. The copious literature on this subject has been summarized and commented upon in the basic reference in the field by Scheflin and Shapiro (1989). In addition to much background, the authors provide an appendix summarizing the law pertaining to forensic hypnosis in all fifty states, federal cases, military cases, and Canada, England, and New Zealand. They give practical advice relating to the preparation for court appearances and actual appearance in court as an expert witness or as a witness. In what follows, we will summarize some of their useful findings.

First, some relevant quotes concerning the roles of the therapist and the law:

> For the clinician, the question as to whether a memory is accurate is less important than the impact of that memory on the individual. Veracity takes second place to the patient's subjective reality (p. 165).

> Psychology favors narrative truth, the law historical truth. Therapists strive for patients' comfort and symptom relief; the law strives for precision, justice, and punishment (p. 232).

The goals of therapy and the law are different. They cross when your client comes to you for the use of hypnosis specifically for memory retrieval which may be immediately applicable to a legal procedure *or* which *may* become applicable. They also cross when material is retrieved by the use of hypnosis whose nature indicates that the material may be of significance in a legal (or criminal) proceeding. To quote further (p. 12):

> In states following the *Shirley* approach, the hypnotherapist must now evaluate far-reaching potentially *legal* events prior to engaging in therapeutic interventions with a client who might be in substantial

mental distress. Hypnosis may have to be rejected as a treatment of choice in order to protect the client's potential legal rights. Therapists find themselves in the position of having to provide full disclosure of potential legal consequences to clients prior to beginning therapy with these clients. Therapists must also decide at that time whether or not they would be willing to be called to court to testify regarding the therapy.

The above citations recommend great caution in the use of hypnosis with clients where there is the potential for legal involvement.

In testimony in the cases State vs. Hurd (1980, 1981) M. Orne developed a series of safeguards for the use of hypnosis in forensic cases. Scheflin and Shapiro summarize these safeguards as follows (p. 79):

1.   The hypnotic session should be conducted by a licensed psychiatrist or psychologist trained in the use of hypnosis.

2.   The qualified professional conducting the hypnotic session should be independent of, not regularly employed by, and not responsible to, the prosecutor, the investigator, or the defense.

3.   Any information given to the hypnotist by law enforcement personnel or the defense prior to the hypnotic session must be in written form or recorded, so that subsequently the extent of the information the subject received from the hypnotist may be determined.

4.   Before induction of hypnosis, the hypnotist should obtain from the subject a detailed description of the facts as the subject remembers them, carefully avoiding adding any new elements to the witness's description of the events.

5.   All contacts between the hypnotist and the subject should be recorded, so that a permanent record is available for comparison and study to establish that the witness has not received information or suggestions that might later be reported as having been first described by the subject during hypnosis. The use of videotape is strongly encouraged but is not mandatory.

6.   Only the hypnotist and the subject should be present during any phase of the hypnotic session, including the prehypnotic testing and posthypnotic interview.

An additional point insisted upon by Orne, and also by Spiegel, was recognized in the *Hurd* case. That point is "the importance of independent verification of hypnotically-induced recollection ... The most we should legitimately expect from hypnotic interrogations is further data which may serve as leads for more conventional data gathering."

Obviously, great caution and care and preparation must be used if you engage in forensic hypnosis.

Since the main use of forensic hypnosis is for memory recall, we should investigate this further. Mark Twain once commented, "When I was a young man I could remember everything, whether it happened or not." Just how reliable is memory recall? The evidence seems to be in favor of the potential for memory distortion in hypnotic suggestion. Scheflin and Shapiro state (p. 81): "The ability of hypnotists to create or implant false memories or inaccurate recollections has been consistently observed and reported, especially with reference to the legal arena." One decidedly relevant point is that skilled interrogators and attorneys who are proficient in the use of leading questions know that the answers they get are strongly influenced by the questions posed and how they are posed. Aren't these practices akin to memory "creation" or contamination? Let us again quote Scheflin and Shapiro:

"Is confabulation an inevitable by-product of hypnotic retrieval?" Our answer is "no." By contrast, suppose we ask, "Can hypnosis lead to confabulation?" That answer is "yes." The harder question requires a comparison between hypnotic retrieval methods and a variety of interrogation methods that use leading questions. Is hypnosis more likely to produce confabulation? No definitive answer is yet supported by available data (p. 167).

From our review of the extant literature on normal witness recall, it seems premature to single out hypnosis for special treatment. No reliable empirical evidence indicates that hypnosis creates a greater number of inaccurate memories, or that the memories achieved under hypnosis are more hard or fixed and thus more impervious to cross-examination (p. 174).

This matter of influencing memory is an important one in the practice of psychotherapy. Is not the powerful technique of *reframing* as applied to past events the creation of new memories by changing how we discern the old events? The NLP techniques of "changing personal history" and "time-line therapy" are based on effectively changing memories by altering *interpretations* of past events. Future pacing and Erickson's method of having a client imagine they are in their own future and looking back at the present through the intervening time to find (have found?) solutions to problems, is an altering of "future" memories. Certainly, Erickson's famous "February Man" case involves the systematic creation of an entirely new past for his client. So the manipulation of memory is a powerful therapeutic technique. You must weigh the benefits to your client against possible legal issues when using the hypnotic intervention.

We close this section with Scheflin and Shapiro's operational definition of hypnosis, particularly as applied to forensic hypnosis (p. 134):

> Hypnosis is an altered state of consciousness, characterized by inten-sified concentration of awareness on certain suggested themes, along with a diminished interest in competing perceptions. Subjects who are hypnotized experience perceptual and sensory distortions and enhanced abilities to utilize normally unconscious mental mechanisms.

G. Guidelines for the Ethical Practice of Hypnosis and Hypnotherapy

In this section we will present a series of guidelines and recom-mendations for the ethical practice of hypnosis and hypnotherapy. Erickson frequently used members of his family for demonstration purposes. Mrs. Betty Erickson was a very good subject, particu-larly in the matter of self-hypnosis. His daughter Betty Alice recently recounted an occasion when she went to a family friend, Dr. R. Pearson, for some personal counseling using hypnosis. She stated that her father *never* did therapy with family members— demonstrations were okay, but doing therapy was considered by Erickson to be improper. In what may be an extreme example we can think of the response of a noted psychotherapist when someone wondered aloud to him about the "bad" behavior of his children, "At work I am a psychologist. At home I am a parent, and I never get the two roles mixed up!" One could, of course, quibble with Erickson's approach by observing that, as a role model and parental-advice-giver and upholder of familial behavioral standards, some of his interactions with his family must have been therapeutic. Erickson was against conscious and deliberate therapeutic interventions with family members.

Erickson was very protective of his clients' rights and sensibilities as the following case exemplifies. He knew that clients withheld information from him, as was their right. A woman came to him at regular intervals over a period of four years, and her request was that having paid for the hour neither he nor she would say a word. Erickson complied with that request until the session when the woman said (Erickson, Rossi, and Ryan, 1986, p. 166), "I am beginning to feel some courage about coming into your office. I am awfully slow about it. There is something I wish I could say to you, but I just haven't the courage to say anything about it. I would like to talk to you about it, but I can't." Since the client opened the discussion, Erickson felt he could talk and he said:

> All right, may I say a few things to you? I would like to offer you some suggestions. I would like to have you listen to the clock so you can't see my face. I would like to have you listen to the clock so you can feel you are not listening to me, and now as you look at the clock, and as you listen to the clock, this is what I am going to say. You want to talk to me about something that is awfully, awfully important to you. You just can't bring yourself to talk on that subject to me, but I can tell you what you can do. You can think it over, as freely as possible, in your mind. It won't be too free, but select the one word—the worst word that you know—the worst possible word that you know connected with that subject—and just say that word to me. Having said it, you don't have to say a single other thing. It will be just the one word. It is the worst possible word, and then the next time you come in, you will feel that the worst has been said.

You will note the extraordinary degree of respect that Erickson showed for his client. He was willing to wait (four years!) until she was ready. Note that Erickson talked about this case at a seminar he presented in San Diego in 1961. His audience wanted to know what that word was, but waited until late in his seminar to ask! Erickson replied (Rossi, and Ryan, 1986, p. 185):

> She thought a while [in that session] and then she said, "Sex."
>
> I said, "That is the worst possible word you can say to me. You really ought to be able to talk freely next time on a number of things."
>
> She said, "I am going to start right now." The worst had been said. *All I wanted to do was to intensify her reaction, to make it very, very specific. And, the worst had been said: "Sex," and she was then free to talk.* I didn't want to give her any explanation. [I wanted] ... to give her freedom to talk, if not this time, then next time. She had control over the next time she came in, and she might talk on a *number of subjects*, because I had said "a number of subjects." You need to protect your patients in every possible regard. I wouldn't want to tell her to talk freely on *that* subject—only a number of subjects.

Perhaps the most important sentence above is, "You need to protect your patients in every possible regard." Just consider the lengths that Erickson was willing to go to in order for that protection to occur!

In the following, we will present various guidelines for ethical practice and discuss them separately. Of course, it is understood that you will also follow the guidelines of your own professional society.

1. Who Should Be Trained?: we recommend that the guidelines of The Milton H. Erickson Foundation be used for the selection of trainees in clinical hypnosis. Training would be open to professionals in health-related fields such as physicians, doctoral level psychologists and dentists who are qualified for membership in, or who are members of, their respective professional organizations. Training would also be available to master's degree level professionals with mental-health-related degrees from accredited institutions. This would include nursing, social work, and mental health counseling. Full-time graduate students in any of the above areas would be eligible for training upon presentation of a letter from their department certifying them as full-time students at the time of training.

These guidelines basically restrict training to health-related professionals with graduate degrees (masters or doctorate) or bona fide graduate students in those areas. Since there are a number of graduate programs which students can be enrolled in as part-time students, and where these students have been formally admitted to graduate student status in an accredited institution, we would interpret the guidelines to include them as trainees.

These guidelines deliberately leave out the kind of "paid-professionals" who work as "counselors" in drug rehabilitation programs and many mental health agencies. Also left out are psychiatric nurses with a bachelor's degree or lower, or any of the non-professional support personnel in psychiatric hospitals.

This also means that the *practice* of hypnosis should not be taught at the undergraduate level in any program. It is conceivable that an undergraduate course could be taught in a psychology department *about* the history, nature, and myths of hypnosis, as long as the students are not given any training in the use of hypnosis. Hypnotic phenomena may be demonstrated in such a course by a qualified professional where this is a *demonstration* and not a training. Group inductions for undergraduates to reduce test anxiety, improve writing skills, or for general relaxation may be done by a qualified and responsible professional.

2. Do No Harm: the most important injunction for anyone in the healing professions is "Above all, do no harm." The client should be at least as healthy when they leave your office as when they entered. You have an absolute obligation to "put your clients back together" before they leave your office, particularly if there have been any abreactions or opening up of old wounds and scars. In the hypnotic state a client may divulge all sorts of traumatic material that they have stored away because they cannot handle that knowledge consciously. It is wise to continue an amnesia for that material until the time when the unconscious mind feels the material may be brought to the light of day. The unconscious mind should be consulted about this. "And, until you are ready and able to handle this information consciously, you can continue to keep it safely stored away. You may not know now, and in what ways and at what times, nor just how much it will be safe to divulge, but as those times develop, you can slowly and safely let the information out in just the right amounts at just the right times, and in just the right ways." This is an important level of protection you can give your clients. Erickson, himself, was very careful about these special memories and worked to consistently protect his clients.

In assigning ordeals or ambiguous functions or homework, the tasks cannot be of such a nature that they would harm the client or others. This is not to say that clients cannot or should not be challenged to test and try and explore and change. Your task is to help them change (if the change is ethical) in ways that the client finds desirable. What are the client's goals for change? How will they know when the sought-after changes have occurred? Just as a lawyer does not prepare papers for a blind trust when a client has come in for help with a divorce, therapists must work within the client's desires. You always have to be alert that your system of values/religion/politics does not dictate the end goals for the client. If there is a conflict in any of these areas that interferes, then you must ethically refer the client to another therapist.

3.   **Respect:** respect must be shown for the client's wishes, value system, beliefs, religion, person, status, and property. Aside from other considerations, the showing of respect and awareness is simply an enhancer of rapport. It also fits with Erickson's utilization principle—you accept the client as is and use whatever they bring into the office to help them. Erickson certainly was showing respect to his grossly obese client when he regaled her in unflattering terms about being an impossible tub of lard. He was showing respect for her intelligence—how could anyone ignore such enormity? She knew it, and Erickson just verbalized the obvious. They could build a relationship and a therapy on the honesty shown in his lambasting of her grossness. Frank Farrelly maintains that therapists, in particular, find it hard to tell a client exactly what the client already knows about him/herself. If you can't trust your therapist to be honest, then why go to him/her? The aggressive verbal challenging done in certain encounter groups such as those dealing with hard drug users is accepted by those present as a mark of respect for the honesty involved. There are many ways to show concern and respect.

Erickson was fond of saying to clients, generally early in their interactions, "Please do not tell me whatever it is that you do not wish to tell me." Among other things, this tells the client that you are not an inquisitive, prying gossip. You may certainly be curious about many things about the client, but you need to show them proper respect by structuring your inquiries so that the client feels free to not respond or keep secret whatever they wish. Questions should be germane to the client's expressed wishes. E.L. Rossi will say something like the following to a client who has started on internal work while he leaves them much quiet time for that work, "And you can just from time to time tell me a word or a phrase that indicates how you are working on that and what is going on." What a gentle way to work!

4. Patient vs. Client: do you think about the person who comes to you for help as a "patient" or a "client"? Patients are "patient" and passive and waiters. The descriptive is used primarily by the physical health professions and psychiatrists. A client is someone who purchases a service and therefore has more control about that service and the relationships involved. Think about the two descriptives and what the implications are to you and those who come to you. We prefer working collaboratively with clients.

5. Legal Matters: there are many aspects to working within what we will call legal matters and they will be considered separately.

   a. Credentials—Your credentials as a therapist should be clearly and openly available. These would include diplomas, evidences of training if relevant, and any certifications or licensures. Some of these credentials will indicate your areas of expertise and training. You should not misrepresent yourself as having training or capabilities that you do not in fact have. Even if it is not required by law where you live, you should have available a list of your expertise and the kinds of problems for which you have competence.

   If you are in training in a particular area, then you must so indicate. You also need to have regular supervision for this training area by someone who is an acknowledged expert or trainer.

b. Informed Consent—The general public has hazy ideas about hypnosis in general, and probably has not heard of the term "hypnotherapy." *Before* using hypnosis, you need to find out what your client knows about the field, and any misconceptions or fears they may have. When hypnosis has been explained to them and they overtly or indirectly accept what you have said, then you can proceed. Some clients will accept the ideas of "relaxation" or "sleep" or "guided imagery" as a description of what you do with your controlled language. If you are known as a hypnotist or hypnotherapist, there is generally no need for written informed consent.

A special problem arises if you work in an institutional setting where the practice of hypnosis is either not permitted or is discouraged. Do you use it anyway and call what you are doing "cognitive restructuring" or "relaxation"? If you cannot persuade your supervisor about your skills with hypnosis or its efficacy, then you are bound to not do any trance work in any guise that another professional would recognize. If operating under such rules is too onerous, then your only ethical alternative is to seek other employment. Hopefully, as mental health professionals become more aware of hypnotherapy, its practice will spread.

Informed written consent is certainly required when a session is either audiotaped or videotaped. The form should clearly state who will have access to the tape and how it will be used.

If there are any observers present, either in the same room, or behind a one-way mirror, or listening in another room, then the client must give clear permission for them to be present.

c. Confidentiality—The client/therapist relationship is a privileged one, and the bounds of these privileges are strictly defined by the law. Since some of the legal constraints are federal and some state, you need to become aware of what they are where you work. In general, your notes and files may not be subpoenaed except under unusual circumstances. Also, you can only be required to testify under special circumstances. You are always free, of course, to defy such rulings if you are willing to face whatever consequences there may be.

It is generally expected that you will not discuss a particular case except in case conferences or with a supervisor. These consultations are considered to be in the client's interest. However, the supervisor and the participants in the case conference are enjoined to maintain confidentiality. Care should be taken to preserve case notes and client files in a secure manner that prevents casual inspection.

d. Minors—Any work with minors, however defined in your state, must be done with the consent of the parents or a parent or legal guardian, preferably in writing. School counselors need to be particularly careful about this.

e. Referrals – Psychotherapeutic—You should refer to another therapist when the client presents problems outside your area of expertise. If you feel that you have taken the client as far as you can towards their desired goals and you know of a colleague who can help them further, then you should refer your client to them explaining your reasons for the referral. If you feel you are getting extra-professionally involved with your client, then you must refer, and also talk this over with a senior therapist. If your client needs psychological or vocational testing which is beyond your area of expertise, then you can refer them to an experienced evaluator with the client's consent.

f. Referrals – Medical—You need to be sensitive to medical complications in any of the psychological problems you encounter. Certainly, someone like Erickson with a medical background could detect many more potential medical problems than an ordinary psychotherapist. If you suspect medical connections, immediately ask the client to check that out with their personal physician. In this era of burgeoning research in areas such as psychoneuroimmunology and mind/body healing, you need to be particularly sensitive when working with clients who have diagnosed medical problems such as cancer, AIDS, ulcers, migraines, etc. Bernie Siegel, for example, rightly insists that the people with life-threatening diseases who come to his support groups also be under medical supervision. It is tempting to use hypnosis and guided imagery for healing and changing physiological or neurological reactions, but this should be done in cooperation with medical practitioners. There is much evidence in Erickson, Rossi, and Ryan (1986) of the kind of mind-body interactions that Erickson was able to influence, but, even with a medical degree, Erickson was very cautious. Hypnosis is frequently used for pain control—this should be done with caution, as well as informing the client's physician if under medical treatment.

g.   **Lawyers**—Your personal or institutional lawyer should be educated about hypnosis and hypnotherapy. Have them read "Trance on Trial" (Scheflin and Shapiro, 1989).

6.   Fees: it has been commented upon many times that, for a world-renowned psychiatrist, Erickson charged very low fees. His office was in his home. Erickson apparently believed that his fees just had to be enough for him and his family to live in reasonable comfort. That tradition has continued via the Milton H. Erickson Foundation and the meetings and conferences they conduct. Certainly you should be aware of what the prevailing fee structure is in your community.

7.   Entertainment: the Society for Clinical and Experimental Hypnosis (SCEH) statement on entertainment is excellent:

"The clinical and scientific utilization of hypnosis is an important contribution to mankind's health. It should not be used as a source of entertainment. No members of SCEH shall offer their services for the purpose of public entertainment nor shall they collaborate with any person or agency engaged in public entertainment. They shall not cooperate with or participate in lectures, demonstrations or publications of lay or stage hypnotists ..."

Hypnosis should only be used by professionals for professional purposes.

8.   Advertising: the SCEH code of ethics states, "No members of SCEH shall offer their professional use of hypnosis via newspapers, radio, television, or similar media." We agree. Telephone and professional directory listings should be accurate as to services offered, training, certification, licensure, and professional credentials. This also applies to business cards and brochures or flyers.

The SCEH code of ethics states the following about publications and appearances: "Members making statements or writing an article for publication in the lay press, or appearing on radio, TV, or similar media, shall behave in conformity with the requirements of their professional society and with the code of ethics of their professional society." We agree. Further, "Members... shall use their influence and prestige to avoid exaggerations or false statements about hypnosis."

9. Extra-Professional Contacts with Clients: the SCEH code of ethics does not deal directly with this area but, in effect, defers to other professional societies. Therefore, we quote below some relevant sections from the American Psychological Association (APA) "Ethical Principles of Psychologists and Code of Conduct," effective December 1, 1992:

1.11 Sexual Harassment. (a) Psychologists do not engage in sexual harassment.

1.17 Multiple Relationships. (a) ... A psychologist refrains from entering into or promising another personal, scientific, professional, financial, or other relationship with such persons if it appears likely that such a relationship reasonably might impede the psychologist's objectivity or otherwise interfere with the psychologist's effectively performing his or her functions as a psychologist or might harm or exploit the other party.

1.19 Exploitative Relationships. (b) Psychologists do not engage in sexual relationships with students or supervisees in training over whom the psychologist has evaluative or direct authority, because such relationships are so likely to impair judgment or be exploitative.

4.05 Sexual Intimacies With Current Patients or Clients. Psychologists do not engage in sexual intimacies with current patients or clients.

4.06 Therapy With Former Sexual Partners. Psychologists do not accept as therapy patients or clients persons with whom they have engaged in sexual intimacies.

4.07 Sexual Intimacies With Former Therapy Patients. (a) Psychologists do not engage in sexual intimacies with a former therapy patient or client for at least two years after cessation or termination of professional services.

The APA standards are quite clear in this area and certainly apply to those who use hypnosis in an ethical manner.

10. Working With Family/Friends/Acquaintances: the APA standard with respect to multiple relationships applies here. To maintain objectivity, it is best to refer these individuals to a professional colleague. The giving of "parental" or "friendly" advice needs to be done with great caution.

11. Self-Disclosure: depending on the client and the circumstance and the timing, self-disclosure may be a useful adjunct to the therapeutic process. But such self-disclosure should be used consciously and deliberately and as part of an overall therapeutic design. You must remember at all times who is the helping professional. This is not to say that it is not sometimes beneficial as part of a treatment plan to deliberately switch roles.

12. Termination: since the client has hired you for a particular purpose, the client can terminate the relationship at any time. However, it is much better for termination to be planned, explained, and agreed to by therapist and client. With the prevalence of single-session therapy (Talmon, 1990), the "traditional" preparation of a client for termination is almost moot. Talmon recommends that you function in each session as if it were the only one or the last one.

Finally, we recommend the careful study of your own professional society's code of ethics. Since the APA standards are so comprehensive, they are good ones to abide by, along with the specific statements with regard to hypnosis and hypnotherapy we have made above.

H. The "Dark" Side of Hypnosis

There is an archetype throughout man's history of evil beings or spirits that can control a person's mind and behavior. One phrase in common usage is being "bent" to the other's will. Another involves literally being taken over by the evil entity as in demonic possession. These ideas cross all cultures and times and are so pervasive that we need to seriously consider the reality of the phenomena. This is particularly so since in the popular mind this form of "mind control" is almost synonymous with mesmerism and hypnosis. Certainly, the kinds of things that stage hypnotists have their volunteers do reinforces the "mind control" idea.

Professional hypno*therapists* may be blinded by their own ethical standards and the ethical standards of their professional societies. Ericksonians, in particular, may have been lulled into a state of comfort by two seminal papers of Erickson (1932, 1939), both of which are found in their entirety in Erickson and Rossi (1980, pp. 493, 498). In the first paper Erickson concludes:

> In summary, then, the literature offers little credible information concerning possible detrimental effects of experimental hypnosis, although replete with dogmatic and opinionated denunciations founded on outworn and untenable concepts of the phenomenon. ... The author's own experience, based on several thousand trances on approximately 300 individual subjects, some of whom were hypnotized at least 500 times each over a period of four to six years, reveals no evidence of such harmful effects. This clinical finding is further substantiated by the well-known difficulties encountered in the deliberate therapeutic attempts to occasion desired changes in the personality. Accordingly, marked changes from experimental hypnosis appear questionable.

In the second paper (1939) Erickson gives 35 detailed accounts of experiments he conducted to influence subjects in the areas of: involving physical or mental injury to the self; involving damage or loss of personal property; giving adverse information about oneself; involving violation of the subjects' moral or conventional codes; violation of personal privacy; experiments involving harm to others; inducing subjects to commit thefts; and experiments involving the direct abuse by the hypnotist of the subject's confidence. Erickson concluded:

> The findings disclosed consistently the failure of all experimental measures to induce hypnotic subjects, in response to hypnotic suggestion, to perform acts of an objectionable character, even

though many of the suggested acts were acceptable to them under circumstances of waking consciousness. Instead of blind, submissive, automatic, unthinking obedience and acquiescence to the hypnotist and the acceptance of carefully given suggestions and commands, the subjects demonstrated a full capacity and ability for self-protection, ready and complete understanding with critical judgment, avoidance, evasion, or complete rejection of commands, resentment and objection to instrumentalization by the hypnotist, and for the aggression and retaliation, direct and immediate, against the hypnotist for his objectionable suggestions and commands. ... *Hence the conclusion warranted by these experimental findings is that hypnosis cannot be misused to induce hypnotized persons to commit actual wrongful acts against either themselves or others, and that the only serious risk encountered in such attempts is incurred by the hypnotists in the form of condemnation, rejection, and exposure.* (Emphasis added.)

We quote Erickson's conclusions in such detail because we took them to be the gospel and happily cited these papers to our students. In effect, we wanted to believe in the validity of his conclusions. With hindsight, could Erickson, a good person and an ethical professional, have found any other conclusions? He himself was not evil or greedy or possessed with the need to control as the character, Svengali, for example, in du Maurier's "Trilby" (1894). (Incidentally, Svengali was the precursor of the many modern hypnotists who use their skills to help clients improve performance, since one of the things Svengali did was to use mesmerism to make Trilby an outstanding singer. The novel is fascinating reading.) Erickson was not ruthless or possessed by an ideology that justified any means to an end. If a hypnotist of Erickson's exceptional skill could not get people to violate their personal codes, then it was just not possible for anyone else to do so, or was it?

There is now much evidence that various governments have used hypnosis in conjunction with other practices to literally take "control" of people's minds. Scheflin (1992), in a brilliant lecture on the "dark" side of hypnosis, has detailed the history and practice of unethical hypnosis. (He has a book in preparation on the subject. Much of this section is due to ideas and leads found in his lecture.) The "show" trials in the former Soviet Union involved political prisoners confessing congruently to crimes they could not possibly have committed. The "brainwashing" carried out by the

People's Republic of China on Korean War prisoners is another example of mind control. This was also practiced by the North Vietnamese. These procedures involved sensory deprivation, drugs, humiliation, sleep deprivation, and abasement, as well as hypnotic reinforcement. Condon's "The Manchurian Candidate" (1988) was not just a piece of fiction.

Could the United States government have become involved in such unethical practices? The answer is "yes" as evidenced in two books, for example, (Marks, 1979; Weinstein, 1990). This involvement apparently started when Estabrooks (1971) called to the attention of the government during World War II the idea that, if it were possible to use hypnosis (as had been known since the turn of the century) to merge multiple personalities, then it would also be possible to *create* a programmable personality that was hidden from the original personality. The CIA funded many research projects in this area under their project code-named MKULTRA. Many of the experiments were conducted on unwitting subjects. There even seems to be evidence of an assassination team that was set along these mind control principles *à la* the Manchurian candidate. One of the most chilling projects funded by the CIA was that of E. Cameron, a Canadian psychiatrist, who used drugs, incredible amounts of ECT, sensory deprivation, and prolonged sleep (up to several weeks, drug-induced) to "de-pattern" psychiatric patients without their consent to a *tabula rasa* state. Then, the patients were restructured by a "psychic driving" process that included hypnosis and continuous repetitive messages delivered by looped audiotapes. (See Weinstein, 1990, for details.) Cameron's totally unethical procedures are actually the "standard" treatment found in modern science fiction for the rehabilitation of criminals!

There is now conclusive evidence that not only does hypnosis have a "dark" side, but that various governments have actually used it for their own nefarious purposes. Knowledge that the "dark" side exists means that individual hypnotherapists and professional societies need to have an extra level of vigilance to protect their clients and themselves.

Exercises

1. Obtain a copy of the ethical standards of your own professional society and study them. Do they have any specific guidelines relating to hypnosis and hypnotherapy?

2. Do you agree with the standards of the Milton H. Erickson Foundation or the SCEH or the ASCH on who can be trained or practice hypnosis and hypnotherapy? What would you change and in what ways?

3. Is it okay to advertise your services? Are there any constraints you would place on yourself?

4. Is it okay to speak to a local group about hypnosis and hypnotherapy? Would it be okay to do a demonstration? What limits would you impose on yourself and the attendees?

5. Does your state have any specific licensing or certification requirements for the practice of hypnosis or hypnotherapy? Do you meet these requirements? Should you work towards getting legal requirements in place? What are the pros and cons about legal requirements?

6. Are you aware of the present status of forensic hypnosis where you live? Certainly check what Scheflin and Shapiro (1989) have listed for your state. Do you routinely tape sessions, use informed consent statements, give out explanatory literature about hypnosis? Have you checked what you do with a knowledgeable lawyer? Do you have a lawyer? How would you go about finding one? Should you get involved in forensic hypnosis? What are the advantages and disadvantages?

7. How secure are your case files? How complete are they?

8. Do you supervise other professionals? Do you regularly use supervision? Are you aware of the legal ramifications in so doing?

9. Do you agree with the APA code on sexual harassment and intimacy with clients? Almost all studies in this area have shown a 5-10% rate of sexual intimacy between helping professionals and their clients. How do you cope with this; with a sexually attractive or provocative client; with your own sexuality? Are clients more vulnerable to sexual advances when they are in trance?

10. Do you have a list of trusted professionals in the helping professions that you can use for referrals? What social service agencies exist in your area? Do you belong to your local professional society? Are you active in it?

11. What do you know about the "dark" side of hypnosis? Do you believe it is possible to control others solely through the use of hypnosis? Are there any circumstances under which this would be ethical? Have you ever been tempted to demonstrate hypnosis at a party? Is "brainwashing" possible? Can a person be regressed/reduced to a *tabula rasa* state? Should you tell your clients about the "dark" side of hypnosis?

12. Do you have professional liability insurance? What does it cover?

13. The questions listed above can be answered individually, but they would better be discussed in a group of peers, perhaps at a professional practices meeting. It is important to openly discuss these issues and obtain the guidance and commentary of your fellow professional. Also, what is the interest of the client in all of this—perhaps, they should be included in the discussions too!

Chapter 21

Trance and Beyond

Rubin Battino, M.S., and Thomas L. South, Ph.D.

We feel that when the history of psychotherapy is written two names will stand out: Sigmund Freud and Milton H. Erickson. Freud will be acknowledged for his "discovery" of the unconscious mind and its psychodynamics. He developed psychoanalysis and many methods for "unlocking" unconscious material so that it could be dealt with in therapeutic ways. His explorations into language, history, mythology, archeology, biography, sex, religion, and humor opened up new ways of studying and appreciating the human condition. However, as a therapeutic method, psychoanalysis has proven to be excessively time-consuming and expensive, as well as frequently ineffective. Erickson, for example, discovered early in his career that the unearthing of unconscious material and its interpretation was not necessary for effective change to occur. You can know "why" you drink or are depressed, and continue to drink and be depressed. It is safe to say that Erickson had little use for psychoanalysis and its practitioners. Erickson was as pragmatic as his farmer roots—he worked for results and not intellectual constructs. Still, Erickson and everyone who followed Freud built on Freud's pioneering genius.

Erickson's genius lay in devising, testing, and fine-tuning the methods of practical and effective psychotherapy. Almost every modern method of psychotherapy has its roots in Erickson's work. One example is Erickson's work with children, couples, and families well before others entered this field. Modern hypnotherapy mainly stems from Erickson's pioneering studies as attested to by his many publications, the workshops he did for dozens of years, the founding of the American Society for Clinical Hypnosis and editing its journal, his many case studies, and the individual and group training he did in his home. Yet, Erickson always resisted codifying what he did, for he knew that such codification stood the risk of becoming dogma. Instead he chose the "guild" approach of apprenticing therapists and, in effect, saying, "Learn from observing and then do it *your* way."

To our minds, Erickson's two major contributions are in his utilization principle, and in what we characterize as "his *precise* use of *vague* language." Growing up on a farm, Erickson recognized that the creatures who gave milk were not all described by being called "cows," but that each and every cow had an unique personality. This is something every farmer knows—to be a successful dairy farmer you must know the individual characteristics of each cow. One of the characteristics of each "name" psychotherapy is a theory of personality and its associated problems that are so accepted as being correct that clients perforce must fit the tenets of the theory and its associated problems. Each theory has its own jargon and descriptives which subtly restrict what can be done to help clients. Erickson welcomed a "resistant" client, for that gave him opportunities to *use* the resistance for the client's benefit, rather than an excuse for (perhaps) criticizing the client for being uncooperative. The utilization principle means that you accept each client exactly as he/she is and use the client's unique character to help him/her to find solutions and ways of behaving that are specific to them. Was a large part of Erickson's success simply due to his interacting with you as a unique individual (rather than with a symptom such as depression)? We think so, and find people endlessly interesting. Who am I going to meet next?

Erickson was an acknowledged master at the subtle and careful and conscious use of language. As a boy, he read the dictionary for enjoyment! Almost all psychotherapy is *talking*. Erickson's mastery of language came from long and intensive study. He told of writing out an induction in 35 pages and then refining and reducing it in stages to a few pages. He was *flexible* enough to feel that he could use the entire 35 pages *or* parts as needed. He would see clients for many hours in one session or in sessions months apart. We have emphasized the precise use of vague language, since this is particularly useful in hypnotic work. "*As* you *sit there*, you *may* find your hand *moving or staying still*." "*And will* your *eyes close when* you *are ready* to *go inside* and *work* on *that* problem, or will they stay open a *while longer* while you *prepare* yourself for *that* inner work?" The indirect, permissive, and cover-all-possibilities language facilitates change and bypasses resistance. It is a common reaction when first encountering Erickson's use of language (and minimal cues) to disbelieve that anyone could be so subtle and yet work in such a conscious manner. It is the design of this book to teach you how to use language in similar effective ways—we learned these linguistic patterns and so can you.

Hypnosis was the medium that Erickson used to facilitate utilization and precise language usage. He was fascinated by the hypnotic state and endlessly explored its capabilities. But, language usage was primary, since he could also do hypnotherapy *without* trance. On the other hand, trance states facilitate change while providing a degree of protection for the client. The popularization of hypnosis for many therapeutic purposes and in many modalities will stand as one of Erickson's major contributions.

What of the future of Ericksonian hypnotherapy and psychotherapy? Erickson's personal philosophy of resisting categorization has let his "followers" explore their own ways of applying his teachings, even though there is a bit of a "cult" atmosphere sometimes apparent. Erickson, of course, had his own expectations (and limitations) as evidenced in the "happy ending" of marriage with children that peppered many of his cases. We just cited Erickson's story of how he pared down a multi-page induction to a page or two. We think that his pioneering work in pseudo-orientation in time has set the stage for the brief and very brief therapies of the present. In fact, we perceive this to be an area of continuing development for the future—a sharpening of therapeutic skills (and expectations!) to shortening the time someone is in treatment.

We shall illustrate this trend with Rossi's work. Recall that Erickson "prepared" his clients for pseudo-orientation in time (as well as other interventions) by a training period which might be ten to twenty sessions. (The *Time Line Therapy* approach of James and Woodsmall (1988) does similar work in the initial session, which may be the only session.) Rossi, in the second edition of "The Psychobiology of Mind-Body Healing" (1993), has refined this work in ten "boxed" interventions he calls teaching tutorials in his Chapter 5. His *expectation* at the outset is that the client will be able to: (1) ratify a decision to do meaningful work; (2) do an inner search for relevant memories and experiences; (3) generate appropriate solution(s) for the presenting problem (which is generally kept private by the client); and (4) ratify that the client accepts and plans to use those solutions. The procedures Rossi uses are invariably anchored by ideodynamic physical movements. This physical involvement is important in concretizing the developed solutions. Sometimes the solution(s) is/are further concretized with a pseudo-orientation in time step. But note that these processes generally take 15–45 minutes (or less!) from start to finish. Rossi's work will be a paradigm for effective brief therapy. Cheek (Cheek and LeCron, 1968; Rossi and Cheek, 1988) has devoted a lifetime to honing ideodynamic signaling (particularly finger signals) along the same lines as Rossi. We feel certain that Cheek's work will continue to be refined and utilized. Similarly, solution-oriented approaches, as characterized by de Shazer's work and building on Erickson's contributions, will continue to become more popular and more refined.

One of us (RB) recalls having great difficulty in finishing reading Volume IV of Erickson's collected papers. He felt during the reading that he was in contact with an exceptional person, and he didn't want that contact to come to an end. Of course, we keep coming across more of Erickson's writings and tapes so the contact continues ...

We trust that this book has fulfilled its design of providing a systematic approach to Erickson's work in an accessible and learnable framework.

It is wise to avoid Procrustean beds!

Chapter 22

Some "Beyonds"

Rubin Battino, M.S.

A. Introduction

In the previous chapter, which was supposed to have been the concluding chapter of this book, we indicated some of the directions we thought would be followed in the future. The "future" of that chapter is *now*, several months later. At the 6th Congress on Ericksonian Methods (December 1994), I realized that this book would not be complete without a brief discussion of some of the "beyonds" I encountered at that meeting and others I reflected upon, and materials I have come upon since that time.

One example of this, which is related to the heavy emphasis on language we have espoused in this book, came at the end of a demonstration Scott D. Miller did on solution-oriented therapy. Earlier I had heard in different sessions two well-known practitioners caution us on the use of the word "try" which implies failure. (Cross-culturally in countries where rugby is popular, "try" has a significantly different meaning!) Knowing that "try" carries the failure implication you can consciously use it *or* avoid its use. Miller used "try" in his demonstration in a way that appeared to be counterproductive to a number of us. When he was asked about this, his response was that the *micro*dynamics of language usage was frequently irrelevant to the *macro*dynamics of the way the overall session was proceeding. In other words, although we need to be consciously careful with language, occasional slips are not disastrous. (It is probably also the case that occasional overly clever and subtle usage may not be as effective as we would like to believe!) Miller's comment carried a sense of relief for me and the reframing, if you accept it, can be a release for you, too.

The remainder of this chapter will be devoted to comments on the centrality of reframing, pause power, Rossi's tutorials, Rossi's new book, and the power of expectations.

B. The Centrality of Reframing

The idea of reframing has been discussed earlier as one of the best methods of achieving second-order change. At the 6th Congress I watched many expert practitioners demonstrate their skills. I was amazed at what I perceived to be *centrality of reframing* in the work of everyone I observed. At one point, I wrote a detailed outline for a long paper on this subject with examples from all the approaches I have studied. It may be useful to prepare this paper at some time, but it would only elaborate on what can be simply said. People get stuck and ask for help because they typically make only *one* interpretation about their lives or circumstances. Reframing changes the meaning and the perspective so that the single interpretation loses validity. Why wait two years before you can laugh at the current situation? Change the meaning of that past or present circumstance *now*. Or, simply, *remove* the old frame (deframing).

O'Hanlon has talked about the importance of reframing with respect to talking about "complaints" rather than "problems" with your clients. The latter are much harder to resolve! So, why not in the initial interview reframe what is presented from a problem to a complaint? I actually prefer the word "concern" to both problem and complaint.

I run my private practice in such a way that I do not have to do diagnoses, i.e. no third-party payments or reports. But I have prepared a universal diagnosis not in the Diagnostic and Statistical Manual which I will use if I have to, and that is that my client is "temporarily troubled." Think how freeing it would be to both you and your clients to use such a diagnosis. I say this because I have encountered too many people whose self-descriptions (like alcoholic, depressive, borderline) have become continuing self-fulfillments.

In the training we do, we have frequently stated that just learning how to reframe is probably worth the cost of the training. In case studies that you read and in demonstrations you observe, please be sensitive to the centrality of reframing—sometimes it is so much a part of the presenter's speech patterns that it goes unnoticed.

C. Pause Power

I submitted a paper to the 6th Congress which had the above as part of its title. This paper did not make the final cut. Since I feel that the main point in that paper is rather important for hypnotherapists, I will make it briefly here.

The neophyte hypnotherapist (and many an experienced practitioner) tends to talk non-stop. One model of doing hypnotherapeutic work is to induce a trance, deepen the trance, deliver the appropriate metaphors or suggestions, and re-orient the client to the present. Once I started doing trancework with a client I used to talk continuously. I was on a roll and didn't want to be disturbed by the client or by pauses. My voice and words were to carry the day. Of course, being a good Ericksonian, I carefully observed the client's *body* language at all times, even adjusting my pattern to appropriately accommodate what I observed. But, I didn't stop talking, and it was rare for me to ask questions of the client while he/she was in a trance. Just my words and observation, continually. I wonder how many of you operate in the same way.

Pauses can be powerful agents of change. Erickson, of course, used pauses and conversed with his clients while they were entranced. The extent of the pauses is not evident in transcripts. Rossi's recent work makes more and more use of long pauses with minimal statements by him. And, his comments tend to verify and continue what he observes in the client's body language. "That's right." "Some more of *that*." "Just let that develop." "The simple courage to stick with that." "Yes." Verbal communication may be requested by saying, "If there is something important I need to know to help you, just let me know by a word or a phrase." "Just a word or a phrase as you continue that." Rossi's assumption is that, once he has given the client permission (overtly or not) to start that inner work, all he needs to do is sit on the sidelines and be an observant cheerleader. He *assumes* the client will do meaningful change work internally. Then, he gives the client *sufficient time* to do that work. We are facilitators and enhancers. Although it is difficult to be silent for several minutes, clients need your silence so that they can do their own focused idiosyncratic inner work. Facilitate their internal reviewing and solutions. And a very good way to do this is to be sensitive to the power of pauses. This understanding has certainly changed my style.

D. Rossi's Tutorials

In the light of Section B in this chapter, it is interesting to note that, at the onset of Chapter 5 "The New Language of Mind-Body Communication: Ten Teaching Tutorials," Rossi (1993) states, "The basic premise for all the approaches outlined in this book is 'Every access is a reframe.'" He further states (pp. 90–91), "Each time we access the SDMLB processes that encode a problem, we have an opportunity to 'reassociate and reorganize' or *reframe* that problem in a manner that resolves it." (SDMLB stands for state-dependent memory, learning, and behavior.) Tutorial 8 is the same as the "fail-safe" moving hands procedure described in some detail in Chapter 10. Although some pauses are indicated in the tutorial directions, it is evident that, when you watch Rossi work with a client, he allows lots and lots of time for the necessary inner work. It might take five or more minutes for hands to come together or for one hand to slowly descend. An occasional comment reflecting body language observations enhances the process and maintains contact with the therapist. You can occasionally speed up the process by stating, "And, knowing just how fast the mind can work, please take all the time you need," but this should be used with caution.

Tutorial 2 (p. 101) follows:

Tutorial 2. The Basic Accessing Question

1. *Time-binding introduction initiating inner search.*
    As soon as your inner mind [creative unconscious, spiritual guide, etc.] knows

2. *Accessing state-bound sources of problem*
    that you can review some important memories related to the source of that problem

3. *Observable behavior signal or problem-solving*
    will your eyes close?

This tutorial may be preceded by a question requesting whether the client is ready to work on that particular problem at this time (checked by some ideomotor signal). Note that the therapist need not know in any detail the nature of the problem (concern), and that therapeutic work is started almost without any preamble. You accept the client's presence as an indication that they are interested in working.

Tutorial 3 (p. 104), goes directly to accessing creative resources. Notice that these are not statements, but questions posed in such a way that the inner mind has much leeway in response. The therapist indicates a caring curiosity.

Tutorial 3. Accessing Creative Resources

1. *Readiness signal for inner work*
   When a deep part of your inner mind knows it can resolve that problem [pause], will you feel yourself getting more and more comfortable as your eyes close?

2. *Accessing and transducing state-bound resources*
   Now your inner mind can continue working all by itself to solve that problem in a manner that fully meets all your needs. [Pause]
   Are there any memories, life experiences, and abilities that your inner mind can use in many ways you may not have realized before?

3. *Ratifying problem-solving*
   When your inner mind knows that it can continue to deal effectively with that problem, will you find yourself wanting to move a bit [pause], and will you open your eyes and come fully alert?

As we summarized in the previous chapter, Rossi has streamlined the therapeutic process to its bare bones. In four steps he expects that his client will be able to: (1) ratify a decision to do meaningful work; (2) do an inner search for relevant memories and experiences; (3) generate appropriate solution(s) for the presenting problem; and (4) accept and plan to use those solutions. Please note the elegant and efficient language in the boxes. These four steps can be adapted to your client with appropriate changes of language and signals. This is a refined hypnotherapy without formal trance induction, regression, deepening, operator-generated therapeutic work, or re-orienting. Nevertheless, clients perforce go into trance to do this work. If using this "beyond" in your work intrigues you, more details may be found in Rossi's book (1993).

E. Rossi's "The Symptom Path to Enlightenment"

E.L. Rossi's new book (Rossi, 1996) is a remarkable attempt to provide a theoretical basis for hypnotherapy (first half) and practical approaches based on that theory (second half). The subtitle expresses much, "The new dynamics of self-organization in hypnotherapy: An advanced manual for beginners."

Many will find Part 1 (the new dynamics of hypnotherapeutic work) difficult to read. In this part he attempts to provide a theoretical basis for hypnotherapy in nonlinear dynamics which is manifested in modern times by the descriptive "chaos theory." This theory has shown that order can arise from chaotic conditions, and that the initial conditions have a profound effect on these apparently random but, in the final effect, organized outcomes. There appear to be critical points of transitions or crises for people who are stuck in a particular pattern of behavior. In nonlinear systems small changes in these critical areas can lead to disproportionate effects. Rossi's tentative formulation is, "... 'hypnotherapeutic work' is the facilitation of the subject's own healing and problem solving capacities in the Self-Organizing Phase Transitions they courageously allow themselves to experience at their subjective 'Edge of Personal Chaos.'" (p. 49) Another quote may help (pp. 64–65), "The important idea is that it is impossible to expect the psychotherapist to know how to suggest, program or predict exactly what is right for the patient. The therapist's role is to engage patients in genuinely creative ideodynamic experiences *live* wherein patients can experience the natural but essentially unpredictable evolution of their own consciousness and behavior." Hypnosis appears particularly suited to enhance this engagement at critical change points: "... the critical dynamics of hypnotherapeutic work involves optimizing potentials for change of rather precarious points of ambiguity in human experience and behavior." (p. 109) Hypnotherapy facilitates internal search processes which enable a patient to reframe their experiences.

Under the heading of "Stress, Healing and the Chaotic Wave Nature of Consciousness," Rossi (p. 131) writes:

> There are four basic hypotheses at the heart of this new concept of stress, healing and the chaotic wave nature of consciousness as well as the essence of hypnotherapeutic work. They begin by locating the ultimate source of the wave nature of life in *(1) the periodic nature of the molecular-genetic-protein loop at the source of life in the cell cycle and (2) the consequent periodic brain-body loop of neuroendocrine self-regulation and mindbody communication.* These two basic hypotheses lead to the next two on the source and resolution of mindbody dysfunctions. *(3) traumatic life experiences or chronic stress can disrupt or desynchronize these natural mindbody rhythms and (4) hypnotherapeutic work can facilitate the adaptation of these complex mindbody rhythms for problem solving and healing.*

On p. 175 Rossi summarizes his approach as follows:

> The integrative chaotobiological theory of hypnotherapeutic work (outlined in this chapter) states that this *something—the basic stuff of hypnotherapy is the entrainment and utilization of the natural psychobiological processes of mindbody communication on all levels from mind to gene that are responsive to psychosocial cues—this is the domain of a hypnotherapy of the future.*

Obviously, Rossi's work is dense and bears close study. Part 1 also contains a fascinating history of hypnosis from Rossi's perspective.

In Part 2 Rossi gives details for a number of hypnotherapeutic approaches which are based on the development in Part 1, although his basic "moving hands" approach was developed earlier (and is described in this book in the chapter on ideodynamic methods). The four stages are now described (p. 194) as "basic accessing questions." Part 2 also gives details on the "hands polarity" and "arms polarity" approaches as well as many case studies and examples of Rossi's elegant and precise use of language. There is an extensive bibliography and a useful glossary.

This new book is daring in its pioneering endeavor to provide a theoretical basis for the effectiveness of hypnotherapeutic work. It bears close study.

F. Expectation Power

The more we watched expert practitioners at the 6th Congress, the more we were aware of the power of *their* expectations for change on the responses of the volunteer subjects. Kay Thompson stated explicitly several times that she felt that her intense personal conviction that her patients would succeed in whatever they came to see her about was a major factor in her success. You have to genuinely believe in the efficacy of your work—if you do things by the numbers, why would a client trust you or gamble their health on you? The establishment of rapport and a collaborative alliance precedes the tutorials or any other process.

G. Some Last Words

By this time you should be able to devise your own set of learning exercises based on the material in this chapter. Kay Thompson stresses practice of the basics (such as becoming skilled at several basic inductions) before attempting advanced procedures. Your effectiveness in using one of Rossi's streamlined procedures will be enhanced by practice in and knowledge of language forms and a variety of inductions. The reason it looks so easy when an expert does something is that they have practiced so much more than we have.

Bibliography

Achterberg, J. (1985). *Imagery in healing: Shamanism and modern medicine*. Boston: New Science Library.

Achterberg, J., Dossey, B., & Kolkmeier, L. (1994). *Rituals of healing: Using imagery for health and wellness*. New York: Bantam Books.

Ader, R. (Ed.). (1981). *Psychoneuroimmunology*. New York: Academic Press.

Ader, R. (1993). Conditioned responses. In B. Moyers (Ed.), *Healing and the mind*. New York: Doubleday.

Andreas, S., & Andreas, C. (1987). *Change your mind, and keep the change*. Moab, Utah: Real People Press.

Bach, S. (1990). *Life paints its own span*. Einsiedeln, Switzerland: Daimon Verlag.

Bandler, R. (1985). *Using your brain - for a change*. Andreas, C., & Andreas, S. (Eds.). Moab, Utah: Real People Press.

Bandler, R., & Grinder, J. (1975). *The structure of magic*. Palo Alto: Science and Behavior Books.

Bandler, R., & Grinder, J. (1975). *Patterns of the hypnotic techniques of Milton H. Erickson, M.D.* Cupertino, CA: Meta Publications.

Bandler, R., & Grinder, J. (1979). *Frogs into princes*. Moab, Utah: Real People Press.

Bandler, R., & Grinder, J. (1982). *Reframing. Neuro-linguistic programming and the transformation of meaning*. Andreas, S., & Andreas, C. (Eds). Moab, Utah: Real People Press.

Barber, J. (1996). *Hypnosis and Suggestion in the treatment of pain*. New York: W.W. Norton & Co.

Barber, J. (1998). The mysterious persistence of hypnotic analgesia. *International Journal of Clinical and Experimental Hypnosis, 46*, 28-43.

Barber, J. & Adrian, C. (1982). *Psychological approaches to pain management*. New York: Brunner/Mazel.

Benson, H. (1975). *The relaxation response*. New York: William Morrow and Co.

Braid, J. (1843). *Neurypnology: or, the rationale of nervous sleep, considered in relation with animal magnetism*. London. Reprinted (1976) by Arno Press, New York.

Buber, M. (1991). *Tales of the Hasidim*. New York: Schocken Books.

Cade, B., & O'Hanlon, W.H. (1993). *A brief guide to brief therapy*. New York: W.W. Norton & Co.

Cameron-Bandler, L. (1985). *Solutions: Practical and effective antidotes for sexual and relationship problems*. San Rafael, CA: FuturePace, Inc.

Chaves, J.F. (1994). Recent advances in the application of hypnosis to pain management. *American Journal of Clinical Hypnosis, 37:2*, 117-119.

Chaves, J.F., & Dworkin, S.F. (197). Hypnotic control of pain: Historical perspectives and future prospects. *International Journal of Clinical and Experimental Hypnosis. 45*, 356-376.

Cheek, D.B., & LeCron, L. (1968). *Clinical hypnotherapy*. New York: Grune and Stratton.

Cheek, D.B. (1982). Some of Erickson's contributions to medicine. In J.K. Zeig (Ed.), *Ericksonian approaches to hypnosis and psychotherapy*. New York: Brunner/Mazel.

Cheek, D.B. (1989). An indirect method of discovering primary traumatic experiences: Two case examples. *American Journal of Clinical Hypnosis, 32*, 41-47.

Cheek, D.B. (1994). *Hypnosis. The application of ideomotor techniques*. Needham Heights, MA: Allyn and Bacon.

Chevreul, M. (1854). *De la baguette divinatoire, du pendul dit explorateur et des tables tourentes, au point de vue de l'histoire, de la critique et de methode experimentale*. Paris: Mallet-Richelieu.

Combs, A., & Freedman, J. (1990). *Symbol, story and ceremony: Using metaphor in individual and family therapy*. New York: W.W. Norton & Co.

Condon, R. (1988). *The Manchurian candidate*. New York: Jove Books.

Cooper, L., & Erickson, M.H. (1959). *Time distortion in hypnosis*. Baltimore: Williams & Wilkins.

Cousins, N. (1979, 1981). *Anatomy of an illness*. New York: W.W. Norton & Co.

de Shazer, S. (1985). *Keys to solution in brief therapy*. New York: W.W. Norton & Co.

de Shazer, S. (1988). *Clues. Investigating solutions in brief therapy*. New York: W.W. Norton & Co.

de Shazer, S. (1991). *Putting difference to work*. New York: W.W. Norton & Co.

de Shazer, S. (1994). *Words were originally magic*. New York: W.W. Norton & Co.

Dilts, R., Grinder, J., Bandler, R., Bandler, L.C., & DeLozier, J. (1980). *Neurolinguistic programming: Vol. I, The study of the structure of subjective experience*. Cupertino, CA: Meta Publications.

Dolan, Y.M. (1991). *Resolving sexual abuse: Solution-focused therapy and Ericksonian hypnosis for adult survivors*. New York: W.W. Norton & Co.

Donaldson, M.M. (1959). Positive and negative information in matching problems. *British Journal of Psychology*, 50, 235-262.

Elliotson, J. (1977). Numerous cases of surgical operations without pain in the mesmeric state; With remarks upon the opposition of many members of the Royal Medical and Chirurgical Society and others to the reception of the inestimable blessings of mesmerism. In D.N. Robinson (Ed.), *Significant contributions to the history of psychology* 1750-1920. Washington, DC: University Publications of America. (Originally published (1843). Philadelphia: Lea and Blanchard.)

Erickson, M.H. (1932). Possible detrimental effects of experimental hypnosis. *J. Abnormal and Social Psychology*, 37, 321-327. (Also pp. 493-497 in Vol. I Collected Papers.)

Erickson, M.H. (1933). The investigation of a specific amnesia. *British Journal of Medical Psychology*, 13, 143-150.

Erickson, M.H. (1937). The experimental demonstration of unconscious mentation by automatic writing. *Psychoanalytic Quarterly*, 6, 513-529.

Erickson, M.H., & Kubie, L.S. (1938). The use of automatic drawing in the interpretation and relief of a state of acute obsessional depression. *Psychoanalytic Quarterly*, 7, 443-466.

Erickson, M.H., & Kubie, L.S. (1939). The permanent relief of an obsessional phobia by means of communications with an unsuspected dual personality. *Psychoanalytic Quarterly*, 7, 471-509.

Erickson, M.H. (1939). An experimental investigation of the possible antisocial use of hypnosis. *Psychiatry*, 2, 391-414. (Also pp. 498-530 in Vol. I Collected Papers.)

Erickson, M.H. (1939b). Experimental determination of the psychopathology of everyday life. *Psychoanalytic Quarterly*, 8, 338-353.

Erickson, M.H., & Kubie, L.S. (1940). The translation of the cryptic automatic writing of one hypnotic subject by another in a trancelike dissociated state. *Psychoanalytic Quarterly*, 9, 51-63.

Erickson, M.H. (1944). Hypnosis in medicine. The Medical Clinics of North America, May, New York Number. (Also pp. 14-27 in Vol. IV Collected papers.).

Erickson, M.H. (1952). Deep hypnosis and its induction. In L.M. LeCron (Ed.), *Experimental Hypnosis*. (pp. 70-114). New York: Macmillan.

Erickson, M.H. (1954). Pseudo-Orientation in time as a hypnotherapeutic procedure. *J. Clinical Exptl. Hypnosis*, 2, 261-283. (Also pp. 397-423 in Vol. IV Collected Papers.)

Erickson, M.H. (1961). Historical note on the hand levitation and ideomotor techniques. *The American Journal of Clinical Hypnosis*, 3, 196-199.

Erickson, M.H. (1964a). The "surprise" and "my-friend-John" techniques of hypnosis: Minimal cues and natural field experimentation. *American Journal of Clinical Hypnosis*, 6, 293-307.

Erickson, M.H. (1964b). Pantomime techniques in hypnosis and the implications. *American Journal of Clinical Hypnosis*, 7, 64-70.

Erickson, M.H. (1964c). Initial experiments investigating the nature of hypnosis. *American Journal of Clinical Hypnosis*, 7, 152-162.

Erickson, M.H. (1964d). An hypnotic technique for resistant patients: The patient, the technique, and its rationale and field experiments. *The American Journal of Clinical Hypnosis*, 7, 8-32.

Erickson, M.H., & Erickson, E.M. (1941). Concerning the nature and character of posthypnotic behavior. *Journal of Genetic Psychology*, 24, 95-133.

Erickson, M.H., & Rossi, E.L. (1974). Varieties of hypnotic amnesia. *American Journal of Clinical Hypnosis*, *16*, (4), April.

Erickson, M.H., & Rossi, E.L. (1976). Two-level communication and the microdynamics of trance and suggestion. *American Journal of Clinical Hypnosis*, 18, 153-171.

Erickson, M.H., Rossi, E.L., & Rossi, S.I. (1976). *Hypnotic realities*. New York: Irvington Publishers, Inc.

Erickson, M.H., & Rossi, E.L. (1979). *Hypnotherapy; An exploratory casebook*. New York: Irvington Publishers, Inc.

Erickson, M.H. (1980). The clinical discovery of a dual personality. In M.H. Erickson, & E.L. Rossi, *Hypnotic investigation of psychodynamic processes*. Vol. III. (pp. 261-270). New York: Irvington Publishers, Inc.

Erickson, M.H., & Raport, D. (1980). Findings on the nature of the personality structures in two different dual personalities by means of projective and psychometric tests. In M.H. Erickson, & E.L. Rossi, *Hypnotic investigation of psychodynamic processes*. Vol. III. (pp. 271-286). New York: Irvington Publishers, Inc.

Erickson, M.H., & Rossi, E.L. (1980). *Indirect forms of suggestion in hand levitation.* Vol. I Collected Papers pp. 478-490.

Erickson, M.H., & Rossi, E.L. (1980). *The nature of hypnosis and suggestion.* Vol. I. New York: Irvington Publishers, Inc.

Erickson, M.H., & Rossi, E.L. (1980). *Hypnotic alteration of sensory, perceptual, and psychophysiological processes.* Vol. II. New York: Irvington Publishers, Inc.

Erickson, M.H., & Rossi, E.L. (1980). *Hypnotic investigation of psychodynamic processes.* Vol. III. New York: Irvington Publishers, Inc.

Erickson, M.H., & Rossi, E.L. (1980). *Innovative hypnotherapy.* Vol. IV. New York: Irvington Publishers, Inc.

Erickson, M.H., & Rossi, E.L. (1981). *Experiencing hypnosis: Therapeutic approaches to altered states.* New York: Irvington Publishers, Inc.

Erickson, M.H., Hershman, S., & Secter, I.I. (1981). *The practical application of medical and dental hypnosis.* Chicago: Seminars On Hypnosis Publishing Co.

Erickson, M.H., & Rossi, E.L. (1989). *The February man. Evolving consciousness and identity in hypnotherapy.* New York: Brunner/Mazel.

Esdaille, J. (1846). *Mesmerism in India, and its practical application in surgery and medicine.* London: Long, Brown, Green and Longmans.

Estabrooks, G.H. (1971). Hypnosis comes of age. *Science Digest.* April, 44-50.

Farrelly, F., & Brandsma, J. (1974). *Provocative therapy.* San Francisco: Shields Publishing Co.

Felten, D. (1993). The brain and the immune system. In B. Moyers (Ed.), *Healing and the mind.* New York: Doubleday.

Frankl, V.E. (1959) (1962, Rev. Ed.). *Man's search for meaning.* New York: Simon and Schuster.

Franklin, B., et al. (1837). *Report of Benjamin Franklin and the other commissioners charged by the King of France with the examination of the animal magnetism as practiced at Paris.* Philadelphia: Perkins.

Furth, G.M. (1988). *The secret world of drawings. Healing through art.* Boston: Sigo Press.

Gilligan, S.G. (1987). *Therapeutic trances, the cooperation principle in Ericksonian hypnotherapy.* New York: Brunner/Mazel.

Gordon, D. (1978). *Therapeutic metaphors. Helping others through the looking glass.* Cupertino, CA: Meta Publications.

Gordon, D., & Meyers-Anderson, M. (1981). *Phoenix. Therapeutic patterns of Milton H. Erickson.* Cupertino, CA: Meta Publications.

Gravitz, M.A. (1988). Early uses of hypnosis as surgical anesthesia. *American Journal of Clinical Hypnosis.* 30, 201-208.

Grinder, J., & Bandler, R. (1976). The structure of magic II. Palo Alto: Science and Behavior Books.

Grinder, J., & Bandler, R. (1981). *Trance-formations; Neurolinguistic programming and the structure of hypnosis.* Moab, Utah: Real People Press.

Grinder, J., DeLozier, J., & Bandler, R. (1977). *Patterns of the hypnotic techniques of Milton H. Erickson, M.D.* Vol. 2. Cupertino, CA: Meta Publications.

Haley, J. (1973). (reissued 1986). *Uncommon therapy; The psychiatric techniques of Milton H.Erickson*, M.D. New York: W.W. Norton & Company.

Haley, J. (1984). *Ordeal therapy.* San Francisco: Jossey-Bass, Inc.

Haley, J. (1985). *Conversations with Milton H. Erickson, M.D. Vol. I. Changing individuals.* New York: Triangle Press (distributed by W.W. Norton & Co.).

Haley, J. (1985). *Conversations with Milton H. Erickson, M.D. Vol. II. Changing couples.* New York: Triangle Press (distributed by W.W. Norton & Co.).

Haley, J. (1985). *Conversations with Milton H. Erickson, M.D. Vol. III. Changing children and families.* New York: Triangle Press distributed by W.W. Norton & Co.).

Hall, E.T. (1959). *The silent language.* New York: A Fawcett Premier Book (Doubleday & Co., Inc.).

Hammond, C. (1990). *Handbook of hypnotic suggestions and metaphors.* New York: W.W. Norton & Co.

Havens, R.A., & Walters, C. (1989). *Hypnotherapy scripts. A neo-Ericksonian approach to persuasive healing.* New York: Brunner/Mazel.

Hilgard, E.R., & Hilgard, J.R. (1984). *Hypnosis in the relief of pain.* New York: Brunner/Mazel.

Jacobson, E. (1938). *Progressive Relaxation.* Chicago: University of Chicago.

James, T., & Woodsmall, W. (1988). *Time line therapy and the basis of personality.* Cupertino, CA: Meta Publications.

Kaptchuk, T. (1983). *The web that has no weaver.* New York: Congdon & Weed.

Klippstein, H. (1991). *Ericksonian hypnotherapeutic group inductions*. New York: Brunner/Mazel.

Kopp, S.B. (1971). *Guru. Metaphors from a psychotherapist*. Palo Alto: Science and Behavior Books.

Kopp, S.B. (1972). *If you meet the Buddha on the road, kill him! The pilgrimage of psychotherapy patients*. Ben Lomond, CA: Science and Behavior Books.

Kopp, S.B. (1983). *The pickpocket and the saint: Free play of imagination*. New York: Bantam Press.

Kroger, S.W. (1977). *Clinical and experimental hypnosis*. New York: Lippincott.

Laing, R.D. (1970). *Knots*. New York: Pantheon Books.

Lankton, S.P. (1980). *Practical magic: A translation of basic neuro-linguistic programming into clinical psychotherapy*. Cupertino, CA: Meta Publications.

Lankton, S., & Lankton, C. (1983). *The answer within: A clinical framework of Ericksonian hypnotherapy*. New York: Brunner/Mazel.

Lankton, S., & Lankton, C. (1986). *Enchantment and intervention in family therapy: Training in Ericksonian approaches*. New York: Brunner/Mazel.

Lankton, S., & Lankton, C. (1989). *Tales of enchantment: A collection of goal-oriented metaphors of adults and children in therapy*. New York: Brunner/Mazel.

LeCron, L.M. (1964). *Self hypnotism*. New York: New American Library.

LeShan, L. (1977). *You can fight for your life*. New York: M. Evans and Co., Inc.

LeShan, L. (1989). *Cancer as a turning point*. New York: A Plume Book (Penguin Books).

Lewis, B.A., & Pucelik, F. (1982). *Magic demystified; A pragmatic guide to communication and change*. Lake Oswego, OR: Metamorphous Press.

Lindner, R. (1955). *The fifty minute hour*. New York: Bantam Books.

Lovern, J.D. (1991). *Pathways to reality: Erickson inspired treatment approaches to chemical dependency*. New York: Brunner/Mazel.

Marks, J. (1979). *The search for the Manchurian candidate: The CIA and mind control*. New York: Times Books.

du Maurier, G. (1984). *Trilby*. New York: Harper and Brothers.

Melzack, R., & Wall, P.D. (1982). *The challenge of pain*. New York: Basic Books.

Mesmer, F.A. (1980). *Mesmerism*. (G. Bloch, Trans.). Los Altos, CA: William Kaufmann, Inc.

Miller, S.D., & Berg, I.K. (1995). *The miracle method. A radically new approach to problem drinking*. New York: W.W. Norton & Company.

Mills, J.C., & Crowley, J.R. (1986). *Therapeutic metaphors for children and the child within*. New York: Brunner/Mazel.

Milton H. Erickson Foundation, *Film of Kay Thompson operation*. Phoenix, AZ.

Naparstek, B. (1994). *Staying well with guided imagery*. New York: Warner Books Inc.

O'Hanlon, W.H. (1987). *Taproots. Underlying principles of Milton Erickson's therapy and hypnosis*. New York: W.W. Norton & Co.

O'Hanlon, W.H., & Weiner-Davis, M. (1989). *In search of solutions. A new direction in psychotherapy*. New York: W.W. Norton & Co.

O'Hanlon, W.H., & Hexum, A.L. (1990). *An uncommon case book. The complete clinical work of Milton H. Erickson*. New York: W.W. Norton & Co.

O'Hanlon, W.H., & Martin, M. (1992). *Solution-oriented hypnosis*. New York: W.W. Norton & Co.

Pert, C. (1993). The chemical communicators. In B. Moyers (Ed.), *Healing and the mind*. New York: Doubleday.

Portenoy, R.H., & Payne, R. (1992). Acute and chronic pain. In *Substance abuse: A comprehensive textbook*. 2nd Ed. J.H. Lowinson, P. Ruiz, & R.B. Millman (Eds.), Baltimore: Williams and Wilkins.

Reiser, M. (1985). Some current issues in investigative hypnosis. *International Journal of Investigative Hypnosis*, 33, 41-56.

Rosen, S. (1982). *My voice will go with you; the teaching tales of Milton H. Erickson, M.D.* New York: W.W. Norton & Co.

Rossi, E.L., Ryan, M.O., & Sharp, F.A. (Eds.). (1983). *Healing in hypnosis. The seminars, workshops, and lectures of Milton H. Erickson (Vol. I)*. New York: Irvington Publishers, Inc.

Rossi, E.L., & Ryan, M.O. (Eds.). (1985). *Life reframing in hypnosis. The seminars, workshops, and lectures of Milton H. Erickson (Vol. II)*. New York: Irvington Publishers, Inc.

Rossi, E.L., & Ryan, M.O. (Eds.). (1986). *Mind-body communications in hypnosis. The seminars, workshops, and lectures of Milton H. Erickson (Vol. III)*. New York: Irvington Publishers, Inc.

Rossi, E.L., & Cheek, D.B. (1988). *Mind-body therapy: Ideodynamic healing in hypnosis*. New York: W.W. Norton & Co.

Rossi, E.L., & Nimmons, D. (1991). *The 20 minute break*. Los Angeles: Jeremy P. Tarcher, Inc.

Rossi, E.L., & Ryan, M.O. (Eds.). (1992). *Creative choice in hypnosis. The seminars, workshops, and lectures of Milton H. Erickson (Vol. IV)*. New York: Irvington Publishers, Inc.

Rossi, E.L. (1993). *The psychobiology of mind-body healing*. (2nd ed.). New York: W.W. Norton & Co.

Rossi, E.L. & Lippincott, B. (1993). A clinical-experimental exploration of Erickson's naturalistic approach: Ultradian time and trance phenomena. *Hypnos*, 20, 10-20.

Rossi, E.L. (1994). New theories of healing and hypnosis: The emergence of mind-gene communication. *European Journal of Clinical Hypnosis*. 3, 4-17.

Rossi, E.L. (1996). *The symptom path to enlightenment. The new dynamics of self-organization in hypnotherapy: An advanced manual for beginners*. Pacific Palisades, CA: Palisades Gateway Publishing.

Scheflin, A.W. (Speaker). (1992). *The illegal, immoral and unethical practice of hypnosis*. (Cassette Recording No. E297-161A,B). Phoenix: The Milton H. Erickson Foundation, Inc.

Scheflin, A.W., & Shapiro, J.L. (1989). *Trance on trial*. New York: The Guilford Press.

Scheinberg, L. (Ed.), *Multiple sclerosis: A guide for patients and their families*. New York: Raven Press.

Selye, H. (1956). *Stress of life*. New York: McGraw-Hill.

Siegel, B.S. (1986). *Love, medicine and miracles*. New York: Harper and Row.

Siegel, B.S. (1989). *Peace, love, and healing*. New York: Harper and Row.

Siegel, B.S. (1993). *How to live between office visits*. New York: Harper Collins Publishers.

Simonton, O.C., Simonton, S., & Creighton, J. (1980). *Getting well again*. New York: Bantam.

Snyder, E.D. (1971). *Hypnotic poetry*. New York: Octagon Books.

South, T.L. (1988). *Hypnosis in childbirth*. In S.R. Lankton, & J.K. Zeig (Eds.), *Treatment of special populations with Ericksonian approaches (pp. 16-24)*. New York: Brunner/Mazel.

Spiegel, D., Bloom, J.R., Kraemer, H.C., & Gottheil, E. Lancet 2 (8668): 888-91, 1989 Oct. 14. *Effect of psychosocial treatment on survival of patients with metastatic breast cancer*. Also, by the same author and colleagues, see: Spiegel, D. Hospice Journal. 8(1-2): 89-119, 1992. *Hypnosis and related techniques in pain management*; Kogon, M.M., Biswas, A., Pearl, D., Carlson, R.W., & Spiegel, D. Cancer. 80(2): 225-30, 1997 July 15. *Effects of medical and psychotherapeutic treatment on the survival of women with metastatic breast cancer*; Spiegel, D. British Journal of Psychiatry - Supplement. (30): 109-16, 1996 June. *Cancer and depression*; Spiegel, D. Supportive Care in Cancer. 3(4): 252-6, 1995 July. *Essentials of psychotherapeutic intervention for cancer patients*; Speigel, D. Cancer. 74(4 Suppl): 1453-7, 1994 Aug. 15. *Health caring. Psychological support for patients with cancer*; Spiegel, D. Seminars in Oncology. 24(1 Suppl 1): S1-36-S1-47, 1997 Feb. *Psychosocial aspects of breast cancer treatment*; Spiegel, D., Sands, S., & Koopman, C. Cancer. 74(9): 2570-8, 1994 Nov. 1. *Pain and depression in patients with cancer*.

State v. Hurd, 173 N.J. Super. Ct. 333, 414 A. 2d 291 (1980); 86 N.J. 525, 432 A. 2d 86 (1981).

Sylvester, S. (1993). Milton H. Erickson, M.D.: The wounded physician as healer. in J. Zeig (Ed.), *Ericksonian methods: The essence of the story*. New York: Brunner/Mazel.

Talmon, M. (1990). *Single-session therapy. Maximizing the effect of the first (and often only) therapeutic encounter*. San Francisco: Jossey-Bass Publishers.

Teitelbaum, M. (1978). *Hypnosis inductive techniques*. Springfield, IL: Charles C. Thomas Publisher.

Thompson, K.F. (1976). A clinical view of the effectiveness of hypnosis in pain control. In M. Weisenberg, & B. Tursky (Eds.), *Pain: New perspectives in therapy and research* (pp. 67-73). New York: Plenum Publishing Corp.

Udolf, R. (1981). *Handbook of hypnosis for professionals*. New York: van Nostrand Reinhold Co.

Wallas, L. (1985). *Stories for the third ear. Using hypnotic fables in psychotherapy*. New York: W.W. Norton & Co.

Wallas, L. (1991). *Stories that heal. Reparenting adult children of dysfunctional families using hypnotic stories in psychotherapy*. New York: W.W. Norton & Co.

Watzlawick, P., Beavin, J.H., & Jackson, D.D. (1967). *Pragmatics of human communication. A study of interactional patterns, pathologies, and paradoxes*. New York: W.W. Norton & Co.

Watzlawick, P., Weakland, J., & Fisch, R. (1974). *Change. Principles of problem formation and problem resolution*. New York: W.W. Norton & Co.

Weeks, G.R., & L'Abate, L. (1982). *Paradoxical psychotherapy: Theory and practice with individuals, couples, and families*. New York: Brunner/Mazel.

Weeks, G.R. (1991). *Promoting change through paradoxical therapy (rev. ed.)*. New York: Brunner/Mazel.

Weinstein, H.M. (1990). *Psychiatry and the CIA: Victims of mind control*. Washington, DC: American Psychiatric Press, Inc.

Weitzenhoffer, A. (1957). *General techniques of hypnotism*. New York: Grune & Stratton.

Weitzenhoffer, A. (1987). *The practice of hypnotism*. Vol. I New York: John Wiley & Sons.

Weitzenhoffer, A. (1987). *The practice of hypnotism*. Vol. II New York: John Wiley & Sons.

Wilber, K. (1993). *Grace and grit. Spirituality and healing in the life and death of Treya Killam Wilber*. Boston: Shambhala.

Wright, M.E., & Wright, B.A. (1987). *Clinical practice of psychotherapy*. New York: The Guilford Press.

Yapko, M.D. (1988). *When living hurts. Directives for treating depression*. New York: Brunner/Mazel.

Yapko, M.D. (1990). *Trance work. An introduction to the practice of clinical hypnosis* (2nd ed.). New York: Brunner/Mazel.

Zeig, J.K. (1980). *A teaching seminar with Milton Erickson*. New York: Brunner/Mazel.

Zeig, J.K. (1985). *Experiencing Erickson: An introduction to the man and his work*. New York: Brunner/Mazel.

Index

Coping
A Practical Guide for People with
Life-Challenging Diseases and their Caregivers
Rubin Battino, M.S.

Coping is a practical guide for those living with or dealing with life-challenging diseases. Detailing the many effective coping strategies that Professor Rubin Battino has encountered during his extensive professional experience—from friends and support groups, from research and from practice—it is written to be thoroughly accessible and informative, inviting you to explore a wide range of techniques and methods that have proved to have a healing influence.

"Coping is an excellent source of information and wisdom, and when they are combined with action and inspiration wonderful things happen."
—*Bernie Siegel, M.D. author of Love, Medicine & Miracles and Prescriptions for Living.*

PAPERBACK   192 PAGES   ISBN: 1899836683

Meaning
A Play Based on the Life of Viktor E. Frankl
Rubin Battino, M.S.

Meaning: a play based on the life of Viktor E. Frankl is a biography in play form. Using many of his own words, the play focuses on the key moments in Frankl's life, it explores his experiences in a Nazi concentration camp, his development of Logotherapy and his insights into the human condition. His book *Man's Search for Meaning* has influenced millions of people worldwide.

Richly illustrated with photographs of Frankl's life and times, including both painful images of imprisonment in the camps and joyful family portraits, *Meaning* presents this extraordinary man's life in a dramatic and readable style. It will appeal to those familiar with Frankl's work, and inspire new readers to learn more about this remarkable man and his contribution to the cause of humanity.

"*Meaning* brings Frankl to life in full dimension—his spirit,
  determination, wisdom, and integrity."
—*Jeffrey K. Zeig, Ph.D., Director, The Milton H. Erickson Foundation.*

"The passionate and poignant bleakness of this magnificent play paints
  vivid pictures with both precision and grandeur. Each person realizes
  anew, the humanness as well as the inhumanity of mankind. Frankl's
  own words responding to the questions we all still have, gives wiser
  and more deeply profound understanding to the meaning of life, then,
  now and for the future. Seeing Frankl's life, in this setting—love and
  life juxtaposed with suffering and death, brings somber joy as we
  realize once again we all can be free, as Frankl always was."
—*Betty Alice Erickson*

PAPERBACK   128 PAGES   ISBN: 1899836837

Metaphoria
Metaphor and Guided Metaphor for Psychotherapy and Healing
Rubin Battino, M.S.

In this groundbreaking book, Rubin Battino provides the reader with the definitive guide to metaphor and its use as a therapeutic tool. This is an essential text for training and professional use, and for *anyone* serious about exploring the potential of metaphor. Conducting a systematic analysis of the effectiveness of metaphor, *Metaphoria* examines:

- the structure of a metaphor: from its essential elements to its optional components
- the delivery of metaphor: from rapport-building and communication skills to the art of effective story-telling
- what makes a metaphor work, with examples of poor and good usage.

Forming a complete reference and resource for the practitioner and therapist, *Metaphoria* investigates:

- the application of metaphors: for children, geriatrics, sleep induction, pain control, trauma, and other purposes
- language forms—the words, phrases and grammatical structure that enhance the content of a metaphor
- the relation of Ericksonian psychotherapy and hypnosis to metaphor
- themes and ideas for metaphor
- the use of metaphors in specific approaches such as: reframing, art therapies, hypnotherapy, healing, preparation for surgery, narrative therapy, solution-focused therapy, and ordeal therapy.

Containing sample scripts and suggestions for basic and advanced metaphors, plus a history of the use of metaphor, *Metaphoria* provides the reader with everything they need to comprehend fully the metaphor's unique properties, and create metaphors for their own unique purposes. The new authority on the subject, *Metaphoria* provides a complete anatomy of the metaphor, and a creative and comprehensive guide to its applications.

"A must-buy and must-read book. Rubin's freshness and honesty is unparalleled, his grasp of the subject matter is uncanny."
—*Stephen Lankton*

CLOTH   376 PAGES   ISBN: 1899836829

USA & Canada *orders to:*

Crown House Publishing
P.O. Box 2223, Williston, VT 05495-2223, USA
Tel: 877-925-1213, Fax: 802-864-7626
www.CHPUS.com

UK & Rest of World *orders to:*

The Anglo American Book Company Ltd.
Crown Buildings, Bancyfelin, Carmarthen, Wales SA33 5ND
Tel: +44 (0)1267 211880/211886, Fax: +44 (0)1267 211882
E-mail: books@anglo-american.co.uk
www.anglo-american.co.uk

Australasia *orders to:*

Footprint Books Pty Ltd
101 McCarrs Creek Road, P.O. Box 418, Church Point
Sydney NSW 2105, Australia
Tel: +61 2 9997 3973, Fax: +61 2 9997 3185
E-mail: footprintbooks@ozmail.com.au